JEWS, FOOD, AND SPAIN

The Oldest Medieval Spanish Cookbook and the Sephardic Culinary Heritage

Hélène Jawhara Piñer

JEWS, FOOD, AND SPAIN

The Oldest Medieval Spanish Cookbook and the Sephardic Culinary Heritage

HÉLÈNE
JAWHARA PIÑER

BOSTON
2022

Library of Congress Cataloging-in-Publication Data

Names: Piñer, Hélène Jawhara, author.
Title: Jews, food, and Spain: the oldest medieval Spanish cookbook and the Sephardic culinary heritage/Hélène Jawhara Piñer.
Description: Boston: Academic Studies Press, 2022. | Includes bibliographical references and index.
Identifiers: LCCN 2022031824 (print) | LCCN 2022031825 (ebook) | ISBN 9781644699188 (hardback) | ISBN 9781644699195 (adobe pdf) | ISBN 9781644699201 (epub)
Subjects: LCSH: Sephardic cooking. | Jews--Food--Spain. | Jews--Food--History. | Antisemitism--Spain--History.
Classification: LCC TX724.2.S47 P558 2022 (print) | LCC TX724.2.S47 (ebook) | DDC 641.5/676--dc23/eng/20220803
LC record available at https://lccn.loc.gov/2022031824
LC ebook record available at https://lccn.loc.gov/2022031825

ISBN 9781644699188 (hardback)
ISBN 9781644699195 (adobe pdf)
ISBN 9781644699201 (epub)

Cover design by Ivan Grave
Book design PHi Business Solutions

Published by Academic Studies Press
1577 Beacon Street
Brookline, MA, 02446, USA

press@academicstudiespress.com
www.academicstdiespress.com

Contents

Impregnadas en cada declaración se entreveían costumbres alimenticias, se escuchaban uno a uno los pasos del Sabbat; la cocina de las grandes ocasiones del pueblo hebreo dejaba escapar su ya peninsular aroma, y desfilaban por las mentes, condensadas en las palabras de estos aldeanos, los pensamientos de incertidumbre e inseguridad ante el paso que habían de dar.

—Carolina Fraile Conde

Sepharad also denotes the reality of a degree of integration unknown elsewhere in medieval times.

—Jane S. Gerber, *The Jews of Spain: A History of the Sephardic Experience*

Acknowledgments

This book would not have been possible without the support of many people: mentors, colleagues, and friends, whom I am fortunate to have met. I would like to express my deepest gratitude to Professor Bruno Laurioux of the Université de Tours. While supervising my doctoral work, he always encouraged me to develop my ideas and believed in my writing. Special thanks goes to Professor Paul Freedman (Yale University) for reviewing the manuscript and sharing his thoughts with me. I would like to thank Professor Massimo Montanari (Università di Bologna) for conversation about this topic and for reviewing my work, and to PhD candidate Filippo Ribbani for sharing information.

I would like to thank Miguel Ángel Motis Dolader (University of Zaragoza and Complutense University of Madrid) for his valuable suggestions and Professor Claude Denjean of the Université de Perpignan Via Domitia (France) for our constructive conversations about Jewish history. I am grateful to Professor Daniel Newman of Durham University (UK) for the documents and information he provided me during my doctoral work. My thanks and sincere respect go to Françoise Sabban, director of research at EHESS (France) and professor emeritus of anthropology (focusing on Chinese food cultures). She has advised and encouraged me throughout my labors.

I would also like to thank my late mentor Professor Emeritus David Gitlitz (Rhode Island University, USA) for his help and support, and the Society for Crypto-Judaic Studies for awarding me the David Gitlitz Emerging Scholar Prize in 2021. I thank Professor Carmen Soares (Universidade de Coimbra, Portugal) for facilitating my access to and understanding of Portuguese-language sources and Enrique Cantera (UNED Madrid), Hilary Pomeroy (University College London), and Elena Romero (CSIC Madrid) for their support, as well as Limor Yungman for her help with Hebrew translations. My thanks also go to Professor David Kraemer, Jewish Theological Seminary Librarian and Professor of Talmud and Rabbinics, for correcting my use of Hebrew terms and liturgical references.

My sincere gratitude also goes to Emmanuel Valency, rabbi of southwest France, for his assistance with understanding the Torah and the Talmud.

I would also like to thank Jordan Finkin, in charge of ancient books and manuscripts at Hebrew Union College (the Jewish Institute of Religion in Cincinnati, USA), for giving me access to historical sources. I thank Corentin Poirier, PhD candidate, who went to the Casanatense in Rome for the Hebrew manuscripts I discuss in this book. I am also grateful to Veronique Jira of the library at IEHCA (Tours) for the photocopies that I requested.

This book would not exist without the support of the Center for Higher Studies of the Renaissance (CESR) in Tours for funding my participation in conferences and the American Sephardi Federation (New York) for awarding me the Broome and Allen Scholarship in 2018. A special thank you goes to my uncle Michel Villain for his interest in this book and financial support. This publication was also made possible because of financial support from the Scientific Council of the IEHCA (European Institute for the History and Culture of Food). I would also like to thank Alessandra Anzani, Kira Nemirovsky, Stuart Allen, Becca Kearnes and Matthew Charlton at Academic Studies Press for shepherding *Jews, Food, and Spain* to publication.

Finally, my deepest gratitude goes to my husband and children for their patience while I was working towards my doctorate and during the writing of this book. Thank you for having always believed in me and for still believing in me.

Foreword

Paul Freedman, Yale University

What had been at one time the largest and most prosperous Jewish diasporic community in Europe was expelled from Spain in 1492. Jews who had at least nominally converted as a result of previous massacres and official pressure, the so-called New Christians or conversos, were permitted to stay, but were subject to surveillance and persecution by the recently established Inquisition. The Holy Office used neighbors and informants to observe and report, among other things, suspicious dining and cooking practices. These included obvious things, such as avoiding pork, but also more subtle indications of "Judaizing," such as cooking eggplant on Friday and then mashing it with cheese and eggs, to be served cold (almodrote de berenjena), or preparing meat stews, such as *adafina*, which was cooked in an oven lit before the beginning of the Sabbath, the pot surrounded by banked up coals so as to stay warm. By the sort of bitter irony that characterizes much of Jewish history, the obsessively detailed reports of the inquisitorial investigations and trials constitute a major source of information about Iberian Jewish cuisine.

In the absence of any Jewish cookbook from the pre-1492 era, it requires arduous research and a creative but disciplined imagination to reconstruct Sephardic tastes from the past and their survival and transmission in communities around the Mediterranean in the early modern period, followed by the even more extensive diaspora in the New World. In an intricate and absorbing study, Hélène Jawhara Piñer presents us with the dishes, ingredients, techniques, and aesthetic principles that make up a sophisticated and attractive cuisine, one that has had a mostly unremarked influence on modern Spanish and Portuguese recipes. Dr. Piñer, who holds a PhD. from the University of Tours in France, tells with finesse an engrossing detective story, tracing connections among cultures, investigating textual witnesses, evaluating repeated words in several languages, attributions (and misattributions), and even late medieval Spanish poetic mockery of stereotypical Jewish foods, such as eggplant and meatballs.

Much has been written recently on Sephardic food, particularly in the United States. While all histories of Jewish communities focus on their formation and exilic dispersion, the historical memory of the Sephardim is strongly connected to food. Among the Ashkenazim, few dishes survived to reflect the Jewish cuisine of medieval France or the Rhineland. The Sephardic communities of North Africa, Italy, and the Ottoman Empire, however, kept not only their versions of the Spanish and Portuguese languages, but preserved a large repertoire of Iberian food traditions and recipes. Piñer's book reconstructs medieval Iberian Jewish cuisine, but it also links it to later practices and memories.

Sephardic identity has been retained and creatively complicated through food as well as religion and language, and the three interact as cultural markers. *Jews, Food, and Spain* is a demonstration of how food relates to historical memory and identity, not just in terms of cultural survival, but for the elaboration of tradition in its deepest and most comforting sense.

The key text in this work of reconstruction and exploration is the *Kitāb al-ṭabīḫ*, which means simply "the book of cooking," a thirteenth-century collection of 462 recipes and the oldest cookery text from the Iberian realms. Written during the thirteenth-century Almohad regime of Islamic Spain (al-Andalus), its author was probably Arabic or, just conceivably, Jewish. Although Hebrew was, of course, the language of Jewish religious ceremony, Arabic was the lingua franca of al-Andalus. The cookbook reflects gastronomic interactions and ambiguities among different religious communities that had been living in proximity and usually in harmony for centuries (the Muslim conquest of Iberia was accomplished between 711 and 717). The shifting balance in favor of the Christian principalities, such as Castile, Portugal, and Catalonia, motivated attempts to stiffen the backbone of the failing Islamic states through austere and intolerant religious uniformity. The Almohads, a Moroccan sect whose peninsular hegemony lasted from about 1147 to 1269, imposed their reform plan by making it all but impossible for Jewish life to continue in the territories they controlled. Maimonides was their best-known refugee victim.

The *Kitāb al-ṭabīḫ* reflects the heritage of shared and borrowed cultures, but, although it has several recipes described as "Jewish," its Sephardic elements, because of the contemporary Islamic mood and policy, are largely hidden and become visible only through comparison and observation across languages and cultures. This is the enterprise that Hélène Jawhara Piñer has bravely and meticulously undertaken. The Jewish elements of the *Kitāb al-ṭabīḫ* have to be gradually unwrapped and deduced from a document produced by a tensely multicultural society. Beyond explicit recipe titles such as "A Jewish Dish of Eggplant Stuffed with Meat" or "Stuffed, Buried Jewish Dish," there are hints of a broader Jewish orientation, such as the inclusion of no less than sixty-nine meatball recipes or a recipe for mock hare using eggplant (hare is licit according to Islamic dietary laws, but forbidden in Jewish regulation).

The legacy of the *Kitāb al-ṭabīḫ* is further complicated by the later oppression, persecution, and eventually expulsion of both the Jewish and Muslim populations after the Christian triumph at the end of the fifteenth century. The Sephardic diaspora and its reception in Islamic ruled states of North Africa and the eastern Mediterranean assured the survival of the cuisine, but its influence remained obscured in Spain itself through a disjunction between unacknowledged culinary borrowing and dangerous, often invented, culinary symbolism. Spanish cookbooks avoided ambiguous ingredients, such as eggplant and exalted pork and other items prohibited by the displaced religions, but they did not actually eradicate cross-cultural culinary traits or legacies.

Food symbolism sometimes did have a real impact on diet and consumption. Dr. Piñer shows how cilantro, common to everyone in the Iberian Middle Ages, became extinguished with the imposition of Christian uniformity, replaced by parsley because cilantro had become a supposedly Jewish herb. In other cases, such as eggplant or meatballs, Christian Spanish cuisine made careful use of them; but nevertheless they were tainted, sometimes comically, sometimes more threateningly, by Jewishness. In addition to discarded and suspicious foods, a third category for Christian gastronomy comprised dishes that are in fact so similar as to be close relatives, even though the Jewish version was considered dangerous. Modern meat stews, *cocidos* and *ollas*, are closely related to the Sabbath *adafina*, but the latter was a prima facie sign of insincere conversion by reason of its cooking method more than its ingredients.

Investigative reporting is not the only purpose or importance of *Jews, Food, and Spain*. The book is also a rumination on cultural heritage. The legacy of medieval society continues to manifest itself in diasporic Sephardic foods, such as *harīsa* (cracked wheat simmered with lamb and flavored with cinnamon), *maqrūd* (fried pastry stuffed with sugar and almonds or dates), *isfenǧ* (a type of fried doughnut, sometimes dipped in honey), and also in the repertoire of modern cuisine. All manner of ubiquitous Spanish ingredients, from dried beef (*cecina*) to marzipan, have Jewish origins.

As Dr. Piñer points out, heritage is something passed down from one generation to the next, but it is subject to shaping and construction, and affected by rupture. Jewish culinary practice is the result of heroic persistence in the face of adversity and dispersal, but also an adaptation to the gaps and erasures imposed by persecution and exile. This book does not exaggerate timeless tradition or posit perfectly intact reconstruction, but rather it displays puzzling correspondences, unexpected paradoxes, and surprise endings, again, in the manner of a mystery story.

The sinuous transformations of recipes and group identity are visible in many parts of the world. In some cases contests over the ownership of symbolically important foods, such as hummus or falafel, between Israelis and Palestinians, are intended to negate common origin or mutual influence. There are generally good-natured disputes over which West African nation has the original or most authentic version of jollof rice, which combines rice with tomatoes, meat, onions, and spices. In other instances, closer to the Iberian case, dishes formerly shared and with no earlier symbolic import are changed into markers of suspicion or contempt. In the Southern United States, the legacy of slavery meant that in a rural, largely poor society, ordinary black and white people tended to eat the same things. A study undertaken in 1943 in South Carolina found that "poor whites eat more like Negroes" than like affluent white people. Their diet included things like chitterlings, collard greens, and other foods that were already in the process of becoming identified solely with African Americans and so mocked or deprecated. While approved Southern dishes such as fried chicken or shrimp perlew (a rice dish with African roots) were presented as "Southern" (i.e., white), those involving organ meat, the extremities of animals (hog's maw, pig's feet), and foraged produce (poke salat or pawpaws) were typified as exclusively as African American, an artificial distinction that became more plausible as whites gained economically.

Returning to the Sephardic world and its broader implications, a peculiar example of unexpected connections is the *mufleta* which appears as *murakkaba* in *Kitāb al-ṭabīẖ* and is included among the updated recipes in the last section of this book. In Moroccan Jewish tradition, *mufleta* is associated with the end of Passover (a festival called *mimouna*). The *Kitāb* has two version of *murakkaba*: semolina-dough crepes are fried and stacked in layers, interlaced with dates in version two. A hole is made in the center and filled with honey and melted butter. At the other side of the world, the *muffuletta* is a sandwich that supposedly originated at the Central Grocery on Decatur Street in New Orleans in 1906. The grocery was owned by Salvatore Lupoo, a Sicilian immigrant, and the name comes from a round Sicilian bread with fennel or anise seeds. The sandwich is made with salami, mortadella, cheese, and a kind of olive salad. Given the Mediterranean exchanges among Spain, North Africa, and Sicily there is probably one or a series of connections. Both dough productions are round, and one sweet, one not. Although hard to prove direct relationships, the likeness of these terms serves to exemplify intricate if incomplete networks, trails, and connections.

Modernized recipes and other writings about Sephardic cuisine emphasize against-the-odds preservation. This does not mean this heritage has been immune from fashion or manipulation. The establishment of the State of Israel and the migration of Jews from Balkan, Turkish, Persian, Bukharan, and Egyptian territories have created a wide set of dining options, as well as a certain amount of crossover. The United States has exploited this pan-Jewish gastronomic possibility by creating "Israeli" restaurants, something rarely found within Israel itself. The success of this current fashion is related to the long-term decline of Ashkenazic food, because of its unhealthful image, overall social assimilation, and the difficulty of executing on a hurried time schedule such classics as noodle pudding or gefilte fish. Lighter, spicier foods deemed "Sephardic," "Middle Eastern," or, above all, "Mediterranean" are, by contrast, wildly popular. Not a whole lot of what is widely diffused today can be drawn from the *Kitāb al-ṭabīẖ* (it too tends to be labor-intensive and requires multiple ingredients), but *pastilla* (a meat pie with spices and sugar) or the Passover matzoh and vegetable pie, *mina,* appear in *Zahav: A World of Israeli Cooking* by Michael Solomonov and Steven Cook. The owners of Zahav, a restaurant in Philadelphia, Solomonov and Cook have brought a largely Mediterranean Jewish eclecticism to the forefront of American culinary attention.

In this brief introduction, I have tried, rather than summarize the work or anticipate too much its conclusions, to sketch some of its implications. The reader will discover a sustained series of arguments about Sephardic cuisine in relation to the *Kitāb al-ṭabīẖ*, as well as an extended discussion of the Sephardic culinary diaspora, with illustrations and recipes from a delightful and intriguing set of flavors and combinations.

Introduction

The present work offers an analysis of a variety of Jewish food—Sepharadic—that existed in Spain at the end of the Middle Ages by way of a reading of the *Kitāb al-ṭabīẖ* (The cookbook), a treatise on Andalusian cuisine. It also reflects on the *Kitāb al-ṭabīẖ*'s status as the foundational text of current Jewish practices in the diaspora. This volume is neither a history of the Sephardic Jews of Spain, then, the narration of which is provided in the scholarship of Jane S. Gerber, Yosef Hayim Yerushalmi, Eliyahu Ashtor, Yitzhak Baer, Myriam Bodian, and others expert on the subject; nor is it an exhaustive study of all the sources that trace the history of the Iberian Jews, be they literary, judicial, notarial, and so on. Rather, this book is an examination of food and cuisine in the light of those texts that address the history of Jews in medieval Spain, principally the first cookbook that covers all periods and territories: the *Kitāb al-ṭabīẖ*.

Starting out as a 2019 doctoral dissertation on medieval history that draws on a multitude of heteroclyte sources, this book inevitably reads some texts and omits others. I hope the reader will excuse me for this. My goal has been to focus on the food of Jews and Sephardim, and understand the conditions under which Jews ate, what they ate, and why they ate it. My guiding intent has been to reflect on the construction of the culinary heritage of present-day Spain. I argue that religion played a key role in the standardization of food in the territory and that it created a culinary ideology. I propose that food was used by hostile non-Jews to identify—and then denounce, mock, and judge—the practices of the Mosaic people. Further, it asks why Jewish cuisine has endured and, thereby, attempts to demonstrate the value of work on the cuisine and Jews of Spain for Jewish studies in particular and history in general.

One of the great difficulties in reconstructing the cooking and dietary habits of medieval Hispanic Jews concerns sources. Several scholars who have written about the Hispanic mediaeval diet have pointed out this problem. This is one reason why studies based on new types of sources are especially welcome, as long as one recognizes the limitations of the evidence.[1]

1 I would like to thank Miguel Ángel Motis Dolader (University of Zaragoza and Complutense University of Madrid [Spain]) for his valuable recommendations.

Analyzing texts that refer to food and cuisine not only deepens our understanding of the diet of medieval Jewish communities, it also helps us increase our comprehension of interfaith relationships and perceptions of the other in Spain during the period. Indeed, the time span this work has to cover makes it possible to address the longevity—and, even more importantly, the survival—of medieval Jewish culinary practices up to the present. How has information about cooking transmitted? How have recipes and culinary practices that originated on the medieval Iberian Peninsula been transposed into other periods, contexts, and territories?

The first cookbook from the Iberian Peninsula—the *Kitāb al-ṭabīḫ*—is an Andalusian medieval treatise, analysis of which means taking the multicultural and multilingual traditions of the area during the Middle Ages into consideration. The specific culinary and dietary requirements of Jews, Muslims, and Christians, then, should be considered when it comes to writing about recipes and food practices. If laws and dietary principles governed the lives of Jews—but also those of Muslims—the history (including the suffering) of the Jews of Spain sometimes shaped them. The *Kitāb al-ṭabīḫ* has been the subject of targeted translations, but there is little scholarship on the recipes it contains and there is even less on their ingredients or the techniques used to make them. Ignoring a people's food is to ignore what defines them. In other words, I submit that there is much more to the culture of the medieval Sephardic Jews than can be found by beginning with the fact that they spoke Arabic. This is all the truer for Jewish cuisine that does not necessarily follow the kosher regulations, but whose recognition as "Jewish" by the surrounding populations, as well as their belonging to what Ariel Toaff describes as "complex paths with their share of reinterpretations," makes them Jewish. Lifestyles, consumption, and culinary practices need to be taken into account too and deserve the same treatment as the ingredients of the recipes which are mentioned.

I hope that this book provides a better understanding of the social history medieval Spain, especially interethnic relations in the country. I also hope that it demonstrates that religion supported the culinary culture of this multireligious society. Studying cuisine is a good way to navigate—without getting lost—a dense and heterogeneous historiography that is crossed by lines of force which testify to aging debates. This work presents identity constituents that are resilient to filiation and coercion. It shows how necessary adaptation forges habits and defines new foods and well-known recipes. It proves how the new preserves the old, that culinary reconfiguration has kept Andalusian Jewishness alive.

Consideration of the persistence of a Jewish tradition—the Sephardic tradition in the case—seems to be essential. The terms "Sephardic" and "Sepharad" have changed in meaning as they have moved from one place to another. Although "Sepharad" exists in the Bible,[2] in reference to a city in Asia Minor, it was not used to identify medieval Andalusia or Muslim Spain until the nineteenth century.[3] Defining what "Sefarad" means is important, then. "Sefarad" is the Hebrew word for Spain. As Jane S. Gerber explains, the word

> was born in Cordoba in the tenth [century] in a luxurious, cosmopolitan, multi-ethnic, hurly-burly land of Berbers, Muslims, Jews and ended in Amsterdam in the seventeenth century, when newly fashioned Jews created a sober and dignified community out of a group of refugees fleeing the Inquisition, creating a new Jew out of a very tragic memory.[4]

She adds that

> there was no single prototype of where a Jew could dwell. It was up to the whims of local authorities, so some Jews lived in city walls, others along the banks of rivers, some in the shadow of the city's cathedral, rarely in the shadow of a mosque since that was not permitted to them. *Sephardim* therefore refers to Jews who lived in Spain and their descendants wherever they managed to get.[5]

By signing his document "Maimon HaSephardi," Moses Maimonides establishes the link that existed between the city where he was born, Cordova in Spain, and the city he moved to and where he died, Fustat in Egypt. This shows that being Sephardic is to belong to a territory, a culture, a history. It is not a static term that refers merely to static Iberian Jews. Jewishness is not simply coterminous with a religion; and he length of time between antiquity and the present is not clear-cut.

---

2 Jane S. Gerber, *The Jews of Spain: A History of the Sephardic Experience* (New York: Free Press, 1992), 2.

3 Michael Brenner, *A Short History of the Jews* (New Jersey: Princeton University Press, 2012), 84; Gerber, *The Jews of Spain*, ix; Jane S. Gerber, "'Cities of Splendour in the Shaping of Sephardi History': A Conversation with Jane S. Gerber," JBS, December 1, 2020, YouTube, 54:32, https://www.youtube.com/watch?v=2vuuD2xdRwQ.

4 Gerber, "Cities of Splendour in the Shaping of Sephardi History": A Conversation with Jane S. Gerber."

5 Ibid.

As I previously said, in this work my aim is not to study in detail the history of the Sephardim of Spain in the Middle Ages from economic, social, and judicial angles, reporting in an almost exhaustive manner the literary and rabbinic sources relating to the life of Iberian Jews. I leave this task to those who specialize in the history of the Sephardim of Spain and who have already accomplished it tremendously. Rather, my purpose is to introduce readers to the existence of a Jewish diet and cuisine revealed in the first cookbook written on the Iberian Peninsula in a climate hostile to the Mosaic communities of Spain. Obviously, nonculinary sources are essential for understanding the context which gave rise to this text, the first that testifies to that Jews had, and have, a unique cuisine.

Various intercultural traditions were formed in the spaces discussed in this book: the Almohad conquest of al-Andalus in Muslim Spain;[6] the *reconquista* of the Iberian Peninsula and the Christian territories; the diasporic Sefarad—the many territories where "culinary ideologies" met. Yet, as Yerushalmi writes,

> anyone attempting a separate study of Jews in Muslim Spain and in Christian Spain will only grasp half of the truth, and perhaps even less about how Spain really was. What would be missing would be the sense of the dynamic interaction between the forces that made the reality in which the synagogue was caught between church and mosque and was in conflict with both.[7]

While this book's three parts are chronological, they focus on the thirteenth to sixteenth centuries, when cookbooks and Inquisition trials, as well as other forms of persecution,[8] provide the richest information concerning the food and culinary practices of Iberian Jews. The book deals with the transformation and standardization of culinary heritages: that of a group, the Sephardim, that of a region: al-Andalus. Then it envisages its distribution during the time of migration and helps to understand what it is to be a Jew among the nations.

---

6 The Almohad was a North African Berber dynasty. It comes from the Arabic term *al-Muwaḥḥidūn*, literally "those who profess the unity of God."

7 Yosef Hayim Yerushalmi, *Sefardica*, 2nd ed. (Paris: Chandeigne, 1998, 2016), 26. Translation by the author.

8 John Tolan, Stéphane Boissellier, and François Clément, *Minorités et régulations sociales en Méditérranée médiévale* (Rennes: PU Rennes, 2010); David Nirenberg, *Communities of Violence: Persecution of Minorities in the Middle Ages* (Princeton: Princeton University Press, 1996).

Methodology and Sources

A Long-Term Perspective

Is a long perspective essential for studying a population and a civilization? Historians have written about Jewish history,[9] but sometimes they have limited themselves to a single theme or period. This is understandable. Jewish history is so vast in scope, both in terms of geography and time, that it is difficult to sum up without altering its meaning. This explains why so many attempts to do so have reached eccentric conclusions. Claiming to be an expert in Jewish history is unwise, then. Thus, it is essential to identify an era (long enough to see development) and a space (the crucial element when studying Jewish history), as deterritorialization is an intrinsic dimension of this history. The territory covered in this book, and which serves as the foundation for the analyses presented here, is Spain. It corresponds to the rise of the dogmatic Muslim Almohad dynasty in the twelfth and thirteenth centuries, an event that a study of the history of Spain and the history of the Jews of Spain must take into account.[10] Why focus on this period? The first reason arises from the existence in the thirteenth century of the oldest source that refers to explicitly Jewish dishes. Second, it corresponds to a religious shift which culminates in the fourteenth century and which marks a radical inflexion point in Jewish, Muslim, and Christian relations. By and large, in history each event must be understood in its own terms. Here, the context is one of economic and social tension ripe for exploitation. This context is even more essential to understand, as what I discuss happened in a multicultural environment over a long period.

Gerber writes: "The beginnings of Jewish life in Spain are cloaked in myth and legend. According to medieval Sephardic traditions, Jews reached the Iberian Peninsula in biblical times."[11] Titus's destruction of Judea and Rome's brutal suppression of a revolt in Palestine in 135 marked the beginning of the westward movement of Jews through the Mediterranean basin. Italy, North Africa, and Spain are three of the several territories where they settled and left evidence of their presence, as the Andalusian tombstones which date back to this period attest. This point will be developed later. A long-term perspective makes it

---

9 See the bibliography mentioned above. The recently published book illustrates this: Pierre Savy et al., *Histoire des Juifs. Un voyage en 80 dates de l'Antiquité à nos jours* (Paris: PUF, 2020). By proposing to consider it through eighty dates, however, the author demonstrates the difficulty of summarizing Jewish history.

10 We will come back of this.

11 Gerber, *The Jews of Spain*, 2.

possible to reflect upon the series of rulers that Spanish Jews were subject to—the Visigoths, the Umayyads, the Almoravids, the Almohads, the Nasrids, and finally Catholic Christians. Cohabitation (eighth to nineth centuries) and the Golden Age (tenth century) gave way to the darkest times of Jewish history on the Iberian Peninsula (611, 1066, 1391, 1492)—the period of persecution that started in the twelfth to thirteenth century. This was when the *Kitāb al-ṭabīḫ* was written.

In order understand the place of food at during a period characterized by intergroup relations of different kinds, such long-term analysis is essential. At that time, Jewish history established its place but, nevertheless, left few written traces. History is generally written by victors, so the Jews' lack of power Spain explains this absence. Still, Abraham Ibn Daud, the Spanish philosopher of Toledo (twelfth century) left behind some written works that express—such as in the *Book of Tradition (Sēfer ha-kabbala,* 1160)—a desire for a recognition and consciousness of Jewish history.[12] He describes the transmission of knowledge among Jews from Mesopotamia to the Iberian Peninsula, thus revealing the existence of a sense of history among Jews.[13] He is one of many Jewish luminaries—Maimonides was the first—to have fled Almohad persecution by going to Christian territories, in particular to Toledo.[14] All in all, when a particular history is a confusion of facts and is marked by a succession of different rulers, food becomes meaningful through both its presence and absence; and food played, and still plays, a key role in Jewish life and religion. In what is considered one of the more famous medieval poems dedicated to Zion, Yehudah Halevi (1075–1141) writes about the situation in Spain under the Almoravids and how he feels as he starts to think of emigrating to Israel:

---

12 Robert Bonfil, "El legado historiográfico de los judíos españoles," in *Moreset Sefarad: El legado de Sefarad*, vol. 2 (Jerusalén: Editorial Magnes-Universidad Hebrea, 1993), 476–493; Sarah Stroumsa, *Andalus and Sefarad: On Philosophy and Its History in Islamic Spain* (Princeton: Princeton University Press, 2019), 96; Gerber, *The Jews of Spain*, 27, 46, 50, 76, 97.

13 Brenner, *A Short History of the Jews*, 84.

14 Yerushalmi, *Sefardica*, 23–24; Moses Maimonides, *On the Regimen of Health*, ed. and trans. Gerrit Bos, with critical editions of medieval Hebrew trans. Gerrit Bos, and Latin trans. Michael R. McVaugh (Leiden and Boston: Brill, 2019), 1; Stroumsa, *Andalus and Sefarad*, 129–131; Gerber, *The Jews of Spain*, 80.

My heart is in the East—
And I am at the edge of the West.
How can I possibly taste what I eat?
How could I keep my promise,
Or ever fulfill my vow,
When Zion is held by Edom
And I am bound by Arabia's chains?
I'd gladly leave behind me
All the pleasures of Spain—
If only I might see
The dust and ruins of your Shrine.[15]

The context of this poem is made clear when Halevi asks, "Have we either in the East or in the West a place of hope in which we can trust?" This implies the existence of a complex situation for Jews in twelfth-century Spain, where he nonetheless could have had "all the pleasures."[16]

Context and Sources

It seems self-evident that the first sources to which a historian must turn when studying the food and cuisine of a people or community will be culinary, that is, primarily cookbooks. For our purposes, it is important to stress that no written Jewish cookbook has been discovered, either in Hebrew or any other language. The culture of the Iberian Peninsula in the Middle Ages is one of the richest in history. The Arabic language was introduced there in 711 and quickly established itself as the language of knowledge, including among Jews. Hasdaï ibn Shaprut (tenth century), Shmouel ibn Alhassan HaLevi, Abraham ibn Ezra, Abraham bar Hiyya Hanassi (eleventh century), and Maimonides (twelfth century) all wrote in Arabic, the lingua franca of Jews in the *Dār al-Islām*[17] in the Middle Ages.18 Hebrew was only used for the liturgy. Consequently, it is the late

15 Peter Cole, *The Dream of the Poem: Hebrew Poetry from Muslim and Christian Spain 950–1492*, introduced, ed., and trans. Peter Cole (New Jersey: Princeton University Press, 2007), 164; Gerber, *The Jews of Spain*, 73. On Halevi's life and poem, see Peter Cole, *The Dream of the Poem*, 143–144; Gerber, *The Jews of Spain*, 60–61, 65, 68–69, 73, 76–78.

16 "Ha-yesh lanu be-mizrah 'o be-ma'arav mekom Tikvah nehi 'alav betuḥim?" See Alexander Kaye and David N. Myers, *The Faith of Fallen Jews: Yosef Hayim Yerushalmi and the Writing of Jewish History* (Brandeis: Brandeis University Press, 2013), 146; Yerushalmi, *Sefardica*, 23.

17 The "house of Islam." Refers to territories under Islamic rule.

18 Yerushalmi, *Sefardica*, 20.

medieval Arabic-language cookbook the *Kitāb al-ṭabīḫ* that is the first place that mentions Sephardic cuisine.

This work has several unique qualities. Written in a thirteenth-century territory under Muslim rule, it was written in Arabic; it was produced in multicultural society riven with strong intercommunity tensions; it records a Spanish Jewish cuisine that has become part of Jewish heritage everywhere. Although Jews were persecuted by the Inquisition, their culinary practices in Christian Spain survived through words. As a result, the Sephardic[19] diaspora gave them a second life in Morocco, the Ottoman Empire, the Middle East, and as far as Latin America. These are the threads that this book patiently intends to pursue.

In this global context, the rejection of Jews also seems to go hand in hand with a less successful Jewish literature than that written during the preceding centuries and which presented—often with great precision—life in the *aljamas*.[20] That is why a linguistic and technical investigation is conducted to track down, through different kinds of sources (dictionaries, literature, trials, cookbooks, etc.) the terms, products, and processes that demonstrate the resilience of the cuisine of the Jews of Spain.

Critical Bibliography

The heterogenous and abundant bibliography this work draws upon points to the variety of fields and sources which our topic demands.

---

19 Sephardim: "Descendants of Jews who were expelled from Spain and Portugal" (https://jewishencyclopedia.com/articles/13430-sephardim); "Jews of Spain and Portugal or their descendants, distinguished from the Ashkenazim and other Jewish communities chiefly by their liturgy, religious customs, and pronunciation of Hebrew: after expulsion from Spain and Portugal in 1492, established communities in North Africa, the Balkans, Western Europe, and elsewhere" (https://www.collinsdictionary.com/dictionary/english/sephardim). Sepharad: "In ancient times 'Sepharad' was believed to be a name for Spain. The *Targum* of Onḳelos renders it אספמיא i.e., "Hispania." Emil G. Hirsch and George A. Barton, "Book of Obadiah," JewishEncyclopedia.com, https://jewishencyclopedia.com/articles/11642-obadiah-book-of; Gerber, *The Jews of Spain*, 2; Brenner, *A Short History of the Jews*, 84.

20 *Aljama*—a term that appears in the Nebrija dictionary of 1495 under two meanings: *aljama de judíos* (*aljama* of Jews), which refers to the synagogue; and *aljama de moros* (*aljama* of the Moors), defined with the terms *concilium punicum*. The *aljama* is a Jewish community (from the Arabic *alǧamā'a*), but also a Muslim community, with its own institutions. In the Middle Ages, it was also a synagogue or a mosque (*alǧamā'a*). See https://dle.rae.es/?id=1trx9rX and https://es.thefreedictionary.com/aljamas. This Spanish term that refers to the quarter where minorities lived. The term is frequently used to designate the Jewish quarter.

Many historians have buckled down to the arduous task of dealing with medieval and later Spanish Judaism. Among the works dealing with this question are those of Abraham A. Neuman (1944), José María Lacalle (1961), Jane S. Gerber (1970), Luis Suárez Fernández (1980), Yitzhak Baer (1981), Haim Beinart (1992), Yosef Hayim Yerushalmi (1998), Uriel Macías Kapón (1992, 1995, 2009), Elena Romero Castelló (1994), Olivia Remie Constable (1997), Joseph Pérez (2005), Robin Vose (2009), and Michael Brenner (2012).[21] Far from arousing only a national interest, Spanish Judaism has been the subject of numerous works like those of Jane S. Gerber, Richard D. Barnett (1971),[22] Robert Singerman (1975, 1993),[23] David Gitlitz,[24] and Sarah Stroumsa (2019). Among the specialized journals dedicated to Iberian Judaism are *Sefarad* (philology, textual criticism of the Bible, Sephardic Jewish history, literature, and culture); *Miscelánea de Estudios Árabes y Hebraicos* (published by the Department of Semitic Studies, University of Granada); *Olivo* (documents and studies concerning dialogue between Jews and Christians; *Hamsa* (relationships between Jews and Muslims); *Bulletin Hispania Judaica* (Iberian Judaism in general); *eHumanista* (a special issue dedicated to Jewish studies); and *Calls* and *Tamid* (Catalan Judaism). The website Aragón. Espacio Sefarad[25] (published by the Provincial Council of Zaragoza) contains much about Judaism in the province of Aragon and *Bibliografía Sefardí* (the Cervantes Institute) is useful for work on medieval Sephardic Judaism.

Along with the renewal of interest in medieval food in general, there has been a great deal of writing on the Iberian Peninsula, in particular on al-Andalus and its cookbooks.[26] The subject of the food of the three communities on the

---

21 More complete references can be found in the article by Vicente Ángel Álvarez Palenzuela, "Judíos y conversos en la España medieval. Estado de la cuestión," *eHumanista/Converso* 4 (2015): 156–191.

22 Richard D. Barnett, ed., *The Sephardi Heritage: Essays on the History and Cultural Contribution of Jews of Spain and Portugal*, vol. 1, *The Jews in Spain and Portugal before and after the Expulsion of 1492* (New York: Ktav Publishing House, 1971).

23 Robert Singerman, *Spanish and Portuguese Jewry: A Classified Bibliography* (Westport: Greenwood Press, 1993). Robert Singerman, *The Jews in Spain and Portugal: A Bibliography* (New York: Garland Publisher, 1975).

24 David Gitlitz, *Secrecy and Deceit: The Religion of Crypto-Jews* (Philadelphia: The Jewish Publication Society, 1996).

25 http://www1.dpz.es/dipu/areas/presidencia/sefarad/NUEVO/ESP/aragonEspacio.htm.

26 Manuela Marín, "Cuisine d'Orient, cuisine d'Occident," in "Cultures et nourritures de l'occident musulman: Essais dédiés à Bernard Rosenberger," ed. Henric Bresc, special issue, *Médiévales*, no. 33 (1997): 9–22; Manuela Marín, "Matériaux pour l'histoire de l'alimentation hispano-maghrébine: 'Alī B. Ibrāhīm al-Andalusī et son Urğūsaï al-fawākih" (Évora: Universidade de Évora, 1986); Évariste Levi-Provençal, *Histoire de l'Espagne musulmane*, vol. 3, *Le siècle du califat de Cordoue* (Paris: Maisonneuve et Larose, 1999), 416–422; Rachel

peninsula during the Middle Ages, and its importance in the history of western Mediterranean basin countries, can be found in texts by David M. Freidenreich (2008, 2011), Olivia Remie Constable (2013, 2018), Sarah Savis-Secord et al. (2022), and Piera Montserrat (2018).[27] All of these scholars discuss material that touches upon food in the late Middle Ages, with particular focus on Christian attitudes towards Muslim and Jewish cuisine.

Jewish food is missing from research into the transmission of al-Andalus's culinary history. Jaume Riera i Sans's,[28] Manuel Sánchez Moya's,[29] and Miguel Ángel Motis Dolader's[30] works are among the few contributions, and they provide

---

Arié, *L'Espagne musulmane au temps des Nasrides (1232–1492)* (Paris: E. de Boccard, 1973), 377–382; Ambrosio Miranda Huici, trans., and Manuela Marín, intro., *La cocina hispano-magrebí en la época almohade Según un manuscrito anónimo del siglo XIII* (Gijón: Trea, 2005); Expiración García Sánchez, "La Alimentación en la *Andalucía islámica," Anejos de Cuadernos de Historia del Islam* (Grenada: Universidad de Granada, 1986), 139–178; idem, "Comida de enfermos, dieta de sanos: procesos culinarios y hábitos alimenticios en los textos médicos andalusí," in *El banquete de las palabras: la alimentación en los textos árabes*, ed. Manuela Marín and Cristina de la Puente (Madrid: CSIC, 2005), 57–87; Manuela Marín and Cristina de la Puente, "La consommation des épices et des plantes aromatiques en al-Andalus," in "Cultures et nourritures de l'occident musulman: Essais dédiés à Bernard Rosenberger," ed. Henric Bresc, special issue, *Médiévales*, no. 33 (1997), 41–54; idem, "La alimentación de los andalusíes: entre las normas médicas y la vida cotidiana," in *El saber en al-Andalus. Textos y Estudios V. Homenaje a la profesora Doña Carmen Ruiz Bravo-Villasante* (Seville: Universidad de Sevilla, 2011), 121–134; idem, "El sabor de lo dulce en la gastronomía andalusí," in *La herencia árabe en la agricultura y el bienestar de Occidente*, ed. Fernando Nuez (Valencia: Universidad Politécnica de Valencia, 2002), 165–204; Lucie Bolens, *La cuisine andalouse un art de vivre, XIe–XIIIe* (Paris: Albin Michel, 1990); Pierre Guichard, "Alimentation et cuisine en Al-Andalus," in *Pratiques et discours alimentaires en Méditerranée de l'Antiquité à la Renaissance. Actes du 18e Colloque de la Villa Kérylos, Beaulieu-sur-Mer, octobre 2007*, ed. Jean Leclant, André Vauchez, and Maurice Sartre (Paris: Académie des Inscriptions des Belles Lettres, 2008), 337–357; Catherine Guillaumond, *Cuisine et diététique dans l'Occident arabe médiéval. D'après un traité anonyme du XIIIe siècle. Étude et traduction française* (Paris: L'Harmattan, 2017); Olivia Remie Constable, "Food and Meaning, Christian understandings of Muslim food and food ways in Spain (1250–1550)," *Viator: Medieval and Renaissance Studies* 44, no. 3 (2013): 199–235.

27 Piera Montserrat, *Forging Communities: Food and Representation in Medieval and Early Modern Southwestern Europe* (Fayetteville: University of Arkansas Press, 2018).

28 Jaume Riera i Sans, "La conflictivitat de l'alimentació dels jueus medievals," in *Alimentació i societat a la Catalunya medieval* (Barcelona: Editorial CSIC, 1988).

29 Manuel Sánchez Moya, "El ayuno del Yom Kippur entre los judaizantes turolenses del siglo xv," *Sefarad* 26 (1966).

30 Miguel Ángel Motis Dolader, "L'alimentation juive médiévale" in *Histoire de l'alimentation*, ed. Massimo Montanari and Jean-Louis Flandrin (Paris: Fayard, 1996); Miguel Ángel Motis Dolader, "Claves e identidades de los judeoconversos de Lleida según los procesos inquisitoriales a finales del siglo xv," *Tamid: Revista Catalana Anual d'Estudis Hebraics* 10 (2014); idem, "Regimen alimentario de las comunidades judías y conversas en la Corona de Aragón en la Edad Media," *Col.loqui d'Història de l'Alimentació a la Corona d'Aragó* (Lleida: Institut d'Estudis Ilerdencs, 1995); Miguel Ángel Motis Dolader et al., "Ritos y festividades de

both interesting and vital insight into medieval Jewish food.[31] The publications of David C. Kraemer, Enrique Cantera[32] and Pilar Bravo Lledó on symbolic cuisine in ancient and medieval Judaism are also highly important. Studies on the Spanish Inquisition that contain research on Jewish food include those by José Ángel Sesma Muñoz,[33] Haim Beinart,[34] Carlos Carrete Parrondo,[35] Dimas Pérez Ramírez,[36] Yiṣḥāq Fritz Baer,[37] and David Gitlitz.[38]

The current dearth of studies about Jewish food in al-Andalus is coupled with the rarity of publications about "Spanish" Jewish cuisine. This perhaps suggests that such books consider Jewish cuisine historically insignificant. Moreover, the abovementioned studies by Cantera, Motis Dolader, and Riera Melis focus only on northern Spain under Christian rule, as is the case in Christopher Kissane's

---

los judeoconversos aragoneses en la Edad Media: la celebración del Yon Kippur o Día del Perdón: ensayo de etnología histórica," *Revista Zurita* 61–62 (1990).

31 These two summaries are restricted to the north of Spain under Christian rule.

32 Enrique Cantera Montenegro, "La carne y el pescado en el sistema alimentario judío de la España medieval," *Espacio, tiempo y forma. Serie III: Historia medieval*, no. 16 (2003); Enrique Cantera Montenegro, "El pan y el vino en el judaísmo antiguo y medieval," *Espacio, tiempo y forma. Serie III: Historia medieval*, no. 19 (2007).

33 José Ángel Sesma Muñoz, *El establecimiento de la Inquisición en Aragón (1484–1486), Documentos para su estudio* (Zaragoza: CSIC, 1987).

34 Haim Beinart, *Records of the trials of the Spanish Inquisition in Ciudad Real*, vol. 3, *The Trials of 1512–1527 in Toledo* (Jerusalem: Israel Academy of Sciences and Humanities, 1981); Haim Beinart, *Records of the Trials of the Spanish Inquisition in Ciudad Real*, vol. 4, *Documents, Biographical Notes, Indexes* (Jerusalem: The Israel academy of science and humanities, 1985); idem, *Records of the Trials of the Spanish Inquisition in Ciudad Real*, vol. 2, *The Trials of 1494–1512 in Toledo* (Jerusalem: Israel National Academy of Sciences and Humanities, 1977); idem, *Records of the Trials of the Spanish Inquisition in Ciudad Real*, vol. 1, *The Trials of 1483–1485* (Jerusalem: Israel Academy of Sciences and Humanities, 1974).

35 Carlos Carrete Parrondo and Carolina Fraile Conde, *Fontes Iudaeorum Regni Castellae*, vol. 4, *Los judeoconversos de Almazán 1501–1505. Origen familiar de los Laínez* (Salamanca: Universidad Pontífica de Salamanca, Universidad de Granada, 1987); Carlos Carrete Parrondo and María José Castaño González, *Fontes ludaeorum Regni Castellae*, vol. 2, *El tribunal de la Inquisición en el obispado de Soria (1486–1502)* (Salamanca: Universidad Pontificada de Salamanca, Universidad de Granada, 1985); Carlos Carrete Parrondo, *Fontes ludaeorum Regni Castellae*, vol. 3, *Proceso Inquisitorial contra los Arias Dávila segovianos: un enfrentamiento social entre judíos y conversos* (Salamanca: Universidad Pontificia de Salamanca, Universidad de Granada, 1986).

36 Dimas Pérez Ramírez, *Catálogo del Archivo de la Inquisición de Cuenca* (Madrid: Fundación Universitaria Española, 1982).

37 Yiṣḥāq Fritz Baer, *Historia de los judíos en la España cristiana* (Zaragoza: Riopiedras, 1998); Yitzhak Baer, *A History of the Jews in Christian Spain* (Philadelphia: Jewish Publication Society of America, 1961).

38 David Davidson and Linda Kay Davidson, *A Drizzle of Honey: The Lives and Recipes of Spanish Secret Jews* (New York: Saint Martin's Press, 1999); David Gitlitz, *Secrecy and Deceit: The Religion of Crypto-Jews* (Philadelphia: The Jewish Publication Society, 1996).

Food, Religion and Communities in Early Modern Europe.[39] It is also imperative to mention *Foreigners and Their Food: Constructing Otherness in Jewish, Christian and Islamic Law*[40] by David Freidenreich, which offers a comparative analysis of Jewish, Muslim, and Christian food practices. Hasia R. Diner's and Simone Cinotto's edited volume *Global Jewish Foodways: A History*[41] tackles similar terrain, but it does not give any particular attention to the Iberian Peninsula during the medieval period. Another reason why Spanish cookbooks that include Jewish food are so scarce is because markers of culinary heterodoxy were established in fifteenth-century Christian Spain. This had an enormous impact on food belonging to Jewish and Muslim culinary practices. Jewish dishes are underrepresented in published cookbooks because Jewish cuisine was erased from the collective culinary memory of the Iberian Peninsula. Furthermore, as Carolyn Nadeau points out, no explicitly Jewish recipes are found in cookbooks after the fifteenth century because Jewish food culture was absorbed into Christian culture.[42] While such recipes are not necessarily explicit, this book illustrates that some nonetheless remain alive in Sephardic culinary practices.

The Structure of This Book—Mirroring History

Part One: The Jews' Place in the Construction of an Andalusian Cuisine (Twelfth to Fourteenth Centuries)

As we have seen, due to the complexity of the subject is difficult to analyze the culinary history of the Jews of Spain and the diaspora. To better guide the reader through the twists and turns of this history, then, *Jews, Food, and Spain* is divided into three sections. Part one seeks to place Jewish food in the broader context of cuisine in Al-Andalus under Almohad rule (twelfth and thirteenth centuries). The historiography shows us how multifaceted the situation was on

---

39 Christopher Kissane, *Food, Religion and Communities in Early Modern Europe* (New York: Bloomsbury Academic, 2018).

40 David M. Freidenreich, *Foreigners and Their Food: Constructing Otherness in Jewish, Christian and Islamic Law* (Berkeley: University of California Press, 2011). See also David Freidenreich, "Sharing Meals with Non-Christians in Canon Law Commentaries, Circa 1160–1260: A Case Study in Legal Development," *Medieval Encounters* 14 (2008): 41–77.

41 Hasia R. Diner and Simone Cinotto, eds., *Global Jewish Foodways: A History* (Lincoln: University of Nebraska Press, 2019).

42 C. Nadeau, "Constructions of Taste in Francisco Martínez Montiño's Cookbook," Culinary Historians of Chicago, Soundcloud audio, 33:20–33:30, https://soundcloud.com/culinaryhistory/constructions-of-taste-in-francisco-martinez-montinos-cookbook.

the Muslim-dominated Iberian Peninsula. Between "hard" social proximity and forced conversions, it is religion—and mainly religious celebrations—that distinguish the cuisines of the territory from one another. Thus, it is unusual to focus on the marks of Jewishness in the *Kitāb al-ṭabīh*. Furthermore, the historical context in which the cookbook was written did not enable it to embrace Jewish recipes. However, the study of this cookbook has proven to be very fruitful. The clues I have discovered in the book reveal scattered traces of Jewish cuisine, that is, a cuisine explicitly designated as Jewish. The combination of a cuisine and a religious practice is unique in Jewish food during this period.

So, what does "Jewish cuisine" mean? The richness and quality of the information contained in the *Kitāb al-ṭabīẖ* make the anonymity of the cookbook even more intriguing. There are enough hints in the *Kitāb al-ṭabīẖ* to conclude that the author was neither Christian nor Berber and knew about medicine and Jewish dietary laws (enshrined in the Laws of Kashrut).[43] Another point highlights the eating habits and practices of Jews and Muslims in the *Kitāb al-ṭabīẖ*. Every cuisine in the cookbook has flagship foods that represent the consumption of the time. Nevertheless, by connecting them with religion, those foods can acquire a symbolism that enshrines them in a system of identity that differentiates communities coexisting in the same territory. Analysis of the way the *Kitāb al-ṭabīẖ* describes how bread, wine, meat, and eggplant are used offer a way to understand what brought the food practices of Jews and Muslims closer together or differentiated them. This lays the groundwork for a reflection on the presence of some of the dishes in the cookbook. Beyond these emblematic foods there are others. They turn out to be full of meaning in their relationship with Jewish cuisine. Finally, this book aims to see the eggplant as a Jewishness Marker. Versatile: this is the word that best describes the eggplant and thereby justifyies the complexity of its study. Its whole existence is steeped in history. It travelled from the Far East to Spain and, in a sense, absorbed the cultures with which it came into contact. The *Kitāb al-ṭabīẖ* discloses, then, the singular place of the eggplant in the history of the culinary practices of Jews. Stuffed or for stuffing, alone or accompanied by meat, is always present in Jewish cooking.

---

43 *Kashrut*: "(Hebrew: 'fitness,' or 'kosher state,) also spelled *Kashrut*, or *Kashrus*, Hebrew *Kashrūt*, in Judaism, regulations that prohibit the eating of certain foods and require that other foods be prepared in a specified manner. The term also denotes the state of being kosher according to Jewish law. Most prescriptions regarding *kashruth* are found in Leviticus, Deuteronomy, Genesis, and Exodus." *Encyclopaedia Britannica*, s.v. "Kashrut," accessed March 30, 2022, https://www.britannica.com/topic/kashruth.

The fourteenth century was one of the most significant periods in Jewish history.[44] Violence against Jews broke out in both the East and West: in Mamluk in 1301 and in France[45] in 1306 when Philip IV the Fair confiscated their property and expelled them. They took refuge in the south of France and in Catalonia where many were massacred in 1322 and 1348.[46] One can read in the records of councils, at the beginning of the fourteenth century, laws that ban Jews and Christians from sharing anything. For example, Christians were not permitted to work in Jewish homes and the two peoples could not eat together. The Spanish Concilium Ocelloduriense[47] of 1313—the council of Zamora—stipulates the following: "[D]o not invite Christians to your meals, nor do Christians eat the food of Jews, nor do they eat their meat, and do not drink their wine."[48]

The war waged by the Spanish Catholic Kings against the Muslims kept Jews in the service of power, and sometimes even in power themselves. For instance, Don Yehudà Abrabanel of Seville provided small biscuit-like cakes and clothes, and guaranteed loans from Genoese traders in order to fund the siege of Algeciras. The Jew Iṣḥac Ibn Ya'iš, the governor of the kingdom of Murcia, was charged with collecting taxes.[49] As for the bloodiest episodes, these surely begin in 1355 with the massacre of twelve thousand Jews in Toledo,[50]an event paralleled anti-Jewish violence in Jerusalem. On June 6, 1391, when the Spanish monarchy was undergoing a period of weakness, Andalusia and Seville witnessed

---

44 Baer, *Historia de los judíos en la España cristiana*, 347–527, 531–610.

45 Nirenberg, *Communities of Violence*; David Nirenberg, "Was There Race before Modernity? The Example of 'Jewish' Blood in Late Medieval Spain," in *The Origins of Racism in the West*, ed. Miriam Eliav-Feldon et al. (Cambridge: Cambridge University Press, 2009), 232–264.

46 Florian Besson et al., *Chrétiens, Juifs et musulmans – Pouvoirs et minorités dans l'espace méditerranéen—Xie–XVe siècles* (Paris: Atlande, 2018), 118–119.

47 Jaqueline Hamesse, ed., *Roma, magistra mundi. Itineraria culturae medievalis: Mélanges offerts au Père L. E. Boyle à l'occasion de son 75e anniversaire* (Turnhout: Brepols Publishers, 1998).

48 Solomon Graysel, *The Church and the Jews in the XIIIth Century*, vol. 2, *1254–1314*, ed. and arranged with additional notes by Kenneth R. Stow (New York: The Jewish Theological Seminary Press, 2012), 269: "non conviden a los christianos en sus comeres, nin los christianos non coman el comer de los judios, sennalada mient que non coman de su carne nin bevan de su vino." Translation by the author.

49 Baer, *Historia de los judíos en la España cristiana*, 349.

50 Concerning 1449 and the Toledan revolt of conversos, see Rica Amran, "El *Fuero real* de Alonso Díaz de Montalvo y la problemática conversa a finales del siglo XV: ¿puntos de vista e influencias de una minoría?" in *Minorías en la España medieval y moderna (ss. XV–XVII)* [Minorities in medieval and early modern Spain (c. 15th–17th)], ed. Rica Amran and Antonio Cortijo Ocaña (Santa Barbara: University of California, 2015), 23–37.

the worst pogrom in Spanish history—the beginning of the persecution of Jews that spread throughout Spain that year.[51] As Henry III wrote,

> most of the Jews who lived there turned to Christians, and many of them died. And . . . as soon as this news was known in Cordoba and Toledo, they [the Christians] did the same, and so in many other places of the Kingdom. It was known from the King that the Jews of Seville, Cordoba, and Toledo were destroyed . . . and that they [the Christians] did the same in Aragon, and in the other cities in Valencia—Barcelona and Lleida—and in other places.[52]

Paradoxically, it was during the fourteenth century that the rural communities of Andalusia experienced their greatest social and demographic growth. Of all the Andalusian *aljamas*, Seville, the capital, is the only one to have subsequently experienced a cultural boom (there were twenty-three synagogues by the end of the fourteenth century) and economic growth (based on tax credits and loans).[53] After the expulsion of Andalusia's Muslims and the allocation of a vast amount of new land to the area, its population did not increase; and this situation was not just limited to Seville. Castile, Aragon, and Mallorca[54] enjoyed a golden period during the second half of the fourteenth century, as is clear from correspondence,[55] but there were underlying interreligious tensions.

A similar demographic situation to that of Seville is observed in Aragon, and in particular in Zaragoza, a city hosting the main Jewish community between the

---

51 On the 1391 Seville pogrom there is an extensive bibliography. Among the numerous works, see: Wolff, "The 1391 Pogrom in Spain: Social Crisis or Not?," *Past & Present* 50 (1971): 4–18; Gerber, *The Jews of Spain*, 113–4, 117; Amran, "El *Fuero real* de Alonso Díaz de Montalvo," in *Minorías en la España medieval y moderna (ss. XV–XVII)* (Santa Barbara: University of California, 2015): 24; Baer, *Historia de los judíos en la España cristiana*, 531–544; Yerushalmi, *Sefardica*, 28.

52 Rica Amran, "Judíos y conversos en las crónicas de los Reyes de Castilla," *Espacio, Tiempo y Forma, Historia medieval* 9 (1996): 259: "É que eran tornados Christianos los mas Judios que y eran, é uchos de ellos muertos. E que luego que estas nuevas sopieron en Cordoba, é en Toledo, ficieron eso mesmo, é asi en otros muchos logares del Regno. E sabido por el Rey como los Judios de Sevilla, é de Cordoba é de Toledo eran destroidos . . . e que ese mismo ficieron en Aragon, é en las cibdades de Valencia, é de Barcelona, é de Lérida, é de otros logares." Translation by the author. See De Cayetano Rosell, ed., *Crónicas de Enrique III*, vol. 3 (Madrid: Atlas, 1953), 259.

53 Baer, *Historia de los judíos en la España cristiana*, 219, 351–52.

54 Ibid., 223.

55 Graysel, *The Church and the Jews in the XIIIth Century*, 304.

thirteenth and fifteenth centuries. The *aljama* in Aragon's capital went through periods of prosperity, decline, and ruin before returning to prosperity. A similar situation characterized Jewish life in Barcelona in the mid-fourteenth century.[56] Many *responsas*[57] from the time raise questions about Jewish-Christian eating practices in the thirteenth and fourteenth centuries, such as the one written by Solomon Ben Adret in 1235 which asks whether Jews should cook meat that has been handled by a non-Jewish butcher.[58]

There were also compulsory conversions of Jews in Sardinia and Sicily in the fourteenth, which prompted many to flee to North Africa.[59] One would have thought that anti-Jewish pogroms would have annihilated the centers—large and small—of Jewish culture in Spain; that the violence would have destroyed families and forced the new *aljamas* to locate themselves elsewhere. But that was not the case. Following the 1391 pogroms in Spain (Andalusia, Castile, Aragon, etc.), Jewish communities in towns and cities maintained their culture. The new *aljamas* were formed in almost the same places where they had been destroyed. Families resettled where attempts had been made to wipe out Jews; thus family lines can be traced in such places from the twelfth century until 1492.[60] Nevertheless, as Yitzhak Baer writes, "The strength of Judaism ended in internal social struggles without content or purpose, in political rivalries and in controversies with detractors of Israel in which their spokesmen were not sufficiently suitable for the religious struggle."[61]

---

56 Ibid., xviii.

57 *Responsa*: "The branch of rabbinical literature comprised of authoritative replies in letter form made by noted rabbis or Jewish scholars to questions sent to them concerning Jewish law" (https://www.collinsdictionary.com/dictionary/english/responsa). The Responsa Project of Bar-Ilan University could be the reference. The RELMIN project, supervised by John Tolan, is also rich because it offers legal texts defining the status of religious minorities in medieval Europe (fifth to fifteenth centuries).

58 Notice no. 252255, projet RELMIN, "Le statut légal des minorités religieuses dans l'espace euro-méditerranéen (Ve–XVe siècle)." John Tolan, *Le statut des minorités religieuses dans l'Europe médiévale*, http://telma.irht.cnrs.fr/outils/relmin/listeextraits/.

59 Besson et al., *Chrétiens, Juifs et musulmans*, 174–177.

60 Baer, *Historia de los judíos en la España cristiana*, 223.

61 Ibid., 347: "Las fuerzas del judaísmo se consumieron en luchas sociales intestinas sin contenido ni finalidad, en rivalidades políticas y en la polémica con los detractores de Israel en la que sus portavoces no se mostraron suficientemente aptos para la lucha religiosa." Translation by the author.

Yet, as David Nirenberg argues,

> The late fourteenth and fifteenth centuries [Iberian history] witnessed massive attempts to eliminate that diversity through massacre, segregation, conversion, Inquisition, and expulsion. In one sense these efforts toward homogeneity were successful. Over the course of the hundred years from 139–1492, for example, all Jews of Spain either converted or were expelled.[62]

The cookbook may be the starting point for later discrimination against Jews on the Iberian Peninsula and, by extension, in the Mediterranean basin.

Part Two: The Legacy of the Multicultural Cuisine of Al-Andalus (Fifteenth to Seventeenth Century)—the Evolution and Perception of Jewish Food

The official expulsion of Jews from Spain in 1492 marked a radical turning point in the food and culinary practices of the Mosaic people. The second part of this book explores the heritage of the multicultural cuisine of Al-Andalus (fifteenth to seventeenth centuries) and focuses on the evolution of Jewish food and the perception that others had of it. The cookbooks written under Christian domination offer an interesting counterpoint. While cookbooks written in Spain under Christian rule are, at first glance, undeniably rich, their contributions are increased tenfold when they are compared with their predecessors written under Muslim rule. The Christian- and Muslim-period books have nothing in common. This dissimilarity demonstrates that religion was used as a discriminatory food tool in the service of power. To be clear, under Christian rule food was

---

62 Nirenberg, "Was There Race before Modernity?" 241–242. Footnote 20 on p. 242 also says that "The population of Jews in the Crown of Aragon dropped from a high of twenty-seven thousand just before the massacres of 1391, to approximately nine thousand at the time of the expulsion of 1492 (and thereafter, of course, to zero). These figures, which are far below those offered by many historians, are meant primarily to illustrate the scale of the decline. They are taken from Jaume Riera, "Judíos y Conversos en los reinos de la Corona de Aragón durante el siglo, XV," in *La Expulsión de los Judíos de España: II Curso de cultura hispano-judía y sefardí de la Universidad de Castilla-La Mancha* [Toledo] (Castilla–La Mancha: Asociación de Amigos del Museo Sefardí, 1993), 78. Riera provides no evidence for them, however. Henry Kamen, in his self-consciously revisionist "The Mediterranean and the Expulsion of Spanish Jews in 1492," *Past and Present* 119 (1988): 30 –55 provides very similar numbers, but also produces no evidence.

used to identify Jews and persecute. The ubiquity of some foods and the absence of others in "Christian" cookbooks stand out by the food and culinary uniformity they offer since the fifteenth century. This was an orchestrated absence, which aimed at erasing any mark of a culinary past marked by the seal of Semitic cultures.

On the other hand, literary works—and documents from Inquisition trials—are surprisingly plentiful in details about the culinary rites and practices of Jews; and they bear witness to the use of food to discriminate against Jews. Iberian literary works offer what cookbooks cannot—a critical perspective. Food is no longer presented as a mere ingredient; in meal scenes it is shown how discrimination is produced through food. Furthermore, the Inquisition tribunals detected Jews by exploiting their wish to maintain their identity through the food they consumed. The goal of Iberian texts, such as the *Libro de Buen amor*, the *Cancionero de Baena*, the *Cancionero del siglo XV*, and the *Cancionero general* was to satirize the way Christians and conversos[63] treated the eating habits of Jews. They mock the mores of the Christian society that stretched from the fourteenth to sixteenth century.

Finally, two major works—*La Lozana andaluza* and *The Provençal Esther Poem*—from Provence and Italy in the southern Mediterranean reveal taboos. The two stories are alike in that they identify Jews (Jewish women, more precisely) in a context where their religion must remain hidden. The women can only be recognized as Jews by how they behave. One must read between the lines, as silence and secrecy are essential for survival in these texts. So, much more than respect for formal religious dietary laws, belonging dwells in the knowledge that is transmitted through gestures.

Once we understand that food is an identity marker, we can see what the food we do or do not eat says about us. The French gourmet and lawyer Brillat-Savarin wrote, "tell me what you eat and I will tell you what you are." This expression is perfectly suited to the study of Spanish Jews as early as the twelfth to thirteenth century, and later in the fifteenth century. Between 1400 and 1700, three trends emerge when examining the relationship between food and Jewish identity. If Jewish holidays were one of the main vectors of culinary transmission, they also harmed their observants. It was in the meals themselves, rather than in recipes, that the absence of pork and the high consumption of eggplant

63 *Converso*: "[A] medieval Spanish Jew who converted to Catholicism, usually in order to avoid persecution from either the Spanish Inquisition or the Portuguese Inquisition" (https://www.collinsdictionary.com/dictionary/english/converso).

and cilantro revealed Jewishness. This is such a symbolic trio of foods that it is noted in judicial documents (trials, etc.) and juridical (responsa,[64] etc.) sources.

Lastly, one must address Inquisition trial documents. Clearly they are not cookbooks, but they do nonetheless capture in writing Jewish skills that were otherwise traditionally transmitted orally. Without any intent, Inquisition tribunals made an inventory of the culinary practices of Jews. There is no extant Jewish cookbook from medieval and early modern times; the centrality of oral transmission in Jewish culture cannot be underestimated. By officially recording their practices, the Holy Office noted that Mosaic food customs were different from those of ruling Christian society and, ipso facto, declared them Jewish. Gradually, Jewish culinary practices were more and more frequently defined in opposition to Christian orthodoxy. These are signs of diasporic Jewish cuisine.

Part Three: Sephardic Jewish Culinary Heritage—Rebirth and the Desire to Recognize a Past Legacy

The final part of the book discusses well-known recipes that demonstrate how the new preserves the old when, through culinary reconfigurations, Andalusian Judaism lives on. I detail the *Kitāb al-ṭabīḫ* dishes common in Spanish Sephardic cuisine. Questioning the permanence of a Jewish and Sephardic tradition is the red thread in the Jewish culinary history of Spain. However, the lack of knowledge and recognition of the Spanish Sephardic culinary legacy in Spain is problematic. Indeed, there are few publications on the subject and it is difficult to inventory cookbooks dealing with Sephardic cuisine. However, in the *Kitāb al-ṭabīḫ* there are dishes that were consumed by the Jews of Spain. This enables reflection on the evolution of their names and ingredients over the long term. Thus, to recipes containing dried beef, oriza, and mufleta, and other Spanish Sephardic, were added those of the diaspora.

What would Jewish culture be without its diaspora? Probably nothing, because the Jewish people are, and have been from the beginning, a people both characterized and enriched by movement. However, the diaspora—an fundamental component of Jewish culture—has only produced a few publications on Sephardic cuisine, although there has been some interest in the Americas. It is all the more necessary, then, to look at those recipes from the *Kitāb al-ṭabīḫ* that

---

64 Isidore Epstein, *The "Responsa" of Rabbi Solomon ben Adreth of Barcelona (1235–1310) as a Source of the History of Spain: Studies in the Communal Life of Jews in Spain as Reflected in the "Responsa"* (London: Kegan Paul, 1925).

exist in the Sephardic culinary heritage of the Mediterranean basin. A thematic analysis carried out around targeted dishes from this region, such as alheiras, boranía, chickpea croquettes, mufleta, mazapan and other emblematic dishes. It reveals that Sephardic food has spread to Morocco, Portugal, Italy, Turkey, the Middle East, and Latin America.

The conclusion of this book concerns illustrated and annotated Jewish recipes. The little information provided by the recipes from the original source made me appreciate my culinary knowledge; the choice of proportions is therefore my own. Three of the six explicitly Jewish recipes from the *Kitāb al-ṭabīḫ*—the "Stuffed, Buried Jewish Dish," the "Jewish Chicken Dish," and the "Jewish Dish of Stuffed Eggplant with Meat"—are described in this chapter. These culinary reconstructions stick as closely to the cookbook—which does not always state the amount of ingredients—as possible. These three recipes were chosen for their presence across time in Sephardic culinary tradition. Furthermore, the Sephardic culinary heritage of the Mediterranean basin is represented through other medieval Iberian recipes, such as oriza, murakkaba, and makrūḍ. They were selected for their significance and also for their connection to festive celebrations. They are the result of culinary reconstructions.

What the reader should bear in mind is the fact that *Jews, Food, and Spain* is a book on food *history*. It aims to trace the culinary history of Jews from facts and sources, from the twelfth century to the present day. It should be read in conjunction with *Sephardi: Cooking the History: Recipes of the Jews of Spain and the Diaspora from the 13th Century to Today*, which is a cookbook to actually be used in the kitchen. It contains recipes prepared by Jews, conversos, and Sephardim which are an integral part of Jewish culinary heritage.

Part One

THE JEWS' PLACE IN THE CONSTRUCTION OF AN ANDALUSIAN CUISINE (TWELFTH TO FOURTEENTH CENTURIES)

The term "al-Andalus" is typically used to refer to the land of the Iberian Peninsula under Muslim rule during the Middle Ages. This great expanse in both space and time, covering nearly eight centuries of history (711–1492), witnessed multiple events that will not fully be addressed in this book. Moreover, the focus here is on al-Andalus in the period that begins with the rise of the Almohads. This was when first cookbook from al-Andalus we know of was written: the *Kitāb al-ṭabīẖ*. The history of al-Andalus is essentially a history of identity. Jews, Muslims, and Christians coexisted and, as power changed hands, they all contributed to the identity of contemporary Spain. Inevitably, this surprisingly multifaceted period[1] produced a cuisine reflecting the diverse cultures that were living side by side. While Christian cuisine is fairly easy to isolate, the boundary between Jewish and Muslim cuisine is blurred. And why would there necessarily be a boundary? Yet, in order to shed light on the long history of Iberian Jews and their food culture, it is important to integrate these features into a general history: that of Spain in the late Middle Ages.

1 This historiographical difference is embodied by Américo Castro, who has a positive outlook on this multicultural and religious cohabitation, and Sánchez Albornoz, who rejects any positive aspects of the mixing of different religious communities). See Américo Castro, *España en su historia; cristianos, moros y judíos* (Buenos Aires: Editorial Losada, 1948); Américo Castro, *La Realidad histórica de España* (México: Editorial Porrúa, 1954); Claudio Sánchez-Albornoz, *España, un enigma histórico* (Buenos Aires: Editorial Sudamericana, 1956); Joseph Pérez, *Histoire de l'Espagne* (Paris: Fayard, 1996); Simon Barton, *A History of Spain*, 2nd ed. (London: Red Globe Press, 2009); Raymond Carr, *Spain: A History* (Oxford: Oxford University Press, 2000).

CHAPTER 1

A Unique "Witness" to Complex Realities

A. What Does the Historiography Say?

As part of the general revival of interest in the history of medieval food,[1] several works have focused on the Iberian Peninsula[2]—specifically al-Andalus[3]—and,

---

1 Charles Perry, Maxime Rodinson, and A. J. Arberry, eds., *Medieval Arab Cookery* (Totnes: Prospect Books, 2001); Bruno Laurioux, "Le goût médiéval est-il arabe? À propos de la 'Saracen connection,'" in *Une histoire culinaire du Moyen Âge*, ed. Bruno Laurioux (Paris: H. Champion, 2005), 305–335; Piera Montserrat, *Forging Communities: Food and Representation in Medieval and Early Modern Southwestern Europe* (Fayetteville: University of Arkansas Press, 2018); Rudolf Grewe, "Hispano-Arabic Cuisine in the Twelfth Century," in *Du manuscrit à la table. Essais sur la cuisine du Moyen Âge essais sur la cuisine au Moyen Âge et répertoire des manuscrits médiévaux contenant des recettes culinaires*, ed. Carole Lambert (Montréal: Presses Universitaires de Montréal, 1992), 142–148.

2 Manuela Marín, "Cuisine d'Orient, cuisine d'Occident:" 9–22; Henri Bresc, "Editorial," "Cultures et nourritures de l'occident musulman: Essais dédiés à Bernard Rosenberger," ed. Henric Bresc, special issue, *Médiévales*, no. 33 (1997): 5–8; Manuela Marín, "La alimentación en las culturas islámicas," in *La alimentación en las culturas islámicas*, ed. Manuela Marín and David Waines (Madrid: Ediciones Mundo Árabe e Islam, 1994), 89–110; Manuela Marín and David Waines, "From al-Andalus to Spain: Arab traces in Spanish cooking," *Food and History* 2, no. 2 (2004): 35–52.

3 Bernard Rosenberger, "Diététique et cuisine dans l'Espagne musulmane du XIIIe siècle," in *Le désir et le goût, une autre histoire (XIIIe–XVIIIe). Actes du colloque international à la mémoire de J. L. Flandrin*, ed. Odile Redon, L. Sallman and S. Steinberg (Saint-Denis: PU de Vincennes, 2003), 175–180; Anne Wilson, "The Saracen Connection: Arab Cuisine in the Medieval West," *Petits propos culinaires* 8 (1981): 13–22; Ambrosio Huici Miranda, "La cocina hispano-magribī durante la época almohade," *Revista del Instituto de Estudios Islámicos* 5 (1957): 137–155; García Sánchez, "Comida de enfermos, dieta de sanos: procesos culinarios y hábitos alimenticios en los textos médicos andalusí," 57–87; idem, "La consommation des épices et des plantes aromatiques en al-Andalus," 41–54; idem, "La Alimentación en la Andalucía islámica," 139–178; idem, "La alimentación de los andalusíes: entre las normas médicas y la vida cotidiana," 121–134; idem, "El sabor de lo dulce en la gastronomía andalusí," 165–204; David Waines, "The Culinary Culture of al-Andalus," in *The legacy of Muslim*

to a lesser extent, on recipe collections from the period.[4] Scholarship has only focused on the history of al-Andalusian Jews; the Jews of medieval Spain, then, require more attention.[5] In other words, few works relate solely to the history of the Jews in this territory and period by highlighting the richness of Jewish culture. Usually, instead, Jewish culture is compared with that of the Muslims and/or Christians. The subject is often discussed in terms of medieval multiculturalism, in which Jews are compared with Christians and, less frequently, with Muslims.[6] This trend is even more pronounced as regards the Iberian Peninsula. The comparatively weak body of historical work on Jews in general was noted by Robert Bonfil in the early 1990s.[7] This dearth of writing explains why Jewish history has been constructed in parallel to, and seldom integrated into, history[8] in the broader sense—a phenomenon supposedly due to the lack of a Jewish "self-consciousness." An explanation can also be found in the fact that Jews were never in a position of power; this has limited the narration of past events to within the Jewish nation. Thus, the *Book of Tradition* (1161) by Abraham Ibn Da'ud Halevi[9] is one of the very few expressions of a desire to

---

Spain, ed. S. Khadra Jayyusi (Leiden: Brill, 1992), 725–738; Bolens, *La cuisine andalouse un art de vivre*; Guichard, "Alimentation et cuisine en Al-Andalus," 337–357.

4 Bernard Rosenberger, "Dietética y cocina en el mundo musulmán occidental según el Kitāb al-ṭabīj, recetario de época almohade," in *Cultura alimentaria Andalucía-América*, ed. Antonio Garrido (México: Universidad Nacional Autónoma, 1996), 13–35; Marín, "Matériaux pour l'histoire de l'alimentation hispano-maghrébine," 297–304; Huici and Marín, *La cocina hispano-magrebí*; Fernando de la Granja, "La cocina arabigo-andaluza según un manuscrito inédito" (PhD diss., Universidad Complutense de Madrid, 1960); Carolyn Nadeau, "From Kitāb al-ṭabīḫ to Llibre de Sent Soví: Continuities and Shifts in the Earliest Iberian Cooking Manuals," in *Forging Communities: Food and Representation in medieval and Early Modern Southwestern* Europe, ed. Piera Montserrat (Fayetteville: University of Arkansas Press, 2018), 21–34.

5 Haïm Zafrani, *Juifs d'Andalousie et du Maghreb* (Paris: Maisonneuve et Larose, 1996); Gerber, *The Jews of Spain*; Eliyahu Ashtor, *The Jews of Moslem Spain*, vols. 1–3 (Philadelphia: Jewish Publication Society of America, 1973).

6 María Filomena Lopes De Baros and José Ramón Hinojosa Montalvo, eds., *Minorías étnico religiosas na Península Ibérica* (Évora: Edições Colibri, 2008); Ron Barkaï, ed., *Chrétiens, musulmans et Juifs dans l'Espagne médiévale: De la convergence à l'expulsion* (Paris: Cerf, 1994); Besson et al., *Chrétiens, Juifs et musulmans*; Charles-Emmanuel Dufourcq, "La coexistence des chrétiens et des musulmans dans Al-Andalus et dans le Maghrib du Xe siècle," in *Actes du 9e congrès des congrès de la Société des historiens médiévistes de l'enseignement supérieur public, Dijon, 1978* (Paris: Société Les Belles Lettres, 1979): 209–224.

7 Robert Bonfil, "El legado historiográfico de los judíos españoles," in *Moreset Sefarad: El legado de Sefarad*, vol. 2 (Jerusalem: Editorial Magnes-Universidad Hebrea, 1993), 476–493.

8 Claude Denjean, "Pourquoi parler de civilisation juive médiévale?" *Cahiers de civilisation médiévale* 62, no. 1, booklet 245 (2019): 17–47.

9 Abraham Ibn Da'ud Halevi, also known as Ravad of Toledo, was born in al-Andalus, in Cordova, in 1110 and died in Toledo in 1180. He was a rabbi, astronomer, historian, doctor,

understand al-Andalusian Jewish history—even if the text has been relegated to the lower depths of the historiography.[10] This lack of attention makes it easy to understand the current state of research into the culinary heritage of Jews in al-Andalus and the Iberian Peninsula. Very few studies exist, and those that do are only a part of the rare works mentioned in the historiography. Consequently, the history of the Jews has been narrated in terms of religion (Judaism) rather than people. The Jews have customs, a literature, philosophical and scientific knowledge, rites, and practices, as well as religion—all of the things, in short, that make up a civilization.[11] This is why the subject of the cuisine and culinary heritage of Jews is so complex.

From reading Sephardic Jewish cookbooks published today, it is clear that Jewish cuisine is a topic that sparks great interest. Yet none of these books, with the exception of *A Drizzle of Honey* by David Gitlitz and Linda Kay Davidson,[12] is constructed against a broader historical background. These cookbooks are generally limited to the narration of facts going back two generations, handed down by Jewish grandmothers who—in the best of cases—jotted down the name of some ingredients on a scrap of paper. In reality, the reasons why Jewish culinary heritage is absent from the general culinary heritage of contemporary Spain lies in fifteenth-century Spain. while recipes are usually passed down orally, cookbooks have left, and continue to leave, a permanent written trace of a culinary heritage that has been transmitted across generations. One of the central aims of this book, then, is to understand why there are so few recipe books of "Spanish cuisine" that acknowledge the place of Jewish food.

As concerns the publication of Sephardic Jewish cookbooks, keep in mind that the Norwegian historian Henry Notaker's *Printed Cookbooks in Europe, 1470–1700: A Bibliography of Early Modern Culinary Literature*[13] includes no recipe books published on Jewish cuisine before the nineteenth century. Notaker's

---

and philosopher, who fled to Toledo after the rise of the Almohads (1147–1269). He is the author of many works, in particular *Sefer ha-Ḳabbalah* (The Book of Tradition), in 1161. There are numerous studies and translations of *Sefer ha-Ḳabbalah*. See G. D. Cohen, trans., *A Critical Edition with a Translation and Notes of the Book of the Tradition by Abraham ibn Daud* (London: Routledge and Kegan Paul, 1969). On Abraham Ibn Daud (Avendauth), see also Gerber, *The Jews of Spain*, 27, 46, 50, 76, 97.

10 Bonfil, "El legado historiográfico de los judíos españoles"; Riera i Sans, "La conflictivitat de l'alimentació dels jueus medievals," 294–314.

11 Denjean, "Pourquoi parler de civilisation juive médiévale?": 17–47

12 Davidson and Gitlitz, *A Drizzle of Honey*.

13 Henry Notaker, *Printed Cookbooks in Europe, 1470–1700: A Bibliography of Early Modern Culinary Literature* (New Castle: Oak Knoll Press and Hes & De Graaf, 2010).

latest volume *A History of Cookbooks: From Kitchen to Page over Seven Centuries*,[14] which is the leading reference book for published cookbooks, contains one chapter on Jewish cookbooks written between 1815 and 1945.[15] It is noteworthy that not one of these cookbooks is in Spanish. Out of 102 titles, one was written in Italian, and almost all of the rest are in German, Polish, Hungarian, Yiddish, Danish and, of course, English. They all refer to Ashkenazi cuisine.[16]

The catalogue of the New York Public Library[17] lists published cookbooks that are categorized by "region." This means that Jewish cookbooks are included in the category "international Jewish cuisine," then "Ashkenazi Jewish cuisine," and finally "Sephardic Jewish cuisine." Various types of dishes (*knishes, gefilte fish, gizado*), the terms "Yiddish," "Ashkenazi," "Sephardic," and place names (Spain, Morocco, Poland, etc.) are used as a basis of classification. Between 1964 and 2011, thirty-one cookbooks of so-called international Jewish cuisine were published. This count does not include translations into other languages. Yet, it should be pointed out that the widespread publication of Jewish cookbooks in the US makes it difficult to update.

The introduction to John Cooper's book *Eat and Be Satisfied*, offers a non-exhaustive but interesting summary of culinary works dealing with the history of Jewish cuisine in the nineteenth and twentieth centuries, along with details about these publications.[18] Other major Jewish cookbooks have recently been published, such as Joan Nathan's *King Solomon's Table*,[19] Jennifer Abadi's *Too Good To Passover*,[20] Leah Koening's *The Jewish Cookbook*,[21] Reyna Simnegar's *Persian Food from the Non-Persian Bride: And Other Sephardic Kosher Recipes You Will Love*,[22] Maguy Kakon's *L'Oriental marocain*,[23] Stella Cohen's *Stella's*

---

14 Henry Notaker, *A History of Cookbooks: From Kitchen to Page over Seven Centuries* (Berkley: University of California Press, 2017).

15 Ibid., 233–245.

16 Ashkenazi Jews are from Central and Eastern Europe.

17 See https://www.nypl.org/collections/nypl-recommendations/guides/jewish-cookbooks-region.

18 John Cooper, *Eat and Be Satisfied* (Northvale, NJ: Jason Aronson INC, 1993).

19 Joan Nathan, *King Solomon's Table: A Culinary Exploration of Jewish Cooking from Around the World* (New York: Alfred A. Knopf, 2017).

20 Jennifer Abadi, *Too Good To Passover: Sephardic & Judeo-Arabic Seder Menus and Memories from Africa, Asia and Europe* (New York: CreateSpace Independent Publishing Platform, 2018).

21 Leah Koening, *The Jewish Cookbook* (New York: Phaidon, 2019).

22 Reyna Simnegar, *Persian Food from the Non-Persian Bride: And Other Sephardic Kosher Recipes You Will Love* (New York: Philipp Feldheim, 2011).

23 Maguy Kakon, *L'oriental marocain. Des siècles d'art culinaire Juif* (Casablanca: La croisée des chemins, 2018).

Sephardic Table: Jewish Family Recipes from the Mediterranean Island of Rhodes,[24] and Ana Bensadon's *Recetas endiamentadas*,[25] and so on. As concerns the list of cookbooks mentioned in the "Sephardic" part of this catalogue, there are forty-two works, only five of which were published in Spain, and nine in Spanish (including one in Ladino). This disparity illustrates the lack of knowledge about, and acknowledgement of, the Spanish Sephardic culinary heritage within the current Spanish culinary history. The complexity of producing an inventory of Sephardic cookbooks is noted in the catalogue of the New York Public Library, as one is invited to consult "the cookbooks of countries or regions such as Algeria, Bulgaria, Greece, India, Iran, Iraq, Italy, the Mediterranean, Morocco, North Africa, Portugal, Spain, Syria, Turkey, Tunisia, Venezuela, and Yemen." This long list of countries where Sephardic Jews live testifies to the extent of the diaspora, a list to which Brazil, Ethiopia, Israel and many others could be added.

It must be concluded that if this topic is of real interest in the US—with chronological and spatial boundaries that are sometimes far removed from those presented in this book—European historians have struggled to research this complex topic. There are only a small number of scientific publications on Jewish food, as well as editions of "Jewish" Spanish cookbooks, produced in Europe. Is this because the topic is inextricably entwined with the horrors of the history of Jews in Europe?

Regarding Jewish cookbooks that are specifically Spanish, there are six publications dated between 1984 and 2003. Two of them are written in French[26] and published in France, three in Spanish[27] published in Spain, and one in English[28] published in the United States. Before 1984, there are no Spanish Jewish cookbooks. Thirty-five years later, only three of these books—explicitly linking Spain to its Jewish culinary history—have been published in Spanish, and the most recent dates back more than ten years ago. How do we explain this lack

---

24 Stella Cohen, *Stella's Sephardic Table: Jewish Family Recipes from the Mediterranean Island of Rhodes* (Hoberman Collection, 2012).

25 Ana Bensadon, *Recetas endiamentadas* (Alcobendas: Nagrela Editores, 2013).

26 Meri Badi, *250 recettes de cuisine juive espagnole* (Paris: Editions Jacques Grancher, 1984); Esther Benbassa, *Cuisine judéo-espagnole* (Paris: Scribe, 1984).

27 Jacinto García and Rosa Tovar, *Un banquete por Sefarad: cocina y costumbres de los judíos españoles* (Gijón: Trea, 2007); Alfredos Juderías, *Alfredos Juderías, Viaje por la cocina hispano-judía* (Barcelona: Seteco, 1990).

28 Davidson and Davidson, *A Drizzle of Honey*; Génie Milgrom's work could also be mentioned. See Génie Milgrom, *Recipes of My 15 Grandmothers: Unique Recipes and Stories from the Times of the Crypto-Jews during the Spanish Inquisition* (Jerusalem and New York: Gefen Publishing House, 2019). However, contrary to what the title suggests, this book does not seem to have been written on the basis of historical sources.

of the Jewish tradition in current Spanish culinary heritage? The only Spanish cookbook that includes Jewish recipes on the same footing as other recipes is Claudia Roden's *The Food of Spain*, where the author writes that "for centuries, Spain erased its Muslim and Jewish history from national memory."[29] Just as Roden provides an account of the Spanish Moorish culinary heritage,[30] she also includes several pages on the culinary heritage of Jews.[31] The fact remains that little current research has been specifically devoted to the food practices of Jews in al-Andalus on the late Middle Ages or early Renaissance. This book aims to fill this gap, by reintegrating Jewish cuisine into the historically transmitted food heritage of Spain.

B. The Coexistence of Jews and Muslims: Nineth to Twelfth Centuries

The Iberian Peninsula has a complex historiography. As early as 70 CE, when the second Temple was destroyed, religious conflict emerged and marked the beginning of the large dispersion of Jews worldwide.[32] The entire southern part of the Iberian Peninsula witnessed the gradual arrival of Jews of the second diaspora from the Roman Empire (70 CE, but mainly 135, when living in Jerusalem was forbidden to Jews).[33] The earliest evidence documenting the presence of the Jewish people on the Iberian Peninsula—and, more specifically, in what we now call "Spain"—is the imprint of a Hebrew seal that measures eighty-seven-centimeters in an amphora that was found in San Agustín de Ibiza in 1907. It dates back to the first century. The two Hebrew letters (דז) are from one to two centimeters. This evidences the existence of a commercial contact between Judea and the Balearic Islands.[34] A second piece of evidence is a Latin engraving (*Iudaea*) on a gravestone in the city of Adra in the Almería province (Andalusia). The engraving mentions the name of a young Jewish girl who died in the second to third century (150–250 CE)[35] at the age of one year, three months, and a day.

29 Claudia Roden, *The Food of Spain* (Harmondsworth: Penguin, 2012); idem, *Le livre de la cuisine espagnole* (Paris: Flammarion, 2012).

30 Ibid. 24.

31 Ibid., 26–31.

32 Jodi Campbel, *At the First Table: Food and Social Identity in Early Modern Spain* (Lincoln: Nebraska Press University, 2017), 72.

33 Ashtor, *The Jews of Moslem Spain*; Gerber, *The Jews of Spain*, 2–4.

34 Alexander Bar-Magen Numhauser, *Hispanojewish Archaeology: The Jews of Hispania in Late Antiquity and the Early Middle Ages Through Their Material Remains* (Leiden: Brill, 2021), xx.

35 In 212, Jews, like other groups, became citizens of the empire.

She was named Annia Salomonula (or Hannah bat Shelomoh).[36] Another grave of a Jewish person was also found in the city of Cordova,[37] also in Andalusia.

The settlement of Jewish communities occurred primarily on the coast and in the south of Spain, most likely due to the large number of tradesmen who were established in ports there in order to better manage their businesses. The situation of the Jewish diaspora in the Roman Empire greatly deteriorated when Christianity became the state religion in the fourth century. In the following century, Jews on the Iberian Peninsula encountered the hostility of the Visigoths, "a barbaric group of people of German origin who had been converted to Christianity,"[38] who in 613 forced Jews to convert.[39] Finally, in 711, Muslims crossed the Strait of Gibraltar, which fostered the liberation of Jews from the oppression of the Visigoths.[40] Beginning in this period, which spans nearly three centuries (711–950), Spain became a spiritual and intellectual center of Talmudic authority and in the teaching of "Spanish Judaism," both of which were characterized by Jewish creativity and Arabic knowledge and culture. It is also important to highlight the distinction between the Umayyad Caliphate of Cordova with that of Baghdad in the tenth century, which led to a "maturing and emancipation of Spanish Judaism, far from the authority of Babylon."[41] Cordova thus became recognized as the most prosperous Jewish center of the Mediterranean in the tenth to eleventh centuries. Still, the importance of Toledo and Granada must not be forgotten.[42] The coexistence of these three religions could also be found in medieval Sicily[43] where there was a small Mosaic[44]

---

36 Yosef Hayim Yerushalmi also mentions this information, but in less detail, in his work. See Yerushalmi, *Sefardica*, 17. See Hispania Epigráfica, "Epitafio de la judía Annia Salomonula," register number 41, http://eda-bea.es/pub/record_card_1.php?page=2&rec=41.

37 See Hispania Epigráfica, ref. CIL II 2232.

38 Yerushalmi, *Sefardica*, 17–18.

39 Ibid., 18.

40 Gabriel Martinez-Gros and Sophie Makariou, *Histoire de Grenade* (Paris: Fayard, 2018), 13.

41 Yerushalmi, *Sefardica*, 17.

42 Gerber, *The Jews of Spain*.

43 Annliese Nef, "La Sicile de Charybde en Scylla? Du tout culturel au transculturel," in *Mélanges de l'École française de Rome—Moyen* Âge, vol. 128.2 (Roma: Ecole française de Rome, 2016), 603–616.

44 Sergio Caldarella, "The Jews of Sicily," *The Philadelphia Jewish Voice*, March 33, 2008; Henri Bresc, *Arabes de langue, Juifs de religion: L'évolution du judaïsme sicilien dans l'environnement latin, XIIe–XVe siècles* (Paris: Bouchène, 2001); Cyrille Aillet explains that there had been large Jewish communities in Sicily since antiquity. See the pedagogical workshop "Retour sur la question médiévale d'agrégation interne: chrétiens, Juifs et musulmans. Pouvoirs et minorités dans l'espace méditerranéen (XIe–XVe siècle)" at the Institut du monde arabe as part of the Rendez-vous de l'Histoire conference, April 12–14, 2019.

community mainly comprised of slaves sent to the island before the destruction of the Temple of Jerusalem in 70 CE.[45]

In *Sefardica,* Yosef Yerushalmi writes that

> if we want to understand the specificity of medieval Spanish Judaism, we can only do so by considering the specificity of Spain. Spain is the only country where, for eight centuries, three major groups—Jews, Christians and Muslims—lived side by side, weaving a network of extremely complex relationships, mixing understanding and fantasy, respect and denigration, mutual influences and incessant wars.[46]

Textual records from two manuscripts found in Cairo's Geniza bear witness to the difficult situation eleventh-century Spanish Jews found themselves in.[47] As Olivia Remie Constable writes, "the intimate details provided by Geniza records reveal aspects of the daily working of these facilities which are unviable in contemporary Muslim sources." It is, first of all, a handwritten letter sent to Ibn Awkal describing the civil war in Cordoba on May 19, 1011 which reveals it;[48] The author of the letter, written in Judeo-Arabic dating from November to December 1057, describes how a Jew was caught by the Berbers. This is a letter from a Jew from Toledo (who emigrated to Jerusalem) to his sister, which there a disturbing allusion to the condition of Jews in al-Andalus.[49] In such complex context, it is always necessary to identify who held the power and which groups were minorities

---

45 Presence confirmed by Pope Gregory the Great in 592. See http://www.jewishencyclopedia.com/articles/11865-palermo.

46 Yerushalmi, *Sefardica,* 26.

47 Concerning commerce and charity in the Jewish community in Cairo in the eleventh and twelfth centuries, see Olivia Remie Constable, *Housing the Stranger in the Mediterranean World Lodging: Trade, and Travel in Late Antiquity and the Middle Ages,* (Cambridge: Cambridge University Press, 2004), 85–88.

48 José Martínez Delgado and Amir Ashur, *La vida cotidiana de los judíos de alandalus (siglos X–XIII)* (Córdoba: UCO Press, 2021), 223 (manuscript T-S 12.218: "En aprietos"): . . . mi señor si hay noticias de Hasday [ben Hala]bo. Él está atrapado en Córdoba donde están en un gran aprieto."

49 Ibid., 85 (manuscript T-S 13j9.4: "Nuevas desde Tierra Santa"): "Ya te he enviado algunas cartas y no sé si las has recibido pues estoy al tanto del desorden en Occidente y de lo que allí ha occurido."

On food and sharing meals with non-Christians, David Freidenreich writes:

> Simon of Bisignano explains in his *Summa* (ca. 1177–79) that the prohibition on Jewish food stems from "curses and hatred for Jewish superstitions" felt by Christians, in this case specifically Christian hatred for superstitions associated with dietary impurity. Although Simon understands the prohibition against unleavened bread found in *Nullus* to refer to all Jewish food, he explicitly rejects the notion that Jewish, or any other food is actually impure. . . . Twelfth- and thirteenth-century commentaries regarding commensality with non-Christians are, thus, characterized by their conservatism with respect to existing legal categories and the contributions of earlier canonists, as well as by their detachment from external developments and, for that matter, realia.[50]

The beginning of the twelfth century (1130) marks the dawn of a new imperium, the Almohad Empire (1130/47–1269), a "prophetic" empire embodied in Ibn Tūmart, which imposed a dogmatic vision of Islam, the aim of which was to "reform the morals of the West."[51] The Jewish and Christian minorities living under Muslim rule thus had to conform to the laws of the Muslim majority. The power of tradition ruled and the only reform possible was that which aimed to increase compliance with the Islamic model. Ibn Tūmart intended to extend this vision of a renewed Islam around the idea of divine unicity (the *tawḥīd*) to the entire *Dār al-Islām*,[52] from China to the Atlantic. Almohad Spain was located between the birthplace of Christianity and the Muslim West that the *Mahdī*[53] sought to reform by adding a messianic dimension to Islam.

---

50 Freidenreich, "Sharing Meals with Non-Christians": 44, 73.

51 Pascal Buresi, "L'Empire Almohade. Le Maghreb et Al-Andalus (1130–1269)," in *Les Empires. Antiquités et Moyen Âge. Analyse comparée*, ed. Frédéric Hurlet (Rennes: PU de Rennes, 2008), 221–237.

52 The author defines the *Dār al-Islām* as Islamic territories from the Middle Ages to the present day. It is at once an overarching structure and a legal framework for exercising power from the Iberian Peninsula to China and the coast of the Indian Ocean.

53 Maribel Fierro, "Le mahdī Ibn Tûmart et al-Andalus: l'élaboration de la légitimité almohade," *Revue des mondes musulmans et de la Méditerranée* 91–94 (2000): 107–124. "The term al-mahdī literally means 'well guided' (by God). Mahdism is one of the paths in the Muslim tradition to legitimize a political leader, especially when the aim is to renew society and eliminate old political-religious elites. Mahdism can be apprehended as the perpetuation of the *khalîfat Allâh* model, that is, the leader is considered a representative of God on Earth. It is the model preserved by the Shiites, whereas Sunnis prefer the *khalîfat rasûl Allâh*

Rachid Bourouiba[54] remarks upon this vision of Islamic dominance in his description of the letters that the *Mahdi* addressed to the Almohad community in the *Book of Mohammed Ibn Tumert* (Ibn Tūmart). When considered in this context—in which, as Pascal Buresi writes, Almohad doctrine embraced "the censorship of mores, the prohibition of wine, the obligation of prayer and *djihād*"[55]—it is not difficult to grasp the tense climate created vis-à-vis minorities living in the land. Moreover, the Almohads extended the process of Arabization and Islamization that the Almoravids[56] had begun in 1042–1147,[57] while favoring Arabic political and literary culture. In line with the idea of *tawḥīd,* the religious and Islamic culture within local society had become the hobby horse of the Almohads. Consequently, the regime has been labeled as "totalitarian."[58] It wished to establish a fundamentalist form of Islam , breaking with the previous Almoravids dynasty. This powerful aspiration led to numerous forced conversions of Christians and Jews in the *Dār al-Islām.*[59] These minorities continued to face a difficult situation between 1238 and 1492 under the Nasrid Emirate (this southern part of the peninsula contained the large city of Granada and it extended to Málaga and Almería). The conversion of non-Muslim minorities in the last bastion of *Dār al-Islām* on the Iberian Peninsula continued while Christians started converting non-Christians in their newly acquired lands.

At this time, the rule of the "those who profess the unity of God" was collapsing, and many Muslims, witnessing the rise of Christianity, took refuge in the Granada of Sultan Mohammed I "The Red" ("*El Rojo*"). Many Jews followed, fleeing both the Christians and the Almohads. During the last two centuries of the *Dār al-Islām* on the Iberian Peninsula, the kingdom of the Nasrid emirs

---

model. Despite everything, at different historical periods and in different forms, this model remerged in the Sunni world, and the Almohad period (twelfth century) was one of them." Translation by the author.

54 Rachid Bourouiba, "La doctrine Almohade," *Revue de l'Occident musulman et de la Méditerranée* 1, nos. 13–14 (1973): 141–158.

55 Buresi, "L'Empire Almohade. Le Maghreb et Al-Andalus (1130–1269)," 221–237.

56 The term "Almoravids" comes from the Arabic term "a*l-Murābiṭūn,* literally "those from the ribats."

57 The Almoravids were a Berber dynasty that ruled from 1042 until 1147. The capital of the empire was Marrakesh. See https://www.universalis.fr/encyclopedie/almoravides/, https://www.lhistoire.fr/les-almoravides-fondent-marrakech.

58 Buresi, "L'Empire Almohade. Le Maghreb et Al-Andalus (1130–1269)," 221–237.

59 Ibid., 145. A letter from Ibn-Tūmart to 'Abd al-Mumīn that states: "Apply yourself to the *djihad* of the veiled infidels [the Almoravids] because it is more important to combat them than to combat the Christians and all the infidels."

turned out to be a heterogeneous concentration of minorities.[60] Christians were usually enslaved, often tortured and condemned to death, while others worked as slaves in the homes of high-level dignitaries. Some converted willingly in order to escape imprisonment (the *elches*,[61] or *tornadizos*).[62] Christian tradesmen, mainly from Genoa, enjoyed special status, as they were exempt from paying tax, the *ğizyah*,[63] in Nasrid territory. The Genoese played another important role through their trade with Jewish families that settled in Granada. As Rachel Arié writes, "Arab sources do not say much about the Jewish community in the Nasrid kingdom between the thirteenth and fifteenth centuries."[64] Dress requirements,[65] specific residential quarters, and the imposed *ğizyah*[66] were all markers of difference that had already been applied under the Almohads and

---

60 Tolan, Boissellier, and Clément, *Minorités et régulations sociales en Méditérranée médiévale*; Sarah Davis-Secord, Belen Vicens, and Robin Vose, *Interfaith Relationships and Perceptions of the Other in the Medieval Mediterranean: Essays in Memory of Olivia Remie Constable* (Cham: Springer Nature Switzerland, 2021); Lopes De Baros and Hinojosa Montalvo, *Minorías étnico religiosas na Península Ibérica* (Évora: Edições Colibri, 2008); Rachel Arié, "Les minorités religieuses dans le royaume de Grenade (1232–1492)," in "Minorités religieuses dans l'Espagne médiévale," ed. Manuela Marín and Joseph Peréz, special issue, *Revue du monde musulman et de la Méditerranée* 63–64 (1992): 51–61: "In the Kingdom of Granada, there was a mixed population composed of descendants of Syrian Arabs, Berbers, and Spaniards converted to Islam, Mozarabs or Arabized Christians, and Jews. Into this ethnic melting pot came Muslim refugees from regions that were reconquered by Christians and North African contributions at the end of the tenth century and in the fourteenth century." Translation by the author.

61 *Elche:* from Hispanic Arabic *ilğ* (captive). It refers to a Christian renegade who converted to Islam. Cf L. P. Harvey, *Muslims in Spain, 1500 to 1614* (Chicago: University of Chicago Press, 2005), 33.

62 From the verb *tornar* in Spanish, *tornadizo* designates someone who changes religion. It is a pejorative term that refers to a renegade and/or a traitor. See Henry Laurens, John Tolan, and Gilles Veinstein, eds., *L'Europe et l'Islam: Quinze siècles d'histoire* (Paris: Odile Jacob, 2009), 69.

63 *Ğizyah* or *ḏjizya* from the Arabic جزية. Refers to the poll tax which, in traditional Muslim law, is levied on non-Muslims [*dhimmis*] in Muslims states [*Dār al-Islām*]. Cf. *Encyclopedia of Islam*, Brill. https://referenceworks.brillonline.com/.

64 Arié, "Les minorités religieuses dans le royaume de Grenade (1232–1492)": 51–61; Erika Spivakovsky, "The Jewish presence in Granada," *Journal of Medieval History* 2, no. 3 (1976): 215–237.

65 Arié, "Les minorités religieuses dans le royaume de Grenade (1232–1492)": 51–61: "From this time, the Jews of al-Andalus were required to wear a yellow headdress instead of a turban and drape a wide belt called a *zunnār*." Translation by the author.

66 Ibid., "This measure, taken between 1314 and 1325 in order to require Jews to pay the legal tribute, remained throughout the fourteenth century, as under the rule of Muhammed V, grandson of Ishmael I, Jews of al-Andalus still wore a yellow emblem." Translation by the author.

earlier,[67] and which endured with the Nasrids. Emmanuelle Tixier du Mesnil and Brigitte Foulon explain that

> during the last days of his rule, Abū Yaqūb Yūsuf (1163–1184] required Jews living on his property to wear special clothes so as to be distinguishable from the rest of the population. It was a black robe with wide sleeves that fell down to the floor. Instead of turbans, Jews also had to wear poorly crafted hats, . . . which fell below the ears. Abū 'Abd Allāh [his son, abandoned this law and] forced them to wear yellow robes and turbans, a custom that endured until 1225.[68]

Nonetheless, Sultan Muhammad V (1354–1391] protected Jews from Christians many times.[69]

As for language, in addition to Hebrew, Jews spoke romance tongues but also and especially Arabic, thus creating Judeo-Arabic, an ethnolect spoken on the Iberian Peninsula, Sicily,[70] and in general by the Jewish communities of the Middle East and North Africa, which testifies to this multicultural coexistence outside of the Iberian *Dār al-Islām*. As Sarah Stroumsa writes,

> Jews living in al-Andalus, as elsewhere, adopted Arabic as their language and developed their own, Jewish version of Arabic culture. . . . Jewish intellectuals were active participants in the court culture. A creative Andalusian Judaeo-Arabic culture flourished, and even Hebrew linguistics and Hebrew poetry in al-Andalus

---

67 In 888, Ibn Tālib, cadi of Kairouan, imposed a distinctive dress code for Jewish (and Christian) *dhimmis*, requiring them to wear a piece of white fabric showing a monkey on one of their shoulders. See Sonia Fellous, *Juifs et Musulmans en Tunisie:* fraternité et déchirements (Paris: Somogy, 2003); In 1118, at the Council of Nablus, dress code restrictions for minorities were mentioned. In 1227, the Council of Narbonne also required Jews to wear special clothes to distinguish them from Christians. On the Iberian Peninsula, kings could excuse certain Jews from wearing them (the sun cross, for instance) if they paid a substantial amount of money. See Besson et al., *Chrétiens, Juifs et musulmans*, 218.

68 Emmanuelle Tixier du Mesnil and Brigitte Foulon, *Al-Andalus: Anthologie* (Paris: Flammarion, 2009), 361.

69 "Despite this prohibition, they benefited from the protection of Muhammad V during the battles that destroyed Castile. The sultan of Granada spared the Jews of Jaén during his raid on the border in 1367, and, having destroyed the city, he brought three hundred Jewish families to his kingdom, sparing them from the fate of the Jews that fell to Henry of Trastamare" (ibid.; translation by the author).

70 Bresc, *Arabes de langue, Juifs de religion.*

> were shaped in the mold of Arabic linguistics and followed Arabic poetical models. . . . The adoption of Arabic high literary culture among Andalusian Christians seems to have been a more protracted and tortuous process. . . . When Arabic did become the language of Christian intellectuals, it was mostly used in domains that are more clearly connected to religious identity.[71]

The many literary writings of Sephardic luminaries such as Maimonides, Shmuel Ha-Nagid, Judah Halevi, Ibn Ezra, Ibn Aqnis, and so many others have made possible to get the measure of the existence of a prolific Jewish literature[72] between the nineth and the thirteenth centuries, as well as to bring to our knowledge the reality of the economic, political, and religious situation in Spain at that time. It explains the flight of many of them to Christian territories in northern Spain.[73] A Hebrew poem that reveals the chaos in which Jews of Spain found themselves in the twelfth century is by of Judah Halevi, who lived part of his life in Toledo under Christian rule:

> O Zion, will you not ask how your captives are—
> The exiles who seek your welfare,
> Who are the remnant of your flocks?
> From west and east, north and south, from every side,
> Accept the greetings of those near and far . . .[74]

As Jane Gerber writes, Judah Halevi "was an innovator in poetry as well as philosophy. . . . His intellectual journey from consummate Spanish poet and courtier to pilgrim and wanderer is mirrored in the conversations of the pagan king and rabbi in his most famous work, the *Kusari*. Composed in the 1130s, it is his most important personal statement on the nature of Jewish history and the Jewish people."[75] Moses Maimonides wrote about religion, medicine, and literature. When many Jews fled to the northern Christian territories, Maimonides and his family fled first to Almería, then between 1159 and 1160 to the Moroccan city

71 Stroumsa, *Andalus and Sefarad: On Philosophy and Its History in Islamic Spain* (Princeton: Princeton University Press, 2019), 15–21. On the topic see also pp. 164–166.

72 Gerber, *The Jews of Spain*, esp. 76–82; Stroumsa, *Andalus and Sefarad*, 19, 23; Yerushalmi, *Sefardica*, 21–22, 24, 27; Brenner, *A Short History of the Jews*, 87. See also Peter Cole, *The Dream of the Poem.*

73 Brenner, *A Short History of the Jews*, 109.

74 Ibid., 88.

75 Gerber, *The Jews of Spain*, 76.

of Fez. He describes the persecution his family endured, and by extension all the Jews of Sefarad his *Mishneh Torah*: "Since we went into exile, the persecutions have not stopped. I have known affliction since childhood, since the womb."[76]

C. Religious Coexistence and Conversion on the Iberian Peninsula (Thirteenth to Fourteenth Centuries)

The arrival of the radical Muslim Almoravides and Almohads changed the rules. "If in previous centuries, Jews had fled Christian for Muslim regions, now they were leaving the Muslim south for the Christian north."[77] Historians[78] have produced numerous theories about the presence and coexistence of the three religions on the Iberian Peninsula. As mentioned earlier, the Mosaic people already occupied the land before the arrival of Christians, and, of course, before Muslims. Manuela Marín offers a different vision of the status of *dhimmi*[79] for minorities who occupied this territory. It was where profits could be made that helped maintain the revenue of the state. The existence of a common idiom played an important role in the relationships between the communities. As a result, the Arabization[80] of Andalusians occurred in two ways. First, through the adoption of Arabic as the language of communication—formal Arabic for the elites, colloquial Arabic for everyone else, which mixed together low Latin and Romance languages.[81] This process of acculturation among elites, even non-Muslims, forged a new Arabic specific to al-Andalus. The second means of Arabization occurred through onomastics. Arabic was used to define an identity, as well as a way to belong to a history. This phenomenon of the voluntary Arabization of Christians and Jews, which was desired just as much to gain access to, and reap the benefits of, the prestige of Arabic culture, started in the nineth century and

---

76 Ibid., 81.

77 Brenner, *A Short History of the Jews*, 85.

78 This historiographic difference is embodied in Américo Castro (who had a positive view of multicultural and multireligious cohabitation) and Sánchez Albornoz (who denied anything positive about the mixing of different religious communities).

79 Concerning the *dhimmī* (ذِمِّي), see note 66 above. See also David Wasserstein, "The Muslims and the Golden Age of the Jews," in *Dhimmis and Others: Jews and Christians and the World of Classical Islam*, vol. 17, ed. Uri Ruben and David Wasserstein (Eisenbrauns: Israel Oriental Studies, 1997), 179–196.

80 Cyrille Aillet, "Identité chrétienne, arabisation et conversion à Cordoue au IXe siècle," in *Les Chrétiens dans la ville*, ed. Françoise Thélamon and Cyrille Aillet (Mont-Saint Aignan: PU de Rennes et du Havre, 2006), 65–77.

81 Federico Corriente, *Diccionario de arabismos y voces afines en Iberorromance* (Madrid: Gredos, 1999).

reached its height in the tenth century. Nevertheless, Christians had a negative view of these conversions because less than one inhabitant out of one thousand knew how to speak and write in Latin at the time.[82]

The birth of the "voluntary martyrs of Cordova"[83] movement, led by Mozarab[84] shows how radical was the reaction to the process of Arabization among Christian elites in the emirate's capital in the nineth century. The later "Mozarabs,"[85] who settled in the northern parts of the Iberian Peninsula in the eleventh century during the Christian invasion (specifically in Toledo after the Christian invasion of 1085), enjoyed this laudatory attribution and it was also used by Alfonso VI. Indeed, the name "Mozarab" was claimed and transmitted by the Mozarabs themselves. However, internal struggles—within a number of neo-Muslim[86] movements that were opposed to the arrival of Christianity—demonstrated that there was a perpetual state of rebellion in various territories, depending on their ruling majority. The situation continued to evolve. It was mainly in the twelfth century, in Cordova and in Toledo (1148), that the forced conversions of Jews and Christians under Muslim rule began.

Sarah Stroumsa points out that, starting in 1066, Granada was the scene of one of the largest anti-Jewish pogroms under medieval Islam. The first expulsion of Jews and Christians from Spain occurred in the twelfth century.[87] Gabriel Martínez-Gros remarks that the uprising in Granada resulted when the Jewish vizier Joseph Ibn Nagrela—son of one of the first Jews in the royal court, Samuel Ibn Nagrela[88]—offered the throne of the city to "a vassal of the Zirids, the king of Almería, Ibn Sumadith, in exchange for continuing to manage his finances. But the conspiracy spread and the conspirators sounded the alarm in the city on

82 Mahmoud Hussein and Philippe Calderon, dirs., *L'âge d'or de l'Islām. L'épopée andalouse* (Paris: France Télévision Distribution, 2001).

83 Pierre Guichard, "La trajectoire historique des mozarabes d'Espagne," in *Mutations, identités en Méditerranée. Moyen Âge et époque contemporaine*, ed. Henri Bresc (Saint-Denis: Bouchène, 2000), 111–122.

84 The term "Mozarab" comes from the Arabic term *musta'rib*, literally "Arabized." It designates Arabic-speaking Christians under Muslim rule in al-Andalus.

85 Jean-Pierre Molénat, "Le passage des mozarabes d'al-Andalus vers l'Espagne chrétienne," in *Passages, Déplacements des hommes, circulation des textes et des identités dans l'Occident médiéval*, ed. Joëlle Ducos and Patrick Henriet (Toulouse: Presses Universitaires du Midi, 2013), 67–76. He writes: "The origin of the etymon is obviously the Arabic *musta'rib*, which can be translated as "Arabizing" or "Arabized"; on the other hand, Simonet insists on the national resistance of those he studies, since he includes converts to Islam, neo-Muslims, usually called *muwalladūn*, or 'renegades.'" Translation by the author.

86 Ibid.

87 Sarah Stroumsa, "Between Acculturation and Conversion in Islamic Spain: The Case of Banū Ḥasday," *Mediterranean International Journal for the Transfer of Knowledge* 1 (2016): 9–36.

88 Martinez-Gros and Makariou, *Histoire de Grenade*, 37.

the night of December 31, 1066.[89] Berbers and Andalusians, brought together for once, launched an assault on the fortress of Alhambra—where Joseph had decided to hide away while awaiting help from the Almerians—killed him, and then proceeded to massacre all the Jews of Granada. Several hundred, perhaps thousands, of them perished in the pogrom, the most important one in Andalusian history."[90] In addition, most Christian populations, finding themselves isolated, gradually converted, thus casting a shadow over the idyllic image of the golden age of coexistence.[91] The conversions reflect the religious and social pressures imposed on Christians and Jews. Yet, in al-Andalus—like elsewhere in Islamic territory—despite the continuous phenomenon of individual Jews converting to Islam, Mosaic communities survived for centuries, whereas Christian communities progressively decreased in certain regions of the south, until they disappeared almost entirely. On this difference, David Wasserstein,[92] who argues that if one considers "the undetermined amorphous mass of the community as a whole," we can observe that "Christians taken as a whole converted to Islam, whereas . . . Jews do not seem to have converted."[93] This could be explained by a united and organized Jewish community nucleus, as well as by the refusal of an assimilation guided by the fear of the dissolution and the loss of the territory's Jewish culture. The Almohads abolished the protective state of the *dhimmis* and forced local Jews and Christians to convert to Islam or flee in exile. Many of those living under Almohad rule converted under these conditions, but the long-term effects on both communities were radically different. For North African Christian communities, this forced conversion meant extinction, and their presence was indeed drastically eliminated from the area. Jewish communities, on the other hand, survived, as they succeeded in preserving their religious identity while feigning conversion.

Beyond their shared status, the Jews and Christians of al-Andalus were two fundamentally different communities both in terms of their social fabric, but

---

89 Alejandro García Sanjuán, "Violencia contra los judíos: el pogromo de Granada del año 459 h/1066," in *De muerte violenta: política, religión y violencia en Al-Andalus*, ed. Maribel Fierro (Madrid: CSIC, 2004), 167–206.

90 Martinez-Gros and Makariou, *Histoire de Grenade*, 40.

91 Emmanuelle Tixier du Mesnil, "La tolérance andalouse a-t-elle existé?" *L'Histoire* 452 (2018): 64–71.

92 David Wasserstein: professor of history, Jewish studies, and classics; Eugene Greener, Jr., professor of Jewish studies.

93 David Wasserstein, "Islamisation and the Conversion of the Jews," in *Conversions islamiques: identités religieuses en islam méditerranéen* [Islamic conversions: religious identities in Mediterranean Islam], ed. Mercedes García Arenal (Paris: Maisonneuve et Larose, 2001), 54.

also in their religious practices. The Jewish community was primarily made up of immigrants and their descendants. After the rise of Muslim rule, other Jews—originating from the east or North Africa—settled in al-Andalus, most often in the cities. One would expect that the local Christian community—which was large and long-established—would have been more resistant to the pressure to convert to Islam compared to the Jewish communities that were spread out across the territory. Moreover, the presence of neighboring Christian kingdoms in the north of the peninsula was a source of religious power that protected the Christians of *Dār al-Islām* from conversion so that they remained Mozarabs. But, in reality, the opposite occurred. Iberian Christian kings, at war with Muslims, shed suspicion on the Mozarabs, and the latter's lack of knowledge about Islam also played a role. Mikel de Epalza suggests that the rural Christian population, isolated from the urban clergy, converted more easily to Islam.[94] The opposite argument is made by Wasserstein,[95] who cautiously writes that "it seems unlikely that the survival of Christianity could have been stronger in rural zones and in the most isolated parts of the peninsula" and that "a large part of the literate class of Christians in al-Andalus converted to Islam." However, whether in cities or in rural areas, the general picture remains: conversation was a widespread phenomenon among Christians, whereas among Jews it was confined to individual cases.

That religious education in Jewish tradition was important is a hypothesis that helps differentiate between the two Semitic communities. Even if knowledge and learning were also vital for Muslims, in Judaism the study of religious texts was, and still is, at the center of tradition. The high level of literacy and knowledge of theology among Jews was combined with a strong and cohesive community. This reinforced the capacity of Jews to resist the pressure to convert to Islam. In the nineth century, they shared knowledge and culture with Muslims.[96] In parallel, they built their own culture by constructing a unique heritage rooted in a history that had been passed down for generations. Jews developed, in Arabic, new literary genres and new forms of Jewish religious expression.[97] Biblical and Talmudic interpretation, Jewish philosophy, theology, mysticism, Jewish literature, and Jewish law were all developed in Arabic—in addition to Hebrew—using the same concepts and models of thought as those

---

94 Mikel de Epalza, Spanish Arabist and translator.

95 Wasserstein, "The Muslims and the Golden Age of the Jews," 179–196.

96 Abdelwahab Meddeb and Benjamin Stora, *A History of Jewish-Muslim relations: From the Origins to the Present Day* (Princeton: Princeton University Press, 2013), 1152.

97 Peter Cole, *The Dream of the Poem*, 576; du Mesnil and Foulon, *Al-Andalus: Anthologie*, 480.

applied by the Muslim rulers in their interpretation of the Quran and Islamic law. There have been many studies about the differences between the Jews and Christians of al-Andalus, as well as the link between their respective degree of acculturation and conversion. Wasserstein underscores the emergence of a Judeo-Arabic culture that was distinct from Christian culture, and asserts that throughout the medieval Islamic world "it was because they possessed a distinct culture that Jews had an identity that allowed them to maintain their own religion and avoid being absorbed into broader society,"[98] just like Jewish community in Provence.

David Abulafia[99] more specifically addresses this question as concerns the Iberian Peninsula, arguing that the "Jews of Al-Andalus and elsewhere did not follow the same path as Mozarabic Christians when it came to Islamization. More simply, there were Arabic Jews, but not Islamized Jews."[100] For Abulafia, "the rather open society of Muslim Spain succeeded in undermining Christianity, while Judaism was reinforced. The mystery of why Jews were acculturated but not assimilated to Islam (unlike many Christians) finds an answer in the existence of common ground between Judaism and Islam in this society."[101] Nevertheless, the Almohads did not believe in the sincerity of the newly converted, and therefore treated the converts as if they were on probation and marginalized them from the community. This was the case whatever a convert's social status.

Let us take the example of Ibn Sahl (1212–1251), who was born into a Jewish family in Seville. Named Abū Isḥaq al-Isrā'īlī al-Ishbīlī, he converted to Islam "at an early age." However, his commitment to his conversion "was subject to much debate, to the extent that there is no certainty about it."[102] Indeed, considerable suspicion about new converts was very common and explains the existence of sources written by Muslims, which offer precise instances where they believed in the sincerity of conversions. Suspicion was particularly manifest in cases of forced mass conversions.

---

98 Wasserstein, "The Muslims and the Golden Age of the Jews," 179–196; See Leonard C. Epafras, "Judeo-Arabic: Cultural Symbiosis of Jews in the Islamicate Contex November," *Journal of Islam and Humanities* 1, no. 1 (2016): 1–14.

99 David Abulafia is an English historian specializing in the history of Italy, Spain, and the rest of the Mediterranean during the Middle Ages and the Renaissance.

100 David Abulafia, "What Happened in Al-Andalus: Minorities in al-Andalus and in Christian Spain," in *Islamic Cultures, Islamic Contexts*, ed. Asad Q. Ahmed et al. (Leiden: Brill, 2015), 540–541. Concerning "Islamized" Jews, see Michael Lecker, *Jews and Arabs in Pre- and Early Islamic Arab* (London: Routledge, 1998).

101 Abulafia, "What Happened in Al-Andalus": 540–541.

102 Du Mesnil and Foulon, *Al-Andalus: Anthologie*, 376.

Thus, even though the Jewish and Christian communities of al-Andalus reacted very differently to the pressure to convert, Jews and Christians belonging to the same social class were equally doubted by the rulers. In the same way, after the Catholic Kings deported Jews in 1492, the newly converted Christians—conversos—that remained on the Iberian Peninsula kept close contact with family members, especially for rituals and food practices, as the stories of the Inquisition trials demonstrate. Trade continued between Jews on the peninsula and Jews in the Mediterranean region (e.g., Genoa) who, for the most part, once again openly practiced Judaism. However, the latter—who were recognized as "new Jews"[103] in Italy and in North Africa—did not wish to officially restart trade under Christian rule in Spain or Portugal. This double religious identity, heralding what is called Marranism,[104] was a secret to neither the Christian authorities nor Jewish community leaders. As a result, Christians and Jews were often considered untrustworthy "new Christians/Jews."

Between cultural assimilation and socio-religious pressure, there were many religious options available to minorities, which introduced further nuance and ambivalence than the term "conversion" strongly implies. Individual conversion tends to be thought of as a break with the past and the choice of another "life"—a sometimes brutal act, or a long decision-making process. But for minorities in Iberian *Dār al-Islām*, the reality was more complex.

Maribel Fierro concurs Sarah Stroumsa on several points. The forced conversion of Jews[105] and Christians was one of the most drastic, while ambiguous, policies implemented at the beginning of the revolutionary movement Almohad.[106] However, an analysis of the status of doctors provides a more nuanced view of minorities. Semitic populations contained medical experts and a number of Jews were treated high-ranking Muslim dignitaries. Yet some

---

103 By "New Jews," I mean that they were living as crypto-Jews before leaving in 1492, and once they arrived in the new territory they were able to restart living more or less openly practicing Judaism.

104 "Marrano" is a term that was used to designate "infamously, from the thirteenth century, but more systematically after the expulsion of Jews in 1492, the Spanish Jew (and sometimes the Arab) who had converted to Catholicism, the *cristiano nuevo* or *crypto-Jew*; the convert being suspected in advance, rightly or wrongly, of remaining faithful to their previous faith and practicing it in secret" (Albert Bensoussan, "Les Marranes," *Atalaya* 14, https://journals.openedition.org/atalaya/1330). Translation by the author. See also Nathan Wachtel, *Entre Moïse et Jésus. Études marranes (XVe–XXIe siècle)* (Paris: CNRS Éditions, 2013), 826; Seymour B. Liebman, *The Jews in New Spain: Faith, Flame, and the Inquisition* (Coral Gables: University of Miami Press, 1970), 21.

105 Maribel Fierro, *Judíos y musulmanes en al-Andalus y el Magreb. Contactos intelectuales* (Madrid: Casa de Velázquez, 2002); du Mesnil and Foulon, *Al-Andalus: Anthologie*, 360.

106 Ibid., 377.

Muslims were in favor of making the social conditions under which minorities were living harsher. Thinkers such as the Sevillian Ibn Khaldūn or Al-Ṭurṭūshī (1059–1126)[107] accentuated the division between Muslims and non-Muslims in line with Ibn Tūmart. They demanded consultations with non-Jewish doctors, a ban on access to higher-level positions for Jews, a prohibition on building churches and synagogues in the *Dār al-Islām,* and conversion to the "real faith"—by persuasion or by force—if non-Muslims were capable of rebelling against Muslims. Some new converts were even accused of having converted for profit. Yet, Ibn Khaldūn and Al-Ṭurṭūshī always respected the pact of the *dîma,* as long as non-Muslims obeyed orders. Jews were also prohibited from insulting Islam or trying to convert a Muslim to Judaism, which was punishable by death. The child of a mixed marriage was Muslim. Jews could not own any property in the city—particularly in Marrakesh—and were sent to Fez (1143), where the first *mellah* (the name for a Jewish quarter in the Arab world) was created. While Christians emigrated towards the northern parts of the Iberian Peninsula, some Jews stayed and converted.[108] Gerber writes that "Maimonides suggested that the persecuted Jew should publicly adopt Islam while maintaining crypto-Judaism and not seek martyrdom unless forced to transgress Jewish commandments in public."[109] When the Almohads no longer needed the *dhimmis* tax, their conversion policy became harsher and Jews had no other choice but to leave or be killed.[110] Perpetual suspicion reigned over the kingdom of the Almohads. Hence, the remarks of Abū Yūsuf Yaqūb al-Mansūr (1184–1199) when he introduced the necessity of different clothing: "If I knew for certain that they became faithful Muslims, I would allow them to mix and intermarry with Muslims; if on the contrary I knew for certain that their conversion was false, I would have the men killed, enslave their sons, seize their property, and offer the loot to Muslims; but as I am not certain of either of these hypotheses, my doubt explains this decision."[111] But some Muslims of the time, like Abd Al-Mu'min (1130–1163), were of a different view. He held that any person who

---

107 Tolan, *Le statut des minorités religieuses dans l'Europe médiévale*; BrillOnline, https://referenceworks.brillonline.com/entries/encyclopedie-de-l-islam/al-turtushi-SIM_7650.

108 Maimonides is known for explicitly stating—in his letter *Obadiah le Prosélyte*—his belief in the capacity of human reason to apprehend truth and that lineage was not an indispensable element of Jewish identity.

109 Gerber, *The Jews of Spain*, 81. See also p. 82.

110 Reinhart Dozy, *Recherches sur l'Histoire*, vol. 1 (Paris: Maisonneuve, 1881), 370. This information appears in a text by Ibn Hamuya, who served Caliph Al-Mansūr (1244).

111 Du Mesnil and Foulon, *Al-Andalus: Anthologie*, 361. Translation by the author. See also Gerber, *The Jews of Spain*, 82.

knew the profession of faith by heart was saved.[112] This separated converts from their ethnicity.[113] Al-Mansūr's (1184–1199) concerns about the authenticity of forced converts led him to externally mark Muslims who were descendants of Jews with a symbol.

Maribel Fierro and Sarah Stroumsa ask why it was more important for Jews to convert than Christians. As both religions believe in a unique God, Christians' cultural, intellectual, and also culinary proximity to Jews likely pushed them to convert and thereby distinguish themselves from their fellow minority. Jews' holding positions of power also constituted a danger for Muslims who often surrounded themselves with Jews in order to play on this ambivalence, with the aim of establishing even stronger Muslim domination.[114] Christians—some of whom were Mozarabs—generally did not hold positions in society that were as important as Jews. As Sarah Stroumsa writes,

> The intellectual history of the Iberian peninsula does not follow a tripartite structure, and the interacting religious cultures are rarely 3, but rather usually 2+1. In al-Andalus from the fourth/tenth to the sixth/twelfth centuries, while Jews were active in almost all aspects of the intellectual and cultural life, the local Christians played a rather marginal intellectual role.[115]

Moreover, their food practices were far removed from those of Muslims. Unlike Jews, they had no dietary prohibitions, apart from some restrictions (Lent and fasting days, for example).[116] But this situation changed. Christians became the majority on the Iberian Peninsula and in Sicily, and Muslims had a minority status. As for Jews, they remained a minority.[117] In 1491, when the Muslims of Spain agreed to surrender, "Muslims were not required to wear a distinctive sign

---

112 In his *Letter on Forced Conversions*, sent to converted Jews in Almohad territory, Maimonides said: "There was never any conversion as remarkable as this one, where the only coercion was to say something."

113 Maribel Fierro, "Conversion, Ancestry and Universal Religion: The Case of the Almohads in the Islamic West (Sixth/Twelfth–Seventh/Thirteenth Centuries)," *Journal of Medieval Iberian Studies* 2, no. 2 (2010): 155–173.

114 Martinez-Gros and Makariou, *Histoire de Grenade*. A Jewish dignitary was introduced to the court of the Nasrids so that, due to his religion and the trust other Jews had towards him, he could take more money from the city's Jews.

115 Stroumsa, *Andalus and Sefarad*, 19.

116 Paul Freedman, *Why Food Matters* (Yale: Yale University Press, 2021), 58.

117 Lopes de Baros and Hinojosa Montalvo, *Minorías étnico religiosas na Península Ibérica* (Évora: Edições Colibri, 2008); Nirenberg, *Communities of Violence*; Tolan, Boissellier, and Clément, *Minorités et régulations sociales en Méditérranée médiévale.*

as provided by the regime of the *dîma* for Christians and Jews in Muslim territory. Jews, who were expelled a few months later, did not receive this right."[118]

The fourteenth century marks a radical turning point in the life of the Jews of Spain, and 1391 can be considered the beginning of the first Sephardic diaspora. This exile continued throughout the fifteenth century, when Jews left Spain to settle in cities around the Mediterranean Basin where small communities were already established, such as those in North Africa, Egypt, Turkey, the Balkans, and Palestine.[119] This political and religious development had repercussions for the food of Spanish Jews and the Sephardim in the diaspora. The Synod of Tortosa in 1359, for instance, stipulated "punishment for eating Jewish or Muslim meat."[120] When pogroms took place in Seville in 1391 and a wave of antisemitism swept the Christian Iberian Peninsula (from Catalonia to Valencia), Jews took refuge in the Nasrid Kingdom, primarily in the capital Granada, where family members or friends working in trade were living.[121] As Rachel Arié writes, "the total number of Jews in al-Andalus, at the end of the fifteenth century, was around 1,500 people, namely a small proportion compared to the Muslim population of the kingdom."[122] The acculturation of Jews in the Granada Kingdom was encouraged. Gabriel Martinez-Gros states that "the very site of Granada, on the Eastern bank of the Darro river, was already home to a Jewish community which favorably welcomed the conquerors [starting in 711], and which would lend the city, up until the eleventh century, the name of 'Granada of Jews.'"[123] Yosef H. Yerushalmi defends the idea that "the very existence of Spanish Judaism rested, in the long run, on the Reconquista. As long as the two protagonists—Christians and Muslims—were engaged in their confrontation, there would be room for Jews. But once the first major episodes of

---

118 Martinez-Gros and Makariou, *Histoire de Grenade*, 104. Translation by the author.

119 Yerushalmi, *Sefardica*, 29.

120 Nirenberg, *Communities of Violence*, 169; John Boswell, *The Royal Treasure: Muslim Communities under the Crown of Aragon in the Fourteenth Century* (New Haven: Yale University Press, 1977), 102. See Olivia Remie Constable, *To Live like a Moor* (Philadelphia: University of Pennsylvania Press, 2017), 185. A complex situation regarding food and Jews already existed in the late thirteenth century in Spain. See Carlos Laliena Corbera, ed. *Documentos municipales de Huesca, 1100–1350* (Huesca: Ayuntamiento de Huesca, 1988), 111.

121 Claude Riveline, *Le monde Juif et l'Islam* (Paris: Akadem, 2005), https://akadem.org/sommaire/cours/juif-et-non-juif-approche-traditionnelle/le-monde-juif-et-l-islam-03-05-2007-6927_4298.php.

122 Arié, "Les minorités religieuses dans le royaume de Grenade (1232–1492)," 51–61.

123 Martinez-Gros and Makariou, *Histoire de Grenade*; Castro, *La Realidad histórica de España*; Claudio Sánchez-Albornoz, *España, un enigma histórico* (Buenos Aires: Editorial Sudamericana, 1956); Pérez, *Histoire de l'Espagne*; Barton, *A History of Spain*; Carr, *Spain: A History*.

the Reconquista were over, a different attitude towards the Jews arose. In the 14th century, there was a general erosion of the legal and social position of the Jews in Spain, and the century ended in a catastrophe."[124]

The religious hostility of the Almohads and the Nasrids towards minorities perhaps only encouraged intellectual competition between the Jewish and Muslim communities—a competition that became a confrontation between two worldviews. In the city of Málaga, reconquered by the Catholic Kings in 1487, Jewish women speaking Arabic could be seen and heard in the streets.[125] Moreover, like their religious peers in Christian Spain, the Jews of al-Andalus often played the role of interpreter. The last sultan of Granada, Boabdil, had two Jewish interpreters, Ysaque Perdoniel and his son-in-law Yuda.

Fluent in Arabic, Jews also translated Muslim philosophical texts, so that all members of the Jewish community could read them. This was also a means of transmitting knowledge through writing. Other forms of Arabic writing was also translated, and, as Aviva Doron notes, "Hebraic poetic creations . . . reflected . . . [a] literary dialogue with Arabic literature."[126]

Knowledge of religious doctrines that governed the Almohad[127] Empire and the Nasrid[128] Kingdom is essential for understanding the coexistence between the ruling class and minorities in *Dār al-Islām* Iberian territory. If this relationship was synonymous with cohabitation and shared values, it also drew a clear line between the two communities. With one purist religious policy replacing another, Christians pursued their goal of religious unity. The dawn of the Spanish Inquisition in 1478 gave the existing Christian rule full power to expel Jews from the territory. Consequently, given such a hostile context, one might wonder whether it is possible to find a trace of Jewish culture in any cookbook produced in the area.

---

124 Yerushalmi, *Sefardica*, 28. Translation by the author.

125 Andrés Bernáldez, *Historia de los Reyes Católicos don Fernando y doña Isabel*. The book was printed by José María Geofrin in Seville in 1870. See Biblioteca Virtual Miguel de Cervantes, https://www.cervantesvirtual.com/obra/historia-de-los-reyes-catolicos-d-fernando-y-dona-isabel/. Known as the "Cura de Los Palacios," Andrés Bernáldez (1415–1513) was famous for these ideas against Jews. He was also the unofficial commentator of the Catholic Kings.

126 Aviva Doron, "Le dialogue littéraire andalou: modèle de dialogue interculturel," *Les routes d'al-Andalus: patrimoine commun et identité plurielle* (Paris: UNESCO, 2011), 11.

127 The term "Almohad" designates a Berber dynasty. It comes from the Arabic term "al-Muwaḥḥidūn," literally "those who profess the unity of God." Amira K. Bennison, *Almoravid and Almohad Empires* (Edinburgh: Edinburgh University Press, 2016), 299–300, 306.

128 Last kingdom of the Iberian Peninsula under Muslim rule (1238–1492).

D. The *Kitāb al-ṭabīẖ*, the "Cookbook" of Cohabitation

What does the term "cohabitation" mean? The *Collins Dictionary* defines it as a "state or condition of cooperating for specific purposes without forming a coalition."[129] Cohabitation is not synonymous of alliance, union, or cooperation, then. To call the *Kitāb al-ṭabīẖ* the "cookbook" of cohabitation is to take it as written proof of the existence of different culinary cultures on the same territory and at the same time. This raises two questions: What is Jewish in this cookbook? Why do Jewish recipes appear in a cookbook written in an anti-Jewish context, whose climax is recognized a century later?[130] "It is a quite reasonable to suggest that the boundary—including the food boundary—between the two Semitic cultures[131] was thin, even though they were radically different from Christian culture.[132] This contrast explains why there are more studies comparing Christians with Jews or Muslims than those comparing Jews and Muslims.

This incessant scholarly competition gave rise to the golden ages of both Muslim and Jewish culture (mainly between the nineth and tenth centuries)—even though the obstinacy of the ethnic-religious separation implemented by the later Berber dynasties limited its full intellectual scope. However, the eleventh century marked a specific turning point in the history of the Muslim West. The process of de-Christianization comes to an end in the Islamic West with the expulsion of the last Christian communities of al-Andalus under the Almohads and Almoravids. The massacre of Grenadine Jews in 1066 indicates the existence of an unfavorable climate for those who opposed the policies developed by the Berber rulers. Nevertheless, in terms of food, this differentiation is not easily identifiable.

---

129 See https://www.collinsdictionary.com/dictionary/english/coalition.

130 Mercedes García-Arenal and Gerard Wiegers, *Polemical Encounters: Christians, Jews, and Muslims in Iberia and Beyond*, Iberian Encounter and Exchange, 475–1755 (Philadelphia: Penn State University Press, 2018); Ross Brann, "The Arabized Jews," in *The Literature of Al-Andalus*, ed. M. Menocal, R. Scheindlin, and M. Sells (Cambridge: Cambridge University Press, 2000): 435–454, https://doi.org/10.1017/CHOL9780521471596.030.

131 On Semitic cultures, see André Pelletier, "De la culture sémitique à la culture hellénique. Rencontre, affrontement, pénétration," *Revue des Études Grecques* vol, 97, booklet 462–464 (1984): 403–418.

132 Kissane, *Food, Religion and Communities in Early Modern Europe*, 13–33; Nancy E. Berg, "Jews among Muslims: Culinary Contexts," in *Global Jewish Foodways. A History*, ed. Hasia R. Diner and Simone Cinotto, intro. Carlo Petrini (Lincoln: University of Nebraska Press, 2019), 70–87.

The *Kitāb al-ṭabīḫ*,[133] which means "cookbook," is the oldest known culinary recipe collection from the Iberian Peninsula. Written in Arabic by an anonymous author, clues contained in the cookbook suggest that it was written in the twelfth to thirteenth centuries, after the "new wave of persecution began" in 1165,"[134] during the period of Islam's domination on the Iberian Peninsula under the Almohad caliphate or immediately after.[135] The "cookbook" has a double feature: a logical structure, with dishes organized by category and an original culinary profile reflecting the multiculturalism of the area. Nothing about the cookbook implies that it includes Jewish recipes. Yet, this is what in-depth analysis reveals.

a. The logical structure of the *Kitāb al-ṭabīḫ*

The "cookbook" begins with a quote from the famous Greek doctor Hippocrates (fifth century BCE): "It is fitting to choose, among food for the sick, that which will be the most pleasing." A quote from his counterpart, Galen (second to third centuries CE), follows, which attempt to explain the words of Hippocrates. Galen highlights the importance of a sick person's appetite: even if the food has no nutritional benefits, it will be good for the patient because he simply enjoys it. The anonymous author of the book insists, in a subsection, on the necessity of choosing foods by presenting recommendations concerning "foods that should be taken alone and should not be mixed with other foods." Details are included that show the author's knowledge of the multiculturalism of Eastern populations. The author explains that food can be similar, but tastes can be different, and it is not because a group or a person denigrates a certain kind of dish or food that everyone should denigrate it. After mentioning a culinary treatise attributed to the ruler Sassanid Anu Širwān/Khosrow I (531–579 CE), the author concludes by providing details about the service order and the consumption of different dishes, thus explaining how one should start and end a meal. Finally, specific attention is given to the dishes named *tafāyā*, because the author writes

---

133 This manuscript has been published and translated many times. See "An Anonymous Andalusian Cookbook of the Thirteenth century," ed. David Friedman and trans. Charles Perry, http://www.daviddfriedman.com/Medieval/Cookbooks/Andalusian/andalusian_contents.htm; Huici and Marín, *La cocina hispano-magrebí*; Guillaumond, *Cuisine et diététique dans l'Occident arabe médiéval*.

134 Gerber, *The Jews of Spain*, 82.

135 As mentioned previously, the term "Almohad" designates a Berber dynasty. It comes from the Arabic term *al-Muwaḥḥidūn*"—"those who profess the unity of God."

that these are the most reputed and that they agree with people of every temperament, especially the melancholic and phlegmatic. Hence, even though the *Kitāb al-ṭabīḫ* is not an entire treatise on medicine or diet—like those written at the same time in the East and the West—the author's knowledge of these fields cannot be ignored.[136]

It is only after this thorough information that the cookbook begins. The recipes do not start with a list of ingredients prior to the instructions. Each recipe is generally introduced by providing information about the preparation (place of origin, etc.) and the type of person the recipe is intended for (convalescents, thin people, etc.). The recipes also include a few rare indications concerning the measurement of ingredients (*ratl, mud,* etc.). Meat is always prepared first. Once the preparation of the dish is finished, instructions are given about those who will enjoy the dish (kings, the people of Ġarb, etc.) and whether there are any variations on the dish (possible garnishes, substituting eggplant for meat, etc.).

The first part includes three chapters of ninety-three recipes, including simple white *tafāyā* called *Isfidbāğa* and *mirqās* (merguez). There is also a section that included a wide range of grilled meats, and another for thick dishes and fermented dishes. The second part includes seven chapters with 220 recipes. There is material concerning the book of Ibrāhīm al-Mahdī,[137] with meat, fish, and vegetable dishes, as well as a section on vegetable dishes. Twenty-one recipes with eggplant are also included. A section dedicated to dishes prepared with different types of fish, meat porridges, couscous, rice, *harīsa,* noodles, and similar dishes leads to another section on *harīsa* by category, followed by one on *rafis* and breads. *Halwa* recipes and other sweets close this second part. The third part contains only one chapter, on 129 recipes using bread and sweets—very sweet dishes, pies, meat and vegetable porridges—as well as meat and fish dishes. The fourth part has no chapters, but includes twenty-four recipes with vegetables and meats. The fifth part does not have any chapters either, but has twenty-seven sweet recipes, while the final part contains no recipes for dishes, but provides a description of fifty-seven preparations for medical purposes, such as drinks and syrups, fruit pastes, electuaries, jams, powders, and grape juices.[138]

---

136 Among these doctors was Ibn Baklarish (eleventh to twelfth century), who lived mainly in Saragossa; his major work was *The Book of Simples.*

137 Ibrāhīm al-Mahdī: Abbassid prince from 817 to 819, poet, singer, gourmet, and brother of Harun al-Rashid. See Laurioux, "Le goût médiéval est-il arabe?"

138 This part is presented in the work of Huici Miranda (five short chapters) and Jean-Michel Laurent, but is absent in the work of Guillaumond. It only contains four chapters in Perry.

b. The culinary profile of the *Kitāb al-ṭabīẖ*

The culinary profile of the *Kitāb al-ṭabīẖ* oscillates between a cookbook and a diet book. It is unique, since it brings together medicine, diet, and food. However, it is not a medical book.[139] Thus, it must be viewed as belonging to its own genre, the polar opposite of the culinary profile of cookbooks written in the same period in Christian areas, as these did not give any dietary recommendations. The quotes from Hippocrates, Galen, and Ar-Rāzī (Rhazes) are the reason why the *Kitāb al-ṭabīẖ* is not presented as a cookbook such as we understand the term today. However, it not only follows in the tradition of cookbooks written in the Muslim East—reflecting the importance given to medical knowledge inherited from ancient Greek philosophers under al-Andalus—but also the tradition of dietary treaties that started to emerge on the Iberian Peninsula in the twelfth century. Cuisine and diet appear to be inherently intertwined. Medicine is even put into the service of food and cuisine.

The anonymous author pays particular attention to different cooking methods. This is especially true for meats, but also for breads, as well for the diets of everyone from nomads to Eastern kings. He insists on the fact that medicine benefits from culinary preparations that, in the end, must be used according to their specific qualities. Appetite, taste, and dietary properties appear as the best ingredients for preparing "good" cuisine. This explains why vinegar, thick syrups, oil, apple, pomegranate and raisin juice, mustard, and spices, as well as medicinal plants are all necessary for making healthy meals. This holds as long as one understands the medicinal properties of each and the constitution of the person who will enjoy the food. The author provides a brief summary of certain foods—those which are frequently used in the book or whose properties are important to know—such as dry cilantro, cumin, chickpeas, saffron, vinegar, and mustard. These details are given in the introduction to the recipes. Specific attention is paid to the aesthetics and taste of the dishes. The author insists on the importance of beautiful and delicious preparations. The place names included further make it possible to locate the dishes included in the *Kitāb al-ṭabīẖ*. It is thus easy to see that a myriad of dishes considered to be superior, and foods that the author recognizes for their qualities, come from the cities of al-Andalus. The *Kitāb al-ṭabīẖ* is all the more unique in that it contains both the food of the elites—thereby implying that the author was close to the royal court—and simple dishes that were common among the lower social

---

139 The cookbook of the East titled *Kanz al-fawā'id fī tanwī 'al-mawā'id*, by anonymous, was probably written by a doctor. I thank Professor Daniel Newman for these details.

classes. This differentiates the cookbook from the other recipe collection of the same period,[140] the *Fuḍālat al-ḫiwān.*[141]

Kitāb al-ṭabīḫ is important because it testifies to the interculturality of the territory where it was produced. Yet even more important is the fact that it contains six explicitly Jewish recipes. These six recipes have been translated as "A Jewish Dish of Chicken" (لون من فروج يهودى), another one bears the same name "A Jewish Dish of Chicken" (يهوديى لون من فروج), "A Jewish Dish of Partridge" (لون من حجلة يهودى), "Jewish Partridge" (حجلة يهودية), "A Stuffed, Buried Jewish Dish" (لون يهودى محشو مدفون), and "A Jewish Dish of Eggplants Stuffed with Meat" (لون يهودى من ناذنجان محشو بلحم).[142] It also contains four dishes whose preparation notes refer to Christian culinary habits. For instance, "A Dish of Large Fish," whose description specifies that it "is part of Christian cuisine"[143] (هو من اطعمة (الروم. The term *rūm* (روم) is used to refer to Christians.[144] The same is true for the information provided in the "Recipe for a Dish of Olives," where it is written: "Take stalks of Swiss chard or vegetables of rūms."[145] Another recipe mentions that Christians share a culinary practice with Berbers, which can be read in the preliminary note on "saffron": "[O]ther people sprinkle ground pepper on the dish before eating. This is what Christians and Berbers do."[146] The last recipe that mentions Christian culinary practices is a sweet dish that the anonymous author says originates from

140 This is evidenced by the many anthroponyms cited in the cookbook, as well as the use of often expensive foods.

141 Ibn Razīn al-Tuǧībī and Manuela Marín, eds. and trans., *Relieves de las mesas acerca de las delicias de la comida y los diferentes platos (Fuḍālat al-Ḫiwān fī ṭayyibāt al-ṭa'ām wa-l-alwān)* (Gijón: Trea, 2007).

142 The English translations of these six titles come from Charles Perry, cited by Friedman, "An Anonymous Andalusian Cookbook of the Thirteenth Century." However, unless otherwise indicated, passages and titles from the cookbook are translated from Guillaumond's version in French: Guillaumond, *Cuisine et diététique dans l'Occident arabe médiéval*, no. 156, no. 158, no. 160, no. 164, no. 169, no. 172.

143 Guillaumond, *Cuisine et diététique dans l'Occident arabe médiéval*, no. 217; idem, "La cuisine dans l'Occident arabe médiéval. Étude de textes" (PhD diss., Université Jean Moulin Lyon III, 1991), no. 316. She proposes a more literal translation: "It's a Christian dish."

144 The term *rūm* refers to Christians of the East, originally tied to Byzantium; but it should be noted that this definition of this term's actually more complex. According to Emmanuelle Tixier du Mesnil, the *Rūm* could be Romans and not necessarily Christians.

145 Guillaumond, *Cuisine et diététique dans l'Occident arabe médiéval*, no. 136; idem, "La cuisine dans l'Occident arabe médiéval," no. 235. This information is not included in Friedman's English translation, but is noted in Guillaumond's French translation.

146 Ibid., no. 8. …

the Copts (Christians) of Egypt: the "the white Eastern *ḥalwa* called 'copte'"[147] (الحلوة . . . هو السماة بالقبيط).[148]

The interculturality of al-Andalus is thus reflected in these different types of foods. Moreover, and this is what is most unique, the author knew the differences between the ethnic groups' tastes, territories, and cultures. His writing helps us to understand and recognize these variations through both the ties that bind the communities and the religions they practice. Further, the fact that the dishes are different from one another is just as important as the fact that these cuisines are perceived to reflect the different religious communities living in the area. Statistical analysis of the recipes in the *Kitāb al-ṭabīḫ* provides more details about the various preparations and ingredients. It brings to light a culinary—but also cultural, social, and political—profile that is completely unexpected; and it unveils the first element of this one-of-a-kind culinary collection.

The culinary profile of the *Kitāb al-ṭabīḫ* can be established by analyzing the food contained in its 462 recipes. I make a distinction between two categories. On the one hand, the 101 sweet dishes, fifty-five of which contain honey and sixty-six sugar (twenty-six contain both). These do not contain meat. On the other hand, the 361 "savory" dishes.[149] Among the latter, there are two subcategories: meat dishes—including 311 recipes (fifty with poultry, forty-one with mutton, etc.)—and fifty dishes without meat. The latter are divided into nineteen fish preparations, four with eggs, eight with various ingredients (including six with cheese), and nineteen with vegetables. This last subcategory is made up of fifteen eggplant recipes and four others with—separately—lentils, gourd, chickpeas, and a "gardener's" recipe. The food diagram below illustrates the predominance of meats (eighty-six percent) within the savory dishes of the *Kitāb al-ṭabīḫ*, while still highlighting the unique inclusion of vegetarian preparations, as these represent fourteen percent of the savory dishes. As fifty-five of the sweet recipes contain honey, and as honey is included in sixty-nine preparations in the *Kitāb al-ṭabīḫ*, we can conclude that honey (eighty percent) is almost exclusively used for dishes that I anachronistically call "desserts" or "pastries." It must be noted that sugar is included in a little more than one-quarter of meat dishes, often as a garnish.

147 Ibid., no. 475. In her PhD dissertation, it is recipe 574, titled "Halwa . . . It Is Called 'Qubbayṭ.'"

148 Nonetheless, it should be mentioned that the correct form is اقباط and that it is in no case it is never a plural in form; and *qubbayt* is an Andalusian Arabic word that means a sweet, honey-based dish cut into bars. I thank Daniel Newman for these details.

149 They do not necessarily contain salt. By this relatively contemporary term, I mean dishes that are not sweet and which are usually main dishes.

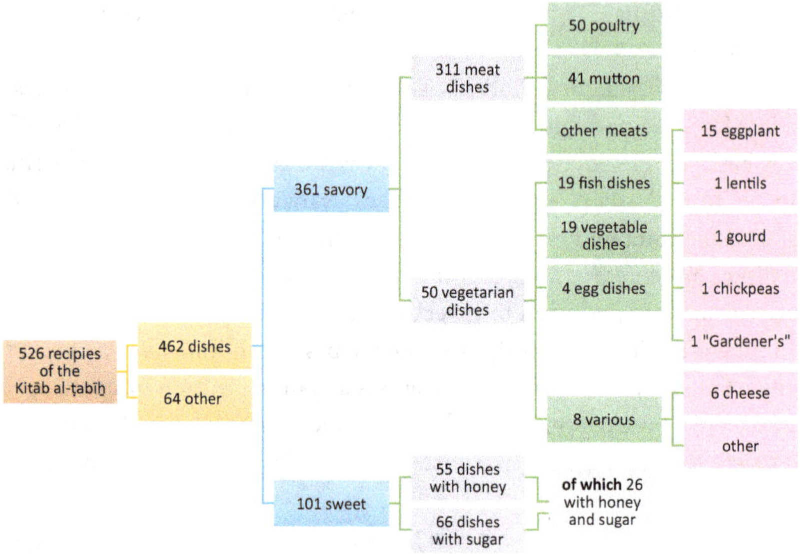

Figure 1. Food diagram of the *Kitāb al-ṭabīḫ*

Thus, even two centuries before the arrival of new products from America, the Iberian Peninsula already enjoyed an enormous food diversity, and all Andalusians had access to the same foods. Yet the food practices of the three communities living in the area turned out to be a marker that differentiated them was a sign of religious identity.

CHAPTER 2

The Jewish Stamp in the *Kitāb al-ṭabīẖ*

Olivia Remie Constable writes:

> Food and food traditions are very striking in the ways in which they encompass both explicitly religious markers of identity . . . and non-religious cultural makers associated with certain regions or ethnic groups. . . . Over time, however, culinary markers of religion and culture that had been understood as separate, though related, in the thirteenth century had become fused—often in uncomfortable ways—by the end of the fifteenth century.[1]

It was at the beginning of this early period that Spain's first cookbook—which contains explicitly Jewish recipes—was written. The association between cuisine and religion is uniquely meaningful in Jewish cuisine; yet this relationship must be further explored. This connection between history and identity comes to the surface in the *Kitāb al-ṭabīẖ* through the recipes that it explicitly designates as "Jewish." Limiting analysis to this fact alone would, however, be a mistake. Indeed, a more nuanced reading reveals the existence of other Jewish recipes hidden in practices or references to ancestral textuality to which the author was clearly not oblivious. But one question emerges above all: Is there an genuine wish in the cookbook to recognize a new culture, that of the Almohads, with the aim of distinguishing it from past dynasties? If this hypothesis is worth considering—and given that elite Jews held high-level positions in Andalusian society,[2] as well as earlier—there is nothing surprising about finding "Jewish"

1 Constable, "Food and Meaning": 201.

2 Fierro, *Judíos y musulmanes en al-Andalus y el Magreb*; Esther Benbassa, "La diaspora juive 1492," *Histoire, économie et société*, no. 3 (1993): 335–343; Maurice Kriegel, *Les Juifs dans l'Europe méditerranéenne à la fin du Moyen Âge* (Paris: Hachette Pluriel Référence, 2006);

recipes in the first known recipe collection written in al-Andalus. Traces of Judaism in the *Kitāb al-ṭabīẖ*, then, should be studied in the light of this unique context, marked by the arrival in 1147 of "a fanatical fundamentalist Muslim dynasty known as the Almohades [who] demanded the conversion of all Jews and Christians."[3] This Berber dynasty, that swept onto the Iberian Peninsula from Morocco, eliminated the status of the *dhimmi* and imposed Islamization. Social practices that differed from the new norm raised many questions; and the goal of these Islamic food restrictions was also to distinguish between Muslims and non-Muslims.

A. What Is Meant by "Jewish Cuisine"?

a. Some Thoughts

"What is food? It is not only a collection of products, subject to dietary or statistical studies. It is also a system of communication, a body of images, a protocol of uses, situations and behaviors."[4] With this in mind, it is necessary, and important, to try to define what I mean by "Jewish cuisine."

If culinary traditions are the last thing that remains as a sign of identity when people have lost everything else,[5] and if "Jewish cuisine" does not exist,[6] why are there certain dishes that have always been prepared and consumed in the same way in Jewish communities regardless of place or period?[7] Is it not true that this cuisine is more complex than a simple collection of recipes over time and across diasporas?[8] If it seems as though the claim that there is a "Jewish cuisine" is very recent, it is worth remembering that people have acknowledged the existence of "Jewish food" at least since the writing of the Torah.[9] The study

---

Enrique Soria Mesa, *La realidad tras el espejo. Asenso social y limpieza de sangre en la España de Felipe II* (Valladolid: Ediciones Universidad de Valladolid, 2016).

3 Gerber, *The Jews of Spain*, 80.

4 Roland Barthes, "Pour une psycho-sociologie de l'alimentation contemporaine," *Annales Économie Sociétés Civilisations* 16, no. 5 (1961). Translation by the author.

5 By this, I mean that despite forced exile or otherwise, and separation from one's family, one will still eat what one is used to.

6 If we hold that Jewish cooking is a simple collection of recipes prepared by Jews, and that they integrated native recipes into their own cooking.

7 This is a question concerning a culinary heritage that is constantly constructed and reconstructed.

8 This is a question that highlights a transmitted heritage.

9 *Torah* means "instruction," "teaching," or "law." "[In] Judaism, in the broadest sense, [it is] the substance of divine revelation to Israel, the Jewish people: God's revealed teaching

of Jewish food has always inspired curiosity and enthusiasm, and continues to do so. Indeed, never before have so many cookbooks containing Jewish recipes been published. Even if this is a US phenomenon in particular, one can point to studies of Jewish food by the European Institute for Food History and Cultures (Tours), the Society for Jewish Studies (Paris), and the Museum of Jewish Art and History (Paris), among other institutions.

If we usually regard cuisine as the art of preparing dishes, "Jewish cuisine" requires us to think about culture and religion, that is, look beyond the fundamentals of cooking. A relationship to history and identity is implicit in these recipes; one must analyze them in terms of ancestral culinary textuality. In short, "Jewish cuisine" has a mnemonic dimension. For Jews, cooking is re-remembering.[10]

Defining "Jewish cuisine" is clearly not an easy task; turning to a few simple criteria is inadequate. Defining this cuisine requires imagining it as a tapestry with no edges: the various food cultures of the territory are its threads. Spain is unique in this sense. If, initially from the fifth to the seventh centuries, this food tapestry was made from two relatively uniform tones of thread—yellow for Christians and blue for Jews—the arrival of Muslims introduced another thread (let's call it green) in the eighth century. While the yellow started to disappear, the cultural proximity of the Semitic populations meant that the blue and green threads sometimes blended together. Nonetheless, Jewish cuisine has a strand that is a unique feature, a strand that is difficult to fray and is, perhaps, indestructible: the food precepts of Kashrut.[11] Nonetheless, the Christian conquest

---

or guidance for humankind. The meaning of "Torah" is often restricted to signify the first five books of the Hebrew Bible (Old Testament), also called the Law (or the Pentateuch in Christianity). These are the books traditionally ascribed to Moses, the recipient of the original revelation from God on Mount Sinai. Jewish, Roman Catholic, Eastern Orthodox, and Protestant canons all agree on their order: Genesis, Exodus, Leviticus, Numbers, and Deuteronomy." See *Encyclopedia Britannica*, s.v. "Torah," accessed 4 April, 2022, https://www.britannica.com/topic/Torah. Many references concerning food precepts with which the Mosaic people must comply are mentioned in the Bible, starting in Genesis (1:29; 2:16–17; 9:3–4; 32:25–33). I will give more details about these references throughout the book and specifically about this case. See *Chumash*, ed. Edmond Safra and trans. Aharon Marciano (New York: ArtScroll Series, 2017), 1372.

10 This deals with the importance of thinking "in more depth about the presentness of the past" and thinking "more explicitly about the significance of the different sites and spaces—and their memories—in the way of interpreting [this includes cooking] and making sense [thinking about why a dish is still cooked] of the world in the present." See Cheryl McGeachan, "(Re) Remembering and Narrating the Childhood City of R. D. Laing," *Cultural Geographies* 20, no. 3 (July 2013): 269–84, doi:10.1177/1474474012462532.

11 David Auerbach says that Jewish identity could be defined as "Jewish Cultural Nationalism," since the Jewish people see themselves as the "chosen people" and regard the Hebrew Bible

coming from the north of the Iberian Peninsula imposed an entirely different food canvas, creating a culinary uniformity across the land. Still, conversos left a unique culinary footprint, which testifies to the survival of the preparation of Jewish dishes. This proves the necessary culinary adaptation that led to a modification of this interlacing food tapestry. All in all, Jewish cooking is originally historical, extremely adaptable, fundamentally transmissible, largely territorial, undoubtedly diasporic, and deeply nostalgic. Trying to define Jewish cuisine as exclusive would be obscure what it actually is. There is a multiplicity of Jewish cuisines—as many as there are communities and diasporas; and the *Kitāb al-ṭabīḫ* enables us to Jewish food in al-Andalus. It is the only cookbook that contains explicitly "Jewish" recipes.

b. The Explicitly Jewish Recipes of the *Kitāb al-ṭabīḫ*

The cookbook is the only recipe collection from the Iberian Peninsula that contains explicitly Jewish recipes. By "explicitly" Jewish, I mean recipes that use the term Jewish (يهودي/ة) in their titles.

The *Kitāb al-ṭabīḫ* contains two chicken recipes (in one, a complete chicken is required; in the other, the bird must be divided into parts) entitled, respectively, "A Jewish Dish of Chicken [with Stuffing]" and "A Jewish Dish of Chicken." There are two partridge dishes (one stipulates a complete partridge; the other calls for the bird to be divided into parts), entitled, respectively, "Jewish Partridge [Stuffed]" and "A Jewish Dish of Partridge." A fifth dish, made with ground meat and meatballs, is called "A Stuffed, Buried Jewish Dish." And, finally, there is a recipe that calls for diced lamb and eggplant: "A Jewish Dish of Eggplants Stuffed with Meat."[12] The table below presents English and Spanish translations of the Arabic names of these recipes.[13]

---

as a "national document." David Auerbach, *Jewish Cultural Nationalism: Origins and Influences* (London: Routledge, 2008).

12 The French translations of the recipes mentioned come from the doctoral work of Guillaumond. I decided not to use the translations that she provides in her latest book *Cuisine et diététique dans l'occident arabe médiéval* due to some inconsistencies. For example, the modification of the term "chicken" into "young rooster," even though the original Arabic is the same: *farūǧ* (فروج). There is no explanation of this decision. Huici Miranda, in *La cocina hispano-magrebí durante la época almohade*; provides titles of recipes that better correspond, in my view, to the literal translation of the original Arabic.

13 The title in Arabic is the original one written in the Colin 7009 manuscript in the National Library of France. The title in English comes from David Friedman's text, elaborated according to notes by Charles Perry, and the Spanish title comes from Huici Miranda (2005).

Table 1. English and Spanish translations of recipe names in Arabic

1. لون من فروج يهودى A Jewish Dish of Chicken [stuffed] Plato de pollo judío	2. لون من فروج يهوديى Jewish Dish of Chicken Plato de pollo judío
3. حجلة يهودية Jewish Partridge [stuffed] Perdiz judía	4. لون من حجلة يهودى A Jewish Dish of Partridge Plato de perdiz judía
5. لون يهودى محشو مدفون A Stuffed, Buried Jewish Dish Plato judío relleno oculto	6. لون يهودى من باذنجان محشو بلحم A Jewish Dish of Eggplants Stuffed with Meat [lamb] Plato judío de berenjenas rellenas con carne

The term لون (*lawn*) means "dish," but also "way" or "color." What is of interest here are the terms يهودى[14] or يهودية, which mean "Jewish." There are a few errors in the writing of the words "Jewish," which are likely mistakes made by the transcriber. As concerns the first dish, there seems to be a diacritical mistake since the "ّ" appear to have been forgotten. By correcting the errors, we can read the letter "ي," which refers to the adjective "Jewish." For the second dish, the transcriber seems to have written the letter "ي" twice, which explains why the two chicken dishes have the same title, even though they are quite different.[15] Let's focus now on the two partridge recipes. The third dish leaves no doubt about the meaning of the name "Jewish Partridge." Note that this time there is no use of the word "dish." The adjective "Jewish" is feminine in Arabic and here refers directly to the word "partridge," which implies that the partridge is Jewish. In light of all the other recipes, two hypotheses can be formed. The first is that the adjective "Jewish" corresponds in these cases to the sex and quantity for the word "chicken," which would mean that in recipes 1, 2, and 3, the chicken/partridge is Jewish. Rather than suggesting that an animal has a religion, "Jewish" here may actually refer to the sacrificial slaughtering of the animals. This would simply mean that the animals were killed according to *shehita*,[16] namely in compliance with Jewish food laws. The second hypothesis is that the adjective "Jewish" corresponds in sex and quantity for the word "dish." Recipe 4 can be interpreted in this way, since it contains both masculine and feminine words that

14 The word "يهوديى" is written as such in Arabic in the manuscript, but this seems to be a mistake made by the scribe.

15 The quality of the microfilm of the Colin manuscript doesn't allow us to learn more.

16 Deut. 12:20–21.

make it possible to more easily identify what the adjective "Jewish" refers to: the noun "partridge" (حجلة) is feminine, even though the adjective "Jewish" (يهودي) that follows is masculine. The word "dish" (لون/"color") is also masculine. Therefore, the word "Jewish" defines the word "dish" and not the word "partridge." Altogether—except for recipe 3, which does not contain the word "dish"—it can be argued that the adjective "Jewish" refers to the word "dish." Indeed, the name of recipes 5 and 6 leave no doubt about this: the adjective "Jewish" is placed right after the noun "dish," thereby describing it in the most direct way possible. If we take these considerations into account, the translations of these recipe names are as follows: "A Jewish Dish of Chicken" (1); "A Jewish Dish of Chicken" (2)' "Jewish Partridge" (3); "A Jewish Dish of Partridge" (4)' "A Stuffed, Buried Jewish Dish" (5); and "A Jewish Dish of Eggplants Stuffed with Meat" (6). These names demonstrate the recognition of a culinary practice different from the more common practice, that is, Muslim; and that the author knew about different customs. But the word "Jewish" might suggest that *non-Jews* described the recipe as such in order to indicate that the preparation style was exclusively their own. Calling a dish "Jewish" may also imply that the dish is a Jewish adaptation of a non-Jewish dish. All in all, the first hypothesis leads us towards the origin of the recipe's preparation, whereas the second hypothesis emphasizes a dish that existed prior to Jewish practices and was adopted by Jews. In the end, both hypotheses are possible, as we don't have enough information. In any case, we shouldn't lose sight of the fact that heritage is not only passed down, but can be constructed and reconstructed. This is one of the essential features of Jewish cuisine.

For these specific analyses, it is useful to refer to the order that Huici Miranda followed to present the recipes in the book *La cocina hispano-magrebí durante la época Almohade.*[17] Thus, we can see that the first five Jewish recipes are presented one after the other. However, 336 recipes separate the sixth and final recipe from the others. This one is isolated, having no obvious connection with the recipes that precede it (or follow it). Yet, in Catherine Guillaumond's reorganization of the manuscript pages, the last explicitly Jewish recipe—"A Jewish Dish of Eggplant Stuffed with Meat"—follows the five previous ones. This creates a thematic coherence with the eggplant dishes that follow, thus constituting a solid set of about twenty recipes.

Among the main ingredients used in these six Jewish recipes are oil, eggs, meat, dried fruit, and cilantro. These ingredients are used in every dish. However, they

---

17 Huici and Marín, *La cocina hispano-magrebí.*

may not seem, at first sight, to be a main feature of Jewish cuisine since they are found in a majority of the recipes in the rest of the *Kitāb al-ṭabīḫ*. Yet, perhaps there is nothing to differentiate between these six recipes and the other in the cookbook. However, pine nuts and rosewater are represented more in these recipes compared to the others and eggs are also used more frequently.

Comparing the two Jewish chicken recipes shows that, while some ingredients are similar overall, they change from one recipe to the next. The style of cooking also varies since, in the first "Jewish Dish of Chicken," the instructions are to roast the chicken, whereas in the other recipe the chicken should be grilled. Further, the proportions of the ingredients used in the Jewish chicken recipes reveals differences. The first "Jewish Dish of Chicken" recipe uses eleven different ingredients while the other uses sixteen. In addition, the frequency with which an ingredient is stipulated varies from one to three times. Recall that in the first recipe the entire chicken is used while in the second it is chopped into pieces. We can draw the conclusion that these dishes are not duplicates, then—even if their titles suggest they are. I followed both of the recipes and can confirm that they are different, both technically and in terms of taste.[18] This is all the more interesting given that these two chicken dishes are similar to a recipe of liver, heart, and chopped entrails served on slices of bread that is still prepared in the Sephardic community today.

Let's turn our attention to the partridge dishes. First, and given the importance of religion in the transmission of any culinary heritage, it should be highlighted that partridge is mentioned in biblical sources.[19] In the *Chumash*[20]—Leviticus/*Vayikra*[21]—it is stated that "contrary to kosher animals and fish, which can be identified on the basis of physical characteristics, the identity of authorized birds is very unclear. The Torah cites twenty-five non-kosher types of birds, meaning

---

18 I am aware that the taste cannot be fully identified, as no quantities are given.

19 Cooper, *Eat and be satisfied*, 259; Lyman Abbott and Thomas Jefferson Conant, *A Dictionary of Religious Knowledge, for Popular and Professional Use: Comprising Full Information on Biblical, Theological, and Ecclesiastical Subjects. With Several Hundred Maps and Illustrations* (New York: Harper & brothers, 1885), 44, 719. See OU Kosher Staff, Kosher, "The Birds of the Bible, or, Solving the Mystery of Which of the Species are Kosher and Which Are Not," accessed April 4, 2022, https://oukosher.org/blog/consumer-kosher/the-birds-of-the-bible-or-solving-the-mystery-of-which-of-the-species-are-kosher-and-which-are-not/; *Qusṭā ibn Lūqā's Medical Regime for the Pilgrims to Mecca: Risālā fī tadbīr safar al-ḥajj*, ed. and trans. Gerrit Bos (New York: Brill, 1992), 89. Jer. 17:11–18.

20 The *Chumash* is one of the names for the Pentateuch. It often presents an arrangement of the text according to its division into parashot. Comments and interpretations are provided in the margins of the original text in Hebrew, but are also translated into another language. I refer here and elsewhere to the 2011 Safra edition.

21 The first is in Hebrew, the second in French.

that all the other ones are kosher."[22] Partridge is not included in the list of forbidden birds. Al-Rāzī[23] (d. 925 or 935) recognized the benefits of consuming this bird and Maimonides also mentioned it.[24] An analysis of the ingredients used in the Jewish partridge recipes shows that they contain the same proportions: fifteen different foods. They also use similar items (citron leaves, mint, pistachios, pine nuts, etc.).

It is worth mentioning that eggs are used in large quantities, as well as, but to a lesser extent, cinnamon and dried fruit. Once again, the meat in the two partridge recipes is prepared differently: in the first recipe (no. 3), the partridge is used in full and stuffed, while in the second it is supposed to be cut into pieces. As before, the style of cooking is also different. the first uses different cooking pots: one that is new with a dough cover and another that is copper and filled with burning coals that must be turned over at the end of cooking. Thus, it can be concluded that these dishes also differ in terms of taste.

To summarize: in these four Jewish recipes using chicken and partridge, the most commonly used ingredient is egg. Halima Ferhat[25] also notes this.[26] Dried fruit, such as pine nuts, nuts, and almonds, are a close second. The importance of citron (including its leaves), as well as vinegar at different stages of fermentation is also interesting. The consumption of eggs—in all forms—is one of the main features of the book. Inexpensive, eggs were available to everyone. They can also be used as a garnish; aesthetics are always important in the recipes. Eggs can be cut in half, in strips, or in a star shape. Sometimes they are hidden under the skin of the meat to add a surprise during the meal, or they are included in the stuffing or stuffed themselves. And let's not forget their powerful coloring ability, giving foods a yellow hue. This multipurpose aspect is found in the two Jewish recipes, since they contain foods (eggplant, meatballs) or methods of preparation (stuffed, buried) and cooking (smothering, dough covers) that I consider to be markers of a Jewish culinary identity, especially since such practices still exist today. These analyses, represented in the graph below, show the

---

22 Lev./Vayikra 11:13–19: *Chumash*, 638–639: Translation from the French text directed by Rav Aharon Marciano.

23 Bos, *Quṣṭā ibn Lūqā's medical regime for the pilgrims to Mecca*, 463.

24 Moïse Maïmonide and Moïse Ibn Tibbon, trans., and Solomon Munter, ed., *Hanhagat ha-Beri'ut (Regimen Sanitas)* (Jerusalem: Mosad ha-Rav Kook, 1957), chapter 1.

25 Moroccan historian and professor at University Mohammed V-Souissi (Morocco).

26 Halima Ferhat, "Le patrimoine gastronomique andalous," in *El banquete de las palabras: la alimentación de los textos árabes*, ed. Manuela Marín and Cristina De la Puente (Madrid: CSIC, 2005), 22.

use of hard-boiled eggs for stuffing, yeast, and other ingredients that enable us to differentiate between the two Jewish partridge recipes.

There are also different cooking methods and styles (for instance, the use of a pot with yeast). The "Jewish Partridge" recipe is especially interesting for this reason. A new pot, in which the partridge is placed, stuffed with giblets, almonds, pine nuts, cinnamon, and two hard-boiled eggs, must be used. The pot must be covered with dough. This technique recalls the Jewish practice—which still exists today—of sealing a dish to ensure that, once the Shabbat[27] meal is prepared on Friday night, nothing else can be added until the next day.[28] This idea should be nuanced, however, given that later on vinegar, citron, mint, and eggs must be added. Still, it is not out of the question that this can be done the next day when the meal is served. Another pot filled with burning embers is placed on top of this container in order to brown the top of the dish. Finally, once the top is golden brown, the pot containing the burning embers is turned around and used to brown the bottom of the dish.

In this "Jewish Partridge" recipe, several pots of different materials (clay, copper, etc.) are used. All of these cooking techniques make this partridge recipe a relatively complex dish. The cooking method required is also unique. Was this dish prepared in compliance with Talmudic law which, during Pessah, required cooking in a new pot that had never been employed before (or for holidays)? Is the second partridge recipe also part of this religious tradition, this time for Shabbat?

Religious practice obviously underpins the recipe. Yet it is possible that, given the porous nature of clay pots, a new pot was recommended so that the different tastes—burned, smoked, fish—would not mix, including during cooking. It is also possible that the taste of earth given off by the pot—which would suit the flavors of the dish—is the reason for using several new pots.[29] A further possibility is that this instruction was part of the recommendations given by al-Arbullī. Indeed, this Andalusian thinker of the thirteenth and fourteenth centuries, author of *Tratado nazarí sobre alimentos: al kalam 'ala l-agdiya,* wrote that

---

27 "Shabath: Hebrew Shabbat, "(from *shavat,* "cease," or "desist"), day of holiness and rest observed by Jews from sunset on Friday to nightfall of the following day. The time division follows the biblical story of creation: 'And there was evening and there was morning, one day' (Genesis 1:5). See *Encyclopedia Britannica,* s.v. "Sabbath," accessed April 4, 2022, https://www.britannica.com/topic/Sabbath-Judaism.

28 See Grewe, "Hispano-arabic cuisine in the twelfth century," 142–148.

29 Danièle Alexandre-Bidon, *Une archéologie du goût. Céramique et consommation (Moyen Âge – Temps modernes)* (Paris: Picard, 2005), 114, 130.

"clay containers should not be used more than once for cooking."[30] However, keep in mind that it is often during religious holidays—which are frequent in Islam and even more so in Judaism—that certain dishes are made following a specific preparation method. To conclude: the "Jewish Dish of Partridge" (no. 4) does not contain hard-boiled eggs or pots that are filled with burning embers, or sugar, cinnamon or almonds. Therefore, it is a very different recipe from the other dish despite an almost identical name.

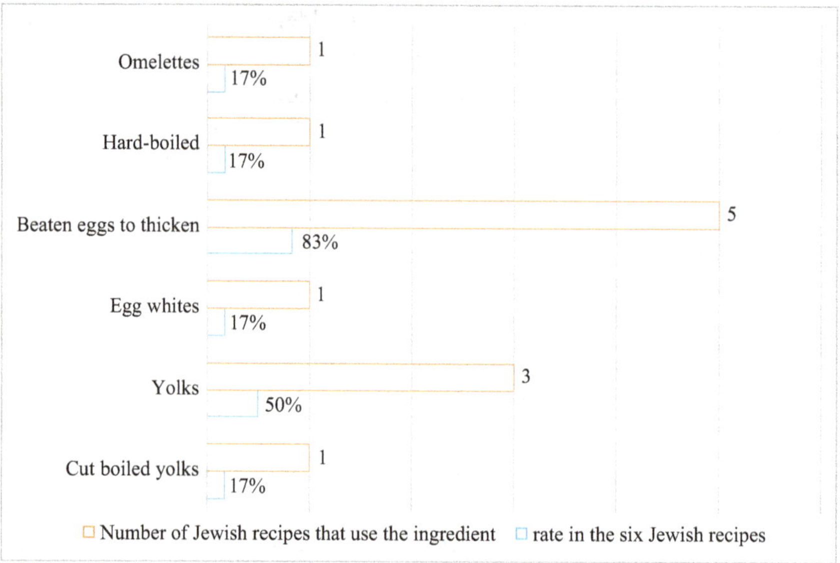

Figure 2. The use of eggs in the six Jewish recipes in the *Kitāb al-ṭabīḫ*

The fifth recipe is the "Stuffed, Buried Jewish Dish." Once again, eggs are used in large quantities. Perfumed rosewater is mentioned twice and pine nuts are added at the end of the preparation, as is the case with the Jewish partridge recipes. The type of meat used is not specified, but we can imagine that it would be mutton, if we consider the meats that are typically used in the recipe collection. I prepared this dish, which looks like a stuffed meat cake with several layers. The process and the recipe are discussed in chapter 11.

The last recipe is called "A Jewish Dish of Eggplants Stuffed with Meat." An examination of the preparation and recipe for this dish—also discussed in chapter 11—reveals that it is the most time-consuming and most difficult to make.

30 Al-Arbulī and Amador Díaz García, ed. and trans., *Tratado nazarí sobre alimentos: al kalam 'ala l-agdiya* (Mojácar-Almería: Arráez, 2000), 148–150; trans. on 82–83. Translation by the author.

Eggs are used in a variety of ways: the whites bind and the hard-boiled yolks are cut into pieces for decoration. This recipe also requires a large number of ingredients. Three different pots are recommended, as though it is important to keep the ingredients from being mixed together. Once again, pine nuts are included in the preparation, as well as rosewater. The addition of acidic liquids at different points in the preparation and in large quantities is noteworthy. These include vinegar *murrī* and marinated *murrī*, which demonstrates the tendency of Jewish recipes to have acidic flavors. However, vinegar also plays an important role in Eastern dishes, such as *sikbāǧ*, the root of Western *escabeche*—foods that are cooked in vinegar in order to be preserved for longer. What also adds to the specificity of these six recipes is the use of pots. Four out of the six recipes call for at least two different pots, which is not typical of the other recipes in the book. Moreover, in two of them, it is specified that the pot must be new.

c. "Buried" Recipes: Other Jewish Recipes?

"Buried recipes" refers to the possibility that in the *Kitāb al-ṭabīḫ* there are recipes that were prepared by Jews in the late Middle Ages, but whose titles do not explicitly include the term "Jewish." The method used to prepare these dishes, as well as their specific ingredients, allows one to identify the practices of this community between the thirteenth and fourteenth centuries. This facilitates the study of the dishes that have survived until the present day, mainly on the Iberian Peninsula and in Morocco. Moreover, this permanence, and the existence of these practices among modern Sephardic Jews, enable us to find Jewish recipes otherwise hidden in the *Kitāb al-ṭabīḫ*.

If we closely examine the content of the recipes in the cookbook, we can see that those that are woven in with the explicitly Jewish recipes have several points in common with the later: the ingredients, types of preparations, recommendations, and so on. For instance, take the example of the recipe "The Making of Cooled Chicken"—chicken stuffed with almonds and hard-boiled eggs that are "hidden" inside the bird, or the "Stuffed Goose" recipe that contains meatballs, almonds, pine nuts, pistachios, stuffed goose and no fewer than twenty-five eggs. This dish is particularly interesting, as it brings together several characteristics of Jewish food, such as the consumption of goose meat,[31] a large quantity of eggs, meatballs, and the culinary technique of stuffing a bird.

31 Lev. 11:13–19: Safra and Marciano, *Chumash*, 638–639. On the association Jew/goose, cf. Pierre De Beauvais, "Bestiaire," in *Bestiaire du Moyen Âge*, ed. Gabriel Bianciotto (Paris:

But the ambiguity remains: How can we determine whether a recipe was made and consumed specifically by Jews or whether it was a part of both Jewish and Muslim practices? When it comes to identifying specifically Jewish recipes, I propose the "preparation of the 'Dish of Hidden Vegetables,'" صنعة البقلية المكر ة. After an in-depth analysis of this recipe and its title, I propose the following name, which is corrected and as close as possible to the original text: "Preparation of Vegetable Balls."

This lamb-based dish is characterized by a large amount of herbs, which gives it a very particular green-black color. The recipe includes cilantro and spinach, but it is also possible to use chard, saltbush, lettuce, and chicory. It is easy to imagine the very dark color of this dish. This stew of spinach and chard with meat is very similar to a dish prepared for Shabbat in the Talmud. It is recommended that the meat is consumed (but one can substitute fried fish for the meat) with spinach and garlic.[32] According to the Talmud, this stew provides many benefits, and it is often mentioned for this reason.[33] From a culinary point of view, it recalls the popular dish *mloukhiya* (الملوخية) that is mainly consumed in Ifriqiya.[34] It is made of Jew's mallow, to which garlic, onions, and oil are added. The greenish-black preparation is cooked for several hours.

Another "hidden" Jewish recipe in the *Kitāb al-ṭabīẖ* has a strong sweet taste—*murakkaba*.[35] This the most revealing of the presence of specifically Jewish recipes in the *Kitāb al-ṭabīẖ*. Reading this recipe, nothing suggests a relationship between the dish and the culinary habits of Spanish Jews, as the ingredients are quite basic. However, the unique confection indicates its true identity: pancakes cooked on one side only that are then turned around; another pancake is placed

---

Stock, 1995); Claudine Sagaert, "L'utilisation des préjuges esthétiques comme redoutable outil de stigmatisation du juif. La question de l'apparence dans les écrits antisémites du XIXe siècle à la première moitié du XXe siècle," *Revue d'anthropologie des connaissances* 7, no. 4 (2014): 971–992, https://doi.org/10.3917/rac.021.0971.

32 Talmud *Shabbat* 118b.

33 I thank the chief rabbi of the southwest of France Emmanuel Valency for providing me with this information.

34 Mainly in Tunisia, Libya, and Egypt. This is still the case in the twenty-first century. It should be mentioned that this dish is mentioned in a source dating from the beginning of the eleventh century, in Hijri 395 (October 24, 1004). In *Itti'ath al-Hunanfa*, Al-Maqrizi cites an order imposed by al-Hakim bi-Amrillah which prohibited the consumption of *mloukhiya* because his enemy, Shiite Mu'awya ibn Abi Sufyan, allowed it. The cookbook *Kitāb al-wusla* (Syria, thirteenth century) proposes four recipes of *mloukhiya* (and two variations). They are made of cilantro leaves, Jew's mallow, onions, garlic, meat, and oil. See Charles Perry, ed. and trans., and David Waines, *Kitāb al-wuṣla ilā -ḥabīb fī waṣf al ṭayyibāt wal-ṭīb/Scents and Flavors: A Syrian Cookbook* (New York: New York University Press, 2017).

35 Guillaumond, *Cuisine et diététique dans l'Occident arabe médiéval*: "Recipe of the *marakība*(?)," no. 285; no. 286 is a variation with dates.

on top; and so on until a small tower is formed on which melted butter and honey are poured before eating. No other recipe included in the *Kitāb al-ṭabīẖ* resembles this one. Far from leading to a teleological argument, the continuity of culinary techniques—as well as the fact that such food practices are still alive today among Jews—one is given a strong hint about where the preparations came from. They have not evolved much—and even if they had, their common foundation would make it possible to identity them. The *murakkaba* in the *Kitāb al-ṭabīẖ* turns out to be the oldest of all the known versions of *moufleta.* Prepared for *Mimouna,* a celebration at the end of Jewish Easter (Pessah), it is identical to a dish still made by Moroccan Sephardic Jews. This prompted me to include the *murakkaba*[36] among the "buried" Jewish recipes in the *Kitāb al-ṭabīẖ*. Other preparations can be added to this list due to their continuity, techniques, and ingredients. In short,[37] these include the "Preparation of Ears,"[38] "Ras Maimun (Monkey's Head)," "Whole Būrāniyya,"[39] and "Panada with Meat and Spinach."[40]

Several recipes in the *Kitāb al-ṭabīẖ* not only disclose Jewish culinary practices, but Muslim ones too. Pies, stuffed dishes, and those that can be consumed as a snack are among the culinary traditions of al-Andalus. For instance, take the *pashtidas* mentioned in the Talmud of Babylon[41] or the "Pie [*mẖbiza*] of Pigeons and Doves."[42] The latter is made of pastry that is put at the bottom of a dish on which cooked pigeons—seasoned with cilantro, onions, and eggs—are placed. Another pastry covers it and the whole thing is sealed with egg whites. The pie that is stuffed with pigeons and called "Preparation of Barmakiyya" (it can also be prepared using doves, chickens, starlings or mutton meat)[43] is similar to the previous dish. In the *barmakiyya,* emphasis is placed on its transportability—the end of the recipe states that it is excellent for travelers. Other preparations, such as the *ka'ak,* the *kuskusū,* the *sanbūsak,* garbanzo croquettes, *muhallabiyya,*

---

36 Recipe described in part 3.

37 Ibid.

38 Guillaumond, "La cuisine dans l'Occident arabe médiéval," no. 445; Huici and Marín, *La cocina hispano-magrebí,* no. 185; Guillaumond, *Cuisine et diététique dans l'Occident arabe médiéval,* no. 346.

39 Guillaumond, *Cuisine et diététique dans l'Occident arabe médiéval,* no. 196.

40 Ibid. no. 240.

41 Talmud Pesachim 74b and Rashi.

42 Guillaumond, *Cuisine et diététique dans l'Occident arabe médiéval,* no. 319.

43 Ibid., no. 92.

and *isfenğ*,[44] testify to a shared culinary heritage belonging to both Jews and Muslims, both in the past and the present day.[45]

One sees, then, the existence of a common foundation that defines al-Andalus cuisine. It seems that the cuisine of Jews and Muslims in the twelfth to thirteenth century in Andalusian Spain was not significantly different in terms of food choice and culinary practices. This observation does not apply to the consumption of bread and wine, as these two foods are intimately linked to the religious practices of Judaism, the precepts of which are regulated by *Kashrut* and whose culinary application is clear from the different religious holidays to which they belong. As for meat, both Jews and Muslims used it in their food. One would think that the shared ban on pork consumption was the reason for this common culinary foundation. It is true that this may explain the similarities between Jewish and Muslim meat dishes. But if there are no major differences between the dishes of Jews and Muslims at that time, the slaughter rules—*shehita*[46]—and sale of meat imposed on Jews in Muslim territories under Almohad domination surely did not facilitate the consumption of it within Mosaic communities.

This also affected commensality. The danger of exposing new converts to mixed eating at festive events was already a reality in the thirteenth century. A situation arose from the context of conversion. "Although a few canon lawyers might object, Iberian Christians in the initial period of territorial conquest (twelfth and thirteenth centuries) apparently had few qualms about sharing a dinner table with Muslims or accepting food from them, even during times of war."[47] The forced conversions of the fourteenth century marked a turning point in culinary and social practices. The fourteenth century paved the way for the laws about interactions between peoples (food, commensality, etc.) that arose in the fifteenth and sixteenth centuries. It is in light of a more nuanced and in-depth reading that the recipes are revealed, particularly through an understanding of the practices or their connection to ancestral texts, which the cookbook's author is clearly familiar with.

---

44 In the fourteenth century, the Sevillian Talmud exegete David Abudarham wrote in the *Sefer Abudarham* (The Book of Abudarham) that the term *isfenğ* is the Arabic name *sufganin*, knowing that the term *sufganin* appears in the *Mishnah* in the third century.

45 These preparations will be analyzed in detail in part three.

46 Claire Soussen, "La cacherout ou le besoin d'une expertise juive en matière alimentaire," in *Expertise et valeur des choses au Moyen Âge*, vol. 1, *Le besoin d'expertise*, ed. Claude Dejean and Laurent Feller (Madrid: Casa de Velázquez, 2013), 37–52.

47 Olivia Remie Constable, *To Live like a Moor*, 112.

B. The *Kitāb al-ṭabīẖ*—Written by an Anonymous Jewish Author?

a. His Origin

Not much is known about the author of the *Kitāb al-ṭabīẖ*.[48] The richness of the information contained in the book makes the anonymous nature of the book even more intriguing. Moreover, meticulous study of the *Kitāb al-ṭabīẖ* uncovers a variety of clues spread throughout the book, which help us to pursue this author with no name. But the medieval notion of authorship was very different from the one we have today. There could have been a sole scribe, who edited several texts together. In the Middle Ages, the boundary between a final work and a manuscript made of different folios was more porous than in other historical periods. Several hypotheses should be considered when thinking about the *Kitāb al-ṭabīẖ*: either the "author" only compiled various texts or there were several authors. Its Jewishness is also under consideration.

The clues that are interspersed throughout the cookbook make it possible to establish that the author was a man from the upper classes of al-Andalus society, before the Christian takeover of Cordova in 1236. He was educated, which can be seen from the numerous literary and dietary references scattered throughout the collection. His knowledge of table art and service, included in the note entitled "How the Service of Dishes is Ordered, and Which Is Fitting to Be First, and Which Last,"[49] confirms his social status. For example, the author writes that "many of the great figures and their companions order that the separate dishes be placed on each table before the diners, one after another; and, on my life, this is more beautiful than putting an uneaten mound on the table, and it is more elegant, shows better breeding, and is modern; this has been the practice of the people in al-Andalus and West—their rulers, great figures, and men of merit since the days of 'Umar b. 'Abd al-'Aziz and the Banu Umayya to the present."[50] The expression "more beautiful" and repetition of the word "more" suggest that the author had the first-hand experience of such dining necessary to make such an observation. Moreover, he refers to the Umayyad Caliphate that emerged in Medina—which ruled from 717 to 720—as well as the Umayyad dynasty, emphasizing their elegance and refinement. This supports the idea that there

48 See *Old cook*, www.oldcook.com.
49 Guillaumond, *Cuisine et diététique dans l'Occident arabe médiéval*, no. 18.
50 "An Anonymous Andalusian Cookbook of the Thirteenth Century."

was a transmission of knowledge surrounding table art that reached the Iberian Peninsula, a tradition that was inherited from Arabs five hundred years before.

These details lead us to the hypothesis that the author is Andalusian and of Arab origin,[51] an idea that is further supported by remarks like "There are others who sprinkle ground pepper over the food when it is cut for eating; this is a practice of the Christians and Berbers. And cinnamon and lavender especially are sprinkled upon food on the plate before eating, but that is for particular dishes, not all."[52] The author was neither Christian nor Berber, then. His awareness of the multiculturalism of al-Andalus strongly suggests that he was Andalusian, most likely from Seville, Cordova, or Jerez,[53] as the following implies: "It's one of the seven cited dishes that we are used to eating at home in the banquets of Cordova and Seville."[54]

The author was familiar with the habits and customs of the communities that lived together, which itself testifies to the land's cultural splendor at the time—a place rich in the knowledge of different traditions and customs. Indeed, the book later reveals that the author lived in Marrakesh[55] before 1198, then stayed in Ceuta, where he was welcomed by an Almohad *sayyid*, between 1202 and 1216;[56] and that he wrote the cookbook in Ifriqiya before the Hafsides period (1207–1574). The following phrase indicates that he did not originate from this region: "It is one of their best dishes. There, they prepare a panada with matzah bread and fatty chickens and some prepare it with fatty mutton meat."[57]

The *Kitāb al-ṭabīẖ*, therefore, should not be read as a simple cookbook. Studying the work is an invitation to deconstruct the concept of the cookbook through literary analysis. It seems to testify to the culinary past of al-Andalus in the thirteenth century, a marker of the existence of a Hispanic-North African cuisine.[58]

Opinions diverge when it comes to the likely profession of the author. According to Bernard Rosenberger,[59] the *Kitāb al-ṭabīẖ* is the work of a doctor.[60] This might explain the book's dietary recommendations and the large number of

---

51 Ibid., 38.
52 Ibid.
53 Guillaumond, *Cuisine et diététique dans l'Occident arabe médiéval*, no. 276, 185.
54 Ibid., no. 18, 79; no. 39, 86–87.
55 Ibid., 38.
56 Ibid.
57 Ibid. no. 242, 169–170.
58 Huici and Marín, *La cocina hispano-magrebí.*
59 Historian, specialist on Morocco.
60 Rosenberger, "Dietética y cocina en el mundo musulmán occidental según el Kitāb al-ṭabīj," 55: "Según algunos detalles del *Kitāb al-ṭabīẖ* suponemos que es obra de medico."

dishes are suggested for staying in good health. Yet dietary manuscripts were not only written by doctors in al-Andalus—just like in the rest of the *Dār al-Islām*.[61] Botanists and agronomists—who were mainly Muslim and Jewish—were also experts on medicine and diet.[62] The same is true, to a certain degree, for cooks and even grammar specialists.[63] According to Daniel Newman,[64] the *Kitāb al-ṭabīḫ* does not resemble a cookbook, at least as regards cookbooks written by doctors in the East during the same period.

In his preliminary study of the work proposed by Ambrosio Huici Miranda,[65] entitled *La cocina hispano-magrebí durante la época Almohade*,[66] Manuela Marín writes that 'Abd al-Ghanī Abū l -'Azm questions the author's identity.[67] He suggests two possibilities. The first is that the author was a professional cook in the employ of royalty. The second is that the anonymous author was a Jew from Andalusia or North Africa. Marín adds that, given the importance of diet and medicine in the text, he believes that the author was a Jewish doctor from Fes, a disciple of Maimonides (1135–1204, Cordova-Fustat) in Egypt, and called Abū l -Ḥaǧǧāǧ Yūsuf b.Yaḥya b. Isḥāq al-Isrā'ilī (d. 1226).[68] Although we can't be certain about the author's name, ~~Marín's~~ work support the hypothesis that the author of the *Kitāb al-ṭabīḫ* was a Jewish Andalusian doctor and could also be a cook. Another question is how well the anonymous author was aware of the interactions between the different ethnic groups of al-Andalus in the thirteenth century. His overall knowledge, especially in the medical field, lends credence

61 For instance, Ibn Shaprūt (Jewish doctor Abd al-Rahman III), Jaén-Cordoue, 915–970; Al-Zahrawi (Abulcassis) (935–1136); Ibn Zuhr (Avenzoar), Seville, 1094–1161; Ibn Rushd (Averroes), Cordova, 1126–1198; Maimonides (Jewish doctor), Cordova, 1135–1204; Moses ben Nahman (Jewish doctor of the twelfth to thirteenth century), Salomon ibn al-Mussalin (Jewish doctor of the thirteenth century); Ibrāhīm ibn Zazār (Jewish doctor of the fourteenth century), etc.

62 For instance, Ibn Bassal (agronomist of the eleventh century), etc. For more details, see Véronique Pitchon, *La gastronomie arabe médiévale – Entre diététique et plaisir* (Paris: Erick Bonnier, 2018).

63 Like Jonah Ibn Ğanāḥ's, Cordova (980–1040). See Paul Fenton, "Jonah Ibn Ğanāḥ's Medical Dictionary, the Kitāb al-Talḫīṣ: Lost and Found," *Aleph* 16, no. 1 (2016): 107–143.

64 Linguistics professor, head of the Arabic Department at the University of Durham, England.

65 Huici and Marín, *La cocina hispano-magrebí*, ~~36, 38.~~

66 Ibid.

67 Statements written in 'Abd al-Ghanī Abū l-'Azm's introduction to the study of the manuscript *Anwā 'al-ṣaydala fī alwān al-aṭima* [Various remedies about different types of foods], which seems to be a copy of the older anonymous *Kitāb al-ṭabīḫ* cookbook: Translation by the author.

68 The *Encyclopedia of Islam* mentions a certain Isḥāq b. Ali b. Yūsuf, from 1146. Results from the 'Abd al-Ghanī Abū l -'Azm are not, however, based on any research presented up until now.

to the idea that he was part of a circle of scholars and that he could not ignore anti-Jewish acts and laws.

b. The Author's Culinary Preferences

The notes in the *Kitāb al-ṭabī* highlight the author's predilection for non-Berber dishes. He was familiar with the culinary practices of the East (Persian and Abbassid)—and the Muslim West (from Constantine to Marrakesh to Toledo)—and this knowledge allowed him to take a critical look at the cuisine that he selected for the cookbook. As a consequence, Berber dishes (*ṣanhāǧī, lamtuniya, kutamia*) are rarely mentioned in the book. That said, it is odd that the author presented the simplest (i.e., socially lower-class) dishes—such as the "Slave Dish," "Country Chicken," the "Servers' Dishes," and so on—in the best possible light. As for royal dishes, there are many of them and they include more detailed descriptions, thus revealing the author's knowledge of the elite world in which he must have mixed.

The high proportion of meat dishes and the richness of detail given for their preparation raises questions about this raw ingredient. Meat was an expensive product.[69] It was not available to everyone and yet it is present in 311 of the 462 recipes in the cookbook. The author's knowledge of dishes in al-Andalus and beyond—Sicily,[70] Constantine,[71] Ifriqiya, and the East[72]—confirms that he was a fine cook. His knowledge of cuisine, a variety of culinary techniques, and table art and service demonstrates his high social status.

c. Clues of Judaism

Among the 462 dishes in the *Kitāb al-ṭabīẖ*, some are not far removed from the principles governing Jewish food laws included in Kashrut.[73] It is no surprise

---

69 Marianne Brisville, "Plats sûrs et plats sains dans l'Occident musulman médiéval. La harīsa comme contre-exemple?" in *De la nature à la table au Moyen Âge: L'acquisition des aliments. Actes du 138e Congrès du CTHS: Se nourrir. Pratiques et stratégies alimentaires, Rennes, 22–26 avril 2013*, ed. Bruno Laurioux (Paris: CTHS, 2017).

70 Guillaumond, *Cuisine et diététique dans l'Occident arabe médiéval*, "Plat à la sicilienne," no. 173.

71 Ibid., "[R]ecette de la *marakība* (?)," no. 285; Guillaumond, "La cuisine dans l'Occident arabe médiéval," no. 384; Huici and Marín, *La cocina hispano-magrebí*, no. 418.

72 Ibid., "[T]afāyā autre manière, à l'orientale"; Guillaumond, *La cuisine dans l'Occident arabe médiéval*, no. 122; Huici and Marín, *La cocina hispano-magrebí*, no. 141.

73 Lev. 10:10; 11:1–30.

that the first of these clues concerns meat, which plays an important role in cultural history.[74] But it is important to remember that the *Kitāb al-ṭabīḫ* contains no pork recipes. Pork is not even mentioned. The significance of religion—and compliance with the food laws that religion imposes—cannot be denied in this al-Andalus cookbook. The absence of port, then, prohibited only in Judaism and Islam, proves that the author is not a Christian.

The recipes in the *Kitāb al-ṭabīḫ* state that the nerves must be removed from meat before it is ground. In the Muslim religion, no directions are provided about removing nerves and/or veins from meat. However, the book states several times that meat should be cooked "without tendons," "without tendons or veins," and even "without nerves." Two recipes are particularly interesting in this regard: the first concerns a preparation made with leg of lamb or mutton, in which the meat used must be without veins (العروق) or vessels, which could contain blood. The book says that they must be scrupulously removed so that no trace is left.[75] It is true that Muslims,[76] like Jews,[77] prohibit the consumption of blood. Nonetheless, such a prohibition, combined with the removal of nerves, suggests a Jewish recipe. As for the other dish, it is a meatball recipe in which the meat used must be "healthy"—meaning without nerves (العصب).[78]

There are twelve similar directives in the cookbook, five of which concern meatballs (*al-bunduq*),[79] three croquettes (*aḥraš*),[80] two a different type of croquette (*isfīriyā*),[81] one a "chicken or meat dish,"[82] and finally *sanbūsak*.[83] This specificity recalls one of the food laws in the Torah: the obligation to remove the sciatic nerve.[84] Let's return to the preparations of "balls" contained in the *Kitāb al-ṭabīḫ*. They appear in the Arabic word *al-bunduq*—from which the Spanish word *albóndigas* is derived—a term which to this day refers to seasoned ground meatballs. In the *Kitāb al-ṭabīḫ*, meatballs must always be prepared with meat that has no veins or nerves; this is the case for *aḥraš*, *isfīriyā* (a sort of croquette),

74 Marie-Pierre Horard-Herbin and Bruno Laurioux, eds., *Pour une histoire de la viande* (Rennes-Tours: PUR et PUFR, 2017).
75 Guillaumond, "La cuisine dans l'Occident arabe médiéval," no. 537; Huici and Marín, *La cocina hispano-magrebí*, no. 270.
76 Quran 2:173; 5:3; 6:145; 16:115.
77 Gen. 9:4.
78 Guillaumond, "La cuisine dans l'Occident arabe médiéval," no. 124, 143.
79 Ibid., no. 124, no. 128, no. 476, no. 478, no. 479.
80 Ibid., no. 126, no. 127, no. 232.
81 Ibid., no. 537, no. 538.
82 Ibid., no. 541.
83 Ibid., no. 480.
84 Genesis 325–33. See Safra and Marciano, *Chumash*, 189.

and *sanbūsaks* (small stuffed foods). According to Enrique Cantera, Jews were condemned by the court of the Inquisition for eating meatballs, making this dish a marker of both culinary and religious identity.[85]

It is interesting to note that the *Kitāb al-ṭabīẖ* contains sixty-nine meatball recipes—a style of dish that is still connected with Jewish cuisine today. Among these dishes, only five are made with fish and one is a recipe with strong sweet flavors. In total, these meatball recipes represent 15.8% of all the dishes in the cookbook and more than 23.5% if the calculation is restricted to meat meals only. This large proportion makes the cookbook all the more unique and imprints it with an undeniable Jewish culinary identity. Indeed, the proportion of meatball dishes in later cookbooks written under Christian rule is much smaller. The presence of religion in the cookbook is obvious.

From this observation, a new hypothesis emerges to explain these results. Jews—and very likely Muslims—ate meatballs and therefore must have enjoyed them; this was probably not the case for Christians. Or, the latter willingly frowned on these dishes because they represented one of the flagship foods of Semitic communities. Given the context of repression initiated by the Inquisition, when all activities not compliant with Christian orthodoxy were monitored, this possibility needs to be considered. I will develop this argument further in the second part of the book.

Analysis of recipes without meat reveals even more secrets.[86] The absence of meat is plain to see, given the large number of vegetable preparations—including Eastern dishes[87]—dating from the same period. The *Kitāb al-ṭabīẖ*, moreover, contains a chapter exclusively dedicated to vegetables. Among the 462 recipes, only 101 have very strong sweet flavors.[88] There are also savory dishes that do not contain meat: nineteen use fish, four use eggs, nineteen are vegetable dishes, and nine are paired with drinks. Thus, there is a total of fifty meatless recipes out of 361 savory ones—a sum of 14%.

An analysis of the vegetable dishes shows that fifteen out of these nineteen dishes are made exclusively from eggplant. Moreover, eggplant is sometimes

---

85 Cantera Montenegro, "La carne y el pescado en el sistema alimentario judío de la España medieval." See analysis in part 2.

86 Massimo Montanari, *La chère et l'esprit. Histoire de la culture alimentaire chrétienne* (Paris: Alma Éditeur, 2017), 59–94.

87 See Rodinson, Arbery, and Perry, *Medieval Arab Cookery*; Ibn Mubārak Shāh, *The Sultan's Feast: A Fifteenth-Century Egyptian Cookbook*, ed., trans., and introduced by Daniel L. Newman (London: Saqi Books, 2020); Limor Yungman, "Beyond Cooking: The Roles of Chefs in Medieval Court Kitchens of the Islamic East," in 15, nos. 1–2 (2017): 85–114, https://doi.org/10.1484/J.FOOD.5.116334.

88 What we call "desserts" today.

used to imitate meat, as is the case in the "*arnabī* recipe"[89] (*arnab* meaning hare). This recipe is one of the major clues about the author's possible Jewish identity. Why propose a hare recipe if, in the end, it doesn't contain any meat? Why use eggplant to replace meat and insinuate, by imitating stuffing, that it contains hare? This would be of little importance if Jews could, like Muslims, eat this animal. However, this isn't the case. According to Kashrut,[90] neither hare—nor any other animal that is not a ruminant with split hoofs—can be consumed. This is a surprising and revealing instance of the author's possible Jewish identity—or, perhaps, Muslim, as he has considerable knowledge about Jewish food laws. But in this case, why not really use hare meat? The clues scattered throughout the cookbook make it possible to sketch a more refined picture of the author's religious profile. In the graph of meatless dishes below—where eggplant emerges as a distinct element—it is interesting that this vegetable holds a strong position among the foods used.

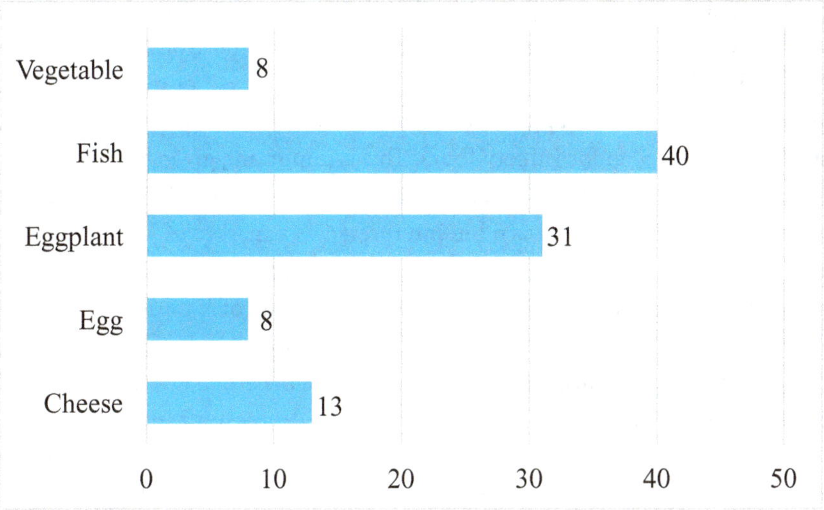

Figure 3. Foods in the meatless dishes of the *Kitāb al-ṭabīḫ*

89 Guillaumond, *Cuisine et diététique dans l'Occident arabe médiéval*, no. 201. Translation by the author.

90 On this question, see Shmuly Yanklowitz, *Kashrut and Jewish Food Ethics* (Boston: Academic Studies Press, 2019).

Why, in a cookbook created by and for the elite,[91] doesn't meat—which is a symbol of wealth and social status—appear in all of the recipes? Vegetables, which were usually the food of the poor, are included in meticulous recipes and have an entire section in the *Kitāb al-ṭabīẖ*. Furthermore, these vegetable dishes are not side dishes, but main dishes, prepared with just as much care as the meat ones. Indeed, in the introduction to the vegetable section, it is stated that "each dish obviously goes with meat."[92]

This is an important reversal. In cookbooks—whether from Andalusia or elsewhere—meat is the main ingredient, with other ingredients featuring in side dishes. Meat could be paired with vegetables, although this this was not often the case. It is important to remember the author's social position. The readership of the cookbook, like the author, were part of the urban social elite. This justifies the use of meat in large proportion in the *Kitāb al-ṭabīẖ*. Yet nothing explains—at first—the presence of vegetable recipes. The author and readers' aristocratic status mean that money didn't prevent meat eating.

The predilection for using eggs is also a culinary marker that is present in Jewish food and practices. This point of view is shared by both Susan Weingarten and Halima Ferhat. The same is true for the frequent use of oil—likely olive oil. Indeed, in the *Kitāb al-ṭabīẖ*, oil is used in 55% of the preparations (254) and in 29% of fried foods (ninety-four). This is important, given that animal fat, *samn* (rancid butter), is used in seventeen recipes and butter in thirty-six. The use and consumption of oil is often interpreted as a marker of Jewish identity, as it is a neutral/*parve* food; this is also true for eggs, which can be prepared with meat. Oil also facilitates compliance with the rules of *Kashrut*. M. A. Motis Dolader contrasts Jews and Christians: "The daily menu of Jews in the Middle Ages is different as regards the preparation and use of certain raw materials from animals."[93] I think that this is also valid, to a lesser degree, for Muslims.

Recipes in which dishes are covered with dough and cooked until the next day also help identify the author's religion. I mentioned this earlier.[94] This culinary technique reflects the preparation of dishes for Shabbat, on Friday night—nothing could be added after sunset and before the next evening.[95]

---

91 Marianne Brisville, "Meat in the Urban Markets of the Medieval Maghrib and al-Andalus. Production, Exchange and consumption," *Food and History* 16, no. 1 (2018): 3–20.

92 Guillaumond, *Cuisine et diététique dans l'Occident arabe médiéval*, no. 175. Translation by the author.

93 Motis Dolader, "L'alimentation juive médiévale," 382.

94 See chapter 2, A and B.

95 Concerning Shabbat, Kashrut, and Jewish practices, see Freedman, *Why Food Matters*, 56.

While the author was certainly not Christian, there is a strong possibility that he was Jewish. All of the above suggests this, even if some uncertainty still exists. Nonetheless, contextualization and pragmatism must be applied here; and the numerous clues, once taken together, point to an increasingly specific profile of the author. There is no reason for Muslims to consume meatless dishes. Neither their customs, celebrations, nor religious obligations prevent it. This is not the case for Jews, though, for whom no dish can contain milk and meat together;[96] the result is a number of dishes that can be described as vegetarian.

The *Kitāb al-ṭabīḫ* is, in this sense, a special case, as it is the only cookbook to contain so many vegetable-based dishes. The increased importance of plant-based foods (vegetables, oil, cereals, etc.) in the daily food practices of Jews is a phenomenon that dates back to antiquity and survives to this day.[97] Moreover, the Torah and the Talmud encourage the avoidance of meat.[98]

Some Jewish holidays do not allow meat to be eaten[99] (for nine days during *Tishabeav*) or even stipulate fasting (*shiv'ah*);[100] and some recipe titles in the *Kitāb al-ṭabīḫ* recall preparations that, to this day, are part and parcel of Sephardic Jewish culinary culture. However, there is much missing information between Middle ages and present. The minority status of Jews, the prohibition on proselytizing, the lack of a Jewish consciousness, and the diaspora explain the loss of these details. The permanence and fervor of faith, encouraged by solid community, make the Jewish religion the cornerstone of enduring practices—including culinary practices—which have survived over time. It is through this lens that the following preparations are considered.

---

96 Ex. 23:19; 34:26; Deut. 14: 21. See Safra and Marciano, *Chumash*, 468–469, 549, 1073.

97 Frugality has been thought to help maintain good health since antiquity. See Ibn Ḫalṣun, "Troisième partie. L'hygiène générale," in *Kitāb al-Aġḏiya (Le livre des aliments)*, ed. Suzanne Gigandet (Damas: Presses de l'Ifpo, 1996), https://doi.org/10.4000/books.ifpo.5507.

98 Genesis 1:29; Safra and Marciano, *Chumash*, 9: "And God said, "Behold, I have given you every plant yielding seed that is on the face of all the earth, and every tree with seed in its fruit. You shall have them for food"; Talmud Sanhédrin 59b: "Adam was not authorized to eat meat"—this authorization was given to Noah after the flood (Genesis 9:3; Safra and Marciano, *Chumash*, 41); Talmud 'Houlin 84a: "The Torah gives a lesson of morality: man must not eat meat without experiencing a particular need. . . . [H]e should only eat it occasionally and rarely"; Isaiah 1:11 and 1:15: "'The multitude of your sacrifices—what are they to me?'" says the LORD. 'I have more than enough of burnt offerings, of rams and the fat of fattened animals; I have no pleasure in the blood of bulls and lambs and goats. . . . And when ye spread forth your hands, I will hide mine eyes from you: yea, when ye make many prayers, I will not hear: your hands are full of blood.'"

99 The consumption of fish is permitted during all Jewish holidays.

100 A practice that is a distinguishing feature of Sephardic food customs today.

The titles of certain recipes in the cookbook and the practices they use clearly point to traces of Jewish cuisine on the Iberian Peninsula. Sometimes, the titles help directly establish the link between dishes and religion; in other cases, one has to read the instructions and the ingredients in order to understand the connection. Take, for example, "Bollo Maimón." This dish has a unique shape that suggests the turban worn by Maimonides. In the *Kitāb al-ṭabīẖ*, this preparation bears the name "Preparation of the Head of Maymūn"[101] (Monkey Head). This is a cake recipe that contains semolina, butter, eggs, oil, and honey. What is most important for our purposes is the baking pan used. It is unique in the sense that the edges are very high and in the center is a cylinder that enables the dough to rise without collapsing into the middle of the pan. In my opinion, this dish has a connection with Moses Maimonides, who is typically represented with a turban on his "head"[102]—a turban with a hole in the middle.

This is not the first time that we come across recipes in which the shape of a turban is used. Moreover, this recipe in the *Kitāb al-ṭabīẖ* clearly refers to a human head. Let's also mention the existence of preparations that endure in the Sephardic culinary heritage. This will be addressed more fully in the second part of this book. In short, it is important to note the "Recipe of the *Marakība* [?],"[103] which matches the current recipe known as *moufleta,* and the "Thin Croquettes with Garbanzos," which corresponds to "Small Simple Croquettes with Garbanzos"[104] (very similar to falafels).

In addition, there are recipes and products which, beyond their nourishment value, play a symbolic role. Analyzing the consumption and culinary practices of Jews and Muslims in the *Kitāb al-ṭabīẖ* sheds light these peoples' respective food systems, which are grounded in religion. The question that likely vexes historians and readers is: "What are explicitly Jewish recipes doing in a cookbook written during the persecution of Jews?" Surely it recognizes Jews and thereby shows an interest in them. To answer the question, must assume that the author of the explicitly Jewish recipes is Jewish and that he did not feel that he was in danger. This enabled the written transmission of these recipes scattered among the 456 others. If the author was a Muslim, these Jewish recipes suggest the existence of Jewish cooking at that same time and in this same territory. It follows, then, that

101 Guillaumond, *Cuisine et diététique dans l'Occident arabe médiéval,* 209; Huici and Marín, *La cocina hispano-magrebí,* "[H]echura de cabeza de mono."

102 While he is not the only one to be represented wearing a turban, Maimonides often appears with a headdress and its shape is a distinguishing feature.

103 Guillaumond, *Cuisine et diététique dans l'Occident arabe médiéval,* no. 285, 188. There is also a variation using dates, ibid., 189.

104 Ibid., no. 32.

in the context of the Inquisition these recipes could be a means in the thirteenth century to identify Jews and indicate a culture different from that of Muslims. If there are multiple authors and the cookbook is a compilation of recipes, the above assumptions still hold true.

Finally, one of the last hypotheses is that, whether the author is Jewish or Muslim, the presence of these six explicitly Jewish recipes testifies to the existence of a cuisine made by an ethnic group (surely other than the one in power), whose culture did not threaten or even interest the government in power.

CHAPTER 3

Jewish and Muslim Food Consumption and Cooking Practices in the *Kitāb al-ṭabīẖ*

> Food is one of the main expressions of cultural identity. This is particularly reinforced when it also marks religious practices, and when it is used as a means of distinction from other communities.[1]

All types of cuisine are constructed around flagship foods that reflect the eating habits of a historical era. Nonetheless, due to religion these foods may take on a symbolic value that roots them in a system of identity, which differentiates communities living in the same territory from one another. The following analyses 462 recipes, including desserts but excluding drinks (fifty-six), sauces, and various mixes (twenty-seven).

A. A Differentiating Food System Grounded in Religion

The previous chapters clearly show that it is often difficult to determine whether a given dish was specifically enjoyed by Jews or Muslims, or whether it was part of the customs of both communities. This may confirm David Freidenreich view that "Islamic dietary law poses [a challenge] to the traditional distinction

1 Silvia Valenzuela-Lamas et al., "Shechita and Kashrut: Identifying Jewish populations through Zooarchaeology and Taphonomy: Two examples from Medieval Catalonia (North-Eastern Spain)," *Quaternary International* 4, no. 330 (2014): 1, https://doi.org/10.1016/j.quaint.2013.12.035.

between Jewish and pagan food practices."[2] It is very likely that on the Iberian Peninsula in the late Middle Ages there was no major difference between Jewish and Muslim cuisine, especially given that ingredients were accessible to both populations. Yet, one difference exists, and the food laws written in the Torah—Kashrut—as well as the various recommendations included in the Quran, call attention to a number of divergencies. The shared prohibition regarding the consumption of pork is a major element that creates ambiguity around the distinctiveness of each food system.

The food market allows us to better understand the topic at hand.[3] Two elements emerge. First, the outside space, which was initially separate due to distribution channels, meant that Jewish butchers had no contact with Muslim ones. Their respective locations in this space were defined, and their displays did not necessarily contain the same products. Second, the baskets. By this, we mean what products the consumer bought in these different distribution channels, whether they came from butchers or other displays. While Kashrut does not impose any food restrictions on the purchase of fruits and vegetables, animals are a another case entirely. In addition to the requirement that they be killed in compliance with distinct slaughtering rituals—*shehita* for Jews and *dhabīḥah* for Muslims—there is a "list," which varies according to religion, of species that can be consumed. In short, even though the market was full of a diverse range of products, in a Jew's basket there would be wine, but no shellfish, rabbit, eels, or snails. By contrast, in the Muslim basket these foods would be included, except for wine.

Of course, neither basket would have contained pork. The market brings to light a second part that, this time, concerns inside space: What happened to the purchased products once they entered the private sphere of the home? In Muslim homes, goods did not receive any special treatment and were mixed together; moreover, there was no required cooking method inherent to Muslim culinary practices. This is not true among Jews. Indeed, the prohibition on mixing milk and meat[4] is the fundamental difference between Jewish and Muslim cooking. As for cooking methods, I will focus on the style used for the Shabbat dish.

---

2 Freidenreich, "Sharing Meals with Non-Christians," 111.

3 I would like to thank Professor Claude Denjean (University of Perpignan, Via Domitia) for this idea.

4 *Bassar be-halav*: "You *shall not boil* a *young goat* in its *mother's milk.*" See Exod. 23:19, 34:26; Deut. 14:21.

The ban on lighting a fire and adding anything to a dish after the beginning of Shabbat until the next evening, required—and still does to this day—special organization. Thus, the food needed to be cooked the previous day, so that the dish could be eaten lukewarm—using dying coals—on Saturday at noon. This type of cooking is specific to Jews and differentiates it from Muslim culinary practices. Indeed, there are numerous written testimonials from the Inquisition trials that describe the lengthy cooking style of the dish that Jews left on the embers Friday night to be eaten lukewarm, with other cold dishes, the following day.

Cooking styles should not be ignored by social history, and the possibility cannot be ruled out that Jewish and Muslim women (it was women who cooked) also worked. Their occupations must have necessitated that the pot remain on a part of the fire so that they could attend to their jobs. While there was no religious stipulation about cooking for Muslims, there was for Jews. Kashrut, then, plays a decisive role in helping us to identify and differentiate these two types of cooking.

B. A Revealing Trio

Analyzing bread, wine, and meat in the *Kitāb al-ṭabīẖ* makes it possible to understand the similarities and differences between Jewish and Muslim food practices. Studies conducted on this eternal food trio lay the groundwork for thinking about the presence of certain dishes in the cookbook.

a. Bread

Since the beginning of the first century, bread has been recognized as the "ideal food for mankind,"[5] as it "contains more nutrients than any other food."[6] Figure 3 shows that bread in every possible form (mashed, in crumbs, etc.) appears in ninety-four recipes, in nine different varieties, representing nearly one-quarter of all recipes. In seventy-nine cases out of ninety-four, bread is made from wheat flour. Most times bread contains yeast, but there are two dishes prepared with

---

5 Montanari, *La chère et l'esprit. Histoire de la culture alimentaire chrétienne*, 39.

6 Jean-Louis Ferrary Celse and Jean-Yves Guillaumin, eds., *De la médecine. Livres I et II* (Paris: Les Belles Lettres, Collection des universités de France Série latine, 1995). Other authors from ancient Rome also wrote on the topic.

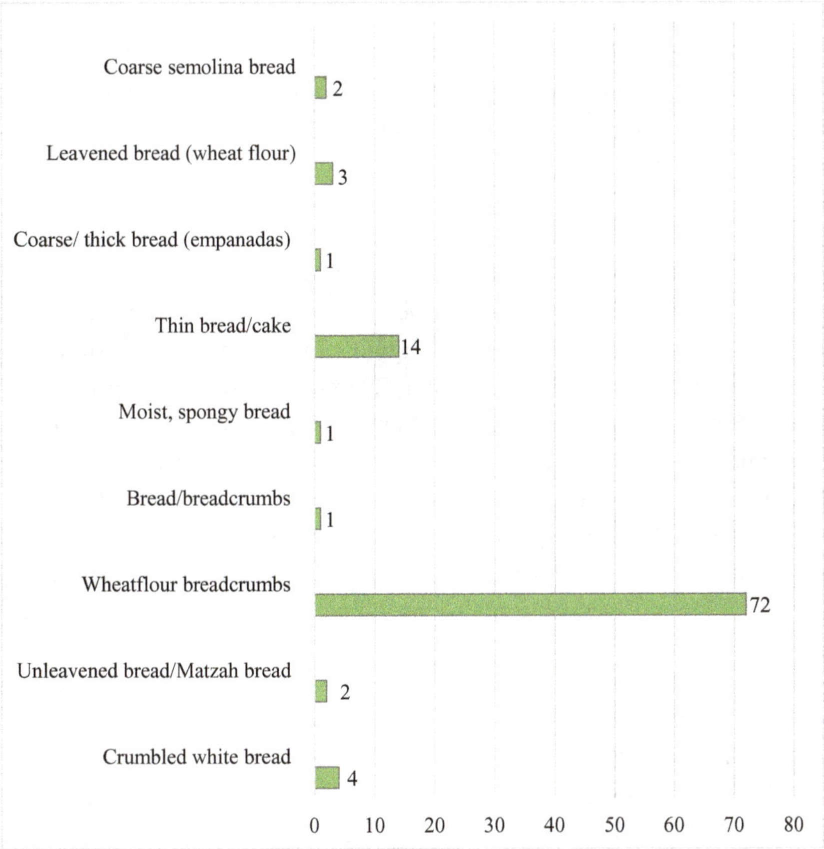

Figure 4. Bread in the *Kitāb al-ṭabīẖ*

unleavened bread (*faṭīr,*[7] فطير in Arabic). Furthermore, in the first preparation, titled "*Tharid* that the People of Ifriqiyya (Tunisia) Call *Fatîr,*"[8] the term *faṭīr* is explicitly used. The other recipe is "Recipe for Folded Bread from Ifriqiyya."[9] In Jewish food, unleavened bread, *matzah,* has a special place in the celebration of Pessah.[10] It is an important part of the celebration because in the Torah it is a

---

7 Mohamed Oubahli, *La main et le pétrin. Alimentation céréalière et pratiques culinaires en Occident musulman au Moyen Âge* (Casablanca: Fondation du Roi Abdul-Aziz Al Saoud pour les Études Islamiques et les Sciences Humaines, 2011), 578. It is written: "*faṭīr*: Azyme." See Maimonides, *On the Regimen of Health,* 53n37.

8 Guillaumond, *Cuisine et diététique dans l'Occident arabe médiéval,* no. 242.

9 Ibid., 173.

10 Freedman, *Why Food Matters,* 57.

reminder that the Hebrews who left Egypt fled so quickly that they didn't have time to let their bread rise.[11] Unleavened bread was thus consumed in al-Andalus—but by whom and why? Muslims, unlike Jews, were not required to eat unleavened bread. If unleavened bread is a good indicator of the food eaten at the time, could it not indicate the presence of Jewish communities in the *Dār al-Islām*?

In *La main et le pétrin*,[12] Mohamed Oubahli studies the consumption of cereal and culinary practices in the Muslim West in the Middle Ages. He examines the *Kitāb al-ṭabīẖ* and *Fuḍālat al-ẖiwān* cookbooks, as well as other sources. He mentions that the flour used to make bread is either semolina (hard wheat) or wheat, but rarely both combined. He counts nine different types of bread consumption in the dishes, the main one being wheat bread crumbs. Wheat flour is used in seventy-nine of the ninety-four recipes: it is a food in and of itself since it isn't used to bread foods or thicken them. This type of flour is not generally recommended in baked goods—given its high gluten content—unless the aim is to make a light, risen bread. *Tarīd* (ثريد) dishes are common in the *Kitāb al-ṭabīẖ* cookbook. These dishes are made of breadcrumbs on which a liquid—often meat broth—is poured.

Rafis and *harīsa*[13] (الهريسة—a crushed wheat mash that can be meat-based or sweet)[14]—are the main dishes that contain bread or related foods. Actually, "only two recipes substitute wheat for rice or breadcrumbs."[15] These are "Rice Harîsa"[16] and "Harîsa Recipe."[17] Bread is generally reduced to crumbs or thin pieces and then covered in broth, becoming so wet that it turns into a gruel. In the *Kitāb al-ṭabīẖ*, there is an entire chapter dedicated to *ṯarīd* and its variations. Huici Miranda has translated *ṯarīd* and *ṯarda* as *sopa* (soup).[18] In *Regimen of Health*, Maimonides writes that "the bread should be made of coarsely ground grain.... It should be clearly raised and salted and well-worked during kneading and baked in an oven. This is well prepared bread according to the physicians; it is the best of foods."[19]

---

11 Exodus 7:34 and 39.

12 Oubahli, *La main et le pétrin*.

13 Ibid., 578: "*Harīsa*: A dish made of wheat and meat cooked together, crushed and kneaded in dough.... They can be made with or without meat."

14 Brisville, "Plats sûrs et plats sains dans l'Occident musulman médiéval," 108.

15 Ibid.

16 Guillaumond, *Cuisine et diététique dans l'Occident arabe médiéval*, no. 262.

17 Ibid., no. 263.

18 Huici and Marín, *La cocina hispano-magrebí*, no. 167, 137.

19 Maimonides, *On the Regimen of Health*, 52; Maimonides, *El régimen de salud. Obras médicas I*, ed. and trans. Ferre (Barcelona: Herder Editorial, 2016), 6, 49.

Of the six explicitly Jewish recipes in the manuscript, three use flour and two use bread crumbs. The "Jewish Dish of Chicken"[20] includes "crumbs rubbed with fine wheat flour," which is not the case in the other "Jewish Dish of Chicken." The "Stuffed, Buried Jewish Dish"[21] also contains fine wheat flour, but not bread crumbs.

In the society of the late Middle Ages, cereals—and products derived from them—always held an important place in food culture, whether Jewish, Muslim, or Christian. As Massimo Montanari notes, "bread unites. . . . But it can also divide, like any food that is imprinted with a strong identity. . . . In the Middle Ages, bread was used to present the 'true' religion to adversaries. During the Crusades, there was a strong ideological tension among Christian authors who claimed bread as a sign of identity and described Muslim bread as a 'badly cooked pancake.'"[22] He continues: "Absurd and fallacious, Christianity's claim over a product that characterized the entire Mediterranean culture is, nonetheless—precisely for that reason—meaningful in terms of the symbolic sentiment and value attached to the consistent materiality of bread."[23] I share this perspective, and it proves to be applicable to the period and territory studied here.

As for pasta, it is typically called *fidawš*[24] (الفدوش), whether long, flat, rolled, cut, and so on. The term corresponds to what is currently known as *fideos* (in Spanish). *Fideos* looks like short spaghetti cut into small sections and is generally used in broth or sauces. A book on important families in Fes provides information about Jewish food in Morocco in the fifteenth century. The book also states that dishes such as *fidāwīsh* were prepared and consumed by Jewish families.[25] The same is true for dishes such as *sha'riyya, tharīd,* and *maqrūt.* It is likely that Muslim families also prepared them, but this source doesn't mention it.

---

20 Guillaumond, *Cuisine et diététique dans l'Occident arabe médiéval,* no. 158.

21 Ibid., no. 169.

22 Massimo Montanari, *Gusti del Medioevo. I prodotti, la cucina, la tavola* (Rome-Bari: Laterza, 2012).

23 Montanari, *La chère et l'esprit. Histoire de la culture alimentaire chrétienne,* 37–38. Translation by the author.

24 Oubahli, *La main et le pétrin,* 578.

25 "Among the *mawālī,* there were those who baked bread and pastries. They roasted meat, made pots for the food and sold it. They pressed olive oil and transported it to sell it, along with soap. They sold salt, fish and lard. They made *fānīd.* They sold remedies and medicinal plants. . . . They were servants in the public baths, carried water and cooked *fidāwīsh, sha'riyya, tharīd* and *maqrūt.*" See Ibn al-Ahmar, "Buyūtāt Fās al-Kubrā (= "Dhikr mashāhīr a'yān Fās al-qadīm")," *Al-Bahth al-'ilmī* 1, no. 3 (1964) (Rabat: Dar al-Mansūr li 'l-Tibā'a wa 'l-Warrāqa, 1972), 56. There is an English translation of this work; see Maya Shatzmiller, "Professions and Ethnic Origin of Urban Labourers in Muslim Spain: Evidence from a Moroccan Source," *Awraq* 5 (1983): 152–153. I thank Professor Newman for this information.

The cooking of different types of bread was mainly done in the *tannūr*.[26] In the *Kitāb al-ṭabīẖ*, it is written that the *tannūr* is the best cooking method because the oven is made of stone. The anonymous author also indicates that "the dishes cooked in this oven are tastier than those cooked in a large oven."[27] This method is still used today in certain regions of Morocco[28] and the Middle East.[29] Doctors, particularly Muslim doctors, recommend using it as part of the theory of moods.[30] Maimonides also specifies in the *Regimen of Health* that oven cooking is best for bread.[31] I counted eighteen recipes for dishes cooked in a *tannūr* and one cooked in a *tannūr* and then on a hot stone that Huici Miranda calls a *rescoldo*.

Let's return to the *matzah* bread, that is, "unleavened Jewish bread." This specific food triggered community conflict, especially among Jews and Christians living in the Muslim territory of al-Andalus. Jewish culinary practices, such as throwing a section of the first bread on the fire, or the need of families, who did not have their own oven or access to a communal one, to bake in a Christian household created divisions between the communities. These divisions would later be used as signs of Jewish identity during the Inquisition. Women removed a small amount of dough, called *challa*, a word which in Latin is *torta*. During Pessah, the only food permitted after meat was a piece of bread which was passed around the table, called *afikoman* (*epikomane* in Hebrew), as in the Greek word *epikomon* (what comes after), which was a dessert. The baking of the bread was a topic of disagreement, as Jews, a minority, did not always have an oven. They needed great ingenuity to bake bread in the ovens of other communities that allowed it. This situation gave rise to denunciations by Christians, who thought that Jews were trying to poison their food.

The following example is very revealing. In 1282, under Christian rule, King Pedro III of Aragon required Jews in the Jewish quarter of Barcelona to bake

---

26 A *tannūr* is a vertical oven made of earthenware or clay. The bread is baked on the sides of the oven. The term comes from the Acadian *tinuru* and the Ugaritic *tnrr*, which means "oven." See Antonella Pasqualone, "Traditional Flat Breads Spread from the Fertile Crescent: Production Process and History of Baking Systems," *Journal of Ethnic Foods* 5, no. 1 (2018): 10–19; P. V. Mankowski, *Akkadian Loanwords in Biblical Hebrew* (Eisenbrauns: Warsaw, 2000).

27 Translation by the author.

28 Mohammed-Habib Samrakandi and Georges Carantino, "Manger au Maghreb. Partie II: approche pluridisciplinaire des pratiques de table en Méditerranée du Moyen Âge à nos jours," *Horizons Maghrébins* 59 (2009).

29 Pasqualone, "Traditional Flat Breads Spread from the Fertile Crescent": 10–19.

30 Oubahli, *La main et le pétrin*.

31 Maimonides, *On the Regimen of Health*, 52; Maimonides, *El régimen de salud*, 6, 49.

their bread in an oven belonging to the widow of Guillem Gruny.[32] In 1390, the Jewish Barcelonan Vidal Brunet was authorized by Queen Violante to bake his bread wherever he pleased.[33] This led to Jews deciding to develop public ovens throughout the city, which users had to pay for; and they developed a quasi-monopoly over them. Remember that it was during holidays that the differences between Jews and non-Jews were the most obvious.

M. A. Motis Doláder argues that "culinary art became a specific activity when religious components were attached to them during particular holidays."[34] As regards bread and/or baking during the week of Pessah, it was impossible for Jews to use an oven where their bread would be in contact with that baked by Muslims or Christians, because the latter would have contained yeast and baking flour. For this reason, King James of Aragon allowed Jews to bake their unleavened bread in their own ovens, without having to pay the usual fee.[35] Massimo Montanari writes: "the symbolic value of bread and wine wasn't born with Christianity . . . they are the creations of human ingenuity, true inventions";[36] and Enrique Cantera observes that bread and wine[37] are the two ingredients that best represent Jewish culture. They are the key to religious celebrations—Shabbat and Pessah are the two most representative holidays—and are undeniable markers of Jewish practices.

Indeed, this fact brings to light a unique recipe in the *Kitāb al-ṭabīḫ:* a braided bread called "The Making of Dafâir, Braids."[38] The term "braids" corresponds to the word *ḍafair* (ضفاير) in Arabic.[39] Braided bread is made of dough molded into hair-like strands. Catherine Guillaumond uses the term "vermicelli," whereas Huici Miranda speaks of *guedejas*[40]—in the recipe that he calls "Hechura de Trenzas."[41] The closest translation of *guedejas* is *peot* in Hebrew. No other source from this period and no other recipe in the book uses this word.

This "braided" recipe closely resembles that for challa, another braided bread made of white flour or semolina that, having been dampened with warm

32 I Sans, "La conflictivitat de l'alimentació dels jueus medievals," 303 (Archivo de la Corona de Aragón, canc., reg. 46, f. 86v, valence, 27/04/1282).

33 I Sans, "La conflictivitat de l'alimentació dels jueus medievals," 303.

34 Dolader, "L'alimentation juive médiévale," 382.

35 I Sans, "La conflictivitat de l'alimentació dels jueus medievals," 303.

36 Montanari, *La chère et l'esprit. Histoire de la culture alimentaire chrétienne,* 31.

37 Cantera Montenegro, "El pan y el vino en el judaísmo antiguo y medieval."

38 Guillaumond, *Cuisine et diététique dans l'Occident arabe médiéval,* no. 336, 208–29.

39 Hélène Jawhara Piñer, "The Sephardi origin of the Challah braided bread," *Meldar: Revista Internacional De Estudios sefardíes* 1 (2020): 65–74.

40 The term *peot* in Hebrew means "lock."

41 Huici and Marín, *La cocina hispano-magrebí,* ~~no.~~ 160, 133.

water, must be kneaded well. Sieved flour is added again, as well as yeast and salt. Hot water must be added several times and the dough kneaded into the same consistency. For each *ratl* (468g) of semolina, five eggs are added and one dirham (3.9g] of saffron. Note that many eggs is used and that it is important that the bread has a yellow color. The recipe then specifies that the dough must be kneaded well, before it is placed in a dish and covered to let it rise. Once risen, fresh oil is added to a pan and heated over the fire. When ready, the braids of risen dough must be shaped into hair braids the size of a hand or smaller. Having coated them with oil, they are fried until they become golden. Once cooked, the bread should be put in a dish and covered with honey and spiced with pepper, cinnamon, and lavender. Sugar is then sprinkled on top.

This dish is unique. Its similarity to the braided bread called challa[42]—well-known today—is very surprising: flour, eggs, yeast, salt, and, of course, the braiding technique that is a special feature of the dish. It would be obvious to anyone that the bread has two surprising features. The first is the size: the braid is smaller than today's *challot*. The second concerns the cooking method, as the braided bread is fried rather than baked. Nonetheless, keep in mind that oil—olive oil mainly—was used by Jews in Spain for both fried foods and other preparations. As it is *parve*,[43] the dish makes it easy to comply with the food laws of Kashrut.[44] Furthermore, Iberian Jews' widespread use of oil made it stand out from Muslims, who used oil but also *smen* (rancid butter)—a practice that is much rarer among Jews.

The use of oil is so important in Jewish Sephardic communities that non-Jews took it that the smell of oil in a city meant that a large number of Jews lived there (this was said of Seville in the beginning of the sixteenth century). The mention of challa bread by the famous Spanish Bible commentator and exegete Abraham Ibn Ezra (1089–1164) affirms that this dish existed and was enjoyed by Spanish Jews as early as the eleventh century. Abraham Ibn also Ezra specifies that it must be "thick."[45] It is interesting that Gil Marks proposes that the bread of Shabbat that was consumed by Ashkenazi Jews[46] from the fifteenth century onwards was enriched and embellished. "The use of oil replicated the

---

42 Also see Daniel Newman's blog: http://eatlikeasultan.com.

43 *Parve* is the term that, in Jewish food laws defined by *Kashrut*, refer to a class of edible substances that don't contain any milk or meat-based products. Foods in this category include things that are grown from the earth, fish, eggs, and non-organic foods. A *parve* food can thus be prepared in contact with other sorts of animal products.

44 Freedman, *Why Food Matters*, 45–49.

45 Gil Marks, *Encyclopedia of Jewish Food* (Boston: Houghton Mifflin Harcourt, 2010), *96*.

46 Ashkenazi are primarily Jews from Eastern Europe.

ingredients of breads prepared in the Temple. Eggs and, less frequently, a pinch of saffron added to the dough resembled the yellow color of cooked manna. Unrelatedly, "the large quantity of oil and eggs produced a softer texture and richer flavor (. . .). The original enriched Sabbath braids were not sweetened."[47] Yet all of this information is already present in the "Braided" recipe of the twelfth century—a recipe prepared solely by Spanish Jews. This is also what makes it unique, as Muslims did not appear to eat this bread and still do not eat it today.

In conclusion, the topic of bread is a complex one—and even more so when seen through the lens of religion. The act of "attaching this or that culinary specialty to the liturgical calendar, linking foods and recipes—the best of them—to religious celebrations, is a way of sanctifying the act of eating, by insisting on its value as an identity."[48] This says it all.

b. Wine

> In the Middle Ages, as in Antiquity, the precedence of wine was absolute and, in the absence of any real competitors, wine had multiple usages that would be difficult to recognize today.[49]

Don't think that the *Dār al-Islām* was always on the margins when it came to drinking wine. In al-Andalus, wine also proved to be one of the most important objects of trade. Tim Unwin[50] argues that the Iberian Peninsula (Cadiz or Jerez) exported sweet wines—with various degrees of alcohol—to England starting at the end of the fourteenth century. Wine also served a therapeutic as well as a social purpose.[51] At this time, when various pogroms erupted, Jews, Christians, and Muslims in al-Andalus already had their own vineyards and engaged in wine

---

47 Marks, *Encyclopedia of Jewish Food, 208.*

48 Montanari, *La chère et l'esprit. Histoire de la culture alimentaire chrétienne,* 221. Translation by the author.

49 Ibid., 43. Translation by the author.

50 Tim Unwin, professor emeritus of geography at Royal Holloway, University of London.

51 See Montenegro, "El pan y el vino en el judaísmo antiguo y medieval;" Pini, "La viticoltura italiana nel Medioevo. Cultura della vite e consumo del vino a Bologna dal X al XV secolo," *Studi Medioevali* 3, no, 15 (1974): 873; Toaff, *Il vino e la carne. Una comunità ebraica nel Medioevo* (Bologna: Il Mulino, 1989), 97–98; Antonio Iván Pini and Ariel Toaff argue that Jewish families from Bologna and Umbria consumed one-half liter per day per person between the tenth and fifteenth centuries.

production. Under Muslim rule, Jews could produce and consume their wine, but selling to Muslims was prohibited.[52]

In Ibn 'Abdūn's *hisba* ordinance no. 116, which dates back to twelfth-century Seville, we read that "glassmakers must be prohibited from making cups intended to contain wine. The same prohibition will apply to potters."[53] The sale of grapes for wine also fell under restriction, and it didn't matter whether the seller was Muslim or not. Thus, in Ibn 'Abdūn's *hisba* ordinance no. 129, it is written that "no one will be allowed to sell large quantities of grapes to someone who we know intends to press to make wine: this is a matter of control."[54]

The many measures taken by the Almohads to control and eradicate the production, sale, and consumption of wine aid our understanding of the social and politico-religious situation in the al-Andalus in the twelfth century. These laws show that Muslims consumed wine and that the ban on the sale of grapes applies to Muslims, Jews, and Christians. One can conclude that al-Andalus was under dogmatic rule at this time, the same kind of governance which saw Maimonides and so many other scholars—Jews, Muslims, and Christians—flee the Almohads. Moreover, Jews' process of manufacturing wine prevented non-Jews from accessing it.

The high levels of immigration and population growth in the thirteenth and fourteenth centuries made it necessary for the *aljamas* of Catalonia, mainly the cities of Barcelona and Girona, to import wine.[55] In order to combat fraudulent importation, the city of Saragossa—a Christian territory—decided in 1370 to prohibit the import of "Jewish wine" (*vino judiego*) from elsewhere. This led to division between the communities, as Christians could no longer go to Jewish taverns to drink wine. Indeed, beyond being in the economic interest of Christians, the aim of this ruling was to prevent proximity between Christians and Jews.

This situation opened up the possibility of bypassing the tax that Christians had to pay to drink wine. In 1391, the Jewish community of Bougie imported

---

52 Alain Huetz de Lemps, *Boissons et civilisations en Afrique, Grappes et Millésimes* (Bordeaux: Presses Universitaires de Bordeaux, 2001), 303.

53 Notice no. 1100, project RELMIN: "Le statut légal des minorités religieuses dans l'espace euro-méditerranéen (Ve–XVe siècle)," Electronic edition Telma, IRHT, Institut de Recherche et d'Histoire des Textes – Orléans, http://www.cn-telma.fr/relmin/extrait1100/. Translation by the author.

54 Notice no. 1101, project RELMIN, "Le statut légal des minorités religieuses dans l'espace euro-méditerranéen (V^e^–XVe siècle)," Electronic edition Telma, IRHT, Institut de Recherche et d'Histoire des Textes – Orléans, accessed July 1, 2018, http://www.cn-telma.fr/relmin/extrait1101/. Translation by the author.

55 I Sans, "La conflictivitat de l'alimentació dels jueus medievals," 303.

the wine of Majorca, a wine produced by *Anusim*.[56] Nonetheless, the most pious Jews of Bougie refused to drink it, arguing that the makers lacked the means to ensure that it was kosher.[57] In 1396, the level of distrust grew and an Oran rabbi received a missive denouncing the fact that Majorcan Jews (whether converted or not) could not control whether Christians intervened in wine production.[58] The same year, the Barcelonan poet and Talmudist Yishak ben Shebet reported that converso Jews couldn't guarantee the kosher status of the wine they drank. Suspicion and animosity towards other communities grew, and wine was increasingly produced and distributed by and for Jews. They could rent their land to Christians and/or buy their grapes, but wine production remained Jewish.

In the *Kitāb al-ṭabīẖ*, wine is rarely mentioned. In the 462 recipes, only four contain wine. Two use blackberry wine, translated as *vino de mirto* by Huici Mirinda, and translated as *murrī de nabīd, vin de dates*, or *nabīd odorant* (in short, any fermented drink) by Catherine Guillaumond. Keep in mind that *murrī*, or in Spanish *almorí*, comes from the fermentation of barley and water over several days. Blackberry is similar to blackcurrant, whose liqueur—which is commonly consumed today in Sicily and Corsica—is obtained by macerating fruits and leaves and adding sugar and/or honey. The word *nabīd* (نبيذ) refers to palm wine, a stronger variety of ordinary palm wine *sharbut* (شربوت). *Nabīd* also designates a fermented drink in which sap macerates with the dates. The fruit from date palms triggers alcoholic fermentation due to the wild yeast that covers the dates.

Even though in ninth-century Ifriqiya, *nabīd* was made from dry raisins, in the eleventh century the word *nabīd* was used to refer to wine made from fresh raisins. The question of whether *nabīd* was lawful or not is not completely resolved, as it is a generic term referring to any type of fruit beverage made from honey, fruit, wheat, or figs. At the same time, it designates any fermented juice coming from fruit which already contains "alcohol." The ordinance of *ḥisba*[59] by Ibn 'Abdūn states that raisins and dates reduced to half their original amounts through

---

56 *Anusim* are Jews converted by force to Christianity. See Liebman, *The Jews in New Spain*, 21.

57 Robert Brunschvig, *La Berbérie orientale sous les Hafsides des origines à la fin du XVe siècle*, vol. 2. (Paris: Maisonneuve, 1982).

58 Dolader, "L'alimentation juive médiévale."

59 *Ḥisba* is a "term which is used to mean on the one hand the duty of every Muslim to "promote good and forbid evil" and, on the other, the function of the person who is effectively entrusted in a town with the application of this rule in the supervision of moral behaviour and more particularly of the markets; this person entrusted with the *ḥisba* was called the *muḥtasib*." *Encyclopaedia of Islam*, https://referenceworks.brillonline.com/browse/encyclopaedia-of-islam-2.

cooking are legal drinks. It is stated that "large quantities of grapes should not be sold to someone who intends to make wine: this should be controlled."[60]

Two other recipes use perfumed wine. It is also noteworthy that in one of the recipes in the *Kitāb al-ṭabīẖ*, the word "wine" is not translated by Huici Miranda: she prefers the term "yeast" or "honey;" whereas Catherine Guillaumond uses the word from the original manuscript for the name of the recipe "Chicken Dish with Wine"[61] (*lawn ḥamrīah* [with wine] *min dǧāǧā*). The term *ḥamr* (خمر), designates something fermented. Wine and yeast correspond to the same word in Arabic. The context defines the appropriate term. Nothing in the recipe justifies Miranda's use of "honey" (*'asl*). Moreover, a note in the margin of the manuscript left by the scribe states that "good Muslims can replace it with honey and the dish will be even better and more delicious."[62] This comment suggest the hypothesis that the scribe did not fully approve of this practice in the thirteenth century or that he was did not like reading and transcribing the term. It may also convey, if the author was not a Muslim, his knowledge of Muslim practices.

This hypothesis is confirmed, for instance, by Maimonides who, particularly in *Regimen of Health*, decided not to integrate wine into Muslim remedies, as he knew that drinking wine was prohibited by Islam.[63] This case also reveals that the term "wine" is indeed the word that was written in the text and corresponds to the recipe's ingredient. This testifies to the fact that it was really consumed at the time. All in all, these details support the possibility that the author was not Muslim and/or that this specification is the mark of wine consumption by Muslims "who are not good Muslims" (as opposed to the expression "good Muslims" in the note).[64]

In the introduction to the grilled dishes, the term *ḥamr* (خمر) is used, which Catherine Guillaumond translates as "wine." She writes that as "grilled foods are the simplest food, they must be cited after the dishes that have to be mentioned, except for wine."[65] The presence of this word, even if I am not able to identify its

---

60 Évariste Levi-Provençal, *Séville musulmane au début du XIIe siècle. Le traité d'Ibn 'Abdun sur la vie urbaine et les corps de métiers* (Paris: Maisonneuve et Larose, 2001), 101. See works written under John Tolan supervision; "Le statut légal des minorités religieuses dans l'espace euro-méditerranéen (Ve–XVe siècle)," Electronic edition Telma, IRHT, Institut de Recherche et d'Histoire des Textes–Orléans, accessed April 7, 2022, http://www.cn-telma.fr/relmin/auteur1507/, see notice no. 1101.

61 Guillaumond, *Cuisine et diététique dans l'Occident arabe médiéval*, no. 111.

62 Ibid.

63 Maimonides, *On the Regimen of Health*, 64n66; Maimonides, *El régimen de salud*, 55.

64 It seems, however, that this detail was included in the body of the recipe in the Rabat copy, *Anwā 'al-ṣaydala*, which dates from the end of the nineteenth century.

65 Guillaumond, *Cuisine et diététique dans l'Occident arabe médiéval*, no. 43, 88.

meaning in the sentence, is further proof of the use of wine in dishes that the author chose to include in the cookbook. In any case, this points to the multiculturalism and likely interculturality of the area, as well as—once again—the author's knowledge of the different cultures living on the peninsula in the thirteenth century. The six explicitly Jewish recipes do not contain wine or its derivatives. Still, even if it's true that a Jewish doctor wrote at least part of the book, expressions like "Inša' Allah" (God willing) that conclude certain recipes cannot be ignored. It is likely that the author, whether converted or not, was displaying his knowledge of Islam. However, it must be mentioned that Judaism also uses this phrase in Hebrew: "Be'zrat Hashem" (*Be'zrat*: with the help of; *Hashem*: God.)

The Christians in power were distrustful of Jewish communities, even though a number of them lived closely among them. Wine was one of the reasons for this distrust, as the production of wine for Jews was exclusively reserved for them, which created a parallel supply chain. For this reason, Christians felt threatened by Jewish wine production, as until the beginning of the fifteenth century Christians were not subject to any ban on buying the drink from Jews. But that changed.

The decree Ordenamiento sobre el encerramiento de los judíos e de los moros on 2 January 1412 "imposed a new regulation marking the segregation of Jews and Muslims."[66] One of the twenty-four provisions was that they were not allowed to sell outside of their quarter, sell food to Christians, or employ them in "their vineyards as servants." This explains why, in 1490, the city of Haro (in the province of La Rioja in the north of Spain) implemented pecuniary sanctions against Christians who bought and consumed Jewish wine. This is stipulated in a source in the Municipal Archives of the city:

> [W]hen certain people went to get wine from the Jewish quarter, and that went against our customs, and even against our Law, they ordered that no one be authorized to go to the Jewish quarter for wine, and the penalty for any person caught going to the Jewish quarter to get wine was sixty maravedis every time, and as the "Ley de Postura" ordered, they would be kept for days in the tower.[67]

---

66 Sonia Fellous, *Histoire de la Bible de Moïse Arragel. Quand un rabbin interprète la Bible pour les chrétiens* (Paris: Somogy Éditions d'Art, 2001), 41.

67 Archivo Municipal de Haro, Actas Municipales, leg. 57, letra AB: "[P]or quanto algunas personas iban por vino a la judería, et esto hera contra nuestros usos et costumbres, et aún contra

These bans and repressions indirectly demonstrate the importance of the actual production and consumption of wine, for both enjoyment and medical reasons, as well as the major role wine played in the country's economy. Despite the religious purism imposed by the Almoravids, and especially by the Almohads, viticulture was never eradicated in Iberian Islamic territory.

c. Meat

> Meat consumption is highly ritualized in Judaism. Jewish dietary laws dictate which species may be consumed and how they must be slaughtered and cooked in order to be kosha (suitable for consumption). This encompasses two aspects: one concerns the composition of food (Kashrut rules), and the other concerns the preparation (Shechita rules). Both are required for the food to be kosher.[68]

A legal text written in Arabic at the end of the tenth century (in Egypt) that could be titled "Buying Meat from Jewish Merchants" contains interesting information. It shows that although business interactions between Muslims and Jews were generally permitted the problem was more about buying meat from Jews. Emre Çelebi explains the disapproval of the Mālikite jurists of North Africa and Muslim Spain about the consumption of this food; yet they did not ban it completely because of the possibilities of impurity that it could present."[69] Another document also hints at the special relationship that existed between North African Jews and Muslims concerning meat selling. It is a *fatwa*[70] dating back to the ninth century and kept in the *Miʿyār* by al-Wansharīsī (fourteenth to fifteenth century) in North Africa. It is called "On Jewish butchers who sell meats

---

nuestra Ley, mandaron que ninguno non sea osado de ir por vino a la judería, so pena de cada uno que se probare que ba por el dicho vino a la judería que pague por cada vez sesenta maravedíes, et, segund manda la Ley de Postura, con los días en la torre." Translation by the author.

68 Valenzuela-Lama, "Shechita and Kashrut," 1.

69 Notice no. 252580, project RELMIN, "Le statut légal des minorités religieuses dans l'espace euro-méditerranéen (Ve–XVe siècle)," Electronic Edition Telma, IRHT, Institut de Recherche et d'Histoire des Textes – Orléans, accessed April 8, 2022, http://www.cn-telma.fr/relmin/extrait252580/. Translation by the author.

70 A *fatwa* is "a formal ruling or interpretation on a point of Islamic law given by a qualified legal scholar (known as a mufti). Fatwas are usually issued in response to questions from individuals or Islamic courts." See *Encyclopedia Britannica*, s.v. "Fatwa," accessed January 13, 2022, https://www.britannica.com/topic/fatwa.

forbidden by Judaism to Muslims." The complex situation addressed in this document is that of Jewish butchers who sell Muslims meats that are banned in Judaism. The answer is that "if Jewish butchers continue to defraud, they will be prohibited from entering not only markets but any place where they can sell their meat."[71] The problems highlighted, though, seem to be more about selling defective merchandise without informing the buyer of its defects than a religious problem regarding the fact that the seller is Jewish.

In the *Kitāb al-ṭabīḫ*, meat and various parts of animals are mentioned 370 times. I counted 311 meat-based recipes. The following graph illustrates the substantial proportion of meat dishes in the 462 recipes included in the cookbook.

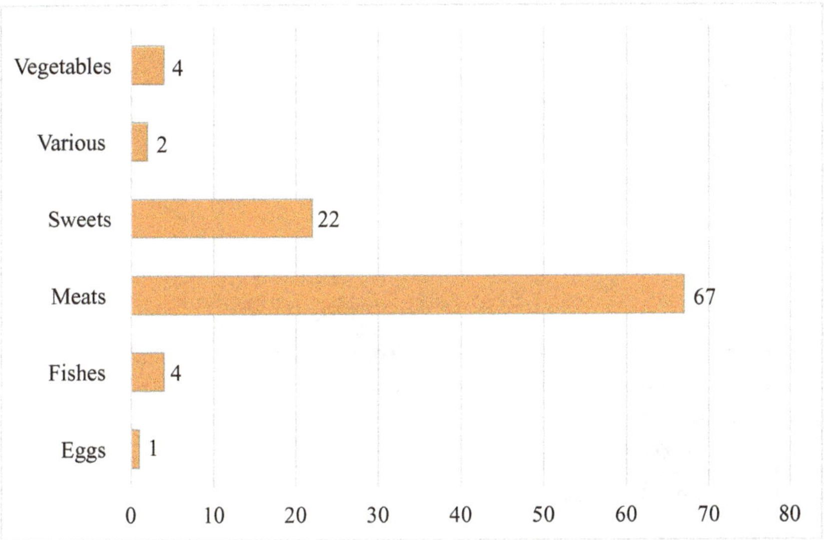

Figure 5. Breakdown and use of the main foods in the *Kitāb al-ṭabīḫ*

I counted twenty-two different types of meat that are mentioned a total of 247 times. The main animals consumed are: hen (including the innards) fifty-two times; mutton (and/or sheep) forty-one times; chicken (including the innards) thirty-two times; and lamb and ram eighteen times. Beef is only rarely included

71 Notice no. 268791, project RELMIN, "Le statut légal des minorités religieuses dans l'espace euro-méditerranéen (Ve–XVe siècle)," Electronic Edition Telma, IRHT, Institut de Recherche et d'Histoire des Textes – Orléans, accessed April 10, 2022, http://www.cn-telma.fr/relmin/extrait268791/. Translation by the author.

in the recipes, used only six times. Pork is never mentioned. The graph below depicts the wide variety of types of meat in the cookbook.

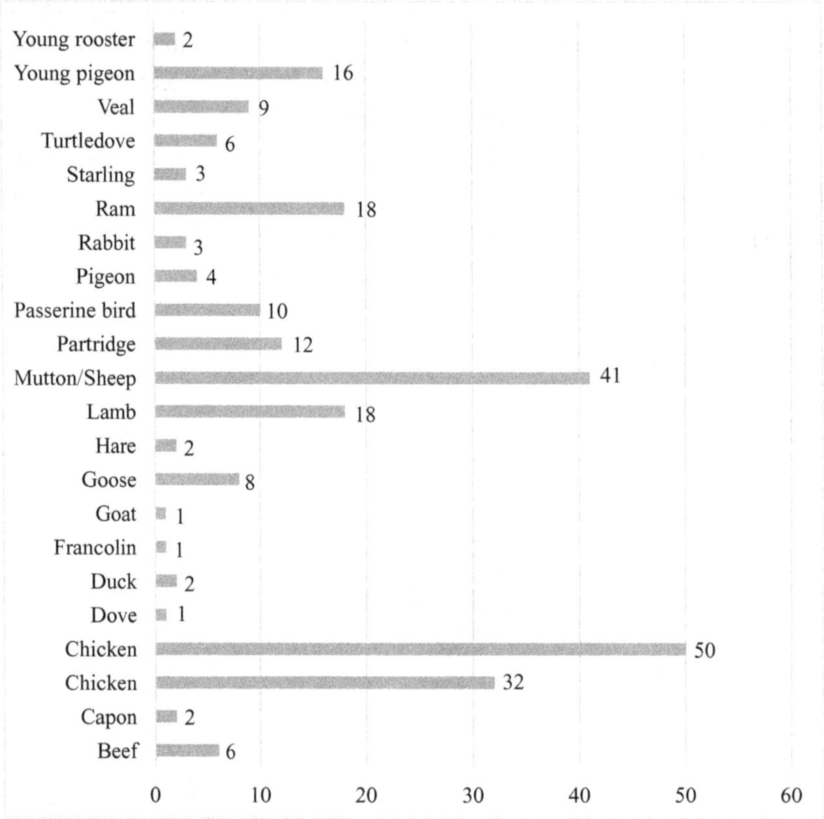

Figure 6. Various meats in the *Kitāb al-ṭabīḫ*

In light of these calculations, it is important to point out that 111 recipes (excluding innards) do not say what type of meat must be used. Finally, twelve recipes are made of innards (kidneys: three; tripe: two; spleen: one; heart: two; liver: 2; etc.). The large variety of animals used in these dishes reflects the author's knowledge and membership of the social elite. It also suggests that a large number of dishes in the book were for the affluent classes, given the price of certain meats. Moreover, the methods for preparing, cooking and preserving foods required substantial equipment found only in urban areas and the wealthiest households.

In theory, for religious reasons Muslims were not allowed to eat animals slaughtered by Jews. Nonetheless, in the ordinance of *ḥisba* entitled *Risāla fī-l-qadā wa-l-ḥisba*, Ibn ʿAbdūn[72] proposes, as González states, that "no Jews should sacrifice an animal for a Muslim. Jews are ordered to have their own cutting tables."[73] Yet he goes even further in his intolerance of the Mosaic people, as he specifies that Muslims have always considered meat sacrificed by Jews to be illegal. The author's comment appears to demonstrate genuine rigidity. In a footnote to the ordinance, the translator adds that it was the Maliki school that considered the consumption of meat sacrificed by Jews as lawful. It is still surprising that the Maliki rite was the one adopted by the Iberian Peninsula before the rise of the Almohads and that it continued afterwards.[74]

Various researchers have written about the consumption of meat under Islamic rule. Expiración García Sánchez[75] observes that at this time the favorite meat among the elites was lamb and, to a lesser extent, veal. Goat meat was not often eaten by the lower classes in al-Andalus, given the dry climate. As for pork, neither Jews nor Muslims were supposed to eat it, in compliance with their respective religious precepts.[76] The most common kind of poultry was chicken, in both Muslim and Christian Spain. Game meat was abundant and was an important source of nutrition in al-Andalus.

The well-known place that meat occupies in this cookbook—as is the case in others of the Muslim West and East—overshadows the vegetable dishes, which are nonetheless numerous. The second cookbook, entitled *Fuḍālat al-ḫiwān* (1238), written by the Andalusian Ibn Razīn al Tuǧībī, contains, like the *Kitāb al-ṭabīḫ*, a chapter dedicated to vegetables. This is not the case for other recipe collections. In cookbooks from the Muslim East produced during the thirteenth century, such as the *Kitāb al-ṭabīḫ*[77] by Al-Baghdādī[78] (1226) and the *Kitāb al-wuṣla* by Ibn Jazzar (Syria), vegetable dishes are not given such prominence.

However, in the *Kanz al-Fawa'id fi tanwi al-mawa'id* (Treasure trove of benefits and variety at the table) dating back to the thirteenth/fourteenth century

---

72 Eduardo Escartín González, *Estudio económico sobre el Tratado de Ibn Abdún. El vino y los gremios en Al-Andalus antes del siglo XII* (Séville: Fundación del Monte, 2006).

73 Translation by the author from Escartín González, *Estudio económico sobre el Tratado de Ibn Abdún*, 83–84.

74 Ibid.

75 Expiración García Sánchez, "La alimentación en la Andalucía Islámica. Estudio histórico y bromatológico," in *Andalucía Islámica*, vols. 4–5, *1983–1986*, Textos y Estudios, eds. J. Bosh Vilá and W. Hoenerbach (Granada: Universidad de Granada, 1987).

76 Lev. 11:17: Safra and Marciano, *Chumash*, 638–639; Deut: 14:8: Safra and Marciano, *Chumash*, 1073.

77 The *Kitāb al-ṭabīḫ* of Al-Baghdādī contains 140 recipes.

78 Al-Baghdādī and Charles Perry, trans., *A Baghdad Cookery Book: The Book of Dishes* (Totnes: Prospect Books, 2005).

and written in Egypt, there are meatless recipes—chickpeas, beans with hazelnuts, and eggplant purée with fermented milk. There are recipes for *tahīniyya* (carrots with sesame butter), *sikbāğ* with eggplant, a fake *mulūkhiyya*, and so on. This is also the case for another cookbook from the same area entitled *Kitāb Waṣf al-Aṭ'ima al-mu'tāda* (The description of familiar foods), which is a compilation of recipes from fourteenth-century Mamelouk (Egypt), written by an unknown author.[79] This cookbook, containing 420 recipes, includes, in particular, a chapter of meatless dishes that does not exist in any other cookbook of the same time. Coptic Christians were the majority in Egypt until the fourteenth century.[80] For this reason, many doctors were still Christian and recommended these vegetable dishes to their patients. It is also possible that some recipes were prepared for the fasting period of Lent—for example, vegetable dishes using eggplant, spinach, or lentils. Keep in mind that Egypt also had the largest Jewish community at the time.[81]

Therefore, any approach to studying food in the medieval Jewish world must consider these various factors, which result from the fact that Jews were a minority. The religious component, then, is key to understanding the habits that governed society under Muslim rule. Kashrut unites culture—that is, food—and religion, and lays down the Jewish food laws which were, and are, more drastic than those governing Muslims. Despite banning pork consumption,[82] a prohibition shared by both religions, Kashrut is much more than a food law: it is a Jewish code of conduct.[83] Detailed study of the culinary techniques and ingredients proposed in the *Kitāb al-ṭabīḫ* reveal the existence of more than six explicitly Jewish recipes.

Beyond the emblematic foods previously analyzed, there is another one which, in veiled terms, is full of meaning in its relation to Jewish cuisine. What

---

79 There are currently two manuscripts kept in Topkapi Palace in Istanbul. One of them ends with a colophon dated November 30, 1373, Cairo. The text was translated into English by Charles Perry and included in Perry, Rodinson, and Arberry, *Medieval Arab Cookery.*

80 The *Kitāb al-ṭabīḫ* includes a recipe linked to the Coptic Christians of Egypt. Cf. Guillaumond, *Cuisine et diététique dans l'Occident arabe médiéval*, no. 475: "The Eastern white *halwa* called 'coptic.'" English translation by the author, from the French translation by Guillaumond.

81 Statements reported by Professor Newman during the 2nd IEHCA international conference in 2016; See Aryeh Graboïs, "La description de l'Égypte au XIVe siècle par les pèlerins et les voyageurs occidentaux," *Le Moyen Âge* 109, no. 3–4 (2003): 529–543.

82 *Coran* (Arabie Saoudite: Présidence générale des Directions des Recherches Scientifiques Islamiques, de l'Ifta, de la Prédication et de l'Orientation Religieuse, Al-Madinah Al-Munawwarah: traduction en langue française du sens de ses versets, révisée et éditée, 2001), s. 2, v. 163; s. 5, v. 1–6; s. 6, v. 118–121; s. 6, v. 44–146; s. 16, v. 116.

83 Lev. 10:16–20; 11:1–47: Safra and Marciano, *Chumash*, 635–645; Deut. 14, 3–21: Safra and Marciano, *Chumash*, 1073–1075.

we know is that under Christian rule, in "early in May 1321, Jaume II allowed the Muslims in Tortosa to build their own *carnicería* in return for an annual payment to the crown; but the location of this new butchery was not established in the original document and this omission would soon cause problems. For some period before the grant, the Muslim community had not had its own butcher and instead bought meat from Jewish butchers."[84] Olivia Remie Constable adds that "a late thirteenth-century ordinance, forbidding Christians in Huesca to purchase meat from Christian and Jewish butchers, suggests that this conveniently situated butchery had attracted some Christian customers."[85] Constable continues:

> [T]he religious valence of food (and especially meat) always created special complexities for legislators and administrators when dealing with Muslim communities and their butcher shops. Unlike bathhouses or fabric shops, where Muslims, Christians, and Jews could share the same spaces and services, though usually at different times, places for selling food were not so easy to partition or regulate. Food shopping was an almost daily necessity, making it impossible for urban administrators to assign one or two days a week during which food stalls and butcher shops were open to minority communities. Sharing was also complicated by the fact that religious communities, food providers, and consumers did not all necessarily agree or cooperate with any one policy. Some people believed that food should only be purchased from a coreligionist, and that meat, particularly, could be rendered unclean by contact with nonbelievers or improper methods of butchering. Meanwhile, other consumers appear to have been perfectly happy to buy meat and other foods from any vendor, of whatever religion, provided that they sold quality goods at competitive prices in a convenient location.

---

84 "There were debates about whether it was permissible for Muslims (and Christians) to buy meat from Jewish butchers. In 1295, a joint ordinance by both Muslim and Christian local authorities in Tarrazona prohibited such sales, but this was later annulled by the king" (Nirenberg, *Communities of Violence,* 172, citing Lourie, "Anatomy of Ambivalence," 43n138). In 1333–34, Muslims in Zaragoza complained to the king that some Muslims were buying from a Jewish butcher, while Christians complained that low prices at Muslim meat stalls were attracting Christian buyers (ibid., 172–73). See Constable, *Live Like a Moor,* 184.

85 *Documentos municipales de Huesca,* 1100–1350, ed. Carlos Laliena Corbera. See Constable, *To Live Like a Moor,* 185.

The interpretation of evidence about butcher shops in medieval Spain is complicated by overlapping religious and commercial interests. While disputes over butchers entailed real and deeply felt religious differences in dietary practices, they often came to the attention of medieval legislators for economic reasons rather than because of strictly religious concerns.[86]

86 Ibid., 118.

CHAPTER 4

Eggplant: The Jewishness Marker

Versatile. This is the word that best describes the eggplant, which alone justifies the complex approach its study demands. The entire existence of this vegetable is already filled with history, as shown by its trajectory from the Far East to Spain and its absorption of the cultures it encountered along the way. Indeed, if any food has experienced a chaotic trajectory, it's definitely the eggplant. Multishaped, multicolored, and multipurpose, the eggplant became an indispensable ingredient in cookbooks on the Iberian Peninsula under Muslim rule. Yet beyond its nutritious and culinary importance, the eggplant has received many pejorative descriptions for being synonymous with Jewish identity.

Peregrino Artusi, an Italian literary figure and gastronome of the nineteenth century, author of *La Scienza in Cucina e l'Arte di Mangiar Bene* (Science in the Kitchen and the Art of Eating Well) published in 1892, wrote that in the early 1800s "eggplants were almost nowhere to be found in the market in Florence; they were despised as being a Jewish food." In praise of the eggplant and those who enjoyed it, he added "[this shows] that just as in areas of the greatest importance, they always had more sense than Christians."[1] The last sentence was erased from the book in 1938—under Mussolini's dictatorship—as leaving it in would have meant giving importance to Jews and highlighting their capacity for reflection, while placing Christians in an inferior light.

To return to my first question about the possible link between food and religion, it is important to look back to the medieval Period. An essential question emerges. How does a food like eggplant reveal relationships that existed between members of the three communities of the Iberian Peninsula under Muslim rule (until the end of the Nasrid Emirate of Granada and the expulsion of Jews in

1 Peregrino Artusi, *La Scienza in Cucina e l'Arte di Mangiar Bene* (Florence: Giunti Gruppo Editoriale, 2017), 222.

1492) and under Christian rule (in the fifteenth to sixteenth century before the rise of the Inquisition)? The consumption and perception of eggplant[2] was different when the Jewish community lived under Islam and under Christianity. An etymological analysis that traces—in parallel—the trajectory of this vegetable from its original land until its arrival on the Iberian Peninsula lays the groundwork for an explanation.

A. At the Roots of Eggplant[3]

a. The Etymology

Unknown to the Greeks and Romans, the eggplant, what Linnaeus defines as the *Solanum melongena L.*, was cultivated by the Mesopotamians[4] at the dawn of the Christian era. It was most likely the cultivated form of a wild *Solanum* from the Madras region in India, the *Solanum insanum*, which would be later known under the name *Malum insanum* or "the mad apple."[5] The name *Solanum oviserum* refers more to the decorative purpose of the plant.[6] The word "eggplant" when referring to *Solanum melongena* appeared in written sources in the early Christian era. Various terms exist in Sanskrit,[7] such as *varrta*, and there are Bengali names, like *bong* and *mohati*,[8] which indicate both its popularity and its multipurpose nature. The name of the eggplant evolved as it travelled from China (500 BCE, according to LiHui-Lin) to India where it was known as *vatinganah*," that which causes flatulence."[9]

---

2 Hilary Pomeroy, "Ojos de Berenjena: Some Literary Links between Food and Religious Identity," *Proceedings of the Thirteenth British Conference on Judeo-Spanish Studies, 7–9 September 2003* (London: University College London, 2006), 137–149.

3 Ibid.; see Andrew Watson, "Eggplant, aubergine, brinjal, Solanum melongena L.," *Agricultural Innovation in the Early Islamic World: The Diffusion of Crops and Farming Techniques, 700–1100* (Cambridge: Cambridge University Press, 2008), 71.

4 Mesopotamia is the region of the fertile crescent. It corresponds, more or less, to the territory of Iraq today.

5 An idea that is shared by the botanist Henri Baillon.

6 As I mentioned earlier, the English word "eggplant" has a different use. Eggplant resembles the scientific name *Solanum ovigerum Dunal* more closely, which, due to the vegetable's multicolor aspect, emphasizes its decorative purpose.

7 Marie-Christine Daunay, "Eggplant," in *Vegetables II: Fabaceae, Liliaceae, Solanaceae, and Umbelliferae*, eds. Jaime Prohens-Tomás and Fernando Nuez (Springer Science & Business Media, 2007), 165.

8 Nina Kehayan, *Voyage de l'aubergine. Préface de Philippe Meyer* (Avignon: L'aube cuisine, 2016); Ernest Klein, *A Comprehensive Etymological Dictionary of the English Language* (1967).

9 Ibid.

A study of these names over the long term reveals that, starting in the fourteenth century, the word was gradually integrated into languages spoken today. Thus, eggplant was called *badin-gan* in Persian[10] in the year 400), which led to *al-badinjan* in Arabic, and then *berenjena* in Spanish. The lexical similarities between the Persian word *bādinğān/bādenjān* and *aubergine* in modern French[11] is relatively clear. This variety of *Solanum melongena L.* of the *Solanaceae* family was already classified by Avicenna (tenth century) and Averroes (twelfth century) well before Linnaeus used the classification.

There was not always a unanimous opinion about eating eggplant. As early as the fifteenth century—and we will see that this is significant—eggplant was named *malum insanum* and *mala insane* by the Italian Renaissance humanist Hermolaus Barbarus.[12] In fact, eggplant was mentioned in the *Novellino* (a thirteenth-century Tuscan cookbook) and in the *Tacuinum Sanitatis* of the fourteenth century. *Mela insana* and *pomo sdegnoso* (disdainful apple) are also used by Scappi in his book *Opera dell'arte del cucinare* (1570). At the same time, it was with the expression *pianta volgare* (common plant) that the translator of Dioscorides and doctor Pietro Andrea Mattioli wrote of eggplants: "They are usually eaten fried in oil with salt and black pepper, like mushrooms."[13]

In 1631, in the treatise that Antonio Frugoli wrote on "delicate fruits to serve at any table of princes and great lords,"[14] he advised that eggplants "must not be eaten, except by people of the countryside or by Jews."[15] This seventeenth-century reference to the Jewish community contributed to the negative image of the vegetable. The Italian agronomist and gastronome Vicenzo Tanara shared this negative perception of eggplants (*melanzani*). He wrote in his masterful work *L'Economia Del Cittadino In Villa* (1674) that eggplant was *mala insana.*[16] He pointed out that they are "a food for the countryside . . . and especially for

---

10 Marks, *Encyclopedia of Jewish Food*, 174–175.

11 Raymond Arveiller, "Les noms français de l'aubergine," *Revue de linguistique romane* 33, nos. 131–132 (1969): 225–244.

12 Michel Pitrat and Claude Faury, *Histoires de légumes: Des origines à l'orée du XXIe siècle* (Editions Quae, 2003), 258.

13 Alberto Capatti and Massimo Montanari, *La cucina italiana. Storia di una cultura* (Roma-Bari: Laterza, 1999), 48: "Mangiansi volgarmente fritte nell'olio con sale e pepe come i fonghi." Translation by the author.

14 "[D]elicati frutti da servirsi a qualsivoglia mensa di Principi e Gran Signori." Translation by the author.

15 Capatti and Montanari, *La cucina italiana*, 49: "[N]on devono essere mangiate se non da gente basa o da ebrei." Translation by the author.

16 Vicenzo Tanara, *L'Economia Del Cittadino In Villa* (Venice: Stefano Curti, 1674), 273; Capatti and Montanari, *La cucina italiana*, 49.

the family, because they are a usual food for Jews."[17] What these words suggest is that Jews are associated with the lowest social category in society—that of the peasantry. Therefore, eggplant and its consumption is considered bad, as are those who eat it.[18]

There were also translations of *malum insanum* as "mad apple" and even "apple of love."[19] I prefer the meaning "unhealthy apple" Was it perceived as "unhealthy" because it made one "crazy with love?" Regarding the phrase "apple of love" to describe the eggplant, the lexicologist Raymond Arveiller suggest that it has a French origin because *amorum pomis* or *pomis amorum* doesn't appear in earlier Latin sources. He proposes that the expression "apple of love" was the invention of the people that believed in the eggplant's aphrodisiac properties.[20]

But what of the usages of the word "eggplant" in Italy? The eggplant is commonly called *melanzana* in Italian. Much has been written about it and, as we previously saw, not only in the field of botany. While *melanzana* is the common Italian term, there is another regional term, specifically from Florence. Artusi mentioned that in this city there were no eggplants in the nineteenth century because it was considered a Jewish food. He adds that it was called *petranciani.*[21] We know that in late sixteenth-century Italy (1572), *mala insana* was called *melanzana* in Lombardy and *petranciani, petonciano-a,* and *pertronciano-a* in Tuscany.[22] These regional terms refer unambiguously to something that causes "flatulence," a meaning that coincides with the primitive Sanskrit etymology *vatin-ganah.*[23] If we connect the name *mala insana* to "Jew's apple," then the negative association between Jewishness and eggplant is obvious.

The bitter taste and gray color of the eggplant are two things one needs to consider, as they emphasize the eggplant's negative qualities. If it is not properly prepared, eggplant can be unhealthy and do more harm than good. Doctors in the Middle Ages paid much attention to the way it was prepared because, if not done

---

17 Capatti and Montanari, *La cucina italiana*, 49: "[V]ivande per campagna . . e massime per la famiglia siccome per gli hebrei sono costumato cibo." Translation by the author.

18 I would like to thank Filippo Ribani for the information he shared with me during the international congress "La comida en la cultura europea durante la Edad Media y el Renaciemiento" at the Instituto Universitario de Investigación en Estudios Medievales y del Siglo de Oro "Miguel de Cervantes" (IEMSO), University of Alcalá de Henrares, Spain, 26–28 May, 2021.

19 Pitrat and Faury, *Histoires de légumes*, 258.

20 Arveiller, "Les noms français de l'aubergine": 226.

21 I thank Massimo Montanari for this information and for our conversation on the topic.

22 Arveiller, "Les noms français de l'aubergine": 228; also see http://www.treccani.it/vocabolario/petonciano/.

23 Maura Carlin Officier, "Eggplant," in *The Oxford Encyclopedia of Food and Drink in America*, eds. Andrew Smith and Bruce Kraig, vol. 1 (Oxford: OUP USA, 2013), 671–672.

correctly, it could be very harmful. For the Jewish doctor Maimonides, eggplant was bad for those following a healthy diet. He writes that "vegetables are generally very bad for all people, especially garlic, onion, leek, radish, cabbage and eggplant."[24] The Muslim Andalusian pharmacologist Abū Marwān (Avenzoar, eleventh to twelfth century) is very clear about this in his book *Kitāb al-agḏiya* (A Treatise on Food), written between 1147 and 1163, during the transition from the Almoravid dynasty to Almohad rule:

> [A]ll doctors agree—and they are right—that as a food it is not advisable to eat eggplant, even if it is not as bad as cabbage. Eggplant as a food does no good. ... As a medicine, it hardens the stomach; it fortifies and tonifies it and is useful against nausea and vomiting, if it is cooked well. The eggplant has two powers—bitterness and astringency—and can therefore just as well soften the stomach, its first [power], or close it [preventing any evacuation], its second [power], or they can both act together, benefiting the stomach, God willing.[25]

All of these explanations account for the eggplant's bad reputation. It is also possible that a connection was made between the grayish color of the eggplant's flesh and the grayish complexion attributed to Jews for eating goose meat and liver. This is apparent in the words of the *scalco* Domenico Romoli (fifteenth century)—the headwaiter and carver responsible for all aspects of the food of Pope Leon X—who wrote that "salted goose is not recommended either, which puts the eater in a bad mood, and since Jews eat it, they have the bad, waxy complexion of melancholics, the color of lead, as well as bad habits."[26]

As for eggplant in the medieval East, it is interesting to notice the connection that the authors of cookbooks make between the vegetable and medicine. In *Scents and Flavors*,[27] Charles Perry connects eggplant and medicine. He writes that "a handful of recipes (for perfumes as well as foods) reference medieval

---

24 Maimonides, *On the Regimen of Health*, 1, 64; Maimonides, *El régimen de salud*, 52.

25 Abū Marwān 'Abd al-Malik Zuhr and Expiración García Sánchez, ed. trans. and intro., *Kitāb al-agḏiya* (Madrid: CSIC, 1992), 85.

26 Domenico Romoli, "Delle Anatre, & Oche, & lor qualità," *La singolar dottrina*. Vol. Ch. XIX (1560), 217–218. Translation by the author from the original Italian text: "Non son laudate ne ancho le Oche salate, che fanno cativi humori in chi le mangia, & perche i Giudei son soliti . . . mangiarne noi gli vediamo di così mala cera melanconici di colore di piombo & di mali costumi."

27 Work by Charles Perry that proposes a bilingual Arabic-English version of the cookbook *Kitāb al-wuṣla ilā l-habīb fi wasf al-tayyabāt wa l-tīb* (The book of friendship or description

medical ideas, such as the need to balance the humors or to match foods to the humoral nature of an individual. Another individual matter was how much store a given diner actually set by medical theory. Doctors may have warned that eggplant caused cancer and madness, but the poet Kushājim, for one, defiantly said, 'The doctor makes ignorant fun of me for loving eggplant, but I will not give it up.'"[28] All of this above helps explain why, in medieval Andalusian recipes, eggplant was always boiled in salt water before preparation. The black water that comes from the purplish color of the skin must be thrown away, as it is "unhealthy." It is easy to understand the precautions taken so that the flesh of the eggplant remained as pale as possible. The color of the vegetable's skin, as well as the color of the water thrown away, were condemned because it tarnished the flesh of the eggplant, making it repulsive. If the eggplant is peeled, the appearance of the flesh is lighter, healthier and thus less harmful and dangerous.

We now come to one of the strangest meanings associated with the eggplant: Jew's apple. This name appeared in England in the seventeenth to eighteenth centuries, when Spanish and Portuguese Sephardic Jews introduced the vegetable. Joseph Vercier[29] refers to the term "Jew's apple" in his mid-twentieth-century *Encyclopedia of Agricultural Sciences*.[30] But the question remains: How and why did this food become intertwined with religion and why is eggplant identified as a Jewish food?

It seems that the English called it Jew's apple because of its popularity with Sephardic Jews.[31] It is also the English who coined the word "eggplant," because the vegetable resembles an egg. However, unlike Americans who kept the word "eggplant," the English use the word "aubergine," from the French. The wide range of names given to the eggplant reflects the multi-purpose nature of the food. Now we will see that the description Jew's apple, which emerged after the period and area that concern us here, is not the only one that ties the food to an identity.

---

of good dishes and perfumes), by Ibn al-'Adīm (thirteenth century, Syria). See Perry and Waines, *Scents and Flavors*.

28 Ibid., xxix.

29 Joseph Vercier, "Culture potagère," in *Encyclopédie des sciences agricoles* (Paris: Hachette, 1965).

30 See Kehayan, *Voyage de l'aubergine*.

31 Details from Bruno Laurioux: "Giacomo Castelvetro, an Italian protestant exiled in England, mentions the eggplant in *A Brief Account of the Fruit, Herbs & Vegetables of Italy* in 1614. He discusses the eggplant as a food consumed by the English aristocracy."

b. The Origin: From India to the Mediterranean Basin[32]

Documents written in Sanskrit, including references to the word eggplant, come from the Indian subcontinent (present-day India, Nepal, Bhutan, and Sri Lanka). The map below allows us to trace the trajectory of the eggplant from this region all the way to the Americas.

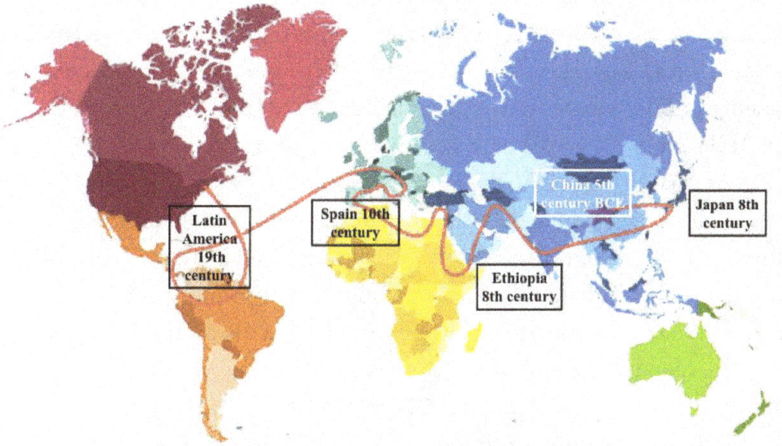

Figure 7. The journey of the eggplant from 500 BCE to the fifteenth century CE

Marie-Christine Daunay,[33] at the French National Institute of Agricultural Research (INRA), notes that the eggplant is mentioned in Chinese agricultural and botany books that were written at about the same time as the Sanskrit documents that mention the vegetable, namely between 0 and 250 CE. Take, for example *The Atlas of Plants of South China*, written under the Jin dynasty of the west (Xi Jin, 西晉, 265–316) or the *Qimin Yaoshu*, an agricultural treatise written in the sixth century.[34] A text by Li Hui-Lin[35] dating from 500 BCE in China also refers the cultivation of eggplant in vegetable gardens in China, but I cannot verify that "what the Chinese classified in the 'grain' category covered in part the

32 Michel Chauvet, *Encyclopédie des plantes alimentaires* (Paris: Belin, 2018), 708 –771.

33 Daunay, "Eggplant," 165.

34 The *Ts'i Min Yao Shu* refers to the work *Qimin Yaoshu*. I thank Mrs. Sabban for her many details and corrections. See also "Eggplant—a Mad Apple with a Dark Liaison," *Vegetarians in Paradise*, accessed April 10, 2022, http://www.vegparadise.com/highestperch67.html.

35 Kehayan, *Voyage de l'aubergine.*

notion of vegetable."[36] According to George Métaillé,[37] it is possible to establish that eggplant—*qiezi*, a species of *Solanum melongena*—arrived from India.

Another Chinese treatise—this time a culinary one[38]—by HU Sihui, the *Yinshan zhengyao*, is interesting because it was written at the beginning of the fourteenth century (1330),[39] that is, one century after the first cookbook from al-Andalus. It mentions a stuffed eggplant dish containing ground meat and orange, whose gustatory value is similar to that of present-day Turkey. Therefore, the vegetable has diverse culinary uses.

The eggplant travelled. Indeed, in the eighth century the eggplant was present in Japan and then moved to Persia. Iranian and Arab merchants then brought it to East Africa. The multiplicity of terms referring to the eggplant confirms its presence in Ethiopia. Moreover, the thinkers Abū Hanīfa[40] of the eighth century and Al Bīrūnī (973–1050) include it in their writings.

The Arab conquest of the Iberian Peninsula made way for the introduction of several edible plants, including the eggplant, which was cultivated in al-Andalus from the ninth century. A variety of sources provide written evidence that the eggplant existed there. Eggplant is mentioned in the tenth century (961) in the *Calendar of Cordova.*[41] Starting in the eleventh century, the *Agronomics Treatises*, called the *Kitāb al-filāḥa* in Arabic, were legion in al-Andalus, and many thinkers—agronomists and botanists like those cited below—wrote about it. In the eleventh century, Abū 'l-Khayr[42] of Seville counted four varieties of eggplant: white, reddish-purple, black, or brown. The doctor and botanist Ibn al-Bayṭār[43] of the twelfth century noted the same. The Sevillian botanist

---

36 Georges Métailié, "Origine des légumes en Chine," in "Dans le numéro thématique Un terrien des îles. À propos de Jacques Barrau", ed. Georges Métailié and Alice Peeters, special issue, *Journal d'agriculture traditionnelle et de botanique appliquée* 42 (2000–2004): 165–186, https://doi.org/10.3406/jatba.2000.3735.

37 Ibid.

38 I would like to thank Mrs. Sabban for information and corrections on this topic.

39 Details from a conversation with Professor Bruno Laurioux: "Territory composed at the time of a Mongol dynasty that dominated China, and on the Western side, the Mongols reached Iraq."

40 See http://www.Iranicaonline.org/articles/badenjan-egeplant-aubergine.

41 The Calendar of Cordova, written under Al Hakam II, mentions eggplant among other foods, such as squash, saffron, and melon.

42 "Abū 'l-Khayr (*Kitāb al-filāḥa*)," The Filāḥa Texts Project, accessed November 1, 2016, http://www.filaha.org/author_khayr.html."

43 Ibn Bayṭār: from Malaga (1190). He mentions in the *Kitāb al-Ǧāmiʿ li-mufradāt al-adwiya wa-l-aġḏiya*, his *Book of Medicine and Simple Foods*, that the culture and consumption of eggplant started in the ninth century, implying this occurred on the Iberian Peninsula.

Ibn al-ʿAwwām[44] (twelfth to thirteenth centuries) wrote about the cultivation of eggplant, as well as providing some recipes for seasoning it to reduce its bitter taste.[45] Out of the six varieties that existed in al-Andalus, he cited four: the Egyptian, the Syrian, the Cordovan, and the "local." He opined that it is like "an egg in the skin of a hedgehog" or "a sheep's heart in the talons of an eagle."[46] In the *Kitāb al-filāḥa*, written in the fourteenth century (1348), the Andalusian agronomist Ibn Luyūn[47] presented the major foundations of his agrotechny of eggplant, cultivated in the south of Spain for, in his words, over four hundred years.

The Arabist historian Manuela Marín wrote that eggplants were very popular in Arab culinary books and that this popularity was reported by European travelers, such as the Frenchman Belon, who visited Egypt in 1547. The latter confirmed that the country's inhabitants ate eggplant in almost every dish and that they were prepared in almost every way possible.[48]

In conclusion, the spread of this *Solanaceae* in the European West occurred in Italy as early as the fifteenth century. The discovery of the new world would then bring it to Central America, Brazil and North America in the nineteenth century.[49]

B. Eggplant in the *Kitāb al-ṭabīḫ*

The *Kitāb al-ṭabīḫ* reveals one of the most interesting histories of the eggplant because of its connection to Jewish culinary preparations and practices. As a

---

44 José Ignacio Cubero Salmerón., ed. and comemtary on the trans. of Banqueri, *El Libro de agricultura de Al Awan* (Sevilla: Junta de Andalucía, 2003), 665.

45 "Ibn al-ʿAwwām (*Kitāb al-filāḥa*)," The Filāḥa Texts Project, accessed November 1, 2016, http://www.filaha.org/author_ibn_al_awwam.html.

46 André Bazzana and Johnny De Meulemeester, "La révolution verte," in *La noria, l'aubergine et le fellah. Archéologie des espaces irrigués dans l'Occident musulman médiéval (IXe-XVe siècles)*. Gand, ARGU 6 [Archeological Reports Ghent University 6] (Cambridge, MA: Academia Press, 2009), 426–427.

47 Ibn Luyūn, Tuǧībī tribe polymath and poet. In his agronomist treatise the *Kitāb al-filāḥa* (1348), Ibn Luyūn presented the major features of his agrotechny of eggplant cultivated in the south of Spain for more than four hundred years in verse (*rajaz*).

48 Pierre Belon, *Voyage en Égypte* (Paris: Klincksiec, 1928), 112a.

49 Louis Albertini, *Apogée des jardins et maraîchages en al-Andalus (Ibérie arabe) Xe–XIVe siècle: nouveaux légumes, fruits et épices. Essor de la cuisine arabo-andalouse* (Paris: L'Harmattan, 2017).

stuffing or stuffed, alone or with meat, eggplant occupies a privileged place in the cookbook. It is because of its inclusion in there that eggplant will appear, three centuries later, at the climax of a subsequent discriminatory process against the Jews of the Iberian Peninsula and, by extension, the whole of the Mediterranean Basin.

a. The Dishes

In the *Kitāb al-ṭabīḫ*, eggplant is the primary vegetable/fruit. Its importance is demonstrated through the many different ways this versatile food is used. The book contains a considerable number of dishes that are prepared with vegetables and/or legumes. As shown in the graph below, celery, salad, carottes, eggplant, onions are included; naturally, there are no tomatoes or peppers, as these foods arrived after the discovery of the New World.

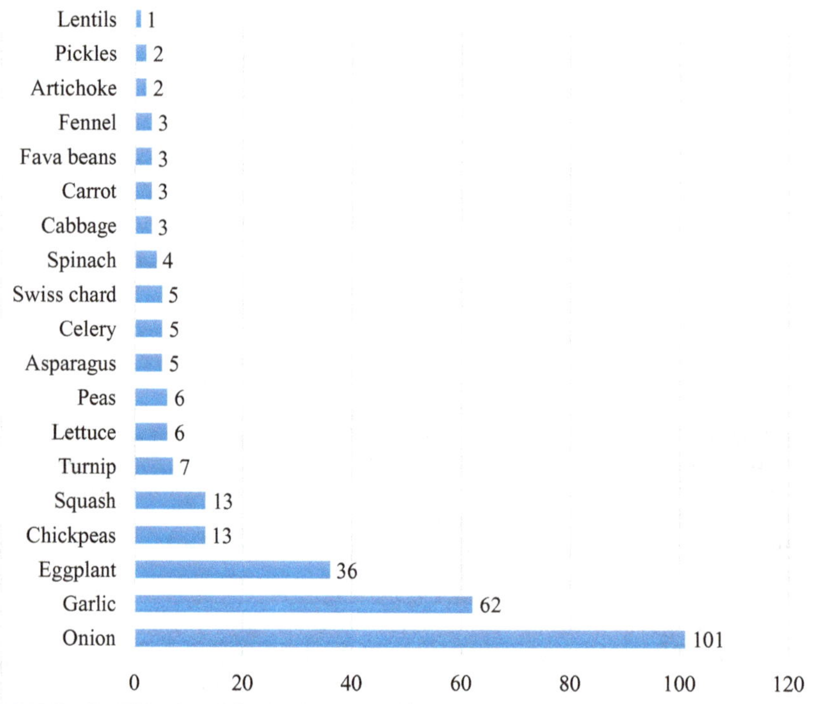

Figure 8. Proportion of dishes in the *Kitāb al-ṭabīḫ* containing vegetables

In addition, two dishes should also be counted: "The Gardener's Dish"[50] and "A Baqliyya of Ziryab's."[51] In all, there are fifteen different vegetables and three legumes: chickpeas, lentils, and beans. The onion is the most frequently used vegetable, as it can also act as a condiment. The same is true for garlic. Our focus, the eggplant, is the most commonly used food in the recipes, excluding condiments. It is the most basic food of all the dishes, including those without meat. Given its versatility, the eggplant is the preferred ingredient for adapting meat dishes. I call it a "stuffing" vegetable because it can be fried, sautéed, boiled, stuffed, or used as stuffing. Out of the thirty-six recipes that contain eggplant, fifteen do not include any meat, that is 42%. The graph below summarizes the multiple usages of eggplant, both in terms of preparations and cooking.

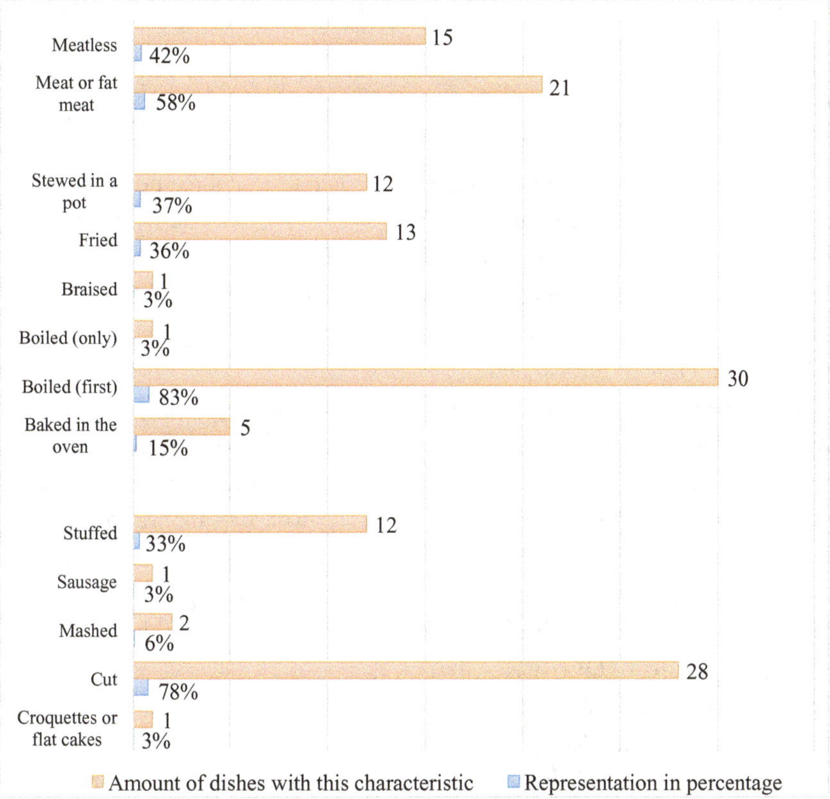

Figure 9. Eggplant characteristics in the *Kitāb al-ṭabīẖ*'s thirty-six recipes

50 Guillaumond, *Cuisine et diététique dans l'Occident arabe médiéval*, no. 215.

51 Ibid. no. 185.

The recipe "A Jewish Dish of Eggplants Stuffed with Meat" thus captures our full attention. Emptied, the eggplant skins are filled with flavored mutton and the eggplant flesh. This dish is characteristic of Jewish cuisine in two ways: it is stuffed and contains eggplant. The use of pine nuts and citron leaves is also a defining feature.

The fact that eggplant is the most commonly used food in the dishes of al-Andalus, and the fact that a wide range of culinary techniques can be used to prepare it, is not an accident. It cannot be ignored that the eggplant, which was inexpensive and had been present on the Iberian Peninsula since the nineth century, was also common in the food practices of the East. However, it would be a mistake to stop there. The eggplant must be analyzed over the long term. By studying the food across several centuries and through different sources, the foundations of the increasingly obvious discrimination against Jews emerge.

b. Eggplant and Later Discrimination

The most flagrant and disconcerting example is found in a recipe of the *Kitāb al-ṭabīẖ*. In the "Preparation of Arnabi"[52] (صفة الارنبى, "A Hare Dish"; *arnab* is the Arabic word for hare), eggplant is used to fool the eater. In fact, the dish contains neither hare nor meat. Why mention hare when, in reality, there isn't any meat at all? Why make the someone believe that they are going to eat hare? Why hare and not another animal?

The answers to these questions may be found in religious food precepts. Muslims have no restrictions on the consumption of hare; but this is not the case in Judaism. The animal, which does not have a split hoof and is not a ruminant, is considered illegal in the food laws of Kashrut. Is it a mere coincidence that eggplant is used to fool the diner into thinking the dish contains hare? Or is it a way for Jews to consume a dish that they are not supposed to eat and thereby bypass a form of discrimination against their identity through food? The question remains unanswered, but it deserves to be asked. This case is even more interesting given that it occurs in the second Andalusian cookbook of the thirteenth century: the *Fuḍālat al-ẖiwān*. Indeed, this cookbook also proposes a recipe—Another Dish Called *Al-arnabī*,"[53] whose title includes the word "hare."

---

52 Guillaumond, *Cuisine et diététique dans l'Occident arabe médiéval*, no. 201. Translation by the author.

53 Ibn Razīn al-Tuǧībī, *Relieves de las mesas acerca de las delicias de la comida y los diferentes platos*, ed. Manuela Marin (Gijón: Ediciones Trea, S. L., 2007), 144–45. Translation by the author. See the recently published Nawal Nasrallah, ed. and trans., *Best of Delectable Foods and Dishes*

Unlike the one in the *Kitāb al-ṭabīḫ*, this dish does contain meat, but not hare meat, as the title would suggest. The color, the dense but malleable texture, the ability to change the appearance and color according to the type of preparation and cooking style, are all features of the eggplant that make it a multifaceted food. If the use of eggplant is a sign of Jewish and Muslim eating habits, and if the use of eggplant to replace hare is a way to identify different food practices, we can't begin to imagine what eggplant would be like in sources under Christian rule.

In the end, Muslim identity was imposed on Jews under the Almohads and until the end of Muslim domination in Spain in 1492—just as Christian identity would be imposed on them upon the official arrival of the Catholic Monarchs and the Inquisition. A sticklerism that prohibited—or greatly complicated—the performance of Jewish rituals both under the Almohads[54] and after. One can imagine, then, that the context in which the *Kitāb al-ṭabīḫ* was written had an impact on Jews when it came time to prepare and cook dishes (according to *Kashrut*) for Jewish liturgical feasts—a daily and essential act that could not go unnoticed by the rulers. This situation captures the challenges that Jews in Spain faced in the twelfth to thirteenth centuries. However, sources that dealing with this question are lacking, if not nonexistent. Was there already a crypto-Judaism that included Jewish culinary practices at the time the *Kitāb al-ṭabīḫ* was written, as there was under Christian rule?

---

from al-Andalus and al-Maghrib: A Cookbook by Thirteenth-Century Andalusi Scholar Ibn Razīn al-Tujībī (1227–1293) (New York: Brill, 2021).

54 Jane S. Gerber uses the term "pogrom" when talking about what the Almohads initiated: "The Golden Age thus began drawing to a close decades before 1147, when the invasion of the zealously fundamentalist Almohad Muslims from North Africa would set off a wave of pogroms and spur Jewish flight" (see Gerber, *The Jews of Spain*, 57).

Part Two

THE LEGACY OF THE MULTICULTURAL CUISINE OF AL-ANDALUS (FOURTEENTH TO SEVENTEENTH CENTURY): THE EVOLUTION AND PERCEPTION OF JEWISH FOOD

CHAPTER 5

The Counterpoint of Christian-Dominated Cookbooks

The French anthropologist Claude Lévi-Strauss defended the idea that it is not enough for food to be good to eat; it should also be "good to think with."[1] Bringing together both the organoleptic and symbolic qualities of food, this idea captures essence of the research presented in this book and invites us to better understand the culinary history of both Spanish Jews, specifically, and modern Spain, in general. Indeed, historical elements must serve as a message for other societies, taking on a pedagogical role. And food should also be included. "Immaterial heritage" stresses food practices that passed on from one generation to the next, the continuity that shapes culinary heritage. In the case of the Iberian Peninsula, this heritage is multicultural, as three cultures lived together on the same territory. This multiculturalism, beyond any controversies about *convivencia*,[2] produced a cuisine—or rather cuisines—which made it possible to identify the way of thinking and the practices of an entire group of people.

A. Christian Rule Versus Muslim Rule

If, from a contemporary perspective, culinary heritage is an economic resource for development and a reaction to food standardization, in thirteenth- to sixteenth-century Spain, food was above all a mark of the identity of a community its space. This multiculturalism has been a part of the culinary heritage of the

1 Claude Lévi-Strauss, *Totemism*, trans. Rodney Needham (Boston: Beacon, 1963).

2 This historiographic difference is embodied by Américo Castro, who has a positive view of this multicultural and religious cohabitation, and Sánchez Albornoz, who rejects that anything positive came out of this mixing of different religious communities.

Iberian Peninsula ever since various elements disappeared or were altered. Thus, there were three cuisines that distinguished Jews, Muslims, and Christians, even if the boundaries between Jewish and Muslim cuisine were sometimes blurry. The cookbooks written in Spain under Christian rule are undeniably rich, and their usefulness increases tenfold when they are compared to earlier cookbooks written under Muslim rule. In fact, the two are polar opposites. The lack of similarities between recipes written under Muslim and Christian rule reveal how religion was a discriminatory food tool in the service of power. Comparing Moslem Andalusian cookbooks with those produced under Christian rule—written in Roman, Castilian, Catalan, and Portuguese—helps us understand how Christian cookbooks were used as an instrument in order to promote and establish food (thanks to the numerous editions of these recipe collections) that was compliant with Christian orthodoxy. Christian cookbooks thus stand in stark contrast to the food and culinary habits of Jews and Muslims.

The first cookbook written under Christian rule, and which can be compared with Andalusian cookbooks, is the *Llibre de Sent Soví.* This is the latest (fourteenth century) of the three Iberian Peninsula cookbooks written in the Middle Ages. I will refer to it by its common title: the *Sent Soví.* The cookbook was written in Catalan in 1324, as indicated in one of the manuscripts, although this date is uncertain. Seventy recipes comprise the common core of the two manuscripts (see ms. 216 at the Historical Library of the University of Valencia), and are supposedly from the fourteenth century.[3]

The *Sent Soví*[4] is known by two other later codices. The first is the *Llibre de totes maneres de potatges* from the fifteenth century (ms. 68 at the University Library of Barcelona), which contains 222 recipes. According to Villanueva, the manuscript comes from the Convent of Saint Catherine in Barcelona.[5] The second is the *Llibre d'aparellar de menjar,* from ms. 2112 in the Library of Catalonia. Composed of 279 recipes, the manuscript was purchased from Babra bookstore and later sold[6] during the Spanish Civil War (1936–1939). The old

---

3 The prologue states that the cookbook was written by "a great cook that served the King of England in 1024" on the advice of Pedro Felipe, who was a royal squire. However, this possibility does not appear to have been taken up.

4 See http://www.unesco.org/new/fileadmin/MULTIMEDIA/HQ/CI/spain_sentsovi_eng_01.pdf, 2–3.

5 Jaime Villanueva, *Viaje literario por las iglesias de España,* vol. 18 (Madrid: Imprenta de Fortanet, 1851), 184–194.

6 The registration proposal form of the *Sent Soví* in the National Memory of the World Register does not mention the location of the deposit.

classification was ms. 2574. The latest edition of the *Sent Soví* was published by Santanach in 2014.[7]

An overview of the ingredients included in the seventy-two recipes sheds light on just how strongly the cookbook—written one century later than the *Fuḍālat al-ẖiwān*—proposes a cuisine specifically for Christians, one that is radically different from that included in former cookbooks. Take, for instance, the use of pork and/or related products, included in 36% of dishes (no pork recipes are found in the *Kitāb al-ṭabīẖ*), whereas only one recipe uses eggplant (1.4% compared to 7% in the *Kitāb al-ṭabīẖ*). The same is true for cilantro (1.4% compared to 60% in the *Kitāb al-ṭabīẖ*). These three foods were not chosen randomly; they are identity markers of both Jewish and Muslim cuisine, and this is the reason why they will be the overarching elements of the explanations that follow, which aim to expose a food and culinary breaking point between the cookbooks written under Christian rule and those written under Muslim rule.

One dish from the *Sent Soví* is especially curious. Entitled "Albergínies,"[8] the recipe consists of slices of boiled eggplant stuffed with grated cheese, garlic, parsley, raisins, marjoram, mint, and onions. After folding a slice over the stuffing, the eggplant is covered with almond milk, broth, and oil. It is then put in the oven on a bed of onions. This preparation resembles today's *almodrote*, enjoyed by Sephardic communities. This comparison is interesting in light of the fact that the *almodrote* dish is similar to "Almadroc"[9] in the Catalan cookbook. The first of the two "Almadroc" recipes is made of grated cheese and garlic, diluted in water. The second is made from almond milk, grated cheese, and cold water. Judicial sources support this observation. Indeed, it should be mentioned here—briefly, as this point will be developed in chapter 8—that the consumption of *almodrote* used as proof of Jewish practices during Spanish Inquisition.[10] The term *almodrote* also appears in the book *Megilat Ha Megale* (1129), written by the Jewish scholar Abraham Bar Hiyya. One can read satirical verses against Muslims, such as ". . . I have almodrote to fight . . ." (. . . almodrote tengo para dar combatte . . .").

But what about the presence of this dish in Andalusian cookbooks? Is it possible to find this preparation's origin? The *Kitāb al-ṭabīẖ* seems to provide some clues. It includes a recipe titled "Boiled Eggplant" that is made of eggplant,

---

7 Anonymous et al., *Llibre de Sent Soví* (Barcelona: Editorial Barcino. Restaurant de les 7 portes, 2014).
8 Ibid., no. 36, 210–211.
9 Ibid., *Llibre de Sent Soví*, no. 25, 204–205, no. 65, 234–235.
10 Freedman, *Why Food Matters*, 57.

vinegar, crushed garlic, oil, and grated cheese. Itis present in a cookbook written in the thirteenth century under Muslim rule, which reappears, with a different name, in a cookbook written in the fourteenth century under Christian rule; and is found again in the trials of the Inquisition to denounce the practices of heretics. This dish also persists among dishes prepared by Sephardic Jews today.

What seems to emerge from analysis of this recipe is that *almadroc* in the *Sent Soví* corresponds to "Boiled Eggplant" in the *Kitāb al-ṭabīẖ*, with the difference that the eggplant has been removed. As for the *albergínies* recipe of the *Sent Soví*, it is related to the "Boiled Eggplant" recipe of the *Kitāb al-ṭabīẖ*. Why does the *Sent Soví* not contain more eggplant recipes? Why is the *Kitāb al-ṭabīẖ* dish—which most closely resembles today's *almodrote*—still enjoyed by Sephardic Jews today and still a part of current Moroccan cuisine?[11] Why is this preparation a part of Sephardic cuisine, but known as "almodrote en flaó"?[12]

Several possibilities should be considered. The first is that the dish in the *Kitāb al-ṭabīẖ* was prepared and consumed by Jews in the thirteenth century, and possibly by Muslims as well. The bad reputation of the eggplant under Christian rule could explain the absence of the recipe from the Catalan cookbook one century later. The fact that this *albergínies* preparation, made of *almadroc* and eggplant, is still enjoyed today by Jews underscores the existence of a Jewish cuisine within fourteenth-century Catalan cuisine. The continuity of this dish in the culinary practices of Spanish Sephardic Jews, as well as Moroccan Jews, under the same name, raises questions about the transmission of culinary knowledge—an entire history. But a history that is only distinguishable by employing a long lens. This prompts a number of further questions. How can this culinary profile, which is so drastically different and yet so close in time, be explained other than by the power of the dominant religion—Catholicism—and the desire of kings to establish a new cuisine? In connection with the political and religious project of the Catholic Kings, then, as well as their successors, a similar observation emerges from analysis of cookbooks written after the *Sent Soví*.

Let's take the example of another cookbook, the *Lybre de Coch*. No manuscript of this text has been found.[13] However, there are several editions, three of

---

11 Herminia Crespo García, *Trabajo de fin de grado: La Judería de Segovia como recurso didáctico. Una propuesta educativa multidisciplinar* (Segovia: Universidad de Segovia, 2014); See *Cocina Marroquí*, November 8, 2013. *Almodrote de berenjenas*. https://decaminoamicocina.blogspot.com/2013/11/almodrote-de-bernejena.html.

12 García and Tovar, *Un banquete por Sefarad*, 278.

13 In *Le livre de cuisine*, Nathalie Peyrebonne writes that "the work was undoubtedly written before 1494, but no edition prior to 1520 seems to have been preserved." For more details,

which are essential for the history of this work—one dated 1520, with the shortened title *Lybre de Coch* (Catalan edition, 203 recipes), one dated 1525, under the shortened title *Libro de cocina* (first edition in Castilian; 236 recipes; printed in seventeen editions between 1520 and 1577), and one dated 1529 with the shortened title *Libro de cozina* (first edition in Castilian, with a number of additions: 243 recipes). Between the first and the last edition in Catalan, and the first editions in Castilian—from 1525 in Toledo and 1529 in Logroño—there are slight differences,[14] particularly as concerns the details about *mazapanes*. This specialty is addressed in greater detail in chapter 9, as it is of utmost importance for measuring the significance of the Jewish legacy in Iberian culinary heritage.

The *Regalo de la vida humana*,[15] a cookbook by Juan Vallés (1496–1563), a former treasurer of Navarre,[16] is known thanks to a sole copy that is stored in the Österreichische National Bibliothek in Vienna; it is categorized under the title *Codex Vindobonensis Palatinus*, ms.11160.[17] This *compedio* is composed of eight large books, but my study will only focus on books five and six, as they contain dishes like "Mazapanes" (marzipan), "Quesadillas," "Empanadas," and "Cecina" (dried beef). These are a part of Jewish culinary heritage.

The *El libro de cocina de la Infanta Doña Maria du Portugal* is a cookbook that contains sixty-one recipes[18] and written like a collection of notes. The online library PhiloBiblon at the University of California, Berkeley, proposes two dates for the manuscript copies: 1480 and 1510.[19] This cookbook from Portugal was found in manuscript I.E-33 in Naples's Vittorio Emanuele III National Library by Alfonso Miola in 1895.[20] It brings together many texts belonging to the

---

see Roberto De Nola and Nathalie Peyrebonne, ed. and trans., *Le livre de cuisine*. Textes de la Renaissance (Paris: Classiques Garnier, 2011), 7.

14 Jeanne Allard, "Nola: Rupture ou continuité?" in *Du manuscrit à la table. Essais sur la cuisine au Moyen Âge et répertoire des manuscrits médiévaux contenant des recettes culinaires*, ed. Carole Lambert (Montréal: Presses Universitaires de Montréal, 1992), 151.

15 Juan Vallés, *Regalo de la vida humana*, ed. and trans. Fernando Serrano Larráyoz, vol. 2 (Pamplona: Gobierno de Navarra-Österreichische National bibliothek, 2008).

16 Huarte De San Juan and Fernando Serrano Larráyoz, "La edición del 'Regalo de la vida humana de Juan Vallés (c. 1496–1563): un proyecto en curso," *Geografía e Historia* 13 (2006): 341–354.

17 Vallés, *Regalo de la vida humana*, 79.

18 Maria Du Portugal and Maria José Palla, trans., *Livre de cuisine de l'Infante Maria du Portugal* (Lisbon: Universidade Nova de Lisboa: Instituto de Estudos Medevais, 2008), 14.

19 The online library PhiloBiblon at the University of Berkeley offers a very detailed description of this manuscript. See *PhiloBiblon*. Dir. Charles B. Faulhaber. Bancroft Library. University of California, Berkeley, 1997–. http://vm136.lib.berkeley.edu/BANC/philobiblon/index.html.

20 In codex I.E 33, there are the texts of six other manuscripts. See the 2006 PhD dissertation by De Souza: http://www.dominiopublico.gov.br/download/texto/cp031055.pdf. Access

Farnèse family.[21] However, the date of the manuscript is problematic: there is no title page and the it contains several styles of handwriting. It is called *O Livro de Cozinha da Infanta D. Maria de Portugal.* The Infanta Maria of Portugal, wife of Alexandre Farnèse, was alive between 1538 and 1577, though. The manuscript may be attributed to her because it is a Portuguese text belonging to the collection of works belonging to the Farnèse family and because she owned it.

The *Libro de Cozinha* shows the food habits of elite Portuguese society at the time. From recipes to advice about health and aesthetics, it appears to convey the Infanta's taste for heterogeneous culinary styles, borrowed in part from a past culinary heritage, that is, from when Portugal and Spain were united. The mark of recipes from the *Kitāb al-ṭabīḫ* and the *Fuḍālat al-ḫiwān* is apparent ("Moorish Chicken,"[22] "Recipe of Moorish Chicken,"[23] "Here Is the Meatball Recipe,"[24]), and some in the *Sent Soví* (e.g., "Blancmange")[25] and later cookbooks.[26] The cookbook is interesting because it is the first one from the Iberian Peninsula written in Portuguese. Its multicultural and multireligious stamp makes it one of the most interesting manuscripts of its kind. Moreover, details in the cookbook suggest that there are "sausage" recipes prepared for Jews. Indeed, this of utmost historical importance, as Portugal witnessed the arrival of Jews who were fleeing the Spanish Inquisition at the end of the fifteenth century. In chapter 10, I explore the sausage dish called *alheira,* in which pork was replaced by chicken or bread.

The cookbook, the full title of which is *Libro del arte de cozina, en el qvual* [sic] *se contiene el modo de guisar y de comer en cualquier tiempo, así de carne, como de pescados, para sanos, enfermos, convalecientes: así de pasteles, tortas, salsas. Como de conservas al uso Español, Italiano, y Tumescent de nuestros tiempos,* was composed by Diego Granado Maldonado and includes 766 recipes.[27] There are three

---

was canceled in December 2020. See https://www.boatos.org/entretenimento/dominio-publico-www-dominiopublico-gov-br-vai-ser-desativado-falta-acessos.html.

21 Marie Josèphe Moncorgé, "Livre de cuisine médiévale en portugais, dédié à l'infante D. Maria de Portugal," *Old cook,* accessed April 4, 2022, http://www.oldcook.com/medieval-livres_cuisine_portugais. It should be noted that this website sometimes includes information that needs to be reviewed, despite the administrators' rigor.

22 Du Portugal and Palla, *Livre de cuisine de l'Infante Maria du Portugal,* recipe no. 2.03, 38.

23 Ibid., recipe no. 2.21, 50.

24 Ibid., recipe no. 2.21, 51. The original title in Portuguese is "boldroegas," which in Mr. Filho's 1963 edition in modern Portuguese (Brazil) was transcribed as "almôndegas" ("albóndigas" in Spanish).

25 Ibid., recipe no. 4.1, 63.

26 Ibid., 13.

27 María Ángeles Pérez Sámper, *La alimentación en la España del Siglo de Oro. Domingo Hernández de Maceras 'Libro del arte de cocina'* (Huesca: La Val de Onsera, Colección Ali Farra Estudios,

editions, the earliest one of which is dated 1599. Let's briefly note "Olla podrida," "Hojuelas," and "Bollo maimon," dishes that evoke certain Andalusian preparations and which are reflected in Sephardic cuisine.

The *Libro del arte de cocina* by Domíngo Hernández de Maceras is also a part of this context. Published in Salamanca in 1607, it contains 180 recipes.[28] The book makes it possible to see changes in the use of certain foods after the Andalusian cookbooks were written. It also questions both the presence of certain ingredients in the cookbooks and the transformation/changes of certain dishes (very slight) that are already in the thirteenth-century cookbooks (but under different names). This is the case for dishes such as "Bollos de clauonia,"[29] "Olla podrida,"[30] and "Mazapán."[31] Furthermore, some dishes are even more unique, as they are included in the chapter on recipes for "Saturday," that is, Shabbat. Thus, some récipes, like "Cómo se ha de guisar el hígado,"[32] "De otro plato de espinacas para servirlas en escudillas,"[33] and "Hormigo de avellanas,"[34] evoke others that are present in Jewish culinary culture. *Albóndigas* (meatballs), *almojábanas,* and *empanadas* (turnovers and pies), which are abundant in Arabic cookbooks, are present in the work of Maceras, but are not dominant. The same is true for eggplant, which only appears in a single cookbook.

The *Recetas experimentadas para diversas cosas* is a cookbook from 1620.[35] It is kept in the BNE (Biblioteca Nacional de España).[36] There are two references in it to the city of Valencia (folios 11v. and 49 v.) and several different proper names, such as "Maria de Mendoza" or "Isabel Vasquez."[37] The cookbook primarily includes cosmetic preparations, like soap, perfume, treatments for hair and teeth, and so on. There are also recipes for preserves. Some of the most

---

1998), 24. Notaker proposes the number of 762 recipes. See Notaker, *Printed Cookbooks in Europe*, 353; see Notaker, *A History of Cookbooks* (Berkeley: University of California Press, 2017).

28 Pérez Sámper, *La alimentación en la España del Siglo de Oro*, 67.

29 Ibid., chap. 55, 217. The dish is also known today as "bollo maimon."

30 Ibid., chap. 54, 217.

31 Ibid., chap 54, 218–219, 239, 241, 258.

32 Ibid., chap. 12, 224. This recipe is in the "Saturday" chapter of recipes. I translate the title of the recipe as "How one should cook liver."

33 Ibid., chap. 5, 231. I translate the title of the recipe as "Another dish of spinach to be served in bowls."

34 Ibid., chap. 7, 231. I translate the title of the recipe as "hazelnuts *hormigo*."

35 See Mariane Saïe, "*Étude des manuscrits 1462, 2019 et 6058 de la Bibliothèque Nationale d'Espagne. Une approche de la cuisine espagnole au début de l'époque moderne*," Master's thesis, Université de la Sorbonne IV, 2007 [under the supervision of Alain Tallon]).

36 See *Biblioteca Digital Hispánica*, http://bdh-rd.bne.es/viewer.vm?id=0000011243&page=1.

37 Jodi Campbel, *At the First Table: Food and Social Identity in Early Modern Spain* (Lincoln: Nebraska Press University, 2017).

interesting notices, as they are connected to Jewish cuisine, are the "Recepta para haçer marçapanes" (folio 11r.), "Recetas para berenjenas de miel" (folio 19r.), the "Receptas de marçapan" (folio 58v.), and, finally, "La manera que han de tener para hazer las rosquillas" (folio 69r.).

What can be taken away from this overview of the common traits between the cookbooks written under Muslim and Christian rulers is that they are completely opposed. The latter cookbooks are only intended for Christian Catholic elites. The importance of diet and medicine disappeared from these cookbooks. Eating well is the only priority, whatever the consequences for health; no recommendations are made about moderation, at least. The *Sent Soví* is very intriguing in this regard. The most recent of the Andalusian cookbooks, it contains dishes that are drastically different from the previous collections. The book laid the foundations for present-day Spanish cuisine. As Jodi Cambell states, "all the religions included food practices as important elements of religion, so after the sixteenth century, when all Spaniards were ostensibly Christian, old Christians viewed the continuation of any of the former Jewish and Muslim food habits as signs of heresy." This favored the emergence of culinary uniformity.

B. The Emergence of Culinary Uniformity

From the omnipresence of some foods to the absence of others, "Christian" cookbooks begin to stand out in the fifteenth century by their food and culinary uniformity—an orchestrated move to erase any trace of a culinary past marked by Semitic cultures, which other sources will later draw on due to antisemitism.

Jacinthe Bessière proposes that "it is the desire to break that proves to be a source of heritage-making. A kind of fracture . . ., invention in the realm of food heritage can result from a situation of difficulty, failure, weakness, or fear."[38] There is no better way of summarizing what occurred in the context of Spain after the arrival of the Catholic Kings. This "desire to break" with the food and cuisine of the time—in order to put the practices of Jews and Muslims at a distance—was born out of the Catholics' fear that that they would no longer command the Iberian Peninsula. The decision to annihilate all traces of its Jewish and Muslim culinary past, even to the extent of recording the practices of Christian heretics, created a "uni-cultural" heritage.

---

38 Jacinthe Bessière, "Quand le patrimoine alimentaire innove," *Mondes du Tourisme* 7 (2013): 37–51.

If a change in tastes was the main reason for this culinary change, we would certainly observe a gradual increase in the use of parsley and a slow decrease in the use of cilantro. However, this is not the case. "Christian" cookbooks demonstrate a dearth—and at times a complete absence—of fresh cilantro and frequent use of parsley, which Muslims knew was called *būšīn* by Christians. For instance, the presence of cilantro in later cookbooks reveals the existence of a past culinary heritage, while the use of parsley indicates the identity of the dominant religious power. These recipes provide an obvious view of the importance of religious pressure on the Iberian Peninsula in the fifteenth century and the need to establish one's identity, particularly through food.[39] The culinary heritage of contemporary Spain reveals the substitution of "Arabic" cilantro with parsley—even though Sephardic Jewish and Muslim communities today continue to use fresh cilantro more than parsley, which was abundantly consumed in the Christian West.

But the cilantro/parsley dilemma is not the only one to point to this culinary break and the desire to uniformize Spain. Eggplant is undoubtedly the food that best helps explain this culinary uniformity. As mentioned previously, the food is omnipresent in the *Kitāb al-ṭabīḫ*. Yet it "disappears" from use in the *Sent Soví*, as well as from all of the cookbooks written under Christian rule. This is not by accident. It is a choice. A choice made by the ruling Catholics, who, let's remember, had the right to censor publications, including cookbooks.

As Fernando Serrano Larráyoz remarks in his analysis of the *Regalo de la vida humana*, the light consumption of olive oil can be explained by its ties to religion. It was only used for fish dishes or on days of fasting when eating meat was prohibited by Christianity. Larráyoz's analysis is all the more interesting if we take a different perspective. It corroborates the view that olive oil was included because of religious food precepts, and not only Christian ones. This argument aligns with the types of dishes in the *Kitāb al-ṭabīḫ* and supports the hypothesis that a Jewish doctor wrote the book. Indeed, keep in mind that the cookbook contains many olive oil recipes, and this vegetable fat simplified the culinary practices of Jewish communities. According to Jodi Cambell,

> while both . . . Jews and Muslims were eventually targeted for their different food practices, perceived as signs of religious difference, they were also both responsible for introducing important elements of cuisine into Spanish cooking. Jewish cuisine in

---

39 Constable, "Food and Meaning."

> Spain relied heavily on soups, especially those based on chickpeas with meat and spices. Catalan bread soups with garlic and thyme are also of Jewish origin, as are milk-based sweets.[40]

She adds that "these ingredients in and of themselves were not perceived as different or threatening, but Jewish and Muslim food practices were strongly associated with their religious identity." Although I agree with this in part, I maintain that it was not the case for all ingredients, particularly coriander and eggplant.

The deletion of any sign of past Jewish or Muslim culture, including food culture, emerges as one of the major aims of the Catholic Kings. This is demonstrated by the introduction of pork in a substantial number of recipes, including recipes described as "Moorish," as well as by the absence of some foods that were deemed an intrinsic part of Semitic cultures. Uniformization was religious, territorial, and culinary. And food—in all its forms—was an instrument used by the Catholic Kings to succeed in this project.

---

40 Campbell, *At the First Table*, 72–73.

CHAPTER 6

Iberian Literary Works: Witnesses to Food Discrimination against Jews

In order to research Jewish recipes and practices from the end of the Middle Ages, and more generally understand their contribution to the culinary heritage of the Iberian Peninsula over the long term, I have drawn on a variety of different sources, thereby creating multiple opportunities for cross-checking. While my main sources are culinary references, they are not the only ones that enable me to address this question and document a community's food practices. I also use literature to supplement and clarify my analyses of the cookbooks. Interpreting literature is more subjective, but it also provides a critical and sometimes even scathing perspective. Further, literary sources offer an at times satirical outlook on the mores of the time, revealing a way of thinking that cookbooks don't. The origin of a given author—and, more specifically, their religion—helps us understand the political and social climate of the period.

A. Food as an Object of Social Criticism

As the fourteenth century was defined by Islamic rigorism Catholic intolerance, one can imagine that tensions between these two rivals had repercussions on the societal and economic life of the three cultures living on the Iberian Peninsula. As Olivia Remie Constable states, "the issue of Christians accepting food from Muslim and Jews, or sharing food with them, had a long history in medieval

Spain and elsewhere in the Mediterranean world."[1] David Freidenreich also argues that "although laws prohibiting such commensality date from the fourth century and remained on the books until the twentieth, the period from the mid-twelfth to the mid-thirteenth centuries constitutes an especially intense time of development in this law, along with Latin canon law more generally."[2] It goes without saying that the minority position occupied by Jews in both Christian and Moslem contexts may explain the pressures and restrictions they faced. As a result, their food habits were affected.

Indeed, the treaty of Libro de las Confesiones de Martín Pérez (1316) stipulated the status and social position that Jews, Christians, and Muslims were to occupy in Christian territory. For example, we read that Christians who worked for Jews or Muslims could not share their food with them. Another decree of 1480 threatened every Christian with a fine, even public punishment, if they bought meat from a Muslim or Jewish butcher. In 1324, ordinances enacted by the bishop of Calahorra ruled that Christians must not enter the houses of Jews or Muslims, or eat their foods (comen de sus viandas); while later in the century Vincent Ferrer preached that Christians should not buy food (conprar d'ells vitualles) from Muslims or Jews."[3] In the year of the official expulsion of Jews from Spain, interactions, including those involving the exchange of food, were outlawed in the multifaith city of Toledo.[4]

Yet these ordinances also show that interactions between religious communities existed. We also know that in the fifteenth century, especially in Aragon, Jews, Christians, and Muslims shared slaughterhouses, but had their own butchers. The sale to Christians of meat slaughtered by Jews—just like cheese and wine—was forbidden.[5]

How, though, does a vegetable, as well as ritualistic practices and culinary techniques, disclose a community's way of thinking. The four Iberian literary works that I will analyze here mention dishes such as *adafina*[6] (a stew that Jews prepared in Spain) and foods like the eggplant, whose consumption had negative associations with Jews. These works were written by or against Jewish

---

1 Constable, "Food and Meaning," 203. See also David Freidenreich, *Foreigners and Their Food: Constructing Otherness in Jewish, Christian and Islamic Law* (Berkeley: University of California Press, 2011).

2 Freidenreich, "Sharing Meals with Non-Christians," 42.

3 Constable, "Food and Meaning," 208.

4 Martínez, "Hacia la configuración del modelo alimentario feudal," 353; Campbell, *At the First Table*, 75–76.

5 Ibid., 75.

6 See below for a detailed description of this dish.

converts to Catholicism. In both cases, through the foods and/or dishes that Jews enjoyed, the texts document discrimination against Judaists. The content of the poem by Crescar du Caylar, for example, illustrates ties with Jewish food practices on the Iberian Peninsula. As concerns *La Lozana andaluza,* it includes a number of Jewish dishes from al-Andalus, while testifying to the distrust that reigned among old and new Christians, as well as between Jewish converts themselves. Conversos were afraid of being condemned for betraying their continued Judaism through their practices, particularly those related to food. Artusi wrote down in the nineteenth century what everyone was thinking in the fifteenth century: "eggplant . . . was despised, for being a Jewish food. . . . [This shows] that just as in areas of the greatest importance, they also had more sense than Christians."[7] That Christians use the act of eating or not eating pork for identification purposes is well established. What is perhaps less certain is the use of this idea by Jews to assert their hatred towards Christians. It is this perspective that is inscribed the prayer that the Spanish converso of the city of Ciudad Real Juan Díaz uttered in 1484:

> Blessed be you, Adonai, who did not make me a pig for Christians to eat, and Blessed be Adonai, my God and God of my fathers, kill them and destroy them and return them to our Law and to our Commandments."[8]

Many literary sources, and not only from Spain, use food, dishes, and meal scenes to criticize Jewish culinary practices, rituals, and celebrations. A fifteenth-century Italian poem titled *Stanze di Lorenzo de'Medici* provides a critical view of a society in which food and culinary practices are associated with the identity of a mocked and ridiculed community. The juxtaposition of foods that are accepted or banned, with the aim of making fun of Jewish customs, is a literary device found in both Italy and in Spain.[9] This anti-Jewish satire provides a lens

---

7 Artusi, *La Scienza in Cucina e l'Arte di Mangiar Bene*, 222. Translation by the author; Capatti and Montanari, *La cucina italiana*, 49.

8 Gitlitz, *Secrecy and Deceit*, 159. See Beinart, *Records of the Trials of the Spanish Inquisition in Ciudad Real*, vol. 1, *The Trials of 1483–1485*, 572: "Bendito Tu, Adonay, en que no me fiste puerco para que me comiese el christiano, y Bendito Adonay, Dio myo y de mis parientes, matalos y destruylos, tornalos a nuestra Ley y a nuestros Mandamientos."

9 Martine Dozon, Contributions à l'étude de la civilisation urbaine en Italie (XIIIe–XVIe). Hommage à Ida Maier (Nanterre: Centre de recherches de langue et littérature italiennes (1974). The regions of Italy evoked through the dishes and wines mentioned here are those of the Adriatic coast, Rome, and Siena, as well as the Island of Giglio in Tuscany. Several allusions are made to the situation of Jewish communities settled in various cities in Italy.

through which to view the condition of this minority group,[10] and meals appear to be the perfect opportunity for criticizing Jews for their rituals.

B. Commensality in Four Literary Works

According to Constable, "prohibitions against accepting and sharing food gained traction during the fourteenth century, although there was still some debate as to whether Muslims and Jews were equally disapproved of as dinning partners. The Siete Partidas[11] ruled that Christians should not eat or drink with Jews, but said nothing of Muslims. In the mid-fifteenth-century Christians were still forbidden to eat together with Jews and Muslims."[12]

Without attempting to be exhaustive, I have decided to analyze how food was presented and represented in six literary works of the fourteenth and fifteenth centuries. My purpose is to highlight the links between food and religion, especially in relation to Judaism. In what follows, then, I aim to identify what food habits can reveal about a Jewish community that lived in Christian Spain and perpetuated the tastes and flavors of Muslim Spain and before. Among these literary works, four were written in Spanish: *Libro de Buen amor, Cancionero de Baena, Copla a Pedro González* and *Cancionero general.* The fifth is a poem written in Avignon in the fourteenth century by Crescas du Caylar, a Jewish doctor from Narbonne. The last text, *La Lozana andaluza,* is an anonymous work from sixteenth-century Rome.

a. *Libro de Buen amor* (The Book of Good love), by Arcipreste de Hita (fourteenth century)

Juan Ruiz, also called Arcipreste de Hita (1284–1351), is known and reputed for his work *Libro de Buen amor* (1330). Only three manuscripts[13] survive, and not a single one in full. *Libro de Buen Amor* was copied in 1330 in the manuscript of Toledo (ms. T). It is an individual manuscript. The G manuscript

10 With the forecast of events between 1465 and 1490.

11 "The Siete Partidas is an extensive Castilian law code commissioned in the thirteenth century and completed in the early fourteenth." See Constable, "Food and Meaning," 205.

12 Siete Partidas, partida VII, title XXIV, law VIII; for English trans. see S. P. Scott, ed., *Las Siete Partidas,* trans. R. I. Burns (Philadelphia: University of Pennsylvania Press, 2001).

13 The BNE provides important details about the work: http://bdh.bne.es/bnesearch/detalle/bdh0000051820.

(ms. G), the date of which is uncertain, as it could be 1342 (according to the Centro virtual Cervantes) or 1389 (according to the Biblioeca Digital Hispánica of the Real Academia Española), was attributed to Gayoso because he owned it. It is an individual manuscript. The Real Academia Española provides a scanned reproduction of the original *Libro de Buen amor* manuscript, known as the *códice Gayoso.* It was copied in the manuscript of Salamanca (ms. S) in about 1417,[14] and is currently in the Biblioteca of Salamanca University.

Three almost identical copies of the T and G manuscripts are in an eighteenth-century codex, currently stored at the Biblioteca Nacional de Madrid, the BnF in Paris, and the Biblioteca de Castilla-La Mancha (BCLM) in Toledo.[15] The Biblioteca Digital Hispánica offers a scanned version dated 1368 (noted on the first page).[16] The Cervantes Institute has also scanned[17] the work.

Libro de Buen amor is composed of more than 1700 stanzas, which narrate the life of the author, whose origins are unknown. As regards the geopolitical context, keep in mind that the Muslim Almohad dynasty in al-Andalus had been replaced by the Nasrid dynasty (1238–1492). However, even though they were no longer present in Castile, it is highly likely that the culinary habits of the Andalusians (primarily Jews and Muslims) persisted.

In this remarkable work, one notices the term *adafina*. By consulting medieval dictionaries, it is first possible to discover whether this term was used extensively at the time enough to be included. If so, the definition would shed light on the point of view of society and the era that produced it. The dictionary by Nebrija,[18] from 1495, is, chronologically speaking, the closest to the period during which *Libro de Buen Amor* was written. However, it does not include the term *adafina*. The same is true for the dictionary by Covarrubias[19] from 1611. The first dictionary to contain the term is the one in the *Real Academia Española* (RAE), the *Diccionario de Autoridades* (1726–1734). There, it is defined as "a

---

14 Centro Virtual Cervantes: https://cvc.cervantes.es/literatura/arcipreste_hita/01/perez.htm.

15 Ibid.

16 Biblioteca Digital Hispánica, http://bdh-rd.bne.es/viewer.vm?id=0000051820.

17 Centro Virtual Cervantes: http://www.cervantesvirtual.com/obra/el-libro-de-buen-amor--0/.

18 Antonio de Nebrija was the first author of a Castilian grammar book (1492). He is also known for his Castilian/Latin dictionary *Dictionarium ex hispaniensi in latinum sermonem* (1495). In 1481, he created one in Latin/Castilian. Bernard Pottier, "Les lexicographes espagnols du XVIe siècle," *Comptes rendus des séances de l'Académie des Inscriptions et Belles-Lettres* 3 (1991): 591–604.

19 Sebastián de Covarrubias wrote the first monolingual Spanish dictionary. See Hans-Josef Niederehe, "La lexicographie espagnole jusqu'à Covarrubias," *Histoire Épistémologie Langage* 8, booklet 1 (1986): 9–19.

kind of stew [*guisado*] that Jews prepared in Spain."[20] This is surprising, given that we know that the term *adafina* is omnipresent in the trials of the Spanish Inquisition in the fifteenth century. In the *Glossaire etimológico de las palabras españolas de origen oriental* (1886), it is reported that Andrès Bernáldez ("Cura de Los Palacios," 1415–1513) said of *adafina* that "it has no other meaning than stew [*puchero*] or pot [*olla*] that Jews [*hebreos*] place at nightfall [*anochecer*]on the stove [*anafe*], covering it with the rest of the coals [*rescoldo*] and embers [*brasas*] to eat it on Saturday."[21]

Let's take a second example. The section titled "Enxiemplo de la abutarda y de la golondrina" in the *Libro de Buen Amor,* stanza 781, includes the following verses:

> Some [men] in their homes are satisfied with two sardines;
> But when they visit foreign inns they ask for exquisite dishes:
> They reject mutton and request *adafinas.*
> They said they would not eat lard without chicken.[22]

It is understood here that *adafina* is a high-quality dish. Moreover, it is not sought after or enjoyed by all people in Spain—only by Jews. The line "they refuse mutton" can be read as expressing a desire to break with the culinary customs of the

---

20 *Diccionario de Autoridades*, vol. 1 (Madrid: Real Academia Española, 1726), 77: *[A]dafina*: "cierto género de guisado de que usaban los judíos en España." It is also stated: "Lat. *Condimentum carnium more Judaico.*" Two literary works are also mentioned. In "Cura de los Palacios, Historia de los Reyes Católicos, fol. 83," one reads: "Nunca perdieron en el comer la costumbre Judaica de manjareros y ollétas de *adafína*," which is translated by the author as follows: "They never lost, in their way of eating, the Jewish habit of adafina dishes and pots." See the facsimile edition at https://archivo.rae.es/index.php/adafina. The second work mentioned is *The Cancionero General.* See also http://web.frl.es/DA.html; Felipe Maíllo Salgado, *Los arabismos del castellano en la Baja Edad Media* (Salamanca: Universidad de Salamanca, 1998).

21 Leopoldo De Eguilaz y Yanguas, *Glosario etimológico de las palabras españolas de origen oriental* (Granada: Edition La Lealtad, 1886): "No tiene otro significado que el puchero ú olla que los hebreos colocan al anachocer del viernes en un anafe cubriéndola de rescoldo y brasas para comerla el sábado." Translation by the author.

22 Julio Cejador y Frauca, *El libro de buen amor* (Madrid: Espasa Calpe, 1967); Louis Michaud study at the Biblioteca virtual Cervantes, http://www.cervantesvirtual.com/obra-visor/el-libro-de-buen-amor--0/html/ff0ec418-82b1-11df-acc7002185ce6064_30.html#I_54_: "Algunos en sus cassas pasan con dos sardinas; / En ajenas posadas demandan golosinas: / Desechan el carnero y piden las adefinas / Desían que no comerían tocino sin gallinas." See Richard Archdekin, *Theologia tripartita universa: complectens perfectam bibliothecam viri ecclesiastici*, 3 vols. (Amstaelodami: Sumptibus societatis, 1737). Translation by the author.

time, specifically with Muslim cuisine, which contained a lot of mutton. In any case, the intention was to use food to differentiate one's group from others.[23]

b. "Respuesta de Juan García contra Juan Alfonso de Baena," in *Cancionero de Baena*, by Juan Alfonso de Baena (fifteenth century)

The collection entitled *Cancionero de poetas antiguos que fizo é ordenó e compuso é acopiló el judino Johan Alfonso de Baena* can be found in the Spanish manuscript 37 stored in the BnF in Paris.[24] The title can be translated as: "*Cancionero* of ancient poets created, arranged and composed by the Jew Juan Alfonso de Baena."[25] It is known today as *Cancionero de Baena*. The manuscript is from about 1465, but the work must have been compiled between 1430 and 1445. The book *El cancionero de Baena: problemas paleográficos*, by José Jurado,[26] pro-

23 Further, in 1450, Andrès Bernáldez (1415–1513), "Cura de Los Palacios," who was an anti-semite and also the unofficial commentator of the Catholic Kings, criticized the culinary customs of Iberian Peninsula Jews in his *Crónica de los RRCC*. He emphasized their food and also mentioned their dishes (including *adefina*), the ingredients they used, and their cooking styles. See fol. 83: "Nunca perdieron en el comer la costumbre judáica de manjares y olleta de adafina y manjarejos de cebollas e ajos refritos con aceite. Y la carne guisaban con aceite y lo echaban en lugar de tocino y de grosura, por escusar el tocino. . . . Y ellos eso mismo tenían el olor de los judíos, por causa de los manjares y de no ser bautizados." My translation: "They never lost, in their way of eating, the Jewish habit of adafina dishes and pots, and dishes with onions and garlic cooked in oil. And they cooked meat in oil which they used instead of lard or fat, to hide the lard. . . . And for this reason, they had the smell of Jews, due to their dishes and because they were not baptized." Cf: http://www.cervantesvirtual.com/obra-visor/cronica-de-los-senores-reyes-catolicos-don-fernando-y-dona-isabel-de-castilla-y-de-aragon--2/html/ffbd03a2-82b1-11df-acc7-002185ce6064.html.

24 Juan Alfonso De Baena, *El Cancionero. (Siglo XV): Ahora por primera vez dado a luz, con notas y comentarios* (La Publicidad, 1851): https://books.google.fr/books?id=wZPEYCYsWQ8C&pg=PA457&dq=Señor,+non+manjedes+manjar+d'Adefyna&hl=fr&sa=X&ved=0ahUKEwiNvNnVyungAhVD2OAKHTI6BwcQ6AEIMTAB#v=onepage&q=Señor%2C%20non%20manjedes%20manjar%20d'Adefyna&f=ffalse.

25 *Judino* is a term which, often in literature, can be used for *judío*, i.e. "Jew." See David Nirenberg, *Neighboring Faiths: Christianity, Islam, and Judaism in the Middle Ages and Today* (Chicago: University of Chicago Press, 2014).

26 José Jurado, *El cancionero de Baena: problemas paleográficos* (Madrid: Editorial CSIC, 1998).

vides a number of details about Alfonso de Baena and this text. While the first printed edition is dated 1851,[27] the latest was completed in September 2018.[28]

In the *Cancionero de Baena* of 1445,[29] compiled by the converted Jew[30] Juan Alfonso de Baena (1406–1454), one finds verses that are part of a debate that started in several poems prior to it. The debate was between Juan Alfonso de Baena and Juan García, and is concluded several poems later. Furthermore, the index of the 1851 edition also refers to pages 455 and 457 in the same volume, and concerns an exchange between Baena and Juan García de Vinuesa. The verses cited below are Juan de Guzmán's response to Juan Alfonso de Baena, advising him not to eat *adafina*:

> My Lord do not eat the *adafina* dish
> Which will give you a strong bitterness,
> And the taste will make you lazy . . .[31]

However, the term *adafina* can take on a different meaning. Indeed, it also refers to "secret,"[32] as the following verse indicates: "Juan García, my secret, I will tell you very quickly."[33]

In other verses,[34] from poem 384 of *Cancionero de Baena*, "Respuesta de Juan García contra Juan Alfonso" (Response of Juan García to Juan Alfonso [de Baena]),[35] eggplant is used describe the eyes of the converso Juan Alfonso de

---

27 "The 'Cancionero de Baena' was first published at Madrid in 1851 by Gayangos and Pidal, with an excellent introduction by the same; and then by Francisque Michel, Leipsic, 1852." http://www.jewishencyclopedia.com/articles/2324-baena-juan-alfonso-de.

28 http://catalogo.bne.es/uhtbin/cgisirsi/0/x/0/05?searchdata1=cancionero%20de%20baena{130}.

29 *Encyclopedia Universalis online*: https://www.universalis.fr/encyclopedie/cancioneros/2-aux-xve-et-xvie-siecles/.

30 http://www.jewishencyclopedia.com/articles/2324-baena-juan-alfonso-de.

31 De Baena, *El Cancionero*, fol. 142, no. 404, 457: "Señor, non manjedes manjar d'Adefyna / El qual gostaredes con grand amargueça. / Por el qual sabor avrés gren peresa/." See *Diccionario histórico (1933–1936)*: http://web.frl.es/DH1936_ARTÍCULOS/A_Cevilla_PDF/Tomo_I_0188.pdf. Translation by the author.

32 See ibid.

33 Francisque Michel, *El Cancionero de Juan Alfonso de Baena*, vol. 2 (Leipzig: ed. de Madrid de 1851, 1860), 98: "Johan Garçia, mi *adefyna* vos daré yo mucho çedo." Translation by the autor.

34 See Brian Dutton, *Brian Dutton Corpus*, fol. 137r, verses 1–5, [ID1509 R 1508]PN1-384(137r) (3x10): http://cancionerovirtual.liv.ac.uk/AnaServer?dutton+0+start.anv+sid=ID1509.

35 Translation by the author.

Baena, because to their black and shiny qualities. He is called "jos de berenjenas," or "eggplant eyes": "Well, you have Eggplant eyes."[36]

c. *La Copla a Pedro González*, in the *Cancionero del siglo XV*, by Rodrigo de Cota (fifteenth century)

In the *Cancionero del siglo XV*[37] (which is different from the *Cancionero de Baena*), there are satirical verses addressed to Pedro González and written by Rodrigo de Cota.[38] These verses refer to Jewish dishes included in Christian banquets, and particularly in the banquet of Diego Aria Dávila's grandson. Rodrigo de Cota—although himself a converso—describes the marriage between a young converted groom and a young Christian bride. Hilary Pomeroy[39] calls attention to the absence of pork and fish without scales. These foods are replaced by eggplant, vegetables, and meatballs—all of which are foods that are a defining feature of Muslim and Jewish cuisine. In his writing, Rodrigo de Cota himself stresses that the banquet is a converso's banquet, as he states that any guest who pronounces the name of Jesus will not be served meatballs:

> At the wedding of the *aljama*
> Nothing hairy was eaten
> Nor fish without scales
> But as soon as the bridegroom was able to
> Lots of eggplant
> And saffron with Swiss chard
> And whoever says "Jesus" during the meal
> Let him eat no *albondiguilla*.[40]

---

36 Uriel Macías, "Ojos de berenjenas, las mil y una recetas," in *La mesa puesta: leyes, costumbres y recetas judías. XVI curso de cultura hispanojudía y sefardí de la Universidad de Castilla-La Mancha: en memoria de Iacob M. Hassán*, ed. Uriel Macías and Ricardo Izquierdo Benito (Cuenca: Universidad de Castilla la Mancha [UCLM], 2010). Translation by the author.

37 The database of the Real Biblioteca of the Patrimonio Nacional provides details on this work: https://realbiblioteca.patrimonionacional.es/cgi-bin/koha/opac-detail.pl?biblionumber=53054; see also library of the Cervantes Institute, which contains a digital copy the original 1475 facsimile held at the British Library: http://www.cervantesvirtual.com/obra/cancionero-del-siglo-xv-.nuscrito--0/?_ga=2.159856189.1678425267.1551535304-1313901290.1493573473.

38 Freedman, *Why Food Matters*, 56.

39 Pomeroy, "Ojos de Berenjena."

40 Brian Dutton, *El cancionero del siglo XV* (MN15-23), c1360–1520, vol. VII. See MN15-23, verses 19-203: "En la boda del aljama / no se comi peliagudo / ni pescado sin escamo

The above verses demonstrate the importance of eggplant as well as meatballs as markers of Jewish culinary identity.[41] As in the poem *Libro de Buen amor* by Arcipreste de Hita, *adafina* is a recurring marker of Jewish culinary identity, like eggplants and meatballs. Even if *adafina* is not mentioned in the previous verses, Carlos Carrete Parrondo[42] writes that meatballs (*albondiguillas*) can be used as a substitute for *adafina* because—whole or cut—they are part of the dish. Hence, meatballs called *albondiguillas* could mean a replacement for *adafina*.[43] The *aljamas*[44] sheds light on the place of the banquet, which also indicates to the reader that the marriage is a Jewish one. An uninformed reader might not grasp the message that hides behind the verse that says that while fish without scales was not eaten, eggplant was consumed as soon as possible. Yet the verses clearly show the family's respect for the food laws of *Kashrut*. A critical view of society is also portrayed here. In fact, it is implied that Jews want to fool others by, whenever possible, eating foods they once enjoy, such as eggplant, Swiss chard, and *albondiguillas*. Once again, culinary practices reveal religious identity, and literature appears to be a subtler means than cookbooks for both conveying a message to an informed public and exposing social prejudice.

d. *Cancionero general*, Compiled by Hernando del Castillo (fifteenth to sixteenth centuries)

The poetry collection *Cancionero general*[45] was written in 1490. It was later compiled in Valencia in 1511 by Hernando del Castillo, which corresponds to the

/ en quantol marido pudo / sino mucha varagena / y açafran con açelguilla / quien Ihesu diga en la cena / que no coma albondiguilla": http://cancionerovirtual.liv.ac.uk/AnaServer?dutton+0+start.anv+ms=MN&sms=65&item=24&entry=ID2804. The term "peliagudo" refers to an animal with long and thin hair. Translation by the author.

41 Pomeroy believes that Muslims could also have eaten meatballs. See Pomeroy, "Ojos de Berenjena."

42 Carlos Carrete Parondo was a Hebraist historian. He is notably the author of the transcriptions of the trials of the Inquisition: *Fontes Iudaeorum Regni Castellae* (*FIRC*).

43 María Isabel Pérez Alonso, "La olla judía el Šabbat: estudio lexicológico y lexicográfico de adafina, ḥamín, caliente(s) y otras denominaciones," *Espacio, tiempo y forma, Historia medieval* 28 (2015): 453.

44 As mentioned previously, *aljamas* is an Arabic term used in Christian Spain to designate the Jewish quarter (and also sometimes the Muslim quarter).

45 See the BnF catalogue: https://data.bnf.fr/fr/16678478/cancionero_general/; See Charles-V. Aubrun, "Le 'Cancionero General' de 1511 et ses trente-huit romances," *Bulletin Hispanique* 86, nos. 1–2 (1984): 39–60.

date of the *princeps*[46] edition. The Cervantes Institute has produced a digitized facsimile of it.[47] *Cancionero general* includes various terms related to Judaism, such as "Talmud," "Torah," and *pueblo judaico*.[48] The word *adafina* is also mentioned when referring to the Shabbat dish. The following verses from *Cancionero general*, "Coplas del Conde de Paredes a Juan Poeta en una perdonança a Valencia," demonstrate this:

> Let us not forget the paten
> Which your mouth came to touch,
> And after kissing it,
> You transformed it, they say,
> Into an eggplant casserole.
> The consecrated altar
> made of hard and delicate stone
> when touched by your hand
> was instantly transformed
> into *ataifor* with *adafina*.[49]

---

46 In 1958, in Madrid, the Real Academia Española hosted a digitized reproduction of the facsimile edition of the *Cancionero general*. In 2002, a new facsimile version was produced with the agreement of the Real Academia Española, this time with a bibliographical introduction, index, and appendices by Antonio Rodríguez Moñino. See the Miguel de Cervantes Virtual Library, https://www.cervantesvirtual.com/obra/cancionero-general--0/. The work is preserved at the Biblioteca Nacional in Madrid and in the BnF in Paris. The site PhiloBiblon, at the University of California, Berkeley gives important details about the work from 1511 and later editions: https://pb.lib.berkeley.edu/xtf/servlet/org.cdlib.xtf.crossQuery.CrossQuery?rmode=philo&everyone=&creator=&title=Cancionero+general&incipit=&explicit=&assocname=&daterange=&placeofcomposition=&subject=&text-join=and&browseout=work&sort=moniker.

47 http://www.cervantesvirtual.com/obra-visor/cancionero-general--0/html/ff8b1982-82b1-11df-acc7-002185ce6064_488.html.

48 See fol. CCXXIIv and fol. CCXXIIIr: http://www.cervantesvirtual.com/obra-visor/cancionero-general--0/html/ff8b1982-82b1-11df-acc7-002185ce6064_462.html.

49 See digitized edition by CORE (COnnecting REpositories), which is an open access data service for research created by the Open University in the United Kingdom. This edition, in modern characters, was produced from the 1511 edition (with an appendix made up from the 1527, 1540, and 1557 editions); La sociedad de bibliofilos españoles, Madrid, num. 215, 1882, copla 969: "No dexemos la patena / á que la boca llegaste, / que luego que la besastes, / se dize que la tornastes / caçuela con verengena. / El ara que es consagrada / Y de piedra dura y fina / De vuestra mano tocada, / En un punto fue tornada / Ataifor con Adafina": https://core.ac.uk/download/pdf/71512832.pdf, 236. The digitized edition of the Real Academia on the website of the Cervantes Virtual Library contains the facsimile version in ancient Castilian characters: http://www.cervantesvirtual.com/obra-visor/cancionero-general--0/html/ff8b1982-82b1-11df-acc7-002185ce6064_462.html folio CCXXIIv. Translation by the author. See Freedman, *Why Food Matters*, 56.

This identifies and designates Juan Poeta as Jewish. Its aim is also to publicly expose Juan Poeta's ability to manipulate people and to "convert" a sacred Christian place (the altar) into an element of another culture, such as the *ataifor* and the *adafina*. Starting in 1495, Nebrija's dictionary describes an *ataifor* as Moorish round table (mesa redonda de moros). The Covarrubias dictionary (1611) states that an *aitafor* is a "flat dish used to serve roast meats."[50] The RAE[51] adds that *ataifor* is also a flat dish used for meats. It cites *Cancionero general*, and states that the poetry was written to call (*motejar*) Juan Poeta a Jew. An *ataifor* serving *adafina* suggest a Jewish and Muslim practice.[52]

The point of these verses is to demonize conversos behaviors. They reveal that the simple act of touching an object transforms what is sacred for Christians into a sign—or rather food—of Judaism, that is, eggplant casseroles and *adafina*.[53] The copla seeks to present Juan Poeta as a pernicious force against Christian orthodoxy. His eggplant-based and *adafina* food is directly connected with his religion. The criticism by Comte de Paredes as to the condition of the converso Juan Poeta appears in the words "kissed" (que la besastes) and "transformed"/"turned into" (*tornastes*)—that is, connected to religion. The aim of the author's words was to demonstrate the deceitfulness of Jews. Once again, food is the element used by Conde de Paredes to assert a false conversion.

In the article "The Habits of Judeo-conversos in Alcalá de Henares," Pilar Bravo Lledó argues that in the sixteenth century "it was the habit of Jews in Castile to prepare *adafina*, a stew [*guiso*] made of chickpeas and mutton and many vegetables, at night between Friday and Saturday, cooking it very slowly; and that they would eat it for Shabbat. The order in which to eat it was, first, the soup, then the meat, and finally the vegetables (which is very similar to our

---

50 Sebastián De Covarrubias and Martín De Riquer, eds., *Tesoro de la lengua castellana o española* (Madrid and Barcelona, 1943 [1611],): *Ataifor*: "plato hondo para servir las viandas guisadas."

51 According to the RAE, *ataifor*, from the Hispanic Arabic *aṭṭayfūr*, derived from the classical Arabic *ṭayfūr*, refers to a small, round table used by the Moors. It also refers to a flat dish for serving meat. Author's translation.

52 The modern Spanish dish, *cocido*, reflects the evolution and, especially, the alteration (since Jews had to add pork to hide their Jewish identity) of the Jewish *adafina* of the Middle Ages.

53 It is important to mention that the *Cancionero general*, in copla 994, also contains the following verses: "Trobar en nunca comer / de lo del rabí devedado / sino manjar trasnochado." The term *trasnochado* is used to describe a dish that has been left ["cooking'] the whole night. It is synonymous with *adafina*. See https://core.ac.uk/download/pdf/71512832.pdf.

pucheros and *cocidos*)."[54] According to Eleazar Gutworth,[55] "meatballs" and even *adafina* have nothing to do with religion. They are evidence of a culinary multiculturalism that has survived in both Jewish and Muslim food traditions. For Javier Castaño, *adafina* could be an Arab-Andalusian dish that Jews in al-Andalus ate during their Shabbat[56] meals. As Remie Constable states, "by the end of the fifteenth century, the Inquisition would look closely at food, not only as a marker of cultural and religious identity, but also for dangers of contact over shared dinner."[57]

C. Unmasked Jewishness

Both narratives—*The Provençal Esther Poem* and *La Lozana andaluza*—compare ways of identifying Jewishness, in this case with regard to women, in a context where religious belonging had to be marked. It is through modes of being and behavior that identification becomes possible. It is not spoken; rather, it is manifest through actions. More than simple compliance with formal religious food laws, belonging involves implicit knowledge, transmitted by gestures that express them. Eating in a certain way is not only a shield against idolatry; it is also a means of discovering God in creation. This raises the question of food as a means of being-in-the-world, just like the question of the relationship to purity.

The examples of Esther and Aldonza help clarify how interrogations were used during the Inquisition. Their stories show that the Inquisition sought out hidden practices. It constantly used the vocabulary of the mask in its attempt to recover buried recipes. The weight of crypto-Judaism remains to be ascertained, whether consciously or unconsciously, whether transmitted or reconstructed from scratch.

If we compare the period of conversions with the narratives about Esther or Aldonza, what is key is not only what is hidden, but also what is unsaid in the

---

54 Pilar Bravo Lledó, "*Las costumbres judeoconversas en Alcalá de Henares.*" Presentation for exhibition at the Museo Casa Natal de Cervantes of Alcalá de Henares in 2012, http://cl.ly/2b1T1D1s0V15: "Era costumbre entre los judíos de Castilla elaborar la "adafina," un guiso de garbanzos con carne de cordero y numerosas hortalizas, en la noche del viernes para el sábado, con una cocción muy lenta, y que se solía comer el Sabbat. La manera de tomarlo era, primero una sopa y después la carne y las verduras (muy similar a nuestros pucheros y cocidos)." Translation by the author.

55 Professor of Judaic-Hispanic history and culture at the University of Tel Aviv.

56 Elena Romero, "*El olor del sábado: la adafina, del Arcipreste de Hita a las versiones 'light'*" (Cuenca: Universidad de Castilla la Mancha, 2010): 215–240.

57 Constable, "Food and Meaning," 184.

recipes that never give proportions because in such matters actions must be connected to words.

a. *The Provençal Esther Poem,* by Crescas du Caylar (fourteenth century)

On the other side of the border, to the north of the Iberian Peninsula, under the rule of the Crown of Aragon, two texts were written and signed[58] by a Jewish doctor born in Narbonne: Crescas (the Provençal name for Israel) du Caylar (descendant of the Tribe of Levi, Caslari). He was forced to leave the royal land of France in 1306 for the neighboring kingdoms of Spain, Italy, Provence, and North Africa.[59] These two poems,[60] were written in Avignon in 1327. They recount the biblical story of Queen Esther, drawing on Talmudic[61] and Midrashic[62] sources, while parodying the text of the *Megillah*.[63] "Israel's retellings of the Purim story are expanded and heavily embellished with material

---

58 Only the final colophon of the manuscript in Hebrew contains the name of the author, Israel ben Joseph, and his city of residence, Avignon, even though he also specified that he also wrote the vernacular version that came before it. See Jaclyn Tzvia Piudik, "Hybridity in the Fourteenth-Century Esther Poems of Israel Caslari" (PhD diss., University of Toronto, 2014), 20. Translation by the author.

59 Susan L. Einbinder, *No Place of Rest: Jewish Literature, Expulsion, and the Memory of Medieval France* (Philadelphia: University of Pennsylvania Press, 2009), 84; Piudik, "Hybridity in the Fourteenth-Century Esther Poems of Israel Caslari," 22.

60 https://www.arlima.net/ad/crescas_du_caylar.html.

61 Sources that are present in the Talmud ("study" in Hebrew). According to the French *Dictionary Larousse*, the Talmud's Oral Law is the "main collection of commentary of the Torah (written law), of which it is both the legal interpretation (the Halaka) and the ethical and homiletical interpretation (the *Haggada*). The Talmud is made up of two pieces of writing: the Mishna and the *Gemara*." In the *Chumash*, the Talmud Yeroushalmi is the "Talmud conceived by Amoraïm d'Eretz Israël in the second, third and fourth century. Although it was called the Talmud of Jerusalem, it was composed in Galilee, since at this time Romans did not authorize Jews to live in Jerusalem." See Safra and Marciano, *Chumash*, 1372.

62 Sources present in the *midrash* which, according to the *Dictionary Larousse* is a "Rabbinic method of exegesis of the Bible which, beyond the literal meaning established in a certain moment in history, seeks a deeper meaning in the biblical writings." Safra and Marciano, *Chumash*, 1369: "Rabbinic literary genre, pieces chosen among the Halachic/Haggadic lessons of Tanaïm and Amoraïm, presented according to the verses of the Torah."

63 *Meguillah*: the scroll. This treaty is the tenth of the Moëd order. Its main subject is, as the name indicates, the reading of the Esther Poem (commonly called the *Meguillah*) during the celebration of Purim; In Safra and Marciano, *Chumash*, 1369, the *Meguillah* is the "Talmudic treaty that belongs to the Sefer Moed."

from Talmudic and apocryphal sources, medieval medicine and philosophy, and references to popular culture,"[64] writes Tzvia Piudik; and Neubauer adds:

> Caslari says, at the beginning of the poem in Hebrew, that he composed the poem in vernacular language for women and children, and then in Hebrew for those who were familiar with the language. Both texts, in Hebrew and in Provençal, are not direct translations. The substance differs only slightly, but the style of presentation is not the same at all. The Provençal poem has a simple and even vulgar presentation; the poem in Hebrew is more refined. The specific character of each of the two idioms, and the difference in the audience to which the poems are addressed, explain these nuances.[65]

These statements summarize the differences that exist between the two poems, including culinary differences, as only the one in Occitan, intended for women, contains the names of dishes.

The first version of the story is an incomplete poem, composed of 448 lines of verse, in vernacular Occitan, but written in Hebrew characters. We know of it today thanks to two manuscripts, one of which is kept in the library of the Jewish Theological Seminary in New York, catalogued under ms. Adler 2039 (f. 23v.–29r.), and the other in the Casatanense Library in Rome, listed in the Hebrew manuscripts, under Heb. 3140, f. 190rb.–192ra.[66] The poem is intended for Jews of Provence who didn't know Hebrew. There are a number of modern editions of the poem and translations into French.[67] It has also been the focus of a PhD dissertation by Susan Milner Silberstein. Published in 1973 and titled "The Provençal Esther Poem Written in Hebrew Characters,"[68] the dissertation examines the manuscript of the Jewish Theological Seminary in New York. The

---

64 Tzvia Piudik, "Hybridity in the Fourteenth-Century Esther Poems of Israel Caslari," ii.

65 Adolf Neubauer and Paul Meyer, "Le Roman provençal d'Esther par Crescas du Caylar, médecin juif du XIVe siècle," *Romania* 21, no. 82 (1892): 195, www.persee.fr/doc/roma_0035-8029_1892_num_21_82_5717.

66 Rome's Biblioteca Casanatense, catalogued as Heb. 3140, f. 190rb-192ra.

67 Nathan Weinstock, *Le 'Livre d'Esther' dans la tradition occitane judéo-comtadine* (Puylaurens: Institut d'Estudis Occitans, 2018). The work contains excerpts from the "Provençal Poem of Queen Esther" by Vidal Crescas du Caylar, and "Queen Esther" by Mardochée Astruc.

68 Susan Milner Silberstein, "The Provençal Esther Poem Written in Hebrew Characters c. 1327 by Crescas de Caylar: Critical Edition" (PhD diss., University of Pennsylvania, 1973) xxvii, 331.

title frequently used in French is *Le roman provençal d'Esther.* Several studies exist on the subject, as the Arlima[69] site indicates.

The second version is in Hebrew and was written in Hebrew characters. This text is composed of 960 lines of verse "in the form of a sacred poem, *Mi Kamokha* ("Who is like you") used as part of the liturgical cycle of *Shabbat Zakhor* ("*Shabbat* [of] remembrance") preceding the celebration of Purim."[70] In the complete version that is included in some manuscripts, there are prayer books (*mahzorim*) and poems that are recited on Shabbat days. This version is more sought after than the one in Occitan and was intended for those who had mastered the sacred dialect. Crescas even stipulates that it was intended for Jewish men.[71] Four manuscripts of the poem exist in Hebrew Union College library in Cincinnati,[72] the library of rare books and manuscripts at Columbia University in New York,[73] the Bodleian Library in Oxford,[74] and the British Library in London.[75] No medieval editions exist (as is the case for the Provençal poem), but there is a modern edition of the Hebrew version. It was created in 1853 in Salonica, titled *Iggeret haPurim,*[76] and was scanned by Virtual Judaica[77] and the

---

69 A fairly complete bibliography was put online by ARLIMA: https://www.arlima.net/ad/crescas_du_caylar.html. See Neubauer and Meyer, "Le Roman provençal d'Esther par Crescas du Caylar," www.persee.fr/doc/roma_0035-8029_1892_num_21_82_5717; Crescas du Caylar, "Roman de la Reine Esther." In *Nouvelles courtoises occitanes et françaises,* ed. Suzanne Méjean-Thiolier and Marie-Francoise Notz, (Paris: LgF, vol. 1, 1997; vol. 2, 2005; vol. 3, 2010), 124–157; P. Pansier, "Le roman d'Esther de Crescas du Cailar," *Annales d'Avignon et du Comtat Venaissin* 11 (1925): 5–18. It is also important to mention the existence of a poem about the Provençal tragedy ("La Tragediou") of Esther de Mardochée Astruc, printed in 1774 and reprinted in 1877 by Sabatier.

70 Tzvia Piudik, "Hybridity in the Fourteenth-Century Esther Poems of Israel Caslari," 32.

71 Ibid., 6: "This second is in the Hebrew for the Jewish men, the work of my hands, in which I glory. Keep silence and listen, Israel, on this very day." https://tspace.library.utoronto.ca/bitstream/1807/74812/1/Piudik_Jaclyn_T_201411_PhD_thesis.pdf.

72 Cincinnati, Hebrew Union College, MS 396, f. 19b-27b. Full version. This is the oldest of all the manuscripts, dated between 1447 and 1455, according to Einbinder, *No Place of Rest,* 85; It was supposedly written in Italy. See Tzvia Piudik, "Hybridity in the Fourteenth-Century Esther Poems of Israel Caslari," 32.

73 New York, Columbia University, Rare Book and Manuscript Library, MS X893 C-J55, vol. 31, f. 75a–87a.

74 Oxford, Bodleian Library, MS heb. e. 10, f. 48r-59r. Full version dating from 1402 and written in Provence.

75 London, British Library, Add. Heb. 19663, f. 21a-32a. Dating from the eighteenth century.

76 *Iggeret haPurim* of "Maestre Koskas," Salonika, 1853: https://www.arlima.net/ad/crescas_du_caylar.html.

77 https://www.virtualjudaica.com/Listing/Details/923587/Iggeret-haPurim-R-Israel-Crescas-de-Caylar-Salonika-1853.

British Library.[78] Finally, there is a dissertation about Crescas du Caylar's Esther poems. Defended in 2014 at the University of Toronto by Jaclyn Tzvia Piudik, the dissertation is titled "Hybridity in the Fourteenth-Century Esther Poems of Israel Caslari." It is available online.[79] Jaclyn Tzvia Piudik writes:

> The texts [by Crescas] are a tapestry of ancient religious legacy and medieval thought, woven from threads of Jewish tradition and secular learning, from medieval belletristic conventions, Midrashic literature and medical writings. This dissertation explores issues of biculturalism and religious identity through Israel's compositional strategies and his modifications to the biblical story. In fact, some of the most difficult questions, and perhaps the most poignant, that arise from the Esther narratives are those of cultural translation and its relationship to identity.[80]

It is not by accident that, of all the books in the Hebrew Bible, the one dedicated to Esther contains the most references to food. Indeed, "the three verses describing the festival of Ahasuerus in the *Megillah* are developed by Crescas in one hundred verses (vv. 63–162), which consist of a long list of dishes, seasoned with dietary comments worthy of a doctor."[81] The *Megillah* of Esther starts:

> This was during the time of Ahaseurus [519 BCE–465 CE] who ruled from Hodou [India] to Couch [Ethiopia], [in] 127 provinces. In those days, during the third year of his reign, King

78 http://explore.bl.uk/primo_library/libweb/action/display.do?tabs=moreTab&ct=display&fn=search&doc=BLL01014495971&indx=1&recIds=BLL01014495971&recIdxs=0&elementId=0&renderMode=poppedOut&displayMode=full&frbrVersion=&frbg=&&vl(488279563UI0)=any&dscnt=0&scp.scps=scope:(BLCONTENT)&tb=t&vid=BLVU1&mode=Basic&srt=rank&tab=local_tab&dum=true&vl(freeText0)=crescas%20de%20caylar&dstmp=1535060793914#, See ms. 1963 according to the BL: http://www.bl.uk/manuscripts/FullDisplay.aspx?ref=Add_MS_19663.

79 Tzvia Piudik, "Hybridity in the Fourteenth-Century Esther Poems of Israel Caslari," viii and 341.

80 Ibid., iii.

81 Bruno Laurioux, "Le festin d'Assuérus: femmes–et hommes–à table vers la fin du Moyen Âge," *Clio: Histoire, femmes et sociétés. Festin de femmes* 14 (2001): 50 n12: "[Neubauer and Meyer] recall other Jewish thinkers from Southern France who also wrote—this time in Hebrew—parodies of the book of Esther, which was the basis of the liturgy of the Jewish celebration of *Purim*." Translation by the author; for medical recommendations, see Neubauer and Meyer, "Le Roman provençal d'Esther par Crescas du Caylar," verse 150: "Aisi con medicina publica"; verse 152: "Per confortar lor estomac."

> Ahaseurus, established on his throne in Suse, the capital, gave a feast for all his princes and servants, the army of Persia and Media [northwest Iran], the nobles and governors of the provinces [united] in his presence, displaying the wealth of his royal splendor and the rare magnificence of his greatness, for many days, 124 days. The drinks [were served] in golden goblets—no two were alike; and the royal wine was abundant, worthy of the king's generosity.[82]

Next, details about other banquets are provided: "Then the king gave a great feast to all his princes and servants [in honor] of Esther,"[83] his new queen ("queen in place of Vashti.")[84] As Bruno Laurioux writes, these are "veritable instances of gastronomical bravery."[85] Esther neither revealed her [Jewish] origin nor her people, as Mordecai ordered her to do."[86] Queen Esther also organized a feast[87] lasting several days for the king of Persia, a feast to which she also invited the Vizier Hamán, who had just ordered the execution of all the Jews in the kingdom. A last feast with offerings was organized to celebrate the end of the threat against Jews in Persia (in the fourteenth day of the month of Adar).[88]

In the story of the *Megillah* of Esther,[89] three banquets are held. In the Provençal poem, the first organized festival (verses 153–154 mention the *neulas encanonadas*)[90] is the one that Ahasuerus gave to celebrate his third year of rule.[91] What is surprising is that, in the Hebrew version, which is addressed to educated Jewish men, there is nothing about this large feast in the poem's 960 lines of verse. The reason is perhaps found in the texts intended audience. It was women who, among their other duties, prepared food. Thus, cooking ideas could be found in the Occitan version, the one for women (who were also the cooks); the more elaborate version in Hebrew, intended for men, therefore had no reason to contain these kinds of details.

---

82 Safra and Marciano, *Chumash*, 1320.
83 Ibid., 1322.
84 Ibid.
85 Laurioux, "Le festin d'Assuérus," 50. Translation by the author.
86 Safra and Marciano, *Chumash*, 1322.
87 Ibid., 1324 and 1326.
88 Ibid., 1324 and 1328.
89 In the *Megillah*, the letter refers to the celebration of Purim, or the festival of "fate," for having conjured the macabre destiny that was supposed to seal the fate of the Mosaic people.
90 Hélène Jawhara Piñer, *Sephardi: Cooking the History: Recipes of the Jews of Spain and the Diaspora from the Thirteenth Century to Today* (Boston: Cherry Orchard Books, 2021).
91 Crescas du Caylar, "Roman de la Reine Esther," 129.

In the fourteenth century, the study of texts, in particular biblical texts, was the domain of men. Women were pushed into the background, in charge of household affairs. We can therefore assume that this was the reason why Crescas du Caylar created a "simplified" version in Occitan for women, and thus introduced elements related to food (which he must have considered to be outside men's interests). This suggests that the Provençal version gave women details about dishes and ingredients so that they could preparing this celebration food for Purim. Even today, cooking for Purim is exclusively done by women.[92]

In her dissertation, Jaclyn Tzvia Piudik writes:

> One of the most remarkable differences between the two versions—one which also illustrates these tendencies with great clarity—is Israel's insertion of the medical material in the Judeo-Provençal text. To be sure, Israel uses the vernacular text to display his literary acumen in his "native" language, but at the same time, it becomes a stage for his expertise as a rationalist physician. . . . Israel, we have seen, was prolific in his description of the foods at Ahasuerus' first banquet, offering his audience a luscious account of the dishes served, their ingredients and preparation as prescribed by the popular dietaries and *regimina sanitatis.* Yet the question that arises about this account from a linguistic perspective is why Israel restricted his medical additions to the vernacular text and chose not to include any of these into the Hebrew version. Indeed, in the parallel section of the Hebrew version, Israel's description of the victuals at the banquet is a mere two lines long, with only the slightest degree of specificity about the menu.[93]

Piudik recomposes the missing words of certain verses in Hebrew by consulting two manuscripts.[94] For instance, she proposes the following translation (the verse in Hebrew is cited below): "Ram and deer, roebuck, lamb / Fatted calves and stuffed swans / steeped in the blood of grapes [wine] he gave to all / some

---

92 Neubauer and Meyer, "Le Roman provençal d'Esther par Crescas du Caylar, médecin juif du XIVe siècle," *Romania* 21, no. 82 (1892): 194–227, verses 153–154; see also Claudine Vassas, *Esther. Le nom voilé* (Paris: CNRS Éditions, 2016).

93 Piudik, "Hybridity in the Fourteenth-Century Esther Poems of Israel Caslari," 185.

94 They are HUC MS. 396, fol. 20a, ll. 77–80) and Bodleian Library, MS. Heb. e. 10, fol. 48v, ll. 77–80.

from here, some from there." The translation of the word "swan" is surprising; I finally chose the word "goose" because it corresponds to the term *וברבורים* that is written. The commentary by Rabbi Saadia Gaon[95] (882–942, an exegete who translated, in particular, the Pentateuch into Arabic)[96] and that by Salomon Ibn Parhon[97] (a Andalusian Hebraic philologist of the twelfth century) about this term, as well as the culinary meaning of the verse, also supports my choice. *אבוסים* means "force-feed" or "fatten" and not "stuffed." Therefore, I would better translate *וברבורים אבוסים* with "forced-fed *geese*" (*barburim avusim*).[98] In this case, the poem refers to the Bible (Kings 5:3), where the list of provisions for the daily dishes of King Salomon is given:

איל וצבי ויחמור שור שה כבשים
עגלי מרבק **וברבורים** אבוסים
לכלם נתן ובדם ענב מתבוססים
אלה מזה ואלה מזה[99]

Of the 448 octosyllabic in the Occitan version of *The Provençal Esther Poem*, one quarter present an enlightening sequence of dishes. This shows the importance of food, both at a symbolic level in terms of the choice of dishes as well as in the ostentatious nature of the banquet. Food is portrayed as a tool that enabled Ahasuerus to establish his power over Suse and beyond. Among the dishes listed by the king of Persia in the Provençal version is *neulas encanoladas* (vv. 153–154).[100] Meyer compares the term *encanonadas* to "cigarettes."[101] For Claudine Vassas, it is a "cake whose pastry, similar to that of a waffle or a wafer, is rolled so as to form a large cylinder, swollen to the size of a 'canon.'"[102] In her study, the anthropologist considers the "*cigares* of Hamán"—associated with the preparation of the Purim celebrations—to be a culinary call-back (for the interrogated

---

95 Rabi Saadia Gaon (Rassag) and Nehemiah Aloni, eds., *Sefer Ha-Egron (hébreu: ספר האגרון Livre de la Collection)* (Jérusalem: Académie de la langue hébraïque, 1969), 200.

96 Safra and Marciano, *Chumash*, 1371.

97 Salomon ibn Parhon, *Maḥberet he-'Aroukh*, Farsbourg (Bratislava, 1844), 11. The characters are in the Rashi script.

98 *Sefarim* proposes "fattened poultry" as a translation: See http://www.sefarim.fr (Prophets), chap. 5, verse 3.

99 The word in Bold type is missing in the Bodleian MS.

100 https://www.persee.fr/doc/roma_0035-8029_1892_num_21_82_5717; Crescas du Caylar, "Roman de la Reine Esther," 134.

101 Neubauer and Meyer, "Le Roman provençal d'Esther par Crescas du Caylar," 194–227, verses 153–154; See Jawhara Piñer, *Sephardi*.

102 Vassas, *Esther*, 95–96.

women who are members of the Sephardic community in Toulouse, France).[103] Susan Einbinder translates neulas encanonadas by "hot wafers that were well rolled."[104] Nelly Labère proposes *orejas de Hamán* as a translation, without, unfortunately, providing a reference.[105] Today, *orejas de Hamán* still means fried pastries prepared by Sephardic Jews in Spain.

All of these considerations make it possible to establish a link between *neulas encanonadas* and a sweet made from thin layers of pastry: *hojuelas*. Moreover, the latter are part of the list of dishes cited by Aldonza in *La Lozana andaluza*. The *hojuelas, cigares of Hamán,* and the *orejas de Hamán,* as well as other rolled pastries, all use the same culinary technique of rolling, a common Jewish practice.[106]

In order to pursue the question of Jewish culinary features and dishes, it should be stressed that *salsa camelina*[107] (cameline sauce) is among the dishes of the feast described by Crescas. Yet, cameline sauce is also part of the Catalan cookbook, *The Book of Sent Soví,* which dates back to the fourteenth century, just like the poem. The recipe specifies that the preparation contains almond milk, chicken broth, ground chicken liver, sugar, pomegranate wine or red vinegar, cinnamon, ginger, clove, spices, nutmeg, and fat. The sauce is served with chicken and capon.[108] Why is a sauce that is described in a poem which parodies Jewish culinary practices and exposes dishes served during a Jewish holiday (Purim)[109] also present in the *Sent Soví*? Did Jews borrow it from the local repertoire? Despite the hypothesis that this sauce is an identity marker of the Jewish Catalan minority in the fourteenth century, it must still be mentioned that cameline sauce was also the most common sauce in the fourteenth-century Latin West. This indicates the complexity of the topic at hand.

As Jaclyn Tzvia Piudik writes, "We are what we speak."[110] Indeed, the dishes that Crescas du Caylar decided to mention as part of the Ahasuerus banquet are not devoid of meaning; quite to the contrary. They reveal the author's Jewish

---

103 Ibid., 107–108, 126.
104 Einbinder, *No Place of Rest*, 99.
105 Analysis borrowed from the work of Nelly Labère. I thank Bruno Laurioux for this information.
106 Jawhara Piñer, *Sephardi.*
107 Neubauer and Meyer, "Le Roman provençal d'Esther par Crescas du Caylar," verse 140.
108 Joan Santanach et al., *Llibre de Sent Soví* (Barcelona: Barcino, 2017), 187.
109 Purim: From the Hebrew term which means "Lots." "English Feast of Lots, a joyous Jewish festival commemorating the survival of Jews who, in the fifth century BCE, were marked for death by their Persian rulers. The story is related in the biblical Book of Esther." See Encyclopaedia Britannica, s.v. "Purim," accessed 10 April, 2022, https://www.britannnica.com/topic/Purim.
110 Piudik, "Hybridity in the Fourteenth-Century Esther Poems of Israel Caslari," 143.

identity, as information is included that only Jews could have been aware of, and this is accentuated by the technique of listing the many dishes. This narrative device is echoed in the one previously cited in *La Lozana andaluza*, when Jewish women set a trap for Aldonza by asking her if she knows of *hormigos* and how she makes them. In addition, the dishes described in *The Provençal Esther Poem* have some points in common with those in the *Sent Soví*. The *neulas encanonadas* recipe proves to be the most important dish in the sense that it has been passed down all the way to current Sephardic Jewish communities.

Overall, Esther and Aldonza raise questions about secrets and parody. It is worth mentioning that there are other texts, some of which are in Catalan, riddled with Hebrew terms, and written in Judeo-Spanish Hebraic characters that also use food as a parody. The play on meanings, in their literal or hidden sense, and humorous commentary go together with the meaning of the ingredients, the dishes, and the order of the meals, that could very well play in the same register, between citations and paratext. Even more than compliance with formal religious food laws, belonging involves implicit knowledge, transmitted by gestures that reveal it. Through these literary texts, we can see that "the secret is not only necessary for reasons of safety, but becomes an essential component of religious fervor itself." In this sense, the words of Nathan Wachtel take on their full meaning.[111] As we will see, this is true in narratives from the trials of the Inquisition.

b. *La Lozana andaluza* (sixteenth century)

Only one single copy is known of the *Retrato de La Lozana andaluza*, which is anonymous and has no typographic information. It is stored under the classification 66.G.30 in the Österreichische Nationalbibliothek in Vienna.[112] Printed in Venice between 1528 and 1530,[113] the first pages state that *Retrato de La Lozana andaluza* was "composed in 1524, thirty days from the month of June, in Rome."[114] In 1857, Pascual de Gayangos[115] attributed "the authorship to Francisco Delicado on the basis of the references contained in the prologue to

---

111 Wachtel, *Entre Moïse et Jésus*, 188.

112 Francisco Delicado, Folke Gernert, and Jacques Joset, eds., *La Lozana andaluza* (Madrid: Real Academia Española, 2013), 479.

113 Ibid., ix and 468.

114 Ibid., folio A3r., 11, 13.

115 Pascual De Gayangos, *Introducción a Libros de Caballería* (Madrid: Rivadeneyra, 1857).

Primaleón."[116] Carla Perugini interprets this as a double composition: the first would have been started in 1524 and then, in 1527, the text would have been revised following the Sack of Rome.[117]

It is important to describe, at least briefly, *Retrato de la Lozana*, given the importance of the relationship that exists between the text and the image.[118] The document, which is 19.5 × 14 cm, is composed of fifty-four sheets of paper in Gothic characters.[119] In the edition of the *Real Academia Española*, there is, in addition to the text of the *principes* edition, studies, notes, an index, a bibliography, and a "reproduction of all of the pages that contain engravings and other illustrations—like a little star or Solomon's knot—to which the text makes explicit reference."[120] This detail is important because of the ambiguity surrounding the probable Jewish identity of the author, Francisco Delicado (1485–1535). Indeed, Carla Perugini sees in this text a return to Judaism by the converso author.[121]

This work has been scanned a number of times and many editions exist, the latest of which is from 2019.[122] In 2003, the Cervantes Virtual Library produced a print version with references to the original folios.[123] In 2011, the same institution also put online work directed by Carla Perugini.[124] To be as comprehensive as possible, I base my analysis on the edition by Gernert and Joset in addition to the digital edition by Carla Perugini (2011). As for the journeys undertaken by Aldonza and its converso origin, the 2004 printed edition and Andrea Zinato's article[125] appear as reference texts.

---

116 Francisco Delicado and Carla Perugini, ed., *La Lozana andaluza* (Alicante: Biblioteca Virtual Miguel de Cervantes, 2011), address. Translation by the author. Original reproduction notes: digitized edition at http://www.cervantesvirtual.com/nd/ark:/59851/bmc2v330.

117 Ibid.; Delicado, Gernert, and Joset, *La Lozana andaluza*, ix.

118 The description provided by Gernet and Joset in the edition of the Real Academia Española is 4° (19.5 × 14 cm), A-M^4 N^2.

119 Francisco Delicado and Carla Perugini, eds., *La Lozana andaluza* (Sevilla: Fundación José Manuel Lara: Clásicos andaluces, 2004), xliv.

120 Delicado, Gernert, and Joset, *La Lozana andaluza*, 468. Translation by the author.

121 Claude Allaigre, "La Lozana Andaluza," *Bulletin hispanique* 12, no. 1 (2010): 41–60.

122 Francisco Delicado and Rocío Díaz Bravo, eds., *Retrato de la Loçana andaluza: Estudio y edición crítica* (Cambridge: MHRA, 2019).

123 Francisco Delicado, *La Lozana andaluza* (Alicante: Biblioteca Virtual Miguel de Cervantes, 2003 [Venice, 1528]). Digital edition based on Antonio Pérez Gómez (Valencia: Tipografía Moderna, 1950): http://www.cervantesvirtual.com/obra/la-lozana-andaluza--0/.

124 Delicado and Perugini, *La Lozana andaluza*.

125 Andrea Zinato, "'¿Y cuándo quiere Usted que partamos?': le mappe virtuali della Lozana Andaluza," *Estratta da quaderni di lingue e letterature* (2008): 179–194; idem, "El viaje de la Lozana andaluza entre Edad Media y Edad Moderna" (forthcoming). On *La Lozana andaluza* and Judaism, see also Francisco Márquez Villanueva, "El mundo converso de la 'Lozana

La Lozana andaluza tells the story of a young Andalusian prostitute from Córdoba (la señora Lozana fue natural compatriota de Séneca),[126] who also lived in Granada, Jerez de la Frontera, Carmona, and finally Seville.[127] She later left Spain[128] to live in Rome, prior to the sack of the city by Spanish troops under Emperor Charles Quint on May 6, 1527. From childhood to marriage, to her life as a prostitute, the story contains a multitude of characters: 125 according to the author.[129] In the end, Aldonza decides to end her life as a courtesan by settling on the island of Lipari.[130]

A number of references and allusions to the Jewish identity of the protagonist are scattered throughout the story.[131] At the beginning of book 9, Aldonza asks about the women around her. She asks Beatriz how long the group of women have been living there (in Rome). Beatriz responds: "Since the year the Inquisition began." Aldonza then asks her "if there are Jews here [in Rome]," and Beatriz answers that there are "Many, and they are our friends."[132]

Food is an omnipresent theme in *La Lozana andaluza.* The reader observes this, indirectly, at the very beginning of the work. Indeed, at first, food is revealed through the questions the women ask Aldonza. These concern her way

---

Andaluza,'" *Archivo Hispalense* 96, no. 291–293 (2013): 31–39; Ruth Pike, "The Conversos in La lozana andaluz," *Modern Language Notes* 84, no. 2 (1969): 30–48; Carolyn Wolfenzon, "La Lozana andaluza: judaísmo, sífilis, exilio y creación," *Hispanic Research Journal* 8, no. 2 (2007): 107–122. I would like to thank Professor Andrea Zinato (Verona University) for these references and for our conversation on this topic.

126 Delicado and Perugini, *La Lozana andaluza,* 15.

127 Delicado, Gernert, and Joset, *La Lozana andaluza,* 13–14; Zinato, "'¿Y cuándo quiere Usted que partamos?' Della Lozana Andaluza," 180.

128 On the Jewish diaspora, see Henry Méchoulan, ed., and Edgar Morin, intro., *Los judíos de España. Historia de una diáspora (1492–1992)* (Madrid: Editorial Trotta, 1992); Israël Salvator, "Les Marranes," *Revue des études juives* T I (118) (1959–60): 29–77; Paloma Díaz-Mas, "Entre el pasado y el futuro: La Cultura sefardí," *Insula* 647 (2000); Paloma Díaz-Mas, *Los Sefardíes. Historia, lengua y cultura* (Barcelona: Riopiedras, 1997).

129 Delicado and Bravo, *Retrato de la Loçana andaluza,* 191.

130 Delicado, Gernert, and Joset, *La Lozana andaluza,* ix.

131 Ibid, "Mamotreto VIII: Cómo torna la Lozana y pregunta," 35n4: "Refrán [las que las sabe las tañe] que se aplica tanto al talento culinario de Lozana como a la treta de Teresa para que la protagonista desvele su condición de conversa." Translation (by the author): "A proverb that applies both to the culinary talent of Lozana, as well as the cunning of Teresa, so that the protagonist reveals her Conversa identity."

132 Delicado, Gernert, and Joset, *La Lozana andaluza,* "Mamotreto IX: Una pregunta que hace la Lozana para se informar," 37: "Lozana: ¿Y cuánto ha que estáis aquí?; Beatriz: Señora mía, desde el año que se puso la inquisición; Lozana: Decime, señoras mías, ¿hay aquí judíos?; Beatriz: Munchos, y amigos nuestros." Translation by the author.

of preparing dishes.[133] There is no doubt about her Andalusian Jewish identity. Knowing whether Aldonza is Jewish or not is essential for the crypto-Jewish women speaking with her. The question of her Jewishness is thus raised at the very beginning of the book when Beatriz says, "I want to know of her [Aldonza] only if she is a converted Jew [*confesa*], because we would speak with no fear."[134] Following Aldonza's replies, the woman exclaims: "She is one of us!"[135] Nonetheless, the women are wary, and in order to dispel any suspicion they set a trap, proposing that Aldonza prepare *hormigos* or make couscous. Aldonza's cooking thus reveals her religious identity. The act is more powerful than words. Beatriz says: "Let's tell [her] that we want to twist [*torcer*] *hormigos* or make couscous and, if she knows how to twist them, this way we will see that she is one of us, and [we will see] if she twists [*tuerce*] with water or oil."[136]

Gernert and Joset specify that "preparing *hormigos* with oil was a recipe of Jews or *conversa*."[137] Perugini defines the dish as a "fried pastry, with honey and breadcrumbs, in the shape of a roll."[138] Thus, skeptical or not, Aldonza answers Teresa's proposition to prepare *hormigos*. The protagonist tells her that with a handful of flour and oil they can fill up an entire basin (*almofía*). When Beatriz finally receives the answer to her questions, her reaction is enthusiastic. As though experiencing a revelation, she cries, "She is one of us !"[139] This response—expected and heard by the others—demonstrates the Jewishness of the Cordovan, as well as the women questioning her.

Food emerges as the most important sign of the protagonist's Jewish identity for the women around her. Yet Aldonza has not said or revealed anything. Her culinary knowledge and cooking techniques have done it for her. These are

---

133 Ibid., *La Lozana andaluza*, "Mamotreto VIII: Cómo torna la Lozana y pregunta;" ibid. "Mamotreto VII: Cómo vienen las parientas y les dice la Sevillana," 33–34; http://www.cervantesvirtual.com/nd/ark:/59851/bmc2v330, 43n221-224.

134 Delicado, Gernert, and Joset, *La Lozana andaluza*, 33; http://www.cervantesvirtual.com/nd/ark:/59851/bmc2v330, 43, 43n221. Translation by the author.

135 Delicado, Gernert, and Joset, *La Lozana andaluza*: "[. . .] es *de nostris !*" 35; http://www.cervantesvirtual.com/nd/ark:/59851/bmc2v330, 45. Translation by the author.

136 Delicado, Gernert, and Joset, *La Lozana andaluza*, 34: "Digamos que queremos torcer hormigos o hacer alcuzcuzú y, si los sabe torcer, ahí veremos si es de nobis, y si los tuerce con agua o con aceite." Translation by the author; http://www.cervantesvirtual.com/nd/ark:/59851/bmc2v330, 43 and 43n221-224.

137 Delicado, Gernert, and Joset, *La Lozana andaluza*, 33n30: "Preparar los hormigos con aceite era receta judía o conversa." Translation by the author.

138 http://www.cervantesvirtual.com/nd/ark:/59851/bmc2v330, 43 and 43n222: "Dulce de fruta, miel y pan rallado, hecho en forma de rollo."

139 Delicado, Gernert, and Joset, *La Lozana andaluza*, 35: "es *de nostris!*"; http://www.cervantesvirtual.com/nd/ark:/59851/bmc2v330, 45. Translation by the author.

decisive for recognizing her Jewish religious identity, especially in a social context where, against the backdrop of obvious antisemitism, any practices linked to Judaism were scrutinized. This happens in parallel with Aldonza's knowledge and preparation of these dishes.

In addition to the *inquisitio* promptly conducted by the conversa women, there is also the scene in book 2 in which Aldonza names for her aunt, with whom she is living because she is an orphan, all the dishes she knows how to make. The many dishes she lists are preparations that her grandmother taught her. It is an enlightening list, and includes dishes and ingredients (*hormigos, nuegados,* eggplants, salted fish stew, etc.) cited in the narratives of the trials of the Spanish Inquisition nearly a century before, as well as, according to some,[140] in Mexican texts.[141] Her grandmother passed on to her the art of cooking and, thanks to her, Aldonza explains that she learned how to "make *fideos* [thin pasta/vermicelli], small stuffed pasties [*empanadillas*], couscous with chickpeas [alcuzcuzú con garbanzos] [...] and round meatballs made with green cilantro [albondiguillas redondas y apretadas con culantro verde]."[142] She praises the cooking talents of her grandmother, renowned in all of Andalusia, and adds that she also knows how to prepare

> *hojuelas, pestiños, rosquillas de alfaxor, testones* of hempseed [*cañamones*] and sesame [*ajonjolí*], *nuégados* [small cakes], *xopaipas* [pastry disks pan-fried in oil], puff pastry [*hojaldres*], *hormigos torcidos* in oil [hormigos torcidos con aceite], *talvinas, zahínas* and turnips without lard and with cumin [nabos sin tocino y con comino], Murcia cabbage with caraway [col murciana con alcaravea], and the resting pot [*olla reposada*], a more delicious one no man has ever tasted. And the *boronía* . . ., and eggplant casserole *mojíes* [cazuela de berenjenas mojí], [and] . . . stew of salted, dried fish [cazuelas de pescado cecial].[143]

---

140 Jawhara Piñer, *Sephardi.*

141 *Ruy Díaz Nieto was a Jew from the sixteenth century. Originally from Porto (Portugal), he was a great connoisseur of Judaism. He travelled in Italy and settled in the city of Ferrara before migrating to Mexico. A trial in which he was sentenced specifies that for Shabbat he ate a fish stew made with chickpeas, eggs, salted fish, fresh fish, and tuna.*

142 Francisco Delicado, *La Lozana andaluza* (Venice, 1528): "[A]prendió de su abuela el arte de guisar y en su poder deprendió a hacer fideos, empanadillas, alcuzcuzú con garbanzos [...] albondiguillas redondas y apretadas con culantro verde," http://www.cervantesvirtual.com/obra/la-lozana-andaluza--0/. Translation by the author.

143 Ibid.: "hojuelas, pestiños, rosquillas de alfaxor, testones de cañamones y ajonjolí, nabos sin tocino y con comino, olla reposada, cazuela de berenjenas, cazuelas de pescado cecial, cabrito apedreado con limón ceutí, pecho de carnero." Translation by the author.

Let's focus on some of the names of these dishes, and in particular the *hojuela*. *Hojuela*[144] is a term that was already present in Nebrija's dictionary in 1495,[145] as well as in the *Diccionario de Autoridades* (book 4, 1734), where it is defined as "a pan-fried pastry [una fruta de sartén], very long [*muy extendida*] and thin [*fina*]."[146] It is not until 1803 that the term *pestiños*—or *prestiños*—was recognized by the RAE in the *Diccionario de la lengua española*. There, it is described as a "pan-fried pastry [una fruta de sartén] in small pieces of dough [*masa*] made of flour [*harina*] and beaten eggs [*huevos batidos*], which once fried in oil [*en aceite*] are soaked in honey."[147] These two pastries are still prepared in Andalusia today. *Hojuelas* are thin strips of narrow, long dough that are rolled up and then fried. *Pestiños* are still made today in the same way: small pieces of dough that are fried in oil and then soaked in honey. This dish has been passed down, unchanged, since the sixteenth century.

These fried pastries are prepared for the Jewish celebration of *Purim* and for the Christian Holy Week. As for *xopaipas*, the current spelling of which is *sopaipas*, these are, according to the RAE, "bigger *hojuelas*" [*hojuelas* gruesas].[148] This term can be found in the *Diccionario de autoridades* in 1739 (book 6). For Gernert and Joset, in *La Lozana andaluza*, *sopaipas* are "pancakes [*tortas*] that are fried in a pan [en la sartén]."[149] As concerns the "*hormigos*, *talvinas* and *zahínas*," Gernert and Joset specify in a note that these dishes "are included in the category of purees [*gachas*] in Arab and Jewish cooking, just like "turnips without lard" [nabos sin tocino] which refer to the same Semitic origin."[150] The term *talavina* is included in Antonio de Nebrija's dictionary from 1495 and later in 1739 (book 6) in the *Diccionario de autoridades*. The inverted dictionary of the RAE (DIRAE) lists it with the same meaning as *atalavina*, a term that only appears in 1611 in the *Tesoro de la lengua castellana o española* by Sebastián de Covarrubias and then in 1726 (book 1) in the *Diccionario de autoridades*. *Talavina* and *atalavina* are defined there as a "puree made of almond milk."[151] The RAE proposes four definitions of the term *hormigo*. While the first is "a puree generally made of

---

144 In the final chapters, I dedicate a section to the *hojuela*.

145 "hojuela de massa tendida .laganum: http://www.rae.es/sites/default/files/Archivos_de_la_BCRAE_Vocabulario_espnaol-latino_Nebrija.pdf.

146 https://dirae.es/palabras/hojuela. Translation by the author.

147 Ibid. Translation by the author.

148 Ibid. Translation by the author.

149 Delicado, Gernert, and Joset, *La Lozana andaluza*, 15n10. Translation by the author.

150 Ibid., 15n11. Translation by the author.

151 See https://dirae.es/palabras/atalvina: *Talvina* comes from Hispanic Arabic: a*ttalbína*, which comes from classic Arabic *talbīnah:* "Gachas que se hacen con leche de almendras." Translation by the author.

maize flour" (keep in mind that maize was only consumed after the discovery of America), the third is the most interesting. It is a "dessert [plato de repostería], typically made of breadcrumbs [*pan rallado*], grilled and chopped almonds and hazelnuts, and honey."[152] *Hormigos* is a dish mentioned in the trials of the Inquisition, and eating it attests to the victim's Jewish identity.[153] Finally, the term *zahína* from the Hispanic-Arabic *saḫína* and the classic Arabic *saḫīnah* is used in Andalusia to refers to a purée of flour that does not thicken.[154] As concerns *olla reposada,* it obviously refers to the *olla* of the *adafina* for Shabbat, which remains on embers the whole night. The importance of eating eggplant, in *boranía,* in a casserole, but also as a confit, as the rest of the listed dishes documents, illustrates its predominant role in Jewish food since the Middle Ages and the transmission of different ways of preparing it. As I've previously remarked, connecting eggplant with Jewish culinary practices is not an isolated case in the literature. It continued at least until nineteenth-century Italy.[155]

In *La Lozana Andaluza,* it is through ways of being and behaving that identification occurs. Nothing is said; actions reveal identity.

---

152 https://dle.rae.es/?id=KeqHrCZ. Translation by the author.

153 *Hormigos* in the inquisition trial of Sigüenza in 1501. See Carrete Parrondo and Fraile Conde, *Fontes Iudaeorum Regni Castellae*, vol. 4, *Los judeoconversos de Almazán 1501–1505. Origen familiar de los Laínez* (Salamanca: Universidad Pontífica de Salamanca, Universidad de Granada, 1987), 26.

154 https://dle.rae.es/?id=cHiVhn9.

155 See Artusi, *La Scienza in Cucina e l'Arte di Mangiar Bene*, 222.

CHAPTER 7

Trends and Evidence: Food as an Identity Marker

The fifteenth century ushered in a new era on the Iberian Peninsula—an era marked by a profusion of cookbooks. It was also marked by Catholic rule, which altered the culinary fabric that existed at the time and replaced it with a single uniform culinary model. Food is one of the bedrocks that allows for the development of identities; and identity at the beginning of the fifteenth century on the Iberian Peninsula was meant to be singular. Attacks on Jews had already taken place (e.g. the pogrom of June 4, 1391 in Seville)[1] and the Inquisition, under the Catholic Kings, began in 1478.[2] It was in this context that a new cuisine took root in Spain, and it swept away the multiplicity of cuisines eaten on the peninsular at the time.

This development can be analyzed looking at three ingredients: cilantro (as opposed to parsley), eggplant, and pork. Because of their common presence (or absence) in cookbooks, their relationship to religion, and the meaning non-Jews gave them, these three ingredients are highly revealing of the changes in cuisine on the Iberian Peninsula of the fifteenth to seventeenth centuries. Beyond simple nourishment, the food we eat—or do not eat—symbolizes who we are. The saying "Tell me what you eat and I will tell you what you are"[3] could not

---

1 See https://www.herodote.net/6_juin_1391-evenement-13910606.php. http://www.akadem.org/medias/documents/1-massacres-1391.pdf; https://journals.openedition.org/atalaya/1240; Philippe Wolff, "The 1391 Pogrom in Spain. Social Crisis or Not?" *Past & Present* 50 (1971): 4–18.

2 Béatrice Pérez, "Aux premiers temps de l'Inquisition: une institution dans la genèse d'un État moderne," in *Aux premiers temps de l'inquisition espagnole (1478–1561)*, ed. Raphaël Carrasco (Montpellier: P. U de la Méditerranée, 2002).

3 Jean Anthelme Brillat-Savarin, *The Physiology of Taste or, Meditations on Transcendental Gastronomy*, ed. and trans. M. F. K Fisher (New York: Vintage Books, 2011), 15. For the French edition, see Jean Anthelme Brillat-Savarin, *Physiologie du goût ou Méditations de gastronomie transcendante*, vol. 1 (Paris: Sautelet, 1826).

be better suited for identifying Jews in Spain in the fifteenth century. In this culinary history, spanning more than three hundred years, three trends and pieces of evidence emerge when it comes to detecting foods that mark Jewish identity practices.

A. Coriander: A Herb Felled by Parsley

Among all the aromatic herbs in Arabic cookbooks, cilantro, *Coriandrum sativum* L.[4] (fresh or dried) is predominant. Expiración García Sánchez classifies cilantro among the herbs that "arrived on the Iberian Peninsula, starting in the Neolithic period and until Roman *Hispania*."[5] Cilantro—the importance of which to the al-Andalus economy is emphasized by E. García Sánchez[6]—and parsley (*Petroselinum crispum* L., or *perejil* in Spanish) expanded the range of aromatic herbs that existed in the area.

Let's focus for a moment on the inclusion of cilantro in old recipe collections from the Iberian Peninsula, such as the *Kitāb al-ṭabīḫ*, the *Fuḍālat al-ḫiwān*, and the *Sent Soví*. The two Arabic cookbooks, the *Kitāb al-ṭabīḫ* and the *Fuḍālat al-ḫiwān*, are organized in the same way, and the *Sent Soví* is in many ways similar. Like most cookbooks of the Middle Ages, these three collections do not give a list of ingredients before cooking instructions. Yet the similarities between the recipe collections written in Arabic and the *Sent Soví* seem to be merely ones of form; the latter's content is very different. The example of cilantro confirms this profound difference. Fresh or dried, cilantro is present in 60% of the 462 recipes in the *Kitāb al-ṭabīḫ*, while parsley is completely absent. In the *Fuḍālat al-ḫiwān*, it is stated that Christians call parsley *būšīn*.[7] This suggests the importance of parsley for Christians, while simultaneously inviting us to consider parsley as *the* distinguishing food within Andalusian communities. In the *Sent Soví*, by contrast, cilantro is only used in a single recipe (1% of the collection), whereas parsley is part of nearly one-quarter of the cookbook (seventeen out of seventy-two

---

4 It is important to specify that the cilantro included in the *Kitāb al-ṭabīḫ* and *Fuḍālat al-ḫiwān* cookbooks—*Coriandrum sativum* L.—is different from the cilantro in *Libro del arte de cocina* by Maceras (1753).

5 Expiración García-Sánchez, Julia María Carabaza Bravo, and J. Esteban Hernández Bermejo, *Flora agrícola y forestal de al-Andalus*, vol. 1, *Monocotiledóneas: cereales, bulbosas y palmeras* (Madrid: Escuelas de Estudios árabes [CSIC Granada], 2012), 20. Translation by the author.

6 Ibid., 24.

7 Ibn Razīn al-Tuğībī and Marín, *Relieves de las mesas acerca de las delicias de la comida y los diferentes platos*, 147, no. 9: ". . . después se cogen cilantro y perejil (que en la lengua de los cristianos se llama *būšīn*)."

recipes).[8] To say that cilantro was a Jewish and Muslim food while parsley was Christian in the thirteenth to fourteenth centuries is undoubtedly not far from the truth.

The question remains, though, as to whether the use of cilantro was perceived as a sign of Jewish or Muslim identity . Was it included among the foods that were banned by Christians? In order to address this question, remember that can be a form of exchange between cultures (in this case, between Muslims and Jews) that does not make the ruling culture feel threatened. Generally speaking, this is what happened in the *Dar al Islām*, as Jews and Muslims shared a certain number of food precepts. If cilantro is often called for by the Arabic-language recipe collections of the *Dār al-Islām*, this is not the case for later cookbooks that were written under Christian rule (in this sense, the *Sent Soví* paved the way).

The use of cilantro in cooking existed before the thirteenth century and was not unique to Jews or Muslims, as it was consumed in antiquity, even if only in small quantities. For example, in the collection of recipes attributed to Apicius, *De re coquinaria*—which contains 468 recipes in a text which seems to have been completed between the end of antiquity and the high Middle Ages—only 20% of preparations use cilantro. Even if this share is low compared to the use of the herb in Andalusian cookbooks, the recipes of Apicius show that it was eaten hundreds of years before the *Kitāb al-ṭabīẖ*. How can this drastic culinary change be explained, if we take into consideration that the cookbooks written under Christian rule are only separated from Iberian Arabic cookbooks by one hundred years (in the case of the *Sent Soví*)? Was there a desire to change the culinary habits of ethnic groups that the ruling power wanted to eliminate? Whatever the case, there are no cookbooks written in Christian territory before the fourteenth-century *Sent Soví*. It is impossible, then, to know whether cilantro was consumed.

Parsley was not a common ingredient in Eastern cookbooks either. As a result, it was consumed by the Islamic elite in neither the east nor in the Muslim West of al-Andalus. However, the case is entirely different with the *Sent Soví*, which was written under Christian rule a century after the *Fuḍālat al-ẖiwān*. In short, there is only one dish made with cilantro[9]—namely 1.38% of all recipes—whereas dishes containing parsley make up one-quarter of the cookbook.[10]

---

8 R. A. Banegas López, "Una anàlisi dels productes i les tècniques de cuina al Llibre de Sent Soví," in *Llibre de Sent Soví*, ed. Joan Santanach et al. (Barcelona: Barcino, 2017), 143.

9 On the other hand, cilantro is used in large quantities in Italian cookbooks.

10 Santanach et al., *Llibre de Sent Soví*, 143.

In the fifteenth century, this change took root and spread. The statistical analyses[11] summarized in the following graph compare the proportions of dishes using cilantro and parsley in three cookbooks from the sixteenth century: *Libro de cozina* by R. de Nola, book six of the *El Regalo de la vida humana* by J. Vallès, and the cookbook of the Infanta Maria of Portugal. The first two collections contain more recipes using parsley than cilantro. The opposite is true for the cookbook of the Infanta Maria of Portugal.[12]

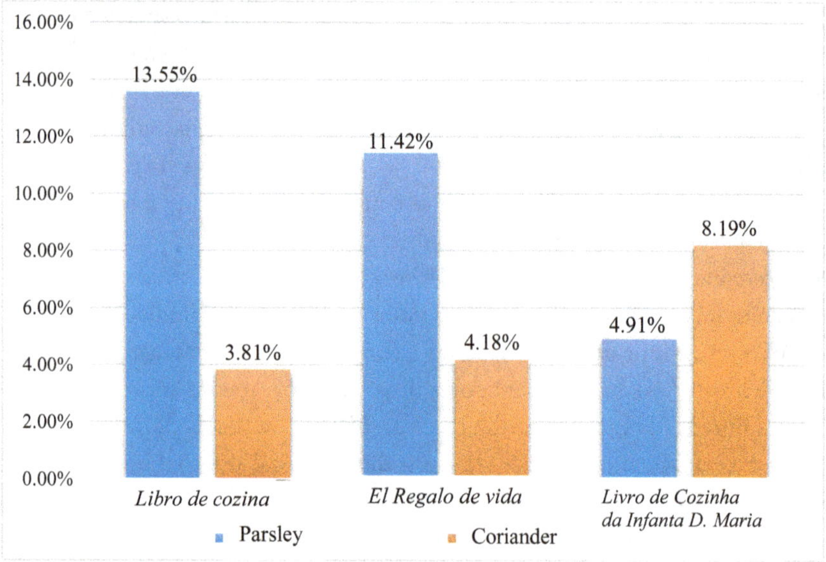

Figure 10. Proportion of dishes using cilantro and parsley in three Iberian cookbooks of the sixteenth century

Let's take as an example the "Moorish Chicken Recipe"[13] from the cookbook of the Infanta Maria of Portugal. Is it the use of mint that makes this dish "Moorish"? Given the information available in cookbooks before the thirteenth to fourteenth centuries from the Iberian Peninsula—the *Kitāb al-ṭabīẖ* and the

11 In *Libro de cozina*, nine recipes out of 236 contain cilantro and thirty-two parsley. Out of the 359 recipes of book 6 of *El Regalo de la vida humana*, 4.18% contain cilantro versus 11.42% for parsley. The *Cookbook of the Infanta Maria of Portugal* has five recipes with cilantro, namely 8.19% of the total cookbook (14.7%, if we don't count fruit jams and cakes), and three recipes with parsley, that is, 4.91% of the total (8.82%, if we don't fruit jams and cakes).

12 My calculations differ from those proposed by Maria José Palla in Maria De Portugal and Maria José Palla, eds. and trans., *Livre de cuisine de l'Infante Maria du Portugal* (Lisbon: Instituto de Estudos Medevais, 2008), 26. To make these calculations, I counted a single use of the ingredient, even if it appears several times in the same recipe.

13 De Portugal and Palla, *Livre de cuisine de l'Infante Maria du Portugal*, recipe no. 2.21, 50.

Fuḍālat al-ḫiwān—I think it's the cilantro that makes this dish appear "Moorish." The preparation consists of chicken fat cut into pieces and placed in a pot with cilantro, parsley, mint, and onion. The book emphasizes the inclusion of "a large quantity of cilantro, parsley and mint and that the parsley is used less than the other herbs."[14] In the "Moorish Chicken"[15] recipe, once again, cilantro is the main herb, acting as an identity marker; in any case, much more so than mint.

In *Libro del arte de cocina* by Maceras[16] (seventeenth century), there are no recipes using cilantro, whereas parsley is used in thirty-seven recipes out of a total of 180, namely 20% of the cookbook. This book proves the end of the use of cilantro on the Iberian Peninsula; parsley takes over at the end of the seventeenth century. The table below offers an idea of the consumption of certain foods—their frequency or absence in recipes and/or the degree to which they mark an identity.

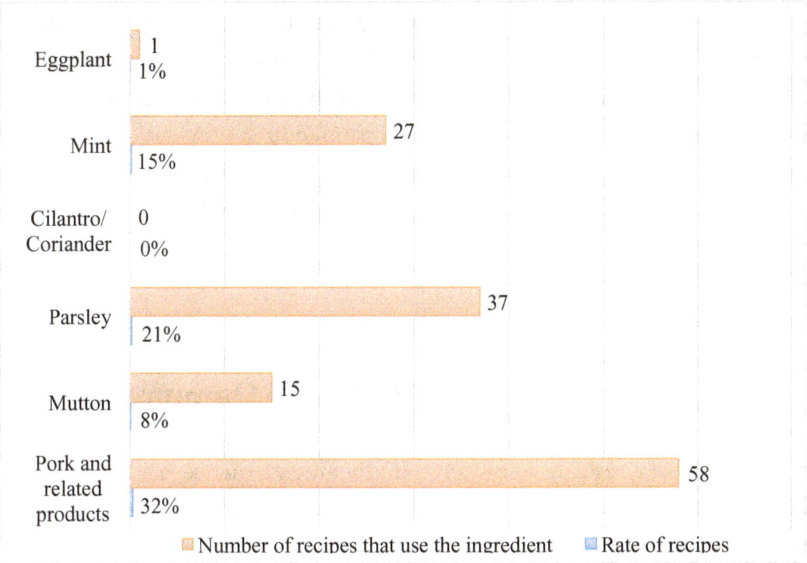

Figure 11. Percentage of recipes including certain foods in *Libro del arte de cocina* by Maceras

Let's focus briefly on three manuscripts written between the sixteenth and seventeenth centuries in Spain,[17] titled *Livro de receptas de pivetes,*[18] *Receptas*

14 Ibid.

15 Ibid., recipe no. 2.03, 38.

16 Pérez Sámper, *La alimentación en la España del Siglo de Oro.*

17 I consulted the Master's thesis of Marianne Saïe, "Étude des manuscrits 1462, 2019 et 6058 de la Bibliothèque Nationale d'Espagne. Une approche de la cuisine espagnole au début de l'époque moderne" (Master's thesis, Université de la Sorbonne IV, 2007), supervised by of Alain Tallon.

18 *Livro de receptas de pivetes, pastilhas e luvas perfumadas y conservas.* (This manuscript is from the sixteenth century. It is stored in the Biblioteca Nacional of Madrid, ms. 1462.

experimentadas para diversas cosas,[19] and *(Libro) en que se allaran facilme [n] te todas receptas y memorias.*[20] The first cookbook—containing fifteen recipes—does not include any cilantro. The other two only include the herb three times each, out of 155 and 157 recipes respectively. Parsley is used even less often. The first manuscript does not mention it at all and the others only have one recipe each that use it. This analysis will be developed. Indeed, the three manuscripts only contain a few food recipes, and are instead filled with preparations for soap, perfume, body and bust care, hair, and so on.

In conclusion, we cannot confirm that the consumption of cilantro was slowly eliminated in favor of parsley, which was used in abundance in cookbooks after the fourteenth century. This change seems to have taken place very quickly, in reaction to what cilantro represented. Cilantro appears to have been a marker of "Arabic" cuisine. Moreover, the introduction of lard in so-called "Moorish" recipes seems to illustrate the necessity and the desire to adapt—transform even—Arab Andalusian culinary practices. The aim was to integrate Arab food into Christian food and customs. However, Christians continued to consume "Moorish" dishes, even though their beliefs banned such preparations. *Libro de cozina* provides, for instance, two recipes that are "Moorish" (*Morisco*):[21] one uses squash and the other eggplant. "Moorish" recipes are not lacking in modern European cuisine, though. Undoubtedly, in this case, it is more a question of stereotypes than real influences.[22]

B. Pork and Religion: From Absence to Omnipresence

The recurrence of questions about food in documents that reveal the relationships between Jews and Christians in the Middle Ages (and particularly those relating to butchery) demonstrates Iberian Jews were concerned about their diet. The Hebrew *responsa* of Salomon ben Adret—the head of the Jewish community of Barcelona in the second half of the thirteenth century—and

19 This manuscript dates from 1620. It is stored at the Biblioteca Nacional in Madrid—ms. 2019.

20 "(Libro) en que se allaran facilme[n]te todas receptas y memorias . . . ansi para guisados, confituras, olores, aguas, afeites, adobos, de gua[n]tes, inguentos, medicinas para muchas enfermedades (titre complet)." This manuscript dates from the end of the seventeenth century, maybe 1679. It is stored at the Biblioteca Nacional in Madrid—ms. 6058.

21 De Nola and Peyrebonne, *Le livre de cuisine*, 82–83, nos. 52 and 55,

22 Joseph Pérez, *Andalousie. Vérités et légendes* (Paris: Tallandier, 2018), 32–45; Martinez-Gros and Makariou, *Histoire de Grenade*, 279–328.

documents related to food practices kept in the Aragonese chancellery registers in the archives of the Crown of Aragon (Barcelona) bear witness to this.[23]

The cuisine in the two Arabic cookbooks written under Muslim rule is primarily identifiable by the total absence of pork (meat, lard, etc.). Paul Freedman writes, "Faith teachings often proscribe certain foods such as pork, or onions, but exalt other foods and rituals as holy."[24] The *Sent Soví* cookbook, which was written in Catalan under Christian rule, breaks with the cuisine of the *Kitāb al-ṭabīẖ* and *Fuḍālat al-ẖiwān*, as a large number of recipes in these books contain pork fat.. Out of the seventy-two core recipes in the *Sent Soví*,[25] only six contain pork meat (including piglet, boar, etc.). The consumption of meat from the pig family was severely limited.[26] But pig fat is used in eighteen recipes and lard is included in two. Pork and related products, then are in twenty-six out of seventy-two recipes, that is, 36% of the cookbook. Further analysis reveals that the percentage is actually higher if one considers the fact that out of eleven very sweet recipes (pastries—two; desserts—four; sweets—five), only two contain pork fat or fat (theoretically from pork). These dishes are called *resoles* and *bunyols* (composed of eggs and grated cheese). Taking these into account we see that nearly 40% of the mainly savory dishes in the *Sent Soví* use pork (sixty-one dishes).

This Catalonian cookbook contains recipes (by stipulating pork, which Jews and Muslims are not allowed to eat) that are very different from those in the *Kitāb al-ṭabīẖ* and the *Fuḍālat al-ẖiwān*. The *Sent Soví* is from of an era and territory that was ruled by Christians. On the Iberian Peninsula, it appears to be the precursor of the *haute cuisine* of Western Christian Europe.[27]

If there is one food in the current culinary heritage of Spain which breaks with the practices of thirteenth-century al-Andalus, it is pork. Human societies are not necessarily black and white, and the prohibition on eating a given food—in this case, pig—must always be contextualized. Al-Andalus and the Iberian Peninsula in the Middle Ages were clearly very different from the Siècle d'or (*Siglo de oro* in Spanish) and Christian Renaissance periods. But an important fact must be taken consideration: the history of Muslim Spain is entirely medieval (711–1492). Neglecting this detail would result in a meaningless conclusion because, even if the territory under examination is the same, the cultures

23 Claire Soussen. "La cacherout ou le besoin d'une expertise juive en matière alimentaire. Expertise et valeur des choses au Moyen Âge," 3.

24 Paul Freedman, *Why Food Matters*, 45.

25 Banegas López, "Una anàlisi dels productes i les tècniques de cuina al Llibre de Sent Soví," 151.

26 Ibid., 160.

27 Ibid., 163.

and religions are different. Only similar things can be compared. The considerable consumption of pork in this territory after the fifteenth century—and its persistence in modern Spanish food—compels us to study ancient culinary sources. The aim here is to shed new light on the repercussions of eating pork in Iberian societies at the time.

Christians in both the East and West saw the consumption pork meat and all parts of the animal, including the fat, as an identity marker. Prohibited in Islam and Judaism, if a person didn't eat pork it was proof that they were a Jew or Muslim. It goes without saying that the political-religious situation of Spain between the eighth and fifteenth centuries influenced the content of cookbooks. Recipe collections play an important role in the transmission of knowledge and practices. In fact, they can be veritable markers of identity. Curiously, despite the fifteenth-century Iberian Peninsula's political and religious culture, shaped as it was by a dogmatic version of Catholicism, some cookbook authors wrote recipes whose titles overtly referenced their Moorish origins.

Thus, a collection of Castilian recipes (twenty-nine)[28] included in the *Manual de mugeres en el qual se contienen muchas y diversas reçetas muy buenas* (dated 1475–1525) has instructions for a Moorish stew (*olla morisca*)[29] made with goat meat, chickpeas, and onions, as well as spices and caraway. In some cases, recipes were associated with Muslims, such as *salsa sarazinesca*, which, however, also contains wine and pork fat (lard). This recipe, known from a Venetian manuscript from the fifteenth century, was passed down from a prior tradition.[30] Alicia Martínez Crespo writes that

> the features of non-Christian food, compared to certain dishes specific to each culture, in addition to the lack of compliance with fasts and days of abstinence ordered by the Church, served many times to reveal the true religion and origin of a number of "converts," and were the motive of many accusations before the Holy Office. The consumption of lard [*tocino*] was one of the most revealing pieces of evidence of conversion to Christianity.[31]

---

28 Alicia Martínez Crespo, ed. and notes, *Manual de mugeres en el qual se contienen muchas y diversas reçeutas muy buenas* (Salamanque: Ediciones universidad de Salamanca, 1995), 24.

29 Ibid., 58.

30 Jean-Louis Flandrin, "Internationalisme, nationalisme et régionalisme dans la cuisine des XIVe et XVe siècle: le témoignage des livres de cuisine," in *Manger et boire au Moyen Âge. Actes du colloque de Nice 15–17 Octobre 1982*, vol. 2, *Cuisines, manières de table, régimes alimentaires* (Paris: Les Belles Lettres, 1984), 75, 91.

31 Martínez Crespo, *Manual de mugeres en el qual se contienen muchas y diversas reçeutas muy buenas*. Translation by the author.

Olivia Remia Constable argues that

> A change in foodways, especially the ingestion of pork and non-halal meat, was one of the signs of Christianization most ardently sought by inquisitors and most bitterly resisted by New Christians. Moriscos (like converted Jews, or conversos) lived in fear of Christian inquisitors, who scrutinized their eating habits and probed to see if they were now cooking with lard and salt pork (tocino) rather than olive oil.[32]

Manuel Espadas Burgos proposes that this explains "the desire to display in Moorish households a piece of ham or lard, which was meaningfully called a medallion (*medalla*)."[33] Thus, cuisine was clearly adapted to the tastes of and ingredients used by Christians—for example, the recipe in *Sent Soví,* which is based on "buckwheat" and includes salted pork fat (*carnsalada*).

The spread of culinary ideas from this new Christian era can be seen through those cookbooks that were eager to differentiate and ban any food that seemed related to Muslim or Jewish culinary habits. Integrating pork into an ethnic minority dish that originally didn't contain it triggered the "creation" of a new dish, a new name, and a new identity. For example, Spanish *cocido*[34] closely resembles the Jewish dish *adafina,* apart from its use of lard. *Ensaimada* is another example. This pastry gets its name from the Arabic term *šaim,* which means "lard." In Catalan, *saim* means "lard." The following story comes from a legend, and thus should not be considered in the same light as the previous research; still, it is important to note that *ensaimada* got its name from a pastry known as *bulema.*

The story goes that when the King James I of Aragon conquered Majorca in 1229, a Jewish pastry maker offered him a *bulema*—a pastry made from risen dough that is rolled into the shape of a snail and made with sheep's milk. This sweet was prepared at the time with olive oil or butter.[35] If, earlier, the name of the dish and the type of fat had changed, the circular shape remained. Today, these pastries are still found in Majorca and across the eastern Spanish coast,

---

32 Constable, *To Live Like a Moor,* 107–108 (Kindle ed.).

33 Manuel Espadas Burgos, "Aspectos socioreligiosos de la alimentación española," *Hispania* 131 (1975): 549. Translation by the author.

34 See https://www.persee.fr/doc/horma_0984-2616_2006_num_55_1_2388.

35 I couldn't find a historical reference for this. Only Miguel Ferrà i Martorrell in his (unpublished) "Ayer y hoy de la cocina mallorquina" explains how *bulema* was made, using the same ingredients as modern *ensaimada,* but with lard replacing butter made from sheep's milk.

but they are made with lard.[36] In this story, as in others, the "real and imaginary are inextricably linked, since no symbol exists without a concrete element to support it."[37]

Analysis of cookbooks written under Christian rule demonstrates the importance of pork meat and related products. In the cookbook of the Infanta Maria of Portugal (sixteenth century), the proportions are close to 8.19% for meat and 18.03% for fat. In *Libro del arte de cocina* by Maceras[38] (seventeenth century), these foods are in 32.2% of the text. For instance, the first recipe, "Small Meatballs," comes from the book by Maceras; it is titled *Cómo se han de hacer albondiguillas*.[39] The meatballs in this recipe are prepared with meat, vegetables, lard (*tocino*), and crushed garlic mixed with spices, eggs, bread crumbs, salt, and vinegar. Eggs are used as a thickening agent. This recipe resembles the one for preparing *albunduq* (a word which is similar to *albóndigas* in modern Spanish) that is in Arab cookbooks, but it leaves out vegetables and, of course, pork.

Meatballs (*albóndigas*) are, therefore, one of the central subjects of my research, as they are already present in Andalusian cookbooks. In *Libro del arte de cozina* by Granado and Maceras, the preparation of this dish differs from the culinary usages of Jews and Muslims present in Andalusian cookbooks. The recipe collection *Arte de cocina, pasteleria, vizcocheria, y conserveria* by Montiño (seventeenth century) includes meatballs made from boar meat. In *Regalo de la vida humana*, pork meat is included in 3.37% of recipes, without counting the 11.47% of recipes that contain lard. Pork fat is also used to make *mazapán* and it is also in the recipe "De torta de mazapán para día de carne."[40] The almond-based sweets in the Andalusian cookbooks, which are similar to *mazapanes*, obviously do not contain pork fat. Only oil from pressed almonds is in the recipes. The other recipe for *mazapanes*, titled "de tortada de mazapán,"[41] doesn't use this ingredient either.

Jodi Campbell writes that "before the fifteenth century and in the rest of Europe it [pork] was largely associated with peasants and the poor, but in Spain its consumption took on greater symbolic value as a proof of Catholic identity.

---

36 "El Pais.com." See José Carlos Capel, "¿La ensaimada mallorquina, un dulce de origen judío?" *El Pais*, February 8, 2019, https://elpais.com/elpais/2019/02/06/gastronotas_de_capel/1549480805_687074.html#?prm=copy_link.

37 Montanari, *La chère et l'esprit. Histoire de la culture alimentaire chrétienne.*

38 Sámper, *La alimentación en la España del Siglo de Oro.*

39 Ibid., chap. 1, 195.

40 Ibid., "De torta de mazapán para día de carne," chap. 59, 219.

41 Pérez Sámper, *La alimentación en la España del Siglo de Oro.* See "De tortada de mazapán," chap. 79, 258.

For Inquisition investigations, the mere avoidance of pork or lard was enough to support an accusation of harboring Muslim or Jewish beliefs."[42] There is a lack of explicit cooking practices. However, the significant number of denunciations—mainly by non-Jewish servants—about converso families cooking with olive oil instead of lard shows that pork was a way to identify people who still clung to their Jewish identities.

The Spanish Inquisition's conviction that a lack of pork consumption identified people as Jews is more complex, however. In the transcripts of trials, the proof of a converso's double religious identity was if they ate pork one day but abstain from it another. The same is true of matza; which is a food indicative of Jewish identity. The case of Pedro Ripoll from the town of Albarracín in the Spanish region of Aragon provides an example of this

> For a while in the 1470s he observed the Sabbath and festivals and kept the dietary laws, but he also attended mass, confessed to a priest, and worked on Saturday. He dealt socially with Jews yet criticized his wife for the same thing. When the Inquisition came in 1480s he began to eat pork for the first time and began to quarrel with his wife about her continued adherence to the old customs. He would not eat matza she bought from the Jewish baker. After a life of continuous stress between the two religions and a sporadic adherence to crypto-Judaism, Ripoll was burned in 1522.[43]

The choice of foods and styles of cooking were markers of ethnic identity. The attempt to impose Christianity altered the culinary heritage of Spain after the fifteenth century. The bid to erase any traces of the past that were not compliant with the prevailing orthodoxy in fifteenth-century Spain created a visible boundary within the Spanish population on the basis of cuisine and food. What people ate, and what they didn't eat, became a marker of religious identity. In this sense, pork played a major role. As Carolyn Nadeau writes, "meat choices, particularly pork, instantly segregated social groups in the early modern period. Vegetables underscored common eating practices across social and ethnic divides, as was the case of eggplant. This is the central taste of Spanish cuisine."[44]

---

42 Campbell, *At the First Table*, 78–79.

43 Gitlitz, *Secrecy and Deceit*, 121–122. See Stephen Haliczer, *Inquisition and Society in the Kingdom of Valencia: 1478–1834* (Berkely: University of California Press, 1990), 215.

44 Listen to the recording of C. Nadeau speaking to the Culinary Historians of Chicago on the topic: "Constructions of Taste in Francisco Martínez Montiño's Cookbook,"

La Olla Podrida

Let's take the example of the dish known as *Olla podrida*. The word *olla* (cooking pot) is common in the abovementioned cookbooks, and it is an integral part of the culinary heritage of modern Spain. *Olla podrida* is a dish which some consider to be the heir of Jewish *adafina*. *Regalo de la vida humana* (sixteenth century) contains a recipe for *olla podrida* among its 359 dishes. The same is true for the book by Granado, which has the recipe "Para hacer una olla podrida."[45] Aside from the use of pork, boar, or hare meat, the latter dish is miles away from the Jewish *adafina*.[46] This recipe is nevertheless intriguing. It is served with "soaked black and white chickpeas (garbanzos negros y blancos), garlic, onions, trimmed chestnuts, boiled *judihuelas* and *frijoles*."[47] The word *judihuelas* is interesting here. *Vocabulista arauigo en letra castellana* by Pedro de Alcalá from 1505 includes an entry in fol. viij,[48] where it is written that *judiguelo fimiète* corresponds to *lūbia* (bean). In this dictionary, the entry *judío/a* refers to a Jewish person and is transliterated as *yahūdi/īa/israelī/īa/barbarī*. It seems that in the sixteenth century the term *judía* did not refer to beans. The meaning of *judihuelas* can also be found in the *Diccionario universal francés-español: Español-francés*[49] by Ramón Joaquín Domínguez, which says it means *judías*. The definition reveals that the word refers to a large bean, but it is important to remember that the current literal translation of the term is "Jews." This may alluding to the fact that the dish was originally prepared by Jews. Maceras and Montiño also propose their own versions of *olla podrida*. However, the "olla podrida en pastel"[50] by Montiño contains a dried meat called *cecina* which, as I previously mentioned, was also a Jewish food.

Much has been written about the possible relationship between dishes from cookbooks under Christian rule and Jewish culinary practices. During a talk

---

Soundcloud recording, 29'30", March 3, 2018, https://soundcloud.com/culinaryhistory/constructions-of-taste-in-francisco-martinez-montinos-cookbook.

45 Diego Granado, *Libro del arte de cozina* (Lleida: Pagès, 1991), 82–83; See Diego Granado, "La 'olla podrida,'" in Sámper, *La alimentación en la España del Siglo de Oro*.

46 In the fifteenth century according to the *FIRC*.

47 Granado, *Libro del arte de cozina*, 82–83.

48 See https://archive.org/details/ARes193062/page/n307.

49 Ramón Joaquín Domínguez, *Diccionario universal francés-español: Español-francés* (Madrid: la Viuda de Jordan e Hijos, 1846), book 5, 474.

50 See the scanned version from 1790, "Olla podrida en pastel," 149–150, https://bibliotecadigital.jcyl.es/es/catalogo_imagenes/grupo.cmd?path=10064851; see the scanned version from 1634, 97–99, https://archive.org/details/hin-wel-all-00002356-001/page/n216; see Julio Valles Rojo, *Cocina y alimentación en los siglos XVI y XVII*, (Valladolid: Junta de Castilla y León, 2007), 57.

in 2018, Carolyn Nadeau briefly mentioned the possibility of a connection between such dishes and Jewish practices. She pointed to the possibility that *olla podrida* is like the *cocido* prepared for Shabbat. She added that unlike the *Kitāb al-ṭabīḫ*, where Jewish recipes are explicitly mentioned, Christian recipe collections do not include any direct references to Jewish cooking. In her opinion, this can be explained by the fact that Jewish culture was integrated into Christian culture and, as a result, it is difficult to ascertain the Jewish origin of a dish.[51]

Transmission is rarely a matter of identical reproduction, but in this case, is it even a question of transmission? I don't believe so, or at least not voluntarily. The Christian fear of social, culinary, linguistic, and so on cultural fluidity led to a transformation of culinary heritage that was grounded in rejection. A new Jewish identity emerged in opposition to this rejection.

C. Eggplant: Paragon of Jewish Cuisine

Eggplant is one of the most versatile foods and the most interesting to analyze. Expiración García Sánchez argues that the *Solanum melongena* L., the variety that was introduced in al-Andalus in the tenth century, is one of the defining vegetables in the Islamic world. Eggplant is used to make a variety of dishes, and its presence is still evident today in the modern culinary heritage of Spain, especially in Andalusian dishes.[52]

Eggplant is the most surprising fruit/vegetable in terms of to its changing place in culinary practices between the thirteenth and the seventeenth century. Fundamental to the eating habits of Jews and Muslims in the eighth century, eggplant was disparaged by Christians for what it signified. Remember that the *Kitāb al-ṭabīḫ* contains thirty-two eggplant recipes and the *Fuḍālat al-ḫiwān* has twenty-two. If many eggplant dishes exist in the Arab cookbooks, this is less frequently the case for later cookbooks. The table below summarizes the various styles of cooking eggplant in Iberian cookbooks after the fourteenth century.

---

51 Nadeau, "Constructions of Taste in Francisco Martínez Montiño's Cookbook," 33'30", https://soundcloud.com/culinaryhistory/constructions-of-taste-in-francisco-martinez-montinos-cookbook.

52 García-Sánchez, Bravo, and Bermejo, *Flora agrícola y forestal de al-Andalus*, 22.

Figure 12. Summary of the styles of eggplant preparations in Iberian cookbooks after the fourteenth century[53]

Boiled [eggplant] recipe	**Recipe of a stuffed dish with eggplant and cheese**	**Same recipe, heated up**	**Eggplant *Mirquas***	**Eggplant croquettes**	**Other dish = eggplant caviar with garlic and cheese**	**Eggplant sau-sages**	**Eggplant pancakes/ tortillas**
Kitāb al-ṭabīẖ (32/462)	*Kitāb al-ẖabīẖ*	*Kitāb al-ẖabīẖ*	*Kitāb al-ẖabīẖ*	*Kitāb al-ẖabīẖ*	*Fuḍālat al-ẖiwān* (22 recipes)	*Fuḍālat al-ẖiwān*	*Fuḍālat al-ẖiwān*
Anonymous	Anonymous	Anonymous	Anonymous	Anonymous	Ibn Razīn al-Tuğībī	Ibn Razīn al-Tuğībī	Ibn Razīn al-Tuğībī
Thirteenth century		Thirteenth century	Thirteenth century		Thirteenth century	Thirteenth century	
Peeled eggplant	Eggplant	Eggplant	Peeled eggplant	Peeled eggplant	Eggplant	Peeled eggplant	Eggplant
Boiled water puree	Salted water	Salted water	Boiled water puree	Boiled water puree	Boiled salt puree	Boiled water puree	Salted water puree
Flour	Eggs	Vinegar	Chopped fat	Breadcrumbs	Cooked garlic	Chopped lard	Breadcrumbs
Oil	Cheese	Grated cheese	*Murri*	Pepper	Finely grated cheese	*Murri*	*Murri*
Beaten eggs	Oil	Oil	Eggs	Eggs	Oil	Spices	Pepper
Fermented breadcrumbs	Almonds	Crushed garlic	Dried cilantro	Cilantro		Eggs	Dried cilantro
			Cinnamon	Cinnamon			Cinnamon
			Pepper	*Murri*			Vinegar broth
			Nard				Oil
			Onion juice				Garlic

Albergínies	***Berengenas en cacuela* p. 81**	***Berengenas espes-sas* p. 81**	***Berengenas ala morisca* p. 82**	***caçuela moxi* p. 110**	***Para berengenas en escabeche* p. 111**	***Berengenas en cazuela moxí* p. 663**	***Berengenas con almodrote* p. 664**
Sent Soví (1/ 72)	*Libro del Coch* (5/236)	*Libro del Coch*	*Libro del Coch*	*Libro del Coch*	*Libro del Coch*	*El Regalo de la vida humana*	*El Regalo de la vida humana*
Anonymous	R. de Nola	R. de Nola	R. de Nola	R. de Nola	R. de Nola	Juan Vallés (1496–1563)	Juan Vallés (1496–1563)
	Ed. 1529	Ed. 1529	Ed. 1529	Ed. 1529	Ed. 1529	–	–
Fourteenth century	Fifteenth century	Fifteenth century	Fifteenth century	Fifteenth century	Fifteenth century	Sixteenth century	Sixteenth century
Eggplant	Eggplant	Eggplant				Eggplant	
Salted water	Meat broth	Meat and veg-etable broth				Salted water	
Onions	Onions	Onions				Oil	
Grated cheese	Grated Aragon cheese	Grated Aragon cheese				Aged grated cheese	
Parsley	Egg yolk	Almond milk				Breadcrumbs	
Eggs	Sauce	Egg yolk				Dried cilantro	
Garlic	Ginger	Dried cilantro				Beaten eggs	
Oil and fat	Mace	Caraway				Pepper	
Spices	Parsley	Nutmeg				Cloves	
Almond milk	Green cilantro	Cloves				Ginger	
Broth	Nutmeg	Cinnamon				Caraway	
Mint	Sugar					Saffron	
Raisins	Cinnamon					Egg yolk	
Marjoram						Honey	

53 The page numbers mentioned next to the recipe titles refer to the pages of the printed editions used for the analyses. These editions have been specified above for the presentation of the cookbook in question.

None	***Berenjenas en cazuela*** **p. 32** **(*Berengenas en caçuela* in *Libro del Coch*)**	***Albóndigas***	***Cómo se han de comer las berengena***	***Cazuelas monjil de berengenas***	***Berengenas (en conserva)***
Cookbook of the Infanta Maria of Portugal	*Libro del arte de cozina* (7/766)	*Libro del arte de cozina*	*Libro del arte de cocina*	*Libro del arte de cocina*	*Libro del arte de cocina*
María of Portugal	Diego Granado Maldonado	Diego Granado Maldonado	Domingo Hernández de Maceras (1607)	Domingo Hernández de Maceras (1607)	Domingo Hernández de Maceras (1607)
	1614	Fried in pork fat	Fried	Fried in fat	
Sixteenth century	Seventeenth century	Seventeenth century	Seventeenth century	Seventeenth century	Seventeenth century
	Eggplant		Eggplant	Eggplant	Eggplant
	Meat broth		Boiled		Confit
	Onions			Fatty lard	Cloves
	Grated Aragon cheese		Grated cheese	Fat	Cinnamon
	Egg yolk		Bread	Parsley	
	Sauce		Spices	Pepper	
	Ginger		Garlic		
	Parsley		Eggs		
	Nutmeg				
	Green cilantro				
	Mace				
	Sugar				
	Cinnamon				

Sent Soví, the first Iberian cookbook to have been written under Christian rule, only includes one *albergínies* recipe,[54] which is baked in the oven. It is made of eggplant, onions, parsley, mint, marjoram, grated cheese, eggs, raisins, cooked garlic, spices, almond milk, broth, oil, and fat. In *Libro de cozina* by Nola, eggplant is used in 2.11% of all recipes (that is, five out of a total of 236). When eggplant is mentioned, it is sometimes linked with Muslims, such as in the recipe "Moorish Eggplant."[55] But there is a contradiction here. On the one hand, eggplant is present in Christian cookbooks, but to a limited degree, and one can imagine that there was some culinary interest in it; on the other hand, the food was disparaged. For example, at the beginning of the sixteenth century, Alfonso de Herrera wrote that the "common opinion is that eggplant was brought to these regions by the Moors, when they left Africa for Spain, and they brought the vegetable to kill [*matar*] Christians."[56] The author adds that "it is therefore the worst herb I have written about." Here, Alfonso de Herrera uses eggplant as a religious weapon for Muslims to kill Christians. He expresses his full contempt for this vegetable, and denigrates its qualities. Note his use of the phrase "common opinion," which suggests that his opinion is shared by all. This example shows the aversion that Christians felt towards Muslims. The association of Jew with eggplant is not presented in such a direct way; it is more implicit, which shows us that literature often captures and encourages cultural and religious discriminations.

In the fifteenth and sixteenth centuries, the style of preparing eggplant changed. In *Libro de cozina* and *Regalo de la vida humana*, eggplant is cooked in vegetable broth and meat. Grated cheese and beaten eggs are added, and cilantro is always included. However, it must be mentioned that as of the fifteenth century some eggplant recipes contained lard. It is possible that this indicates of a desire for Jews and Muslims to differentiate themselves from the culinary habits of Semitic people.

Libro del arte de cocina by Maceras[57] is part of this trend, as it only includes a single recipe entitled "Cómo se han de comer las berengenas"[58] (in three

---

54 Santanach et al., *Llibre de Sent Soví*, 211, no. 36.

55 De Nola and Peyrebonne, *Le livre de cuisine*, 82.

56 "Común opinión del vulgo es, que las verengenas fueron traídas a estas partes por los Moros, quando de África passaron en España, que las trajeron para matar con ellas a los Christianos"; "Así como es la más mala de todas las yerbas que he escrito." Translation by the author. See Biblioteca Digital de Castilla y León, book 4, 247–249: "Delas berenjenas," chap. 38, fol. Cxxxiiij: http://bdh-rd.bne.es/viewer.vm?id=0000050739.

57 Sámper, *La alimentación en la España del Siglo de Oro*.

58 Ibid., 236.

versions). In the first variation, the eggplant is boiled and then fried. Grated cheese, bread, spices, and garlic are then added. The entire mix is crushed and eggs are placed on top. There are a number of similarities between this recipe and the *Alberginies* dish in *Sent Soví* (boiled eggplant, grated cheese, garlic, eggs, spices, and parsley).[59] The transmission of this recipe throughout the late Middle Ages seems more than plausible.[60] Yet the other two variants are surprising. It is the only such case in this cookbook. The "Cazuelas monjil de berengenas" dish, which I translate as "Monastic Eggplant Stew," is made of eggplant, fat, lard, pepper, and parsley.[61] This dish is associated with Christianity, even though theoretically, monks did not eat meat. In this dish, pork is the food that distinguishes it from the first version; it does not seem to be recorded in any of the other cookbooks analyzed. The last variation on eggplant is a confit. It is prepared as a preserve using cloves and cinnamon.[62] Note that this eggplant confit recipe is part of the culinary heritage of Sephardic Jews in living beside the Straits of Gibraltar, as well as in Morocco and as far as the Dominican Republic.[63] The cookbook of the Infanta Maria of Portugal (sixteenth century) does not contain any eggplant recipes. The only vegetable mentioned is lettuce, which is prepared as a preserve.

Now let's look at how the eggplant is represented in three manuscripts: *Livro de receptas*,[64] *Receptas experimentadas*,[65] and (*Libro*) *en que se allaran facilme [n] te todas receptas y memorias* [...],[66] the texts previously used to compare the uses of cilantro and pork. The first cookbook does not contain eggplant (0/15), and the second contains seven recipes with this vegetable (7/155). The last manuscript of 157 recipes includes five dishes with eggplant. With a total of twelve usages, it is just one short of equaling squash (*calabaza*) and carrot (*zanahoria*).

---

59 Let's remember that in the *Fuḍālat al-ḫiwān* there is a recipe with ingredients like boiled eggplant, grated cheese, garlic, eggs, and oil that is called "Other Dish," which I call "Eggplant Caviar with Garlic and Cheese."

60 This recipe, "Cómo se han de comer las berengenas," has much in common with the one in the *Kitāb al-ṭabīḫ* called "Boiled Eggplant Recipe." I have compared these recipes with *Cazuelas de berenjenas* recipes in collections from the fifteenth, sixteenth, and seventeenth centuries; see Sámper, *La alimentación en la España del Siglo de Oro*, 236.

61 The Spanish terms are: *Carnero, vaca, tocino, pies de Puerco, testuz, longanizas, lenguas de vaca*; there are also chickpeas, garlic, turnips, if they are in season. The dish is cooked for a long time with spices, grape mustard, and parsley.

62 Sámper, *La alimentación en la España del Siglo de Oro*.

63 Piñer, *Sephardi*.

64 This manuscript dates back to the sixteenth century. It is stored in the Biblioteca Nacional in Madrid, ms. 1462.

65 This manuscript dates back to 1620. It is stored in the Biblioteca Nacional in Madrid, ms. 2019.

66 This manuscript dates back to the end of the seventeenth century, maybe 1679. It is stored in the Biblioteca Nacional in Madrid, ms. 6058.

This confirms that that eggplant was of little culinary interest on the Iberian Peninsula in the sixteenth to seventeenth centuries.

In the wake of Nola's book, eggplant was frequently cooked in a meat-based broth and flavored with onions; this broke with the style of eating fried eggplant that was widespread in Muslim and Jewish communities, and with the place of eggplant in Andalusian recipe collections. With this change, eggplant was regularly prepared as a confit after the sixteenth century.

In addition to the share of eggplant-based recipes in Iberian cookbooks, there is also the symbolic value of eggplant dishes in literary sources. Let's remember the verse *Cazuelas de berenjenas* [eggplant stew] from *Cancionero general*: "Coplas del Conde de Paredes a Juan Poeta en una perdonança a Valencia." *Cazuelas de berenjenas* could be the most emblematic dish of the conversos of Spain. Its name has stayed the same throughout the centuries and is found in nearly all cookbooks from the Iberian Peninsula. *Libro de cozina* by Nola also contains a dish called *Cazuela moxí*, which Peyrebonne translates as *poêlon mojí*.[67] The word *mojí*, it is of Arabic origin, like *jabalí*. It comes from the term *muhsí* which means "stuffed." This word was often used to name an eggplant-based dish, and the *Tesoro de la lengua castellana o española* by Covarrubias[68] mentions the dish. Another recipe in *Libro de cozina* is a casserole dish called "Eggplant Casserole" (*Berengenas en caçuela*)[69] in the 1529 edition. As for *Regalo de la vida humana,* there are only two eggplant recipes: one called "Berengenas en caçuela moxí"[70] and the other *berengenas con almodrote*.[71]

The same is true for *Libro del arte de cozina* (seventeenth century). It is important to remember that the above recipe, which is in the *Kitāb al-ṭabīḫ* under the name "Boiled [Eggplant] Recipe" has been passed down for centuries and has not changed much. The thirteenth-century recipe, which contains eggplant, vinegar, cheese, oil, and garlic, was modified by adding eggs, parsley, or dry cilantro, and sometimes cinnamon. Cervantes mentions *Cazuela mojí* in his play *Los baños de Argel,* and we know that he also associated Muslims with eggplant in some of his other work. Another change also seems unique. As early as the

---

67 De Nola and Peyrebonne, *Le livre de cuisine,* 110, no. 11,.

68 Covarrubias and de Riquer, *Tesoro de la lengua castellana o española.*

69 De Nola and Peyrebonne, *Le livre de cuisine,* 81, folio xli, no. 50.

70 Vallés, *Regalo de la vida humana,* 663, no. 231, (chapter 123, folio 263v.). Translation by the author: "Cut the eggplant into two equal pieces, boil in salt water, cook, strain and press the eggplant. Put the boiled eggplant in a casserole dish with oil. Add aged grated cheese and breadcrumbs, and then add the eggplant. Cook. Add dried cilantro, caraway and pepper, cloves and ground ginger, beaten eggs. Cook. Pour the mixture into a casserole dish with oil and add the beaten eggs, pepper, cloves and saffron. Mix."

71 Vallés, *Regalo de la vida humana,* 664, no. 232.

fifteenth century, in the Nola cookbook, but also in the seventeenth century in *Libro del arte de cozina* by Diego Granado, eggplant—almost completely absent in latter cookbook—is not cooked in salt water, but rather in meat broth that is often spiced with onion. This is the case for the *Berenjenas en cazuela*[72] recipe.

If we focus on the permanence of eggplant in literary sources, we can see that eggplant *almodrote* was often associated with Iberian Jews. *Regalo de la vida humana* by Juan Vallés (sixteenth century) also contains a recipe called *Almodrote,*[73] which is made of raw chopped garlic with grated cheese (*queso rallado*) sprinkled on top; the ingredients are then crushed together. Water is wrung out until the mixture becomes thicker.[74] This preparation is a dish that is still enjoyed today by Sephardic Jews during Shabbat. As Paul Freedman writes, "Eggplant, chickpeas, onions, garlic and chard were eaten (during the Inquisition period) by everyone, but nevertheless typified as Jewish."[75]

---

72 Granado, *Libro del arte de cozina*, 32–33.

73 Vallés, *Regalo de la vida humana*, folio 245r., chap. 49, no. 292.

74 Vallés, *Regalo de la vida humana*, folio 245r, chap. 49, nos. 8 and 292 Translation by the author.

75 Paul Freedman, *Why Food Matters*, 56.

CHAPTER 8

The Trials of the Inquisition: Written Witnesses of an Oral Transmission of Jewish Skills

Without wishing it or knowing it, the censors of the Inquisition Tribunal—completely unprecedentedly and for the first time explicitly—carried out an inventory of Jewish culinary practices. Sources dating from the Inquisition are filled with narratives that bring together religion and food. Indeed, these stories relate the daily practices, including eating habits, of Jews that enable religious identification. Food, but also culinary techniques, were recorded during the trials of the Inquisition, making it possible to give an overview of the dishes and practices of the Mosaic people starting in the fifteenth century. By establishing the Spanish Inquisition (1478–1834), the Catholic Kings created a database that resulted in the creation of what might be, if not the first Jewish cookbook, then a large and precise notebook of Jewish food and culinary practices. This information is contained in the trials of the various cities of Spain, Venice,[1] and all the other cities where the Inquisition tried conversos (Mexico, Brazil, etc.).

The in-depth research conducted by Carlos Carrete Parrondo at the beginning of the 1980s begins with the creation in 1478 of the Tribunal of the Inquisition (from the Latin term *Inquisitio*: inquiry) by the Catholic monarchs Isabella of Castile and Ferdinand of Aragon. The Inquisition was intended primarily to scrutinize conversos, as well as to spread and maintain Catholic orthodoxy.[2] Béatrice Pérez, in her *Inquisition, pouvoir et société. La province de Séville et ses judéoconvers*

1 After the Edict of Expulsion of Jews from Spain in 1492, many left for Italy, mainly Rome and Venice.

2 J. Pérez, *Histoire de l'Espagne*, 363.

sous les Rois Catholiques,[3] Enrique Soria Mesa's, *La realidad tras el Espejo,*[4] and the edited volume *Los judeoconversos en el mundo ibérico*[5] thoroughly address the issue of Jewish converts to Christianity in Andalusia and throughout the Catholic world. The eight volumes of *Fontes Iudaeorum regni Castellae*[6] (abbreviated to *FIRC*) contain full transcriptions of the various testimonies presented before the tribunals. Carrete Parrondo, in various volumes that he produced in collaboration with other researchers like María José Castaño González (vol. 2) and Carolina Fraile Conde (vol. 4, also provides transcripts of the trials. These come with brief notes that shed light on the historical and geographical context of the denunciations, as well as interpretations of the texts.

The trials of the Inquisition in the diocese of Soria (1486–1502)[7] are the richest sources of information in terms of food. The trials stand out for their linguistic wealth, with terms in Latin, Castilian and Hebrew, and contain very interesting historical and culinary details. The first folio (folio 937 v.) dates from 1490 and narrates an event which a witness says he saw "ten or eleven years" before—namely between 1479 and 1480—in a village neighboring the town of Soria, located two hundred kilometers north of Madrid. This retroactive memory is not an isolated case. Other people on trial related facts dating "over thirty years,"[8] "more than forty years,"[9] and even "fifty years"[10] before—that is, before 1440. The names of dishes are repeated in different trials, particularly *adafina.*

The transcriptions of the Inquisition trials of the Arias Dávila family of Segovia[11] are complete. In this city, located 180 km south-west of Soria, the Arias Dávilas were powerful. The crux of the trial concerned Bishop Juan Arias Dávila, the son of the conversa Elvira González and the converso Diego

---

3 Béatrice Pérez, *Inquisition, pouvoir et société. La province de Séville et ses judéoconvers sous les Rois Catholiques* (Paris: Honoré Champion, Collection Études d'histoire médiévale, 2007).

4 Soria Mesa, *La realidad tras el espejo.*

5 Béatrice Pérez, "Conversos sevillanos a principios de la época moderna. ¿Élites financieras o familias relacionadas?," in *Los judeoconversos en el mundo ibérico,* ed. Enrique Soria Mesa and Antonio Díaz Rodríguez (Ediciones Universidad de Córdoba, UCO Press, 2019).

6 Fontes Iudaeorum regni Castellae—a Latin phrase I translate as "Jewish sources of the Kingdom of Castile." I should add that I did not personally consult these sources.

7 Carrete Parrondo and Castaño González, *Fontes ludaeorum Regni Castellae,* vol. 2. The authors of the book refer to file 28/73 (incomplete) in the Archivo Real de Simancas (AGS), Patronato Real, Inquisición, and that it corresponds to folios 937r.–1121v.

8 Ibid., 21.

9 Ibid. no. 23, 29: [Q]ue ha más de quarenta años."

10 Ibid. no. 111, 59.

11 Parrondo and González, *Fontes ludaeorum Regni Castellae.*

Aria(s) Dávila, a royal accountant. This transcription illustrates the seemingly contradictory relationships between members of the Jewish community of Segovia and these new conversos. The *Adafina* dish also appears a number of times.[12]

The trials concerning the conversos of Almazán, especially those of the Lainez family, contain rich information too.[13] Many trials narrate facts that go back several dozen years before 1505. Almazán is a small city, thirty-five kilometers south of Soria. Almazán is, after Soria, the city with the second most important Jewish *aljama* in the province (in terms of Jews and conversos). These trials, like the ones, previously mentioned, aimed to get more information about Castilian Judaism. It is through the lives of the ancestors of Diego Lainez—the second general official of the "Society of Jesus"—that we follow the trials, led by four members of the clergy, of one hundred Jewish converso families who had lived in five streets of the city of Almazán between 1501 and 1505. They shed light on the history of a society in which religious pressure was omnipresent. The trials of the Judeo-converts of Almazán contain a wealth of information about food. If they provide details about synagogue and funeral rites, they shed even more light on the dishes prepared and enjoyed by Jews.[14]

Another unique judicial source is *The Trials of the Holy Office of Venice against Jews and Judaists*. The fifth of the fourteen volumes has the original title *Processi del S. Uffizio di Venezia contro ebrei e giudaizzanti (1579–1586)*.[15] Although this volume is much later than the trials of the previously cited *FIRC*, it reveals the existence of dishes prepared by crypto-Jews in Venice, food that is identical to those mentioned in the Inquisition trials of the conversos of Spain. Some refer to fish dishes,[16] others to sweet foods. As concerns the latter, the most obvious is marzipan; it is cited a number of times in these trials.[17] Keep in mind that

---

12 The analyses by Carrete Parrondo are based on important material dating back to the sixteenth century, present in the Inquisition file 1413 n. 7, held in the National Historical Archive (AHN) in Madrid.

13 Parrondo and Conde, *Fontes Iudaeorum Regni Castellae*, vol. 4.

14 The majority of sources from this volume (5) are found in the Diocesan Archives of Cuenca (ADC), and concern Inquisition files 748/5-6, mainly the folios from 22r. to 39v.

15 Pier Cesare Ioly Zorattini, *Processi del S. Uffizio di Venezia contro ebrei e giudaizzanti*, vol. 5, *(1579–1586)* (Florence: Ed. Olschki, 1980–1999), 69–71, 84, 100, 106, 117–118, 142. Title translated by the author.

16 Ibid., 84 (folio 63v. "[S]pesso de la tonina, credo di Spagna"—which I translate as: "Often of tonine, from Spain I believe"), 106 (91r. "[P]esce salato" (salted fish).

17 Ibid., 69 (folio 44r.: "[U]n pocho de marzipan," which I translate as "a little marzipan"); ibid. 71 (folio 46v.: "[H]aver magnato perri, ceriese, marzipan," which I translate as "[H]aving eaten pears, cherries, and marzipan"); ibid., 117 (folio 107r.: "[C]ose fate de zucharo et sempre de queste cose che son cose tonde che dentro ve è pasta de marzapane," which I

after the expulsion of Jews from Spain, some chose exile in Italy (mainly Rome and Venice), as testified to by the converso Francisco Delicado in 1528. Due to its similarity with the *Fontes Iudaeorum Regni Castellae* and the parallel that can be established with the *La Lozana andaluza,* the action of which takes place in Rome in the sixteenth century, this Italian judiciary source makes it possible to "prove" the existence of dishes made by Jews. They were perceived as Jewish since their preparation and consumption were denounced to the Holy Office. The trials of the Inquisition in Venice also testify to the current transmission and enduring presence in Jewish culture of certain dishes which were already a part of history five hundred years earlier.

To conclude, even if the following statements cannot be viewed in the same light as the other explanations provided here, and even though this is a study and not a source, it is also worth mentioning the book by David Gitlitz and Linda Kay Davidson titled *A Drizzle of Honey: The lives and Recipes of Spanish Secret Jews.* This is not an ordinary cookbook. It contains dishes adapted from the testimonies in the trials of the Inquisition. The book offers recipes made by Spanish and Portuguese Jews, as well as by Sephardic Jews from Mexico, Brazil, and several countries where the Holy Office governed. The sources on which this book is based are scrupulously referenced at the end of the volume.

Reading about the trials of the Inquisition throws up a surprise. The accused were almost always women who had been denounced by other women (often servants or neighbors). These accusers propagated stories about Jewish practices on Iberian soil and beyond. Let's keep in mind that the food of Jews and Muslims had aroused Christian animosity since the beginning of the Spanish Inquisition in 1478. Christians spied on the culinary preparations and practices of "heretics," practices which were perceived as proof of their heresy. Eradicating these practices must have made it possible to promote social and religious conformity and unity.[18] However, the permanence of certain Jewish culinary dishes and techniques reveals rifts in the Inquisition system, while at the same time showing the tenacity and the power of transmission within Jewish culture. As proof of this, fear of the prevailing orthodoxy was not sufficient to eradicate the culinary knowledge possessed by women, which spread well beyond the borders of Spain.

---

translate as "Things made of sugar; these things are always round and have marzipan inside"). The importance of the term "always" shows that *marzapane* was frequently consumed by Jews and Italians during this period.

18 Constable, "Food and Meaning."

A. *Adafina*

In volume 2 of *FIRC,* which contains the transcription of the trials of the "Inquisition tribunal in the diocese of Soria (1486–1502),"[19] the *adafina* dish is cited a number of times. The fact that the dish was eaten during Shabbat is mentioned in at least eight trials,[20] but this is not the only dish. *Adafina* appears to be the only food that indicated heresy, as though it made the accusation clear and thus proved that the person who ate it was Jewish. An good number of trials contain other accusations regarding food. Like *adafina,* there is also unleavened bread (*pan cenceño*),[21] kosher wine (*vino caser* or *vino judiego*), and kosher meat (*carne caser*). Food practices were also mentioned with regard to the preparation of meat, as in trial 404 where it is reported that Juan Sanches's wife "cleansed [the meat], by removing the mutton fat and the [sciatic] nerve of the leg of lamb."[22] Jewish celebrations—the dates of which were also known to the inquisitors (since they themselves could have been conversos)—were the ultimate indicators of the faith. Of course, the timing of these celebrations made it possible to verify the information of the accusers and thus identify Jews. But, in particular, the specific culinary techniques and preparations made it possible for the Inquisition to corroborate the veracity of the denunciations regarding Jewish practices. Thus, Pessah,[23] Purim,[24] Yom Kippur,[25] Sukkot (*cabañuelas*), and obviously Shabbat are the most frequently mentioned celebrations. It goes without

---

19 Parrondo and González, *Fontes ludaeorum Regni Castellae,* vol. 2. The authors of the book specify that it is file 28/73, in the Archivo Real de Simancas (AGS), Patronato Real, Inquisición.

20 Parrondo and González, *Fontes ludaeorum Regni Castellae,* vol. 2. Ibid., 17, no. 2; 28, no. 20; 44, no. 68; 50, no. 87; 59, no. 111; 65, no. 122; 173, no. 419; 174, no. 423.

21 Ibid., 18, no. 5; 174, no. 422

22 Ibid., 167, no. 404.

23 Ibid., 18, no. 5; 155, no. 373. *Passover*: "Hebrew *Pesaḥ* or *Pesach,* in Judaism, holiday commemorating the Hebrews' liberation from slavery in Egypt and the 'passing over' of the forces of destruction, or the sparing of the firstborn of the Israelites, when the Lord 'smote the land of Egypt' on the eve of the Exodus. Passover begins with the fifteenth and ends with the twenty-first (or, outside of Israel and among Reform Jews, the second) day of the month of Nisan (March or April)." See *Encyclopaedia Britannica,* s.v. "Passover," accessed 15 April, 2022, https://www.britannica.com/topic/Passover.

24 Parrondo and González, *Fontes ludaeorum Regni Castellae,* 2:22, no. 9.

25 Ibid., 2:60, no. 111. Yom Kippur: In "Hebrew 'Yom Ha-Kippurim,' in English 'Day of Atonement,' most solemn of Jewish religious holidays, observed on the tenth day of the lunar month of Tishri (in the course of September and October), when Jews seek to expiate their sins and achieve reconciliation with God. Yom Kippur concludes the '10 days of repentance' that begin with Rosh Hashana (New Year's Day) on the first day of Tishri." See *Encyclopaedia Britannica,* s.v. "Yom Kippur," accessed April 15, 2022, https://www.britannica.com/topic/Yom-Kippur.

saying that periods of fasting, and therefore the lack of cooking and eating, were just as indicative of the survival of Jewish practices. For example, take trial 122 of the *FIRC*, vol. 3, which establishes a link between *adafina* and Andalusia, as it is stated that "Juan Açan [and perhaps his wife] went to Andalusia, in a place called Segura"[26] (city to the northeast of autonomous region). Juan Açan asked, we learn, his wife if she would prepare adafina "like Jews prepare it . . . they cook it from the afternoon until the next morning, and eat it another day."[27] In the *FIRC*, it is rare to find details about place name besides Castile. It is even more uncommon to be able to identify a connection between a dish and a place. In fact, this example shows the presence of a Jewish community in Andalusia, just like the existence of links between this community and that of Castile.

Multiple references to *adafina* are also found in volume 3. Once again, *adafina*[28]—a dish that is also known under different names, such as *caliente*,[29] *hamín*,[30] *aní*, and *trasnochado*—is a marker of Judaism, just like the act of fasting (*ayunaba*.)[31] In trial number 17, new information about food is provided. It is written that "Diego Arias claimed to be sick on Saturdays to avoid going to mass and locked himself in a room all day, only to leave at night, and didn't eat anything all day just dried fruit and almonds and at night he ate a roast chicken."[32] The trials in this volume also report the existence of Jewish butchers (carnicería de los judíos)[33] and details regarding the ritual of preparing the dead the consumption of specific foods during such occasions,[34] such as unleavened bread

---

26 Parrondo and González, *Fontes Iudaeorum Regni Castellae*, 2:65, no. 122: "Juan Açan fueron all Andaluzía, a un lugar que se llama Segura." Translation by the author. In this volume (155, no. 372), another Converso is discussed whose Jewish practices were discovered and who returned to Andalusia and died there. It is very likely that this was his birth region. It is worth noting that a city named Segura de la Sierra also exists in Andalusia in the province of Jaén, but other cities named "Segura" are located in the provinces of León (Castilla y León) and Badajoz (Extremadura).

27 Ibid., 65, no. 122: "que le fiziese una adafina como la fasían las judías . . . desde un día tarde hasta otro día de mañana, e que así otro día la comieron." Translation by the author.

28 Parrondo, *Fontes Iudaeorum Regni Castellae*, 3:22, no. 9; 23, no. 10; 27, no. 23; 27, no. 24; 116, no. 222; 117, no. 225; 138, no. 246; 140, no. 247; 144, no. 249.

29 Ibid., 98, no. 169.

30 Ibid., 21, no. 9.

31 Ibid., 21, no. 6.

32 Parrondo, *Fontes Iudaeorum Regni Castellae*, 3:25, no. 17: "Que el dicho Arias que se facía doliente los sábados a causa de no ir a la iglesia e que se encerraba en una cámara todo el día, que no salía hasta la noche, e que no comía sino pasas y almendras entre día y que a la noche comía una gallina asada" (sic). Translation by the author.

33 Ibid., 21, no. 6.

34 Ibid., 24, no. 15; 26, no. 20.

and salad.[35] Once again, the food eaten during religious holidays like Easter/Passover—fried eggs with sardines and unleavened bread[36]—held a special place in denouncing Jewish-related practices.

The fourth trial in volume 4 (leg. 748/5–6, folio 28r.), held in Almazán on June 3, 1505, immediately addresses the theme of food. It narrates the moment when Aldonza[37] (the wife of Pedro Lainez) asked her black slave Angelina to prepare them a cooking pot (*olla*) with turnips (*nabos*)[38] and a piece of grated cheese (una ralladura de queso).[39] Later in the trial (June 5, 1505), Aldonza was seen by this witness while she was sitting in the entrance of the kitchen: "She had on her knees, on her skirt, a white sheet of cloth and on this, the hoof of a sheep or ram, round, and she had split it down the middle with a knife next to her; and with her nails or fingers she was trying to remove all of the fat and a long vein[40] and with the other hand she held it.[41]

Pork (and the strategies used by conversos to avoid eating it, or even entering into contact with a dish that contained pork) is important in this trial, as in others. The desire of these new Christians to avoid putting lard[42] in their pots, in the same way they avoided using utensils that had prepared pork-based dishes, revealed their status as crypto-Jews.[43] There are also many transcriptions of dishes for Shabbat in the trials. I will only mention here the custom of consuming "eggs on Friday."[44]

It is also in volume 4 (ADC, file 749/15, fol. 21r.–v.) that *adafina* is presented in detail. Even though it is not explicitly named in the trial, the clues about dish leave no doubt. A witness narrates that Catalina, the wife of Alvaro de Luna, had

---

35 Ibid., 29, no. 28.

36 Ibid., 30, no. 30; 116, no. 220; 141, no. 247.

37 We can't help but think of Aldonza, the protagonist of *La Lozana andaluza*, discussed earlier.

38 There is a recurring presence of turnips (*nabos*) in the *ollas* (pots). See ibid., 78, no. 143.

39 Parrondo and Conde, *Fontes Iudaeorum Regni Castellae*, 4:19, no. 4. Translation by the author.

40 On removing the sciatic nerve (*landrecilla* or *b[r]inças*), see ibid., 20, no. 4; 21, no. 4; 73, no. 134; 78, no. 143.

41 Parrondo and Conde, *Fontes Iudaeorum Regni Castellae*, 4:20, no. 4, 20: ". . . asentada a la entrada de la . . . cozina y tenía ençima de las rodillas, *en sus faldas un panno blanco de lienço* y ençima dél una pierna de carnero o macho redonda y la tenía hendida por medio, y un cuchillo junto con ella y con las uñas o dedos de la mano ella estaba quitando toda la gordura e una vena larga y con la otra mano la tenía." Translation by the author. Other similar descriptions are provided: see 78, no. 139; 78, no. 143; 80, no. 147.

42 Concerning the rejection of the consumption of lard (*tocino*), there are a number of elements. See ibid., 21, no. 4; 22, no. 4; 64, no. 107; 64, no. 108; 66, no. 119; 77, no. 124; 70, no. 131; 72, no. 134; 74, no. 134; 77, no. 136; 80, no. 146; 86, no. 166; 87, no. 165; 91, no. 173.

43 Parrondo and Conde, *Fontes Iudaeorum Regni Castellae*, 4:72, no. 134, 72; 73, no. 134; 77, no. 136; 74. no. 138.

44 Ibid., 91, no. 173. Translation by the author.

asked her to prepare two pots: one for them and the other for her and the other servants. She asked her

> not to put lard in the pot that was cooking for her and her husband, only meat and sometimes chickpeas and other times vegetables; and she asked her to put a wooden spoon in this pot and an iron spoon in the other, and the spoon from the first pot must not be put in the other; and she asked that the meat for her and her husband be washed very well, and when chard was added to the pot that was cooking for her masters, Catalina Laynez required they be washed with water and salt, and then put in the pot. . . . And they had a cow killed and the meat from the head, heart and innards was cooked, and once cooked, the witness chopped it at the request of their master and they added dry cilantro to the meat and their master put some in the cow's innards and left it to dry and later they ate it.[45]

The last step that is mentioned evokes meat sausages that are left to dry. Today, a small paté of beef seasoned with herbs and spices is still included in Sephardic *adafina* preparations.

B. *Cabaheas*

In the trials of the Inquisition, sausage dishes frequently come up. This was easy to identify, as the cow head had to be cooked, chopped up after cooking, and then prepared. But it is also the fact that these sausages had to be dried that attracted the attention of the denunciators. Sausages without pork, called *cabaheas*,[46] thus appear to be mentioned for the first time ever in an account of a Spanish Inquisition trial. This preparation does not appear in any cookbook at

45 Ibid. ". . . que no echase tocino en la olla que se guisaba para ella y su marido salvo la carne e algunas veses garbanzos e verdura otras veses; e que le mandaba pusiese en aquella olla una cuchara de palo, e en la otra una cuchara de fierro, e que no llegase la cuchara de la una olla en la otra; e mandaba lavar mucho la carne parra ella e a su marido, e quando habían de echar berzas en la olla que se guisaba para sus amos, le mandaba Catalina Laynez que las lavase con agua y sal, e después las echase en la olla . . .E que mataron una vaca e de la carne de la cabeça e del corazón e baço echaronlo a cozer e, cozido, lo picó este testigo por mandado de su ama, e echaron culantro seco en la carne e así lo echó su ama en las tripas de la vaca e las pusieron a secar e comían después dellas." Translation by the author.

46 Ibid., 23 and 23n3, no. 4; 30, no. 18; 31, no. 19; 32, no. 25; 37, no. 39; 42, no. 52; 67, no. 124.

the time—nor at any other period—at least not under this name.[47] For example, one account describes that Catalina Lainez ate *cabaheas* in the presence of a witness.[48] Trial 18 specifies that another witness saw the daughter of Baray practice Jewish prayers and eat "*cabaheas* many Saturdays" [*muchos sábados*].[49] The last reference of *cabaheas* relates to Catalina Lainez, denounced by a witness who lived with her "five or six months" [*çinco o seys meses*], who said that she had asked them to "make a stew without pork" [*guisar la olla syn tocino*], to "wash the meat well" [*lavar mucho la carne*], and that she "made [Catalan] *cabaheas* from the head and heart of a cow [*e fasya cabaheas de cabeça e coraçón de vaca*] and the innards of a cow [*e baço de vaca*] and that she cooked and chopped them with cilantro [*e lo cozía e picaba con cilantro*]."[50] Trial 52 gives further information about the cooking technique. They are "hung" [*colgadas*][51] likely to be dried, as trial 25 tells us that they are "smoked" [*sahumar*].[52]

C. *Albóndigas*

The trials concerning the Judeo-Converts of Almazán[53] name dishes that include meatballs. These have slightly different titles depending on the size of the balls. In this sense, the *albondequexos* dish comes in first place. Indeed, the records of trial 52 define them as raw ground meat that is mixed with spices and eggs which, once chopped and shaped into balls [*bodoques*], are fried in a pan [*sartén*] with oil or in a pot.[54] The term *albondequexos* refers to *albóndigas*,[55] which are seasoned meatballs that are fried and cooked in a pot. In the same trial, a dish of mutton innards is also mentioned [*alvillos de carnero*] and chopped spleen [*baço picado*] with hard-boiled eggs [*huevos cozidos*] and the whites of chopped egg [*alburas picadas*]. Full egg yolks [*yemas enteras*] were put in the innards to

---

47 The question of Jewish sausage will be discussed in more detail in the last two chapters of this book.

48 A. D. C, Inquisición, leg. 749/15, fol. 18v.; Carrete Parrondo and Fraile Conde, *Fontes Iudaeorum Regni Castellae*, 4:23, no. 4.

49 Ibid., 30, no. 18. Translation by the author.

50 Ibid., 67, no. 124.

51 Ibid., 43, no. 52. Translation by the author.

52 Ibid., 32, no. 25. Translation by the author.

53 Ibid., Translation by the author.

54 Ibid., 43, no. 52. Translation by the author.

55 These "albóndigas," or beef meatballs made with spices, are also mentioned in *FIRC*, vol. 4, 31, no. 19.

make "small pancakes" [*torterillos*].[56] Finally, there is a dish which was reported to have been prepared for the Christian Holy Week, which coincides with the dates of Jewish Easter (Pessah).[57] It concerns "small rolls"[58] [*rollillos*] made from an egg-based dough, similar to the preparation of round "tortillas," made of pepper [*pimienta*], honey [*miel*], and oil [*azeite*], and baked in the oven [*horno*].[59]

The report of the Inquisition trial against Fernando de la Chica is of the utmost value. It outlines the following facts: "Other Shabbat foods were meatballs [*albóndigas*], stews [*caçuelas*] and eggplant [*berenjenas*], all accompanied with lots of vegetables [*hortalizas*]. Fernando de la Chica was accused of cooking and eating *adafina*."[60] The narrative summarizes, in two sentences, the daily practices of Jewish culinary habits. These practices were so revealing of Jewish identity that the Holy Office registered them in writing. Indeed, Fernando de la Chica was accused of having cooked and eaten *adafina*, but there is also mention of other dishes made during this period, such as *albóndigas*. Recall that the *Kitāb al-ṭabīẖ* contains an considerable number of recipes made of meatballs, which are related to Jewish culinary practices. Carolina Fraile[61] and Miguel Ángel Motis Dolader[62] also provide detailed information about conversa society, specifically that of the Castilian-Aragonese.

Of course, other dishes beyond the most emblematic ones were also tied with Judaism. Let's take for example the dish called *cogüerço*,[63] which was prepared in the home of a Jewish family member and then brought to a funeral banquet. There is also the dried beef meat dish called *çesina*,[64] as well as a myriad of other dishes, such as *hormigos* (pastries), *nuegados* (honeyed pastries), *empanadas* (stuffed pastries), *pasteles de carne* (meat pie), le *pan ceceño* (unleavened bread),

---

56 Parrondo and Conde, *Fontes Iudaeorum Regni Castellae*, 4:43–44, no. 52. Translation by the author.

57 Ibid., 38, no. 39. Translation by the author.

58 Ibid., 32, no. 25. Translation by the author.

59 These rolls seem to be similar to the "neulas encanonadas" mentioned in the *Provençal Esther Poem* of the Jewish doctor Crescas du Caylar mentioned earlier.

60 "Otras comidas sabáticas eran las albóndigas, las caçuelas y las berenjenas, todo acompañado con muchas hortalizas. De preparar y comer adafina fue acusado Fernando de la Chica." AHN, Inquisición, 140, no. 7. Translation by the author.

61 Carolina Fraile Conde, "Las costumbres judaizantes de la comunidad conversa de Almazán a finales del siglo XV y principios del XVI" (Universidad Pontificada de Salamanca, II: Archivo General de Simancas, Archivo Histórico Nacional, 2012): https://core.ac.uk/download/pdf/50598289.pdf.

62 Motis Dolader, "L'alimentation juive médiévale"; Motis Dolader, "Regimen alimentario de las comunidades judías y conversas en la Corona de Aragón en la Edad Media." See bibliography.

63 Parrondo and Conde, *Fontes Iudaeorum Regni Castellae*, vol. 4:77, no. 137.

64 Ibid., 79, no. 146.

and so on. These were frequently part of the dishes recorded in the trials of the Inquisition and for which Jewish converts to Christianity were denounced. In short, "man is probably as big a consumer of symbols as of food."[65] The documents of the Inquisition represent a rich written source the contain much about things deemed questionable by the Holy Office, precisely for their association with the practices and culinary habits of supposed "heretics." Through their food, through their unique culinary techniques, Jews were condemned for not complying with the prevailing orthodoxy.

65 Jean Trémolières, *Biologie générale*, 4 vols. (Paris: Dunod, 1969), *462. Translation by the author.*

Part Three

SEPHARDIC JEWISH CULINARY HERITAGE: BETWEEN REBIRTH AND THE DESIRE TO RECOGNIZE A PAST LEGACY

"For the most part, . . . Sephardic communities worked hard to blend in with their neighbors (keeping in mind that they has been established in Spain for centuries), and except for specific dietary restrictions of their religion, the foods they ate were not recognizably distinctive,"[1] writes Jodi Campbell. Transmission is rarely a matter of exact reproduction. When studying food, a major difficulty is changes to the names of recipes. How do we disentangle the history of dishes which, because of history, politics, and religion, have evolved or radically changed? After all, food is a major part of our contemporary understanding of the Jewish past. Let's start at the beginning, with the first source that includes explicitly Jewish recipes.

The cuisine presented in the cookbooks of the thirteenth century reflects the culinary art of the multiculturally rich al-Andalus. A culinary kaleidoscope, the dishes in the *Kitāb al-ṭabīḫ* are profoundly rooted in this unique part of Southern Spain and in a historical period marked by religious intolerance. It is hard to believe that this cuisine endured. And yet . . .

---

1 Jodi Campbell, *At the First Table*, 73.

CHAPTER 9

Dishes Common in Spanish Sephardic Cuisine

Questioning the permanence of a Jewish and Sephardic tradition is central to this culinary Jewish history of Spain. The lack of knowledge and recognition of the Spanish Sephardic culinary legacy within Spain's current food culture is highly problematic. The meagre publications and the difficulty of inventorying cookbooks dealing with Sephardic cuisine make the task of writing this history even more difficult. Perhaps studying Sephardic food prompts guilt about what Jews have experienced across the centuries, especially in Spain.

A thorough survey leads to an understanding of the reasons for the spread of the Sephardic Jewish culinary heritage. It explains why Andalusian culinary heritage has been maintained in the diaspora from Spain, where religious holidays were a means of differentiating communities. A culinary investigation reveals what dishes from the *Kitāb al-ṭabīḫ* that were consumed among the Sephardic of Spain, while also allowing us to see the evolution of their names and ingredients. *Cecina, oriza, almodrote,* and Shabbat dishes (*olla, dafina*) are presented, alongside sugar and honey dishes such as *hojuela, orejas de Hamán,* and *mazapanes,* as signs of a past Iberian culinary heritage.

A. An overview of Sephardic Jewish Cookbooks

The Norwegian historian Henry Notaker's *Printed Cookbooks in Europe, 1470–1700: A Bibliography of Early Modern Culinary Literature*[1] does not refer to any published cookbook related to Jewish cuisine before the nineteenth century. His recent *A History of Cookbooks: From Kitchen to Page over Seven Centuries,*[2] which

1 Notaker, *Printed Cookbooks in Europe.*
2 Notaker, *A History of Cookbooks.*

is *the* study of published cookbooks, contains a chapter[3] on Jewish cookbooks that were published between 1815 and 1945. None of these were written in Spanish or Judeo-Spanish. Out of the one hundred and two titles, one is written in Italian; almost all of them were written in German, Polish, Hungarian, Yiddish, Danish, and, of course, English, and they all focus on Ashkenazi cuisine.[4]

The catalogue of the New York Public Library[5] categorizes cookbooks by "region." This means that Jewish cookbooks are included in the category "International Jewish Cuisine," then "Ashkenazi Jewish Cuisine," and finally "Sephardic Jewish Cuisine." This categorization underscores the degree to which the diaspora is an integral part of Jewish culture and history. Various types of dishes (*knishes, gefilte fish, gizado*), or the terms "Yiddish," "Ashkenazi," "Sephardic," or even place names (Spain, Morocco, Poland, etc.) are used as the basis of classification. Between 1964 and 2011, there are thirty-one cookbooks of so-called "international" Jewish cuisine. This count does not include translations into other languages. Yet it is important to point out that the widespread publication of Jewish cookbooks in the US makes it difficult to update this list. The introduction to John Cooper's *Eat and Be Satisfied* proposes a non exhaustive summary of Christian cookbooks dealing with the history of Jewish cooking in the nineteenth and twentieth centuries, along with details about these publications.[6]

It is worth briefly noting the number of cookbooks mentioned in the "Sephardic" part of this catalogue. There are forty-two, of which only five were published in Spain. Eight are written in Spanish, and one in Ladino.[7] The difficult task of producing an inventory of recipe books dealing with Sephardic cuisine is acknowledged by the New York Public Library catalogue, as one is invited to consult the cookbooks of countries or regions such as Algeria, Bulgaria, Greece, India, Iran, Iraq, Italy, the Mediterranean, Morocco, North Africa,

---

3 Ibid., 233–245.

4 Ashkenazi are primarily Jews from central and Eastern Europe.

5 New York Public Library: https://www.nypl.org/collections/nypl-recommendations/guides/jewish-cookbooks-region.

6 Cooper, *Eat and be satisfied*, xii–xx.

7 *Ladino* language, also called "Judeo-Spanish," "Judesmo," or "Sephardi," is a Romance language spoken by Sephardic Jews living mostly in Israel, the Balkans, North Africa, Greece, and Turkey nowadays. It is a very old form of Castilian Spanish with some Hebrew elements (as well as Aramaic, Arabic, Turkish, Greek, French, Bulgarian, and Italian). Ladino originated in Spain, and was carried to its present speech areas by the descendants of Spanish Jews who were expelled from Spain after 1492. Ladino preserves many words and grammatical usages that have been lost in modern Spanish (sic) See *Britannica*, https://www.britannica.com/topic/Ladino-language.

Portugal, Spain, Syria, Turkey, Tunisia, Venezuela, and Yemen. This long list of countries where Sephardic Jews live testifies to the extent of the diaspora—a list to which Brazil, Ethiopia, Israel, and many other countries can be added.

In short, this disparity illustrates the lack of knowledge and acknowledgement of the Spanish Sephardic culinary heritage within current Spanish food history. As I discussed in the introduction, the relatively small amount of Jewish historiography in general, combined with the fact that Jewish history has often been constructed in parallel to, and sometimes in reaction to, history in the broader sense, undoubtedly explains the small number of Iberian, and hence Sephardic and southern, publications. A Jewish "self-consciousness," which never existed in written form, has resurfaced strongly among Sephardic Jews through food, meals, celebrations, and the culinary preparations required for such events, thus making cuisine an emblem of identity filled with nostalgia for a culture that Mediterranean Jews carry on to this day.

B. "Savory" Dishes in Medieval Arabic Cookbooks

I have chosen the following preparations based on two criteria: their inclusion in the medieval cookbooks and the fact that they currently belong to the culinary heritage of modern Spain. But there is another essential criterion too: transmission. The task here is to regard the transmission and production of these recipes as an integral part of the culinary habits of Sephardic Jews, even though they were not explicitly recognized as Jewish in al-Andalus. Despite the fact that the use of concepts such as "savory" and "sweet" medieval cuisine is debatable, I have decided to present them in two distinct parts, as this corresponds to the contemporary period.

a. *Cecina*, or Dried Beef

Cecina is the term used in Spain today to refer to dried beef. Beyond its gustatory interest, the preparation was used to preserve and transport meat more easily. But what do the texts say about the origin of this dish, and to what degree is it part of the al-Andalus cookbooks, the *Kitāb al-ṭabīḫ* and the *Fuḍālat al-ḫiwān*? The first question asks why dried beef endured in the culinary heritage of Spain.[8]

8 "Inventario dieta mediterránea: IDIME: https://www.inventariodietamediterranea.com/cecina-sello-c/

This fact could be seen as peculiar, given that pork-based cold meats have reigned for several centuries—in areas under Christian rule and more generally since the end of the fifteenth century—as a major Spanish food.

Let's consider for this analysis the religious division of Iberia. In contrast with neighboring countries like (northern) France, Italy, and England, where "one of the most important meats was beef," in Catalonia at the end of the Middle Ages there was, "among the Kings of Aragon," a "prevalence of mutton."[9] Catalonia's "preference for mutton [was] shared with other Mediterranean regions of the Iberian Peninsula, such as the Kingdom of Valencia or the Kingdom of Murcia," which reflects the habits of the rest of Europe. Indeed, pork was frequently eaten as a salted dish, whereas beef and mutton were consumed fresh.

As concerns the consumption of these meats on Muslim territory, let's consider what the Arabic-language cookbooks contain. The *Kitāb al-ṭabīẖ* has 311 meat-based recipes and mentions the meat of twenty-two animal species. Beef is only present in six recipes, two of which discuss the possibility of replacing it with mutton. As for mutton, it is included in forty-one dishes, and there are an additional eighteen lamb preparations. This demonstrates an strong appetite for this type of meat, even if it can't be ruled out that a lack of pasture land contributed to the reduced consumption of beef. If cow meat was not a favorite of the communities living on the Iberian Peninsula in the Late Middle Ages, why was so much time spent making dried beef? How and why did dried meat, present in Andalusian cookbooks of the thirteenth century, span so much time and become a part of the culinary heritage of Spain?

Let's examine more closely the six beef recipes in the *Kitāb al-ṭabīẖ*. They are all prepared in a pot, and no dried beef recipe is included. However, the *Fuḍālat al-ẖiwān* has one. This cookbook, which appeared only several decades after the *Kitāb al-ṭabīẖ*, contains a recipe called "Eleventh chapter, about the preparation of dried beef."[10] This is how it is prepared:

> The mean is cut into long pieces, as thin as possible. Put them in a vat with a lot of thick vinegar and pure ground salt. Stir occasionally, from the morning until noon. Then, sprinkle pepper,

9 Ramón A. Banegas López, "Évolution de la consommation de viande de mouton en Catalogne au long du Moyen Âge. La reconstruction d'un modèle alimentaire," in *Pour une histoire de la viande. Fabrique et représentations de l'Antiquité à nos jours*, ed. Bruno Laurioux and Marie-Pierre Horard-Herbin (Rennes-Tours: Presses Universitaires de Rennes et Presses Universitaires François Rabelais, 2017).

10 Ibn Razīn al-Tuǧībī and Marín, *Relieves de las mesas acerca de las delicias de la comida y los diferentes platos*, 305–306. Translation by the author.

> cilantro, cumin grains, caraway, and murri. Beat the mix and turn it several times until the spices have been absorbed. Taste it, and add salt or other spices if needed. Leave for the rest of the day and the night. Then, hang a rope in the sun and hang [the meat] until the afternoon. Remove the rope and wrap it in cheesecloth with something light. Then hang it again the next day on the rope, for several days, until it is dry and has lost all its moisture. Put it aside somewhere dry and out of the sun. [*Cecina*] can be made with just a little water and salt, dried in the sun.[11]

The author continues:

> I saw, in the *Kitāb al-talẖīṣ* by Ibn Ǧanāḥ, a recipe that the author calls *al-namkasūd,* which is a recipe of salted meat and crushed salt. The difference between this recipe and the dried meat [*cecina*] recipe is that *namkasūd* is made with a boar, whole or cut in half; the meat stays tender and fatty, and when you press on top your hand sinks and you can cut it like it were fresh meat, not like cutting dried meat [*cecina*]. Whoever wishes it can do it, and should try.[12]

The problem here concerns the identity of Ibn Ǧanāḥ and how a recipe of dried meat can be directly connected with a dish from medical-pharmacological literature. Entitled *Book of the compendium*[13] [*Kitāb al-talẖīṣ,* كتاب التلخيص],

---

11 Ibid.: "Capítulo undécimo, sobre la confección de la cecina. Se corta la carne en fragmentos alargados, lo más finos que se pueda. Se ponen en una artesa con vinagre espeso en suficiente cantidad y sal pura molida y se remueve de rato en rato, desde la mañana hasta el mediodía. Después se le espolvorea pimienta, cilantro, cominos, alcaravea y almorí desleído. Se bate todo y se le dan vueltas hasta que absorbe la especias. Se prueba y, si falta sal u otra cosa, se le añade. Se deja así el resto del día y la noche. Después se suspende una cuerda al sol y se deja en la cuerda hasta después de mediodía. Se retira de la cuerda y se tapa en un cedazo con algo ligero. Después se vuelve a poner en la cuerda al sol, al día siguiente, y así durante varios días, hasta que se ha secado y perdido toda la humedad. Se retira a un lugar donde no le dé el sol y que no sea húmedo. Se puede hacer también solo con agua y sal y secado al sol. He visto, en el *Tratado de la explicación de los medicamentos,* de Ibn Ǧanāḥ, una receta que el autor llama *al-namkasūd,* que es una receta de carne salada con sal machacada. La diferencia entre esta receta y la cecina es que el namkasūd se hace de un carnero entero o partido en dos mitades; la carne queda blanda y grasa, cuando la aprietas te untas la mano y el cuchillo la corta como si fuera carne fresca, no como se corta la cecina. Quien lo desee, puede hacerlo, y que lo experimente."

12 Ibid.

13 Translation by the author. Paul Fenton uses the term "Compendium." See Fenton, "Jonah Ibn Ǧanāḥ's Medical Dictionary, the Kitāb al-Talẖīṣ: Lost and Found," 108.

this text is written in Arabic by an Andalusian Jewish author of the eleventh century, who knew Arabic[14] and Hebrew: Yonah Ibn Ğanāḥ (ca. 980–1040).[15] Hebrew texts refer to him as Rabbi Yōnāh or Rabbi Marinus. Thus, even if this these are difficult problems, they deserve to be addressed: Is this recipe of dried beef by a Jewish thinker, who was neither a cook nor a gastronome, connected with the widespread consumption of dried beef in Sephardic communities of Hispanic origin?

The Bible exegete and lexicographer[16] Yonah Ibn Ğanāḥ also quotes the Jewish Egyptian doctor and philosopher Isaac al-Isrā'īlī (ninth to tenth century) in the *Kitāb al-talḫīṣ*. It is important to stress the originality of the *Book of the Extract*, as well as the major role played by Jewish thinkers in the discipline of pharmacology.[17] Thus, even if distance is required so as to avoid reducing the writings of Ibn Ğanāḥ to a representative example of Jewish cooking, the possibility cannot be excluded that the dried meat recipe of Ibn Ğanāḥ, adopted by Ibn Razīn al-Tuğībī in the *Fuḍālat al-ḫiwān*, is actually representative of the food and culinary habits of Andalusian Jews. Unfortunately, the work of Ibn Ğanāḥ[18] has not survived.[19] However, commentary about the treaty, in particular by Maimonides, provides some information.

---

14 However, Ibn Ğanāḥ said himself that he did not have a perfect mastery of classical Arabic. In this work, the entries are written in various languages (Arabic, Roman, and different Berber, Syriac, and Persian dialects), but not in Hebrew. Paul Fenton writes that the reason for this is, perhaps, the need to adapt to Muslim readers. It also explains the lack of Talmudic sources, which are nonetheless filled with botanical references. See Fenton, "Jonah Ibn Ğanāḥ's Medical Dictionary, the Kitāb al-Talḫīṣ: Lost and Found," 115 and 117.

15 José Martínez Delgado, "Ibn Janāḥ, Jonah (Abū' l-Walīd Marwān)," in *Encyclopedia of Jews in the Islamic World*, ed. Norman A. Stillman (Leiden: Brill, 2010), https://referenceworks.brillonline.com/entries/encyclopedia-of-jews-in-the-islamic-world/ibn-janah-jonah-abu-l-walid-marwan-COM_0010730?s.num=2&s.au=%22Mart%C3%ADnez+Delgado%2C+José%22%22. "Despite his great influence, we have little information about the life of Jonah (Abū ʾl-Walīd Marwān) ibn Janāḥ beyond what can be extracted from his writings. He was apparently born in Cordova between 985 and 990. The names that appear in later works have given rise to considerable discussion. His Hebrew name is thought to have been Jonah (Heb. dove), based on his Arabic surname, Ibn Janāḥ (winged). His designation in Latin sources, Rabbi Marinus, is apparently derived from his Arabic personal name, Marwān."

16 Yonah Ibn Ğanāḥ had already written a bilingual biblical Hebrew dictionary in the eleventh century, the *Kitāb al-uṣūl* (*The book of origins*). See Yonah Ibn Ğanāḥ, *The Book of Hebrew Roots*, ed. and trans. A. Neubauer (Oxford: Clarendon, 1875). The *Kitāb al-uṣūl* was written in Zaragoza after his forced exile from Cordova following the repressions by Sulaymān b. al-Ḥakam. The dictionary includes medical, philosophical, literary, and botanical references.

17 Fenton, "Jonah Ibn Ğanāḥ's Medical Dictionary, the Kitāb al-Talḫīṣ: Lost and Found," 107, 140.

18 María Ángeles Gallego, *El judeo-árabe medieval: edición, traducción y estudio lingüístico del Kitāb al-taswiʿa de Yonah ibn Ğanāḥ* (Bern: Peter Lang AG, 2006), 5.

19 Ibid., 7.

The term *al-namkasūd*, used in the *Kitāb al-talḫīṣ*, is of Persian origin and it is found especially in medical literature, such as the works of Ṯābit b. Qurra (ninth century), al-Rāzī (ninth to tenth century), and Ibn al-Bayṭār (twelfth century).[20] This is a unique recipe when we consider that Ibn Ǧanāḥ is person mentioned in the entire work of Ibn Razīn al-Tuǧībī. Moreover, Ibn Ǧanāḥ is only cited to compare the dried meat recipe that the *Fuḍālat al-ḫiwān* contains and the one proposed by the Jewish thinker. In short, if the recipe in the *Fuḍālat al-ḫiwān* is not very different from the one that appears in the *Kitāb al-ṭabīḫ* by Ibn Sayyār (tenth century),[21] it seems wise to examine later sources (fifteenth to sixteenth centuries) for the presence of dried beef[22] in order to determine if there is a link between this preparation and Iberian Jews. In this sense, judicial sources are essential.

The culinary techniques used by conversos proved to be a decisive element in accusations against Jewish practices during Inquisition. These were rigorously recorded in the trials and their frequency—even more than what people said—were proof of Judaism. There are a multitude of testimonies concerning dried beef. It is often written that the preparation of the meat consisted in drying it in the sun and smoking the salted meat in order to better preserve it.[23] This practice was compliant with Jewish Law, as the meat had to be washed, sometimes several times, and generously salted so that as much blood and fat[24] as possible were removed, as well as the sciatic nerve. These numerous religious dictates could not possibly have gone unnoticed by the Inquisition, which declared them to be proof of Jewish practices. In this way, Don Gonzalo, a jeweler from the city of Soria, was sentenced by because in his home

> they prepared dried beef [*çeçina de vaca*], and it was the custom at the time to prepare dried meats [*çeçinas*] in this city and to prepare them, as Jews do; the wife and daughters of Gonçalo the jeweler removed blood from . . . the meat.[25]

---

20 See introduction to Ibn Razīn al-Tuǧībī and Marín, *Relieves de las mesas acerca de las delicias de la comida y los diferentes platos*.

21 Ibid. Kaj Öhrnberg and Sahban Mroueh, eds., *Ibn Sāyyār al-Warrāq*, كتاب الطبيخ *Kitāb al-ṭabīḫ* (Helsinki: Finnish Oriental Society, 1987), 233.

22 Brined, spiced beef that is dried or smoked, called *cecina* in Spanish, resembles today's *pastrami*, with the difference that pastrami is coated in spices. On this topic, see also Freedman, *Why Food Matters*, 60.

23 Cantera Montenegro, "La carne y el pescado en el sistema alimentario judío de la España medieval," 34.

24 Lev. 7:22–25.

25 Carrete Parrondo and Castaño González, *Fontes Iudaeorum Regni Castellae*, vol. 2, 50: ". . . fazían çeçina de vaca, e quera en tienpo que suelen fazer çeçinas en la dicha çibdad, e que

In the above it is clear that Jews were removing the blood as commanded by the precepts of the Torah.[26] From the beginning of the Inquisition in 1478, the transcripts of the trials are full of stories in which conversos were denounced for having removed the nerve from the meat[27] right before salting it (the step before drying). This practice was so commonplace among Iberian Jews, at least from the fifteenth century, that it became a marker of Jewish identity. Removing the nerve, salting, and brining, all steps involved in making dried meat, were registered in the judiciary sources and reveal Jewish practices and food during the period. Thus, Constanza Nuñez and her servant Alonso were described

> splitting the thighs of goats in two, putting salt, and removing the sciatic nerve inside [*landrezylla*] and fat[28] [*sebo*] and throwing it away; and he knows that it was the sciatic nerve [*landrezylla*] because he saw them remove it; . . . when they were Jews they split the thighs to salt, brine and dry them [*ceninarlo*].[29]

---

para las ainsí fazer estavan purgando la. . . carne, como los judíos fazen, su muger e fijas de . . . Gonçalo, platero" (AGS, Patronato Real, Inquisición, dossier 28/73, folio verso 981). Translation by the author.

26 On the prohibition against eating fat and blood, see Safra and Marciano, *Chumash*, 617; Lev. 7:22–27.

27 The sciatic nerve was commonly called in Spanish "landrecilla." See Ricardo Múñoz Solla, "Los conversos judaizantes de Berlanga de Duero (s. XV-XVI)," vol. 3 (PhD diss., Universidad de Salamanca, 2003), 882–883; Cantera Montenegro, "La carne y el pescado en el sistema alimentario judío de la España medieval," 22: Inquisition trial against María Rodriguez, Pedro Rodríguez's wife, who was living close to Berlanga de Duero (1526–1528; 1547): ". . . que a la dicha Mari Rodríguez le vido sacar las dichas landrezillas estando presentes las dichas personas, que por lo menos fueron dos o tres vezes. Y la dicha landrezilla le paresge que sería de la manera de la carne de una molleja de abe, que no se sabe determinar en ella porque sacándola la dicha Mari Rodríguez la arrojava luego. Y que de las dichas piernas las sacava de la pared de abaxo dellas, donde estava el huesso de la anguilla" (ADC, Inquisición, leg. 101/1448); See Carrete Parrondo and Castaño González, *Fontes ludaeorum Regni Castellae*, 2:85: ". . . que todas las vezes que tra/an pierna de carnero de la carnegería vio este testigo cómo Ynés, donzella, fija de Yñigo López e María Hermosa . . ., ques de más de veynte años, tendía las dichas piernas por medio y las sacava la landrezilla y la echava, la qual estava en medio de la pierna, ques redonda, como negrilla; y este testigo le dezía que por qué la sacava y la echava, y la susodicha dezía . . . que porque non hera buena. Lo qual le vido este testigo fazer cada vez que trayan piernas." (ADC, Inquisición, leg. 748/5-5, fol. 31v.).

28 On the prohibition against eating fat see Lev. 7:22–25. See Safra and Marciano, *Chumash*, 616–617.

29 Parrondo and González, *Fontes ludaeorum Regni Castellae*, 2:91, no. 186: ". . . abrían por medio las piernas de cabrones e cabras, que echavan en sal, e les sacavan de enmedio la landrezylla e sebo e lo echavan; e que sabe que hera la landrezylla porque lo a visto sacar . . . quando heran judíos abrían las piernas para salgar e çeçinallo." (AGS, Patronato Real, Inquisición, leg. 28/73, fol. 1068r.). Translation by the author.

The term *sebo* refers to the fat that covered the meat, which Jews removed. The words *brinças* and *binças* in the transcripts of Inquisition trials also refer to when this fat was used in large quantities.[30] Eating dried meat (at least this type of dried meat) was a common practice among Spanish Jews, whether conversos or not. Sources from the beginning of the sixteenth century from the city of Almazán also testify to this. The consumption of dried meat was maybe as important as pork was for Christians. These hypotheses are verified if we look at the number of times the word *cecina* appears in the judiciary sources from the tribunals of the Spanish monarchy. Here is one more example supporting this fact:

> Maria Ortíz, from Biscay, near Almazán . . ., says that in the areas around San Miguel, one year, while this witness went to see Grauiel Nuñes and his wife in San Torcas, other people brought a suckling pig and a piece of pork lard [*toçino*]; the wife of Grauiel Nuñes, grocer [*tendero*], never wanted to eat that, and she asked beforehand . . . her aunt, a new Christian [*tornadiza*], to give her meat [*carne*] and dried beef [*çesina*].[31]

From the sources from the Inquisition, we can say that Jews indeed used beef to make dried meat. One noteworthy example concerns Martín de Ortega, who wanted to kill a cow to make dried meat. This was denounced by an anonymous accuser, who stated that the Judeo-converso Pedro Laynes did not want to kill the animal "as Christians do, but cut [its neck] with a sharpened knife."[32]

In sum, beef that was salted, brined, dried, or smoked was a part of the culinary rites and practices of Spanish Jews at the end of the Middle Ages. This is still the case today, even if its consumption has spread beyond the Jewish community (which does not exclude the possibility that non-Jews could also have eaten it). Is this, then, one of the reasons that dried meat endured in the culinary heritage of modern Spain? Most likely, yes. Indeed, the technique for preparing and drying meat presented in the *Fuḍālat al-ẖiwān* is the same as that included

---

30 Parrondo and Conde, *Fontes ludaeorum Regni Castellae*, 4:72–73, no. 134: ". . . y con vn cuchillo la estaua quitando las brinças questauan ençima de la carne"; 78–79, no. 143: ". . . su ama a este testigo antes que echase la carne en la olla que la desvenase e quitase las binças para que estouviese más linpia."

31 Parrondo and Conde, *Fontes ludaeorum Regni Castellae*, 4:79, no. 146. Translation by the author.

32 Parrondo and Conde, *Fontes ludaeorum Regni Castellae*, 4:73, no. 134: ". . . quería matar vn buey para çeçina y que . . . Pero Laynes no lo consentió matar como matan los christianos, syno atrauesado, con el cuchillo syn mellar." (ADC, Inquisición, leg. 749/15, fol. 3v.; anonymous accusation, Sigüenza 1501, in ibid., leg. 749/14, fol. 46v. Translation by the author.

in the IDIME (Inventario de la DIeta MEditerránea) to prepare dried meat, called *Cecina Sello C.*[33] Brined, pickled, and spiced, the meat is dried in the sun to remove all the moisture. It is then stored in a dry place away from light, under a cheesecloth, where it continues to mature for several days, or even months, before cutting.

b. Dishes for Shabbat

Adefina, Aní, Trasnochado, Hamín, Caliente, albondiguillas. These are different terms that refer to the same dish: the food that Jews prepared on Friday night for Shabbat in Spain. According to the *Diccionario de la lengua española de la Real Academia Española,* the word *adafina* comes from the Hispanic-Arabic term *addafína* and the classical Arabic *dafīnah* means "buried." It is a pot that Hebrews prepared on Friday night, during preparation covered with a hot stone (*rescoldo*) and embers, to be eaten on Saturday. *Dafūn* is the verb which, in Arabic, means to "bury" or "hide," and whose root is the same as the Hebrew *ŝ.f.n,* "hide," although this is not surprising since both languages are Semitic. *Dafina,* دفينة, thus refers to the adjective in the female singular, meaning "buried." *Ad-* is added to produce "that which is buried," *ad-dafina,* hence the word *addafina,* الدفينة.

i. *Adafina*[34]

Adafina is a Jewish Spanish dish par excellence, prepared on Friday night for Shabbat. It is cooked "buried" beneath a hot stone, which, keeps the dish hot for a long time. In the *Kitāb al-ṭabīḫ,* this culinary technique often employs a pot covered in coals in order to keep the dish relatively hot for the next day without needing to touch it. In the "Jewish Partridge" recipe, it says,[35] "Put a potsherd or copper pot full of burning coals on it." In the "Stuffed, Buried Jewish Dish,"

33 IDIME, "Cecina," accessed 4 April, 2022, https://www.inventariodietamediterranea.com/cecina-sello-c/.

34 De Eguilaz y Yanguas, *Glosario etimológico de las palabras españolas de origen oriental*: "Del ár. hisp. *addafína,* y este del ár. clás. *dafīnah* 'enterrada', pues lo es en el rescoldo. Es una olla que los hebreos preparan el anochecer del viernes, cubriéndola con rescoldo y brasas, para comerla el sábado."

35 Guillaumond, *Cuisine et diététique dans l'Occident arabe médiéval,* 140–141, no. 169.

it says, "Then take a new pot and put in a spoonful of oil. . . . Then cover it with burning coals."

However, it is another recipe of the *Kitāb al-ṭabīẖ* that is particularly intriguing. This one concerns a dish with the title *madfūn*, or "Stuffed Buried Jewish Dish." Charles Perry's notes about this dish confirm this. He specifies that the "Stuffed Buried Jewish Dish" is "A version of adafina (from an Arabic word meaning 'buried treasure,' related to the word *madfûn*, 'buried,' which is found in the name of this dish), the Sephardic equivalent of the Ashkenazi dish *cholent*, which could be left in the oven overnight on Friday so that Jewish housewives wouldn't have to violate the Sabbath by cooking."[36] The *Kitāb al-ṭabīẖ*, then, appears to contain the first written *adafina* recipe.

As soon as the Inquisition began, trial records were filled with stories that mention the term *adefina*.[37] It is the most frequently used word when referring to Friday night culinary practices in the homes of conversos. This leads to two essential insights: first, the existence of a dish that is specific to Iberian Jews, and second, the knowledge and acknowledgement by non-Jews of a specifically Jewish dish. For instance, consider the final reports written by an *el fiscal* (inspector, prosecutor) concerning the Arias Dávila family. Beyond the statements transcribed in the accusations, the first obvious sign of Judaism was not the recitation of prayers or ways of dressing, but, rather, culinary habits, with the eating of *adefina* being the most commonly mentioned:

> [A]nd she withdrew and returned to the Jewish Law under which she had been born and raised, by saying, doing and acting many different times, in many different places and moments, events and gestures, rituals and ceremonies of the Jewish Law, according to which they are accustomed to saying and doing, and we know and are certain that Doña Elbira Goncález, was accustomed to and followed the Jewish Law, that she had cooked [*guizar*] and prepared Jewish dishes, like *adefinas* and other dishes made by Jews, with her ceremonies and rituals and she brought them [these dishes] cooked in Jewish homes on Friday for Saturday and they ate them [*adefinas*] cold, secretly, in hiding.[38]

---

36 "An Anonymous Andalusian Cookbook," no. 42, http://www.daviddfriedman.com/Medieval/Cookbooks/Andalusian/andalusian_footnotes.htm#fnB41.

37 Freedman, *Why Food Matters*, 57.

38 Parrondo, *Fontes Iudaeorum Regni Castellae*, 3:140: fol. 71 r., paragraph 247: ". . . e se redujo e tornó a la dicha ley de los judíos en que abía nacido e se abía criado, diciendo, faciendo e obrando por muchas e diversas veçes, en diversos lugares e tiempos dichos, obras e fechos,

Adafina/adefina are the terms used in judiciary sources. Carlos Carrete Parondo explains that in the trial against the Arias Dávila family, the word *adafina* is employed to describe the dish "that Jews left [to cook] on Friday night, by covering it with a hot stone [*rescoldo*] and coals, to be eaten on Saturday." He adds that "it is also called *hamín* and *caliente*."[39] The transcripts demonstrate that *adafina* was generally brought to the house of a family member, "cooked in the Jewish quarter on Saturday,"[40] and "consumed every Saturday."[41] The preparation and consumption of *adafina* was also perceived by Christians to be a conspicuous sign of Judaism and a rejection of what Jews and conversos represented for them. A letter written to King Ferdinand in 1516 states that "nearly all the residents of this city [Seville] smell Jews [*huelen a judíos*], them, their houses and the doors of their houses [*ellos, sus casas y las pertas de sus casas*], because they are gluttons [*tragones*] and pigs [*comilones*], and they nourish themselves with casseroles [*olletas*], garlic [*ajos*] and *adafinas*."[42]

ii. *Aní*

Among the dishes served for Shabbat is *aní*, which is an equivalent term for *adafina*. It is found, for instance, in the transcripts of the Inquisition of Valencia under the rule of the Catholic Kings (1479–1504):

> [*Aní*] . . . means something hot, which was usually made with fatty meat [*carne gorda*], chickpeas [*garbanços*], fava beans [*habas*], beans [*judías*] hard boiled eggs [*huebos duros*], and any other vegetables; the dish cooked all night on Friday [*toda la noche del viernes*], because Jews [*porque los judíos*] on Saturday [*el sábbado*] could not cook [*no podían guisar de comer*]; and this

---

ritos e ceremonias de la dicha ley de los judíos, según que ellos suelen y acostumbran decir y açer, que se prueba y está probado la dicha doña Elbira Goncález, teniendo afiçión e siguiendo la dicha ley de los judíos, faía guisar e guisaba manjar de judíos, así como adefinas e otros manjares por manos de judíos e con sus ceremonias e rictos e ge los trayan guisados de cassa de los dichos judíos del viernes para el sábado e las comían los sábados frías, secreta e ocultamente." Translation by the author.

39 Parrondo, *Fontes Iudaeorum Regni Castellae*, 3:22, no. 9n5: ". . . adefina: es el guiso que los judíos colocan el viernes por la tarde, cubriéndolo con rescoldo y brasas para comerlo el sábado; también se le denomina 'hamín' y 'caliente.'"

40 Ibid., 22. Translation by the author.

41 Ibid., 23, no. 10. Translation by the author.

42 *Nuevo Diccionario histórico del Español*, entry no. 9: http://web.frl.es/fichero.html. Translation by the author.

> cooked dish [*aquel guisado*] stayed hot [*estava caliente*] on the hearth [*en el fogaril*] until meal time on Saturday [*fasta la hora de comer el sábado*].[43]

The identity and uniqueness of *adafina* is revealed through what it hides. It is a buried dish, a "treasure"[44] that must be not be displayed for all to see.

Aní has all the features of the dish that is today called *olla podrida*. Jews used to prepare it with "fatty meat, chickpeas, fava beans, beans [*judías*], hardboiled eggs and any other vegetables."[45] This preparation has a lot in common with the *olla podrida* recipe recorded by the Spanish writer Emilia Pardo Bazán. She considers it to be the paragon of Spanish cooking. Among the ingredients listed by the writer, the term "bean" merits some attention. The Spanish term is *judía* (or *alubia*, *lūbiyā* in Arabic). The similarity between the terms *judía* meaning "bean" and *judía* meaning "Jew" arouses curiosity. Does a relationship exist between this vegetable and Jews? It is interesting given that the kind of bean called "black-eyed pea"—known as *Vigna unguiculata* and *melanophthalmus DC*,[46] the only one which preceded the use of beans in the old world—is called *lūbiyā širkiyyah*.[47] This term is used by the Andalusian agronomist Abū 'l-Khayr al-Ishbīlī to refer to the "bean of the heretics" (or polytheists). From the perspective of Islam, "polytheists" are Christians or Jews. The *Dictionary of Andalusi Arabic: Phraseological and Etymological Perspectives*[48] by Federico Corriente, Christophe Pereira, and Ángeles Vicente explains that the root of the word شرك (the group of letters ŠRK) is related to *širkiyyah* (polytheism). However, the fact that this author mentions it does not mean that it was cultivated in al-Andalus, since it

---

43 Ramón Santa María, "Ritos y costumbres de los hebreos españoles," *Boletín de la Real Academia de la Historia*, leg. 299 (1893): 187: "Item el aní, que quiere decir cossa caliente, que se acostumbraba á hacer con carne gorda, garbanços, fabas, judías, huebos duros, y de otro cualquier legumbre; lo qual todo cocía toda la noche de el viernes, porque los judíos el sábbado no podían guissar de comer; y aquel guisado estava caliente en su fogaril fasta la hora de comer el sábado; y anssí el guisar de este aní hera principio de la guarda de el sábbado en signifficación que los judios guardaban manna de un día para otro, y todo el dicho manna se les tornava gusanos, salvo lo que cozían el viernes para el sábbado, porque aquello no se bolvía gussanos, y por aquel resppeto los judíos hacían el aní el viernes para el sábbado." See Davidson and Davidson, *A Drizzle of Honey*, 148, 324.

44 The term *adafina* was also used in Iberian poems to refer to the "treasure."

45 Santa María, "Ritos y costumbres de los hebreos españoles." See Davidson and Davidson, *A Drizzle of Honey*, 310.

46 *Encyclopédie des plantes alimentaires*, 420

47 *Diccionario Etimológico Castellano en Línea.*

48 Federico Corriente, Christophe Pereira and Ángeles Vicente, eds., *Dictionnaire du faisceau dialectal arabe andalou. Perspectives phraséologiques et étymologiques* (Berlin: De Gruyter, 2017), 705.

could have been read about in another source and not direct observed. It is highly likely, though, that this variety already existed at the end of the eleventh century in al-Andalus. It could also prove the uses of black-eyed pea in Jewish dishes.

Let's look at what the judiciary sources say about *olla*. The following, which describes how *olla*[49] was prepared, was written in 1523, but narrates events that occurred fifty years before in Toledo, and thus before the Tribunal of the Inquisition was established there:

> [They showed him a pot [*olla*] for cooking [*guisar*] . . . in which they put chickpeas and fava beans [*avas*];[50] and the fattiest meat that could be found or breast [*ubre*], and they put it in the pot, and they added eggplants if they were in season, and dry cilantro and caraway and cumin and pepper and onion; and these spices, they called them scents [*güesmo*], and the pot [*olla*] was cooked [*guisar*] the night before until meal time the next day; when they wanted to cover it [*cubijar*] before nightfall, they put slices of Swiss chard [*cochas*] chopped and crushed, and if they didn't have any, they put radish leaves.[51]

This dish, both in terms of its content and cooking technique, appears to bring together the whole of Iberian Jewish cuisine of the Middle Ages. The word *güesmo* refers to the particular smell[52] that comes from preparing the pot. This dish is no other than *adafina*. The text recalls the words of Caesar to Rabbi Joshua, recorded in the Babylonian Talmud (450–550 CE), Shabbat 119a:8:

> The Roman emperor said to Rabbi Yehoshua ben Ḥananya: Why does the fragrance of a cooked *Shabbat* dish diffuse? He said to him: We have a certain spice called dill [*shevet*], which we place in the cooked dishes and its fragrance spreads. The emperor

---

49 Davidson and Davidson, *A Drizzle of Honey*, 155.

50 The term is not listed in the *Tesoro de la lengua castellana o Española*, by Covarrubias, 1611, http://fondosdigitales.us.es/fondos/libros/765/244/tesoro-de-la-lengua-castellana-o-espanola/.

51 Davidson and Davidson, *A Drizzle of Honey*, 311, 311n38, and 323; See Pilar León Tello, "Costumbres, fiestas y ritos de los judíos toledanos a fines del siglo XV," in *Symposium Toledo judaico (Toledo 20–22 abril 1972)*, 2 vols. (Toledo: Centro universitario de Toledo, 1973). 2:67–90.

52 I would like to thank Professor Elena Romero for shedding light on the meaning of this word.

> said to him: Give us some of it. He said to him: For anyone who observes *Shabbat,* the spice is effective, and for one who does not observe *Shabbat,* it is not effective.[53]

It is noteworthy that the atmosphere of a home where Shabbat is respected makes everything become delicious. Indeed, the word formed by the letters Shin Beth Tav means both dill (which reads as *shevet*) and Shabbat. Rabbi Yehoshua ben Ḥananya puns of the two meanings to poetically capture the deliciousness of *Shabbat,* sweet and good like *shevet*[54] perfume.

iii. *Ḥamín*

The Shabbat dish *adafina* is also known by a third name: *ḥamín.* This is the accusation of heresy and apostasy made against the Jew Juan Sánchez Exarch that occurred on November 30, 1484. The term *ḥamyn* is recognized for being "truly (*verdad*), by all the people (*fama pública*), a well-known (*voz común*) converso dish."[55] It resembles the previously mentioned *aní* dish. *Ḥamín/Hamín* is derived from the Hebrew *ḥam,* which means "hot" (ḥam, חם);[56] *hamía* can also be used.[57] The main feature of this dish is not so much what it contains as the way it is cooked. Ariel Toaff writes that *ḥamin* was known during the Italian Renaissance as *frizinsal* in Piedmont, Reggio Emilia, Veneto, and Mantua; he adds that at the

53 אמר לו קיסר לרבי יהושע בן חנניא מפני מה תבשיל של שבת ריחו נודף אמר לו תבלין אחד יש לנו ושבת שמו שאנו מטילין לתוכו וריחו נודף אמר לו תן לנו הימנו אמר לו כל המשמר את השבת מועיל לו ושאינו משמר את השבת אינו מועיל לו. See https://www.sefaria.org/Shabbat.119a.8?ven=William_Davidson_Edition_-_English&vhe=William_Davidson_Edition_-_Vocalized_Aramaic&lang=bi. The commentary by Jastrow specifies: a. fr. 119a ת׳ אחד יש לנו וכ׳: "[W]e have a certain spice the name of which is Sabbath."

54 I would like to thank the chief rabbi of the Southwest of France, Emmanuel Valency, for this analysis.

55 Bernardino Llorca, "La Inquisición Española Incipiente. Nuevos Datos Sobre Su Primera Actuación," *Gregorianum* 20, no. 1 (1939): 130: "Item más dice y propone el dicho promotor fiscal que el dicho reo denunciado e infamado a costumbrado y costumbra comer según que el fecho comió y come per cerimonia judayca del sábado, vn comer vulgarmente llamado *Hamyn,* que judíos en su casa. E assi es verdad, voz común y fama pública." The note about the word *Hamyn* indicates that it is undoubtedly the same thing as *ḥamía,* a special dish that Jews ate on Saturday, which can be grasped from the context. The note adds that there is no doubt about the connection between this dish and the *ḥamán* fasting; Montenegro, "La carne y el pescado en el sistema alimentario judío de la España medieval," 33.

56 See Romero, *El olor del sábado.* Translation by the author.

57 Llorca, "La Inquisición Española Incipiente": 135: ". . . e que por obseruación del dicho día del sábado comía *hamía* e otros comeres de carnes quisadas del viernes paral sábado." Translation by the author.

end of the eighteenth century, the poet and writer from Mantua, Samuel Romancelli, mentioned *ḥamin*, given its ties to Moroccan Jews.[58]

Food and *ḥamin* in particular are well described in Spanish trials. One example among many others is found in Inquisition trials from Lleida at the end of the fifteenth century. We read that Aldonça Sisona, widow of Manuel Sisón, "on Saturdays ate *ḥamin* and *ḥamin* eggs, which were sent [to her] by this Jewish woman."[59] Eating *ḥamin* Friday night for Shabbat was a converso practice, which is also underscored in a trial transcript from the same city, Lleida. So we learn that Aldonça Garreta, Jaume Joan Garret's wife, "on Friday afternoons lit many fires and put clean tablecloths on the table and we ate *ḥamin*, which we enjoyed bringing together from the Jewish quarter."[60]

iv. *Caliente*

Additional evidence of the many terms that refer to *adafina* comes from the word *caliente* (Spanish for "hot"). Starting in 1480, the word was used to refer to dishes prepared by Jews in the province of Segovia. Moreover, each time that the term *adefina* is referred to in the *Proceso Inquisitorial contra los Arias Dávila segovianos*, which was held at the end of the fifteenth century in Spain, a note from the editor refers to trial number 9 of the book.[61] References to the *caliente* dish are frequent, making it clear proof of continuing compliance with Mosaic law by accused conversos. Here is an excerpt from one of the trials

> Another then said that, next Friday, the afore mentioned Diego Arias supplicated the father of this witness to prepare him a *caliente* for Saturday, using a half dozen eggs, and his father told him that it contained bad meat, and he answered: "This is how it is made." And his father made it for him, and had the witness send it to him, and he gave it to Diego Arias, who ate it in front of

58 Ariel Toaff, "Pranzi quotidiani, di sabato, di festa," in *Mangiare alla giudia: la cucina ebraica in Italia dal Rinascimento all'età moderna*, ed. Ariel Toaff (Bologne: Il Mulino, 2000), 132–133.

59 Dolader, "Claves e identidades de los judeoconversos de Lleida según los procesos inquisitoriales a finales del siglo xv," 112: "y en dias de sabado [ha] comido hamin y huevos de hamin, los quales [le] enviava la dicha judía." Translation by the author.

60 Ibid., 114: ". . . los viernes a las tardes encendia muchas lumbres y ponia manteles limpios en la mesa y comiendo hamin, el qual nos faziamos traher aparejado de la juderia."

61 Carrete Parrondo, *Fontes ludaeorum Regni Castellae*, 3:22, no. 9n5: ". . . adefina: es el guiso que los judíos colocan el viernes por la tarde, cubriéndolo con rescoldo y brasas para comerlo el sábado; también se le denomina 'hamín' y 'caliente.'"

> the witness, while he waited to bring back the pot [*puchero*] that contained the dish, as well as the bowl that he had brought.[62]

Whether *caliente* or *ḥamin*, both terms refer to the same dish: *adafina*. They have something significant common: the distinguishing feature is the heat of the dish.

v. *Trasnochado* and Meatballs

Here is a final example of the terminological diversity of *adafina*. It is found in the word *trasnochado*, which can be translated as "all night long."[63] The word appears the poem *Cancionero general de Hernando del Castillo*, which dates from the end of the fifteenth century.[64] While this term refers to the dish, it is important to stress that its defining feature is the way it is cooked: all night long. This clearly refers to the preparation of the dish for Shabbat.

Beyond *adafina*, meatballs were also associated, in the eyes of old Christians, with the culinary habits of Jews on the Iberian Peninsula. These two foods were regularly mentioned in Inquisition trials, as when Guimor Fernández, of Guadalajara, was accused in 1523 of having "followed Jewish rituals, by making *adafina* and meatballs in the same way as Jews, and by observing *Shabbat*."[65] The same year, in Toledo, Blanca Ramírez was accused of acting in a Jewish manner. The following is stated in the judgment:

> On Friday night, she put [in a pot] some meatballs [*pelotas*] that had been cooked and sautéed [*sancochadas*] and another pot

---

62 Ibid., 98, no. 169: "Otrosí dixo que luego, el biernes adelante, el dicho Diego Arias rogó a su padre de este testigo que le ficiesse facer un caliente para el sábado y le echasse en él medio deçena de güebos, e su padre le dixo que abía mala carne, e le dixo: 'Tal qual/ así se aga/'. E su padre le fiço façer, e lo inbió con este testigo e lo dió al dicho Diego Arias e lo comió en su presencia de este testigo, porque esperó allí para llebar el puchero en que yba y la escudilla que abía llevado." See Davidson and Davidson, *A Drizzle of Honey*, 322, no. 148. Translation by the author.

63 Translation by the author.

64 Hernando Del Castillo, *Cancionero general*, 2 vols. (Madrid: Sociedad de Bibliófilos Españoles, 1882), poem no. 997; see https://bibliotecadigital.jcyl.es/es/consulta/registro.cmd?id=3708: ". . . que contiene muchas obras de diuersos autores antiguos con algunas cosas nueuas de modernos, de nueuo corregido e impresso Martin Nucio" (quoted from the edition of 1557), poem 364: ". . . porque nadie nos reproche trobar papillos rellenos en los viernes en la noche trobar en sangre coger de lo que aueys degollado trobar en nunca comer lo del rabi deuedado fino manjar trasnochado;" See Delicado, Gernert, and Joset, *La Lozana andaluza*: "trasnochado," mamotreto/chapter 34. Translation by the author.

65 Davidson and Davidson, *A Drizzle of Honey*, 312n74. Translation by the author.

> [*olla*] of Spanish chard with spices and chickpeas, and when they went to bed, they left a candle lit on the pot [*olla*], and the next day, on Saturday, they uncovered the pot and they ate it.[66]

To conclude, the use of a Semitic term (*adafina/ḥamin*) to signify a typically Jewish culinary specialty eaten during Shabbat may be surprising,[67] as this celebration of the sacred day[68] marks the application of one of the ten commandments[69] in the Hebrew Bible. But remember that Jews were Arabized and that at the end of the Middle Ages disagreements were primarily between Jews and Christians. The more issue question concerns the reasons for the terminological diversity of the Shabbat dish *adafina.* Does it reflect an attempt to conceal the preparation from the Inquisition? The specificity of all of these terms for the same dish is revealed by what isn't seen. More than the ingredients, the very features of the dish make *adafina* the Jewish Shabbat dish.

Let's look at these words more closely. The term *a-dafina* refers to the content of a dish that is not seen. It is buried, hidden, and must not be uncovered to reveal the culinary treasure that is hiding there. The terms *ḥamin* and *caliente* do not refer to ingredients either. Rather, they draw attention to the purpose of the dish: to reheat is prohibited once Shabbat begins. As for the term *trasnochado,* it refers to the very essence of the Shabbat dish that had to cook all night until the next morning. *Adafina* is the very essence of Jewish cuisine, and the word's use undoubtedly underscores the existence of a dish specific to Jews. Yet, beyond this, it is also a reflection of a historical period—that of Spain in the fifteenth to sixteenth centuries. *Adafina,* moreover, never stands out for its ingredients. What is not seen has a smell; what is not seen must remain buried; what is not seen cooks all night long; what is not seen warms the body. Nothing is said, but the actions speak for themselves.

However, the term *adafina* is absent from Iberian recipe collections after the thirteenth century until it reappears in contemporary Andalusian[70]

---

66 Ibid., 312n71: "El viernes en la noche, echava vnas pelotas cozidas e sancochadas e otra olla de açelgas con sus espeçias e garvanços, e quando se yvan acostar dexavan vna caldera sobre la dicha olla con lunbre, o otro día, sábado, hallavan descocha la dicha olla e comían della." Translation by the author.

67 Pérez Alonso, "La olla judía el Šabbat: estudio lexicológico y lexicográfico de adafina, ḥamín, caliente(s) y otras denominaciones," 453.

68 Ex. 35:3: "You shall kindle no fire throughout your settlements on the sabbath day." See https://www.sefaria.org/Exodus.35.3?lang=bi&aliyot=0.

69 Deut. 5:12: "Observe the sabbath day and keep it holy, as the LORD your God has commanded you." https://www.sefaria.org/Deuteronomy.5.12?lang=bi&with=all&lang2=en.

70 Luis Benavides Barajas, *Al-Andalús, la cocina y su historia* (Motril: Dulcinea, 1992).

cookbooks, even though it is still prepared by Spanish and Moroccan Jews.[71] Indeed, *adafina* or *dafina* or *daf* is a dish that has always been prepared by Moroccan and Spanish Sephardic Jews, who continue to call it *ẖamín*[72] or *sẖina* (a word from the Moroccan-Arabic *sẖon,* which means "hot"). But today, *adafina* is not acknowledged as being a part of the national culinary heritage of Spain, even though it was eaten by Jews on the Iberian Peninsula. Dishes like *olla* and *cocido* are, however, recognized as being part of contemporary national dishes. Have their origins been the focus of past research? The answer is clear. The fact that *adafina* was not included in dictionaries between 1770 and 1884 (the official end of the Spanish Inquisition was 1834) suggests a possible avenue of exploration.[73]

c. *Oriza* (*Harīsa*)

"It was the most popular dish of al-Andalus,"[74] argues the historian Rachel Arié in reference to *harīsa.* Of course, we are not referring to the spicy condiment. However, there is one point in common between these two preparations. The name *harīsa* indeed comes from the Arabic *harīs,* هريس, which refers to something that is ground or crushed.[75]

The main ingredient in this dish is wheat. The wheat is cooked until the grain cracks. The *Kitāb al-ṭabīẖ* includes a *harīsa* recipe in which only oil is used, in addition to cracked wheat and soaked bread. The author specifies that the dish is difficult to digest. No animal fat is used—neither butter nor *samn*—only vegetable fat. The *Kitāb al-ṭabīẖ*[76] contains two *harīsa* recipes. The first is called rice *harīsa.*[77] It contains rice that must be left to expand the day before and that cracks from the large amount of water it has absorbed. The recipe specifies that

---

71 Jawhara Piñer, *Sephardi.*

72 For *hamín,* see above about "the dishes of *Shabbat.*" See Romero, *El olor del sábado.* She writes: "In the Talmud, *adafina* is known under the generic name *ḥamín,* which the Hebrew dictionary groups under the name *ḥam,* "hot," and is defined as 'comida caliente que se guarda la víspera del sábado en un horno o semejante para conservarla caliente para la comida del sábado.'" Translation by the author.

73 *Nuevo Diccionario histórico del Español*: http://web.frl.es/fichero.html.

74 Rachel Arié, *Éudes sur la civilisation musulmane* (Leiden: Brill, 1990), 146.

75 Ariel Toaff, "Le couscous et l'histoire des juifs en Italie," in *Couscous, boulgour et polenta. Transformer et consommer les céréales dans le monde,* ed. Hélène Franconie, Monique Chastanet, and François Sigaut (Paris: Karthala, 2010).

76 Guillaumond, *Cuisine et diététique dans l'Occident arabe médiéval,* 177.

77 Ibid., 178.

chicken breasts or mutton should be added, and then the pot is covered and cooked. Mutton fat and cinnamon are added at the end of the preparation.

The interesting thing here is the cooking alternative that is proposed. It is possible to cook the dish in the oven all night in a sealed pot. Two elements indicate that the cooking methods in the recipe collection should not be ignored. First, because this practice went against the recommendations of the *muḥtasib*,[78] the person in charge of monitoring the practices (food and sales) of the bazaar, asked that *harīsa*(s) be consumed the day they were prepared in order to prevent the preparation being altered. The second is the alternative cooking technique: cooking it all night in a sealed pot. These are two essential features of Shabbat dishes. As for the second *harīsa* recipe in the *Kitāb al-ṭabīẖ*, it is called "Recipe for Harīsa Made with White Bread Crumbs Instead of Wheat."[79] This alternative gives the impression that the dish was originally prepared with wheat. Finally, no *harīsa* dish is mentioned in Iberian recipe books after those written in Arabic.

The historian Mohamed Oubahli asserts that *harīsa* was still prepared at the beginning of the twentieth century by Spanish Jews in Tangiers, but that the dish has declined in popularity. He adds that the word is still used by Jews to refer to a wheat preparation cooked in oatmeal broth with butter and meat.[80] The precepts of Mosaic Law prohibit the mixing together of milk and meat. Yet there is the possibility that these rules were not always obeyed to the letter.

What is curious is the enduring presence of this dish in the culinary heritage of Moroccan Jews. Indeed, the *harīsa* dish in the *Kitāb al-ṭabīẖ* strongly recalls—both in its cooking style and ingredients—the *(h)oriza* dish of contemporary Sephardic Jews. The terminological proximity between *harīsa* and *(h)oriza* supports this argument. It is true that while the name changed somewhat, the content is almost identical: grains of wheat that are cooked all night long in a broth with meat and vegetables and eaten the next day.[81]

---

78 Brisville, "Plats sûrs et plats sains dans l'Occident musulman médiéval," 112–113.

79 Guillaumond, *Cuisine et diététique dans l'Occident arabe médiéval*, 178.

80 Oubahli, *La main et le pétrin*, 578–579.

81 Jawhara Piñer, *Sephardi*; Claudia Roden, *Le livre de la cuisine juive* (Paris: Flammarion, 2012), 394, 397; Mois Benarroch, *Andalusian in Jerusalem* (Lulu: independently published, 2017), 152; Michael Asheri, *Living Jewish: The Lore and Law of Being a Practicing Jew* (Pune: Everest House, 1980), 148, 402.

C. "Sweet and Honeyed" Dishes in the Medieval and Early Modern Period

a. *Hojuela/Tsapiẖ*

The term hojuela appears in various medieval Spanish dictionaries, such as that by Nebrija[82] (Spanish-Latin) in 1495. It is defined as "Hojuela de massa tendida. Laganum" and notes that the dough [*massa*] is spread out [*tendida*]. The term *laganum* refers to *tracta,* a kind of stretched dough which can be used as pasta too.[83] The term *hojuela* is also described in detail in *Tesoro de la lengua castellana o española* by Covarrubias in 1611.[84] It derives from the Latin term *lagana* and specifies that it is a dough [*massa*] stretched [*estendida*] very thinly [*muy delgada*], like leaves [*hojas*], from which it gets its name. Covarrubias also defines *hojuela* as a "razor" [*lamina*] of dough [*massa*], like *laganum.* His definition concludes with an expression which means "cherry on the cake." Indeed, Covarrubias describes it as "one thing [*cosa*] that has everything we need [*que tiene suficientemente lo que le basta*] and if another thing is added to improve it [*si sobre aquello se le añade cosa que la mejore*], we say commonly that it is honey on the *hojuela* [*dezimos vulagarmente que es miel sobre hojuela*]." If we believe Covarrubias, the term *hojuela* gets its name from the Spanish word *hoja,* that is, "leaf."

As for cookbooks, the *Kitāb al-ṭabīẖ* contains a recipe for "The Preparation of Ears." This is a dessert fried in oil. In the edition of *Libro del arte de cozina de Diego Granado Maldonado* published in Madrid in 1599, there is a recipe for

---

82 Antonio De Nebrija, *Gramática sobre la lengua española. Vocabulario español-latino* (Madrid: Real Academia Española, 1494), fol. b ii vo: "Hojuela de massa tendida. Laganum."

83 Susan Weingarten, "The Debate about Ancient Tracta: Evidence from the Talmud," *Food & History* 2, no. 1 (2004): 21–40; C. Perry, "What Was Tracta?" *Petits propos culinaires* 12 (1982): 37–39; idem, "Tracta/Trachanas/Kishk," *Petits propos culinaires* 14 (1983); idem, "Trakhanas Revisited," *Petits propos culinaires* 55 (1997): 34–39; Bruno Laurioux, "Des lasagnes romaines aux vermicelles arabes: quelques réflexions sur les pâtes alimentaires," in *Hommes et campagnes médiévales: L'homme et son espace. Études offertes à Robert Fossier*, ed. Elisabeth Mornet (Paris: Publications de la Sorbonne, 1995); idem., *Une histoire culinaire du Moyen Âge* (Paris: Honoré Champion, 2005); Bruno Laurioux and Martin Bruegel, eds., *Histoire et identités alimentaires en Europe* (Paris: Hachette littératures, 2002]; Silvano Serventi and Françoise Sabban, *Pasta: The Story of a Universal Food* (New York: Columbia University Press, 2002); B. L. Ullman, "Horace Serm. I, 6, 115 and the History of the Word *Laganum*," *Classical Philology* 7, no. 4 (1912).

84 Covarrubias and De Riquer, *Tesoro de la lengua castellana o española*: "hojuela," fol. 474 vo.

hojuelas.[85] This is also true for *Libro del arte de cocina* by Domingo Hernández de Maceras, published in 1607, which has three recipes.[86]

Hojuela is a pastry that is often manipulated into the shape of stretched-out ears. It is enjoyed today by the whole of Spain, mainly during Easter[87] (although it can be found throughout the year).[88] *Hojuela* is also a part of Sephardic culinary heritage, including in America. The pastry is prepared for celebrating the Jewish holiday of *Purim,* and alludes to the cut-off ears of the vizier Hamán, who wanted to execute Persian Jews. This fact is even more interesting when we realize that the *Kitāb al-ṭabīẖ* includes a fried, sweet recipe called "Preparation of Ears."[89] There is also another recipe, "Recipe of Ğawzīnaq," which refers to a dish called اذانين القاضى [ears of the *qadī*/judge]. "Ears of the Judge" is connected to the phrase *hojuela de massa tendida,*[90] included in *Vocabulista arauigo en letra castellana* by Pedro de Alcalá (1505). *Hojuela de massa tendida* translates into Arabic as *utnēi al cādi*[91] (*oudnin al qādī* in modern Arabic, i.e. "ears of the *qādī*/judge").

The link that exists between *hojuela* and Jews is an ancient one, and the dictionary by Covarrubias (1611) offers an explanation. Discussing manna (*maná*), Covarrubias defines *hojuela* as a kind of jam or sap that is quickly shaped into balls before it solidifies, like to gum balls that are consumed for medical purposes. Covarrubias's explanation refers to the biblical *maná,* which God gave to nourish the Hebrew people when they crossed the dessert after leaving Egypt (Ex. 16:31).[92] In the *New American Standard Bible,*[93] it is written: "The house

---

85 Granado, *Libro del arte de cozina,* 403.

86 Sámper, *La alimentación en la España del Siglo de Oro,* 241, 257, 261, 357.

87 *República de las ideas,* https://gastronomiaycia.republica.com/2011/04/20/receta-de-hojuelas/; *Recetas gratis,* https://www.recetasgratis.net/receta-de-hojuelas-12531.html; *El aderezo,* https://www.eladerezo.com/recetas/hojuelas-de-la-abuela-germana.html.

88 *Las 1000 mejores recetas de cocina* (Madrid: Editorial Optima, 2001).

89 Guillaumond, "La cuisine dans l'Occident arabe médiéval," no. 445; Huici and Marín, *La cocina hispano-magrebí,* no. 185; Guillaumond, *Cuisine et diététique dans l'Occident arabe médiéval,* no. 346.

90 Pedro De Alcalá, *Vocabulista arauigo en letra castellana* (1505), *Internet Archive,* accessed April 15, 2022, https://archive.org/details/ARes193062/page/n299, page 301.

91 In the *Kitāb al-ṭabīẖ,* there is a recipe called "Recipe of Ğawzīnaq" (Guillaumond, *Cuisine et diététique dans l'Occident arabe médiéval,* 195–196, no. 302), which mentions the preparation for اذانين القاضى (ears of the qadī/judge). Guillaumond writes that "The preparation of ğawzīnaq" is also called "A Mouthful of Qadī." I believe, nonetheless, that the "ears of the qadī/judge" only concern the thickening of the syrup which is used to soak the ears of qadī/judge, since the *ğawzīnaq* and ears of the judge preparations differ in every aspect.

92 Covarrubias and de Riquer, *Tesoro de la lengua castellana o española,* 96: ". . . era el manná en la hechura como granos de culantro blanco, en sabor como hojuelas o hojaldres con miel." Translation by the author. According to Rachi's commentary, "cilantro" is a "round grain, and not white."

93 *New American Standard Bible* (place: The Lockman Foundation, 2020).

of Israel named it manna, and it was like coriander seed, white, and its taste was like wafers with honey." The Spanish term used for "wafers with honey" is none other than *hojuelas con miel*.[94] This is a peculiar translation because it uses the term *hojuela* to designate a preparation which today is necessarily still made with honey. This is highly interesting if we note that a glossary of non-Hebrew words in the Torah and translated into Ladino—such as in the *Sefer Heshek Shelomo*, first published in Venice in 1588, uses the term *binuelos* for "wafers with honey" (*tzapihit* in Hebrew).[95] *Bimuelos* are the emblematic Jewish pastries nowadays eaten for celebrating the Jewish holiday of Hanukkah.[96] As concerns "honey wafer," Rashi writes that it is "dough fried in honey, called *isqeritawan*."[97] My hypothesis is that the pastry named *hojuela*[98] has roots in the Bible, where it is called *tsapiẖ*[99] in the Torah. In the commentary on Ex. 16:31 by Rabbi Isaac Abarbanel (1437–1508), he claims that *tzapihit* in the verse about manna is "a food made from flour cooked in oil, in the shape of a *tzapahat* [a pitcher] of water eaten with honey. And it is like the *rekikim* [cakes] made from dough in the shape of ears cooked in oil, and they are dipped in honey, and they are called ears. So is the *tzapihit bidvash* [in this verse]."[100] It is likely that this dish, enjoyed

---

94 "Biblia Reina Valeria," *Biblia Online*, https://www.biblia.es/reina-valera-1960.php: "Y la casa de Israel lo llamó Maná; y era como simiente de culantro, blanco, y su sabor como de hojuelas con miel." For the English/Hebrew version, see "Sefaria," https://www.sefaria.org/Exodus.16?ven=The_Koren_Jerusalem_Bible&lang=bi&aliyot=0. For the text in French/Hebrew with Rashi's commentary, see Sefarim, Exodus 16:31: http://www.sefarim.fr.

95 Ty Alhadeff, "Manna from Heaven: Bumuelos, a Sephardic Hanukkah Treat," Stroum Center for Jewish Studies, accessed December 25, 2016, https://jewishstudies.washington.edu/sephardic-studies/manna-from-heaven-bumuelos/.

96 Hanukkah is a Jewish holiday also known as the "Festival of the Lights." According to the Torah, Hanukkah is an eight-day Jewish celebration that commemorates the rededication during the second century BCE of the Second Temple in Jerusalem, when Jews rose up against their Greek-Syrian oppressors in the Maccabean Revolt, and means "dedication" in Hebrew. It begins on the fifth of Kislev on the Hebrew calendar, and usually falls in November or December.

97 Dough called *isqeritawan* in the language of the Mishnah ('Challa 1.4; Bikourim 1.2 and 2.3 as well as in the *Targoum Onqelos*. See Sefarim, Exodus 16:31: http://www.sefarim.fr.

98 וַיִּקְרְאוּ בֵית-יִשְׂרָאֵל אֶת-שְׁמוֹ, מָן; וְהוּא, כְּזֶרַע גַּד לָבָן, וְטַעְמוֹ, כְּצַפִּיחִת בִּדְבָשׁ

99 The rabbi of Bordeaux Emmanuel Valency specifies that "In the Mishnah treaty 'Challa 1.4 three different wafers are discussed: *soufganin* which, according to Bartenoura's commentary, are wafers made of flexible dough (or fried pancakes, according to another explanation); *doubchanin* which are wafers cooked in honey (another explanation: the dough is kneaded in honey); the *estrikin* which are wafers whose dough is even more flexible than the *soufganin*. The term is used for the Aramaic translation by Onkelos for *tsapi'h*."

100 See The Schechter Institutes, http://www.schechter.edu/why-do-ashkenazic-jews-eat-hamentashen-on-purim/: "Eliezer Ben Yehudah quotes Rabbi Isaac Abarbanel's commentary to Exodus 16:31. The Abarbanel (Spain, Portugal, Italy 1437–1508) says that *tzapihit* mentioned in the verse about manna is "a food made from flour cooked in oil, in the shape of a *tzapahat* [a pitcher] of water eaten with honey. And it is like the *rekikim* [cakes] made from

by Jews and possibly by Muslims, was transmitted and eventually adopted by Christians.

In poetry and literature, there are pastries named *hojuelas* in Aldonza's *La Lozana andaluza.* The dish is one of many culinary preparations that the protagonist discusses, dishes that she knows how to make because her grandmother taught her when they were living in Seville and Granada. This shows the importance of transmission, particularly of food knowledge, for the topic at hand: the culinary heritage of Spanish Jews. Transmission was oral, intergenerational, and shared among Jewish women—both in Spain and beyond—demonstrating a deterritorialization that is inherent to Jewish culture. Finally, verses by Ḥayim Yom-Tob Magula in his *Las malas costumbres* [Bad habits] should be highlighted. This eighteenth-century book vigorously criticizes the author's fellow Jews for having wavered from the straight path dictated by Mosaic law.[101] There is a verse that mentions *hojuelas* as a dish that is traditionally consumed for Purim: "Comer en Purim hijuelas, y en Ḥanuká bimuelos."[102]

The Spanish expression "como miel sobre hojuela" is listed by IDIME as something that cannot be improved. The Inventory of the Mediterranean Diet also specifies that this expression means *hojuela,* a typical dish in Castilla y León, which is enjoyed during the period of Lent.[103] Today, *hojuela* is a fried pastry that is a common feature of Easter in Andalusia, a celebration whose dates overlap with Jewish Easter, during which *fijuelas* (also known as *hojuelas)* are commonly enjoyed.[104]

b. *Mazapán*

Rarely have the origins and etymology of a dish been shrouded in so much mystery. *Mazapán, marzipan, massapan, massepain, mauthabān, marzabān, maçapães,*

---

dough in the shape of ears cooked in oil, and they are dipped in honey, and they are called ears. So is the *tzapihit bidvash* [in this verse]" (ed. Avishai Schotland [Jerusalem, 1997], 245–246). This interpretation was taken from *Metzaref Lakesef* by Rabbi Yosef ibn Kaspi to Exodus 16:31 (1279–1340). Indeed, these two rabbis are describing a food that is similar to *hamentashen,* but that food had no connection to Purim whatsoever."

101 Elena Romero, "Canciones y coplas sefardíes de contenido gastronómico," in *La mesa puesta: leyes, costumbres y recetas judías. XVI curso de cultura hispanojudía y sefardí de la Universidad de Castilla-La Mancha: en memoria de Iacob M. Hassán,* ed. Uriel Macías and Ricardo Izquierdo Benito (Cuenca: Universidad de Castilla la Mancha, 2010), 184.

102 Elena Romero and Carmen Valentín, *Seis coplas sefardíes de "castiguerio" de Hayim Yom-Tob Magula. Edición crítica y estudio* (Madrid: CSIC, 2003), 57–174.

103 IDIME, "Miel sobre hojuelas," accessed April 15, 2022, https://www.inventariodietamediterranea.com/miel-sobre-hojuelas/.

104 *Fijuela o fazuelas.* See Clara Pérez Villalón, "El País," *El Comidista,* 27 March 2018, https://elcomidista.elpais.com/elcomidista/2018/03/14/receta/1520989775_726854.html.

and so on: the plethora of different names for this dish reflect the diversity of the populations that were eating it.

A sweet almond paste, which the Spanish today call *mazapán*, is among the food that is considered an integral part of the culinary heritage of modern Spain.[105] Rudolf Grewe's work highlights the presence of a similar kind of preparation in the *Kitāb al-ṭabīẖ*, and he is surprised that the dish has no specific name, whereas the word *mauthabān* is of Arabic origin.[106] A historian of the nineteenth century, Armand Pierre Caussin de Perceval, thinks that *el-mauthabān* comes from the root *wathab*, which in Himyaritic means "sitting down." This term refers to King Amr Dhou-l-Awād (third century) who was nicknamed *El-mauthabān* because he only moved around sitting down.[107]

Grewe's point merits attention. This almond sugar paste is regularly used in the *Kitāb al-ṭabīẖ* and is paired with drinks. Preparations are sometimes shaped in the form of flowers, oranges, or pears. The recurrence of this food and the multiple ways it is used in the cookbook leads us to wonder why it doesn't have a name. Various explanations have been given. Sweets such as marzipan "were invented by Arabic-Persian doctors," and certain works use the term—*lauzinaj*—to describe the sweet.[108] However, what most scholars seem to agree on is the Arabic origin of the word "marzipan."[109]

Let's return to the inclusion of the sweet almond paste in the first cookbook of the Iberian Peninsula. In the *Kitāb al-ṭabīẖ*, five types of sweet dishes contain almond paste. The first preparation is called *ka'ak* (كعك). It is made of sugar and pruned ground almonds that are reduced to a paste, as well as camphor, nard, cloves, mastic, and rose water. This stuffing, which has elements in common with today's *mazapán* (the current Spanish term), is then placed inside rings made of flour, semolina, and oil. The recipe specifies that oil-based paste is better than paste made of *smen* (rancid butter) because the smells bad and gives a bitter

105 IDIME, "Mazapáan de Toledo," accessed April 15, 2022, https://www.inventariodietamediterranea.com/mazapan-de-toledo-i-g-p/.

106 Grewe, "Hispano-arabic cuisine in the twelfth century," 147; Armand Pierre Caussin de Perceval, *Essai sur l'histoire des Arabes avant l'islamisme: pendant l'époque de Mahomet, et jusqu'à la réduction de toutes les tribus sous la loi musulmane* (Paris: Firmin Didot, 1847), 106.

107 De Perceval, *Essai sur l'histoire des Arabes avant l'islamisme.*

108 Liliane Plouvier, "Regards nouveaux sur la cuisine provençale du bas Moyen Âge: le témoignage des livres de cuisine," *Revue Provence historique* 54, no. 218 (2004): 438–439—"The *Liber* is nonetheless concerned about marzipans and almond paste, *lauzinaj* in Arabic." Translation by the author.

109 Maxime Rodinson, "Venice and the Spice Trade," in *Medieval Arab Cookery*, ed. A. J. Arberry, Maxime Rodinson, and Charles Perry (Totnes: Prospect Books, 2006), 211–213; Maxime Rodinson, *Recherches sur les documents arabes relatifs à la cuisine* (Paris: Geuthner, Revue des études islamiques, 1950).

taste to the dish. These little "cakes" are then shaped into birds or gazelles and cooked in the oven.

A variation on *ka'ak* is *ẖaškalān* (خشكلان). This recipe, "Preparation of *ẖaškalān*,"[110] is similar to the one described above, except that it is shaped like a horn (half-circle), ring, or pancake, fried and then sprinkled with sugar or nard. In the recipe in the *Kitāb al-ṭabīẖ*, the author says that this is how the dish is called in Béjaïa in modern day Algeria. Another recipe, which doesn't have a fixed name but is referred to as "Another Variety of It,"[111] is the same as the one described above. However, rose water and camphor are still added. It is then used to stuff a pastry made from flour, semolina, and oil. These sweets crushed with a special device, after which they are fried and soaked in rose water. The final preparation using sweet almond paste, without any ingredients other than those previously mentioned, is "Preparation of *Ğawzīnaq*" (جوزينق).[112] It is intriguing that even though the word *ğawz* means "nut," the recipe does not contain nuts. The size of the sweet is that of a nut, rather. This is, once again, a pastry stuffed with sweet almond paste, and shaped as a rose, flower, and so on. It is then fried and soaked with honey, rose water, julep,[113] and mastic. These recipes in the *Kitāb al-ṭabīẖ* thus demonstrate that sweet almond paste was used as a stuffing to fill pastries made from flour, semolina, and oil. Baked in the oven, but usually fried, the aesthetics of the food are important since it can be molded into different shapes.

However, sweet almond paste is called by a different name when another ingredient is added: starch. The difference is considerable. In this case, *mazapán* is no longer used as a filling, but is a pastry all on its own, whose unique quality is that it is dried before cooking used. Adding starch creates what is called, in the *Kitāb al-ṭabīẖ*, *qāhirīya* (قاهرية). The cookbook contains five such recipes.[114] The first is called "Preparation of *Cairotes*."[115] It is made of sugar that is cooked until it turns into syrup.. Then peeled and grounded almonds are added. Once the pastry is soft and oily, nard, cloves, rose water, and a little camphor are added. The mix must be dry in order to form small piles, which are left to dry.

---

110 Ibid., no. 193, no. 297.

111 Ibid., 195, no. 301.

112 Ibid., 195, no. 302,

113 "Centre National des Ressources Textuelles et Lexicales," http://www.cnrtl.fr/definition/julep. From the Arabic *ğulāb*: "Potion made of water and syrup"; "Pharmaceutical preparation, made of distilled water, orange blossom water, syrup, Arabic gum, etc., used as an excipient for some medical substances."

114 The *Kitāb al-waṣf*, a fourteenth-century Egyptian cookbook, includes a *qāhirīya* recipe that is the same as the one in the *Kitāb al-ṭabīẖ*. See Charles Perry, "The Description of Familiar Foods," in Arberry, Rodinson, and Perry, *Medieval Arab Cookery*, 433.

115 Guillaumond, *Cuisine et diététique dans l'Occident arabe médiéval*, no. 303.

The way in which this method differs from the previous preparations is that the sweets must be soaked in a thick starch-based liquid and left to dry. They are then fried and coated in rose syrup, julep syrup, or honey. The following recipe, "*Cairotes* in the Oven,"[116] is made from *mazapán,* to which flour and starch are added in order to make it more solid. After adding spices, camphor, and rose water, small piles of paste are made and placed on a plate to be put in the oven. The Sunny *Cairotes*"[117] recipe also uses *mazapán* paste with spices. After shaping them into little mounds, they are placed in liquid starch and left to dry in the sun until the coating of starch dries. Finally, the last recipe is "*Cairotes* Called *Ṣābūniya,*"[118] which are shaped like little pieces of soap (*ṣābūn).* This preparation, known in Marrakesh[119] according to the *Kitāb al-ṭabīẖ,* is almost identical to the previous one. However, the coating, made from a thick sweet rose and julep syrup, forms three layers around the *cairote.*

These four *mazapán* recipes, to which starch is added—so that the sweet almond paste can be eaten alone and not as a filling—are similar to today's *mazapán,* with one exception. Although it was not always the case, *mazapan(es)* are today very often molded in a specific way, typically in the shape of a piece of fruit. This is the case of the last sweet almond paste recipe in the *Kitāb al-ṭabīẖ,* listed under the name *sanbūsak*[120] (سنبوسك), the recipe that most closely resembles today's *mazapán.* Particular attention must be paid to the shape. The sweets are to be molded into the form of mini loaves or balls representing oranges, pears, or apples. These round shapes are very important. The text of the recipe in the *Kitāb al-ṭabīẖ* states that these sweets are to be served with drinks and that they are, in the East, called *sanbūsak*(s). Presenting the almond paste in a conspicuously elegant way confirms that the *Kitāb al-ṭabīẖ* contained recipes for elites, even "kings," from Marrakesh (where they were prepared at the house of Abū Yusuf al-Mansūr) or the East.

Some Eastern cookbooks from the Middle Ages refer to this almond paste preparation. For instance, the *Kitāb al-wuṣla* (thirteenth to fourteenth centuries, Syria)[121] contains recipes called *lawzīnağ,* which are simply variations on

116 Ibid., no. 304.
117 Ibid., no. 305.
118 Ibid., no. 306.
119 The *Kitāb al-waṣf* includes a *ṣābūniya* recipe that is the same as the one in the *Kitāb al-ṭabīẖ.* See Charles Perry, "The Description of Familiar Foods," 456.
120 Guillaumond, *Cuisine et diététique dans l'Occident arabe médiéval,* no. 307.
121 Perry and Waines, *Scents and Flavors,* 162–163 (recipe 7.47) and 168–169 (recipe 7.62).

sanbūsak preparations included in many other cookbooks.[122] The first *lawzīnağ*[123] recipe is made from one third shelled, ground almonds and two-thirds sugar. The mix must be ground until it melts (without water). The almonds are then added until the preparation thickens. After forming a lump, it is divided into pieces. A little bit of rose water and a lot of musk are then used to flavor the dish. It is possible to add starch to make it pleasantly crunchy. The other *lawzīnağ*[124] recipe in the *Kitāb al-wuṣla* is described as "dry." It is made of one-third coarsely ground almonds, one-third fine sugar, and one-third rose water. This is all dissolved over heat. Once the mix has thickened, more sugar is added and it is removed from the heat. This recipe is, for instance, mentioned in the early cookbook of the tenth century by al-Warraq.[125] The raw variety is also present in a recipe collection from the eleventh century,[126] written by the Baghdadi doctor Ibn Jazla, under the name *lawzīnağ* Farisi (meaning the Persian city of Fars in modern day Iran).

These details raise more questions about the origin of the dish. If this preparation of sweet almond paste also existed in the East,[127] does this mean that it originated from there? The *Kitāb al-ṭabīẖ* tells us that these sweets are named as such in the Muslim East. But why would the Eastern term have been used in the Muslim West? Let's stress the fact that *sanbūsak*(s) are also known in the *Kitāb al-ṭabīẖ* as fried dishes, with a triangular shape, stuffed with meat, spices, and eggs.[128] Furthermore, this is the name that is still used for this savory dish, enjoyed today worldwide.[129] *Sanbūsak*(s) no longer refer to almond paste.

---

122 Personal communication. I would like to thank Daniel Newman for this precious information.

123 Perry and Waines, *Scents and Flavors*, 162–163 (recipe 7.47).

124 Ibid., 168–169 (recipe 7.62).

125 Nawel Nasrallah, *Annals of the Caliph's Kitchen: Ibn Sayyar al-Warraq's Tenth-Century Baghdadi Cookbook* (Leiden: Brill, 2007), chapter 99.

126 This could be the work of ibn Jazla, which was translated into Latin in the fourteenth century under the name *Liber de ferculis et condimentis* by Jamboninus de Crémone. It does indeed contain a *Lauzime* recipe made with almonds, sugar, and rose water. In Western Latin cuisine, there are several *Losanges* recipes. See Maxime Rodinson, "Sur l'Etymologie de 'losange,'" *Studi orientalistici in onore di Giorgio Levi Della Vida* 2 (1956): 425–435.

127 A Syrian cookbook from the thirteenth century, the *Kitāb al-wuṣla ilā al-ḥabīb* includes four recipes, two of which are sweet preparations. See Perry and Waines, *Scents and Flavors*, 77; Perry, Rodinson, and Arberry, *Medieval Arab Cookery*, 133, 134, 136, 141. The *Kitāb al-waṣf* also mentions savory and sweet variations on *sanbūsak*(s); See Perry, Rodinson, and Arberry, *Medieval Arab Cookery*, 354, 379, 382, 384, 386, 456.

128 Guillaumond, *Cuisine et diététique dans l'Occident arabe médiéval*, no. 308.

129 Maxime Rodinson specifies that *sanbūsak*(s) are prepared and enjoyed today particularly in Syria and Lebanon: Maxime Rodinson, "Studies in Arabic Manuscripts Relating to Cookery," in Arberry, Rodinson, and Perry *Medieval Arab Cookery*, 136n3.

Some modern dictionaries compare marzipan with other dishes. The Redhouse dictionary, for instance, defines *ma'mūniyya* as *marzipan.*[130] In the *Supplément aux dictionnaires arabes,* Dozy agrees, adding that *ma'mūniyya* is a dish associated with the Spanish *bollo maimon* (referred to above), which he calls *marzipan,*[131] eaten with preserves. In *A Drizzle of Honey,*[132] David Gitlitz and Linda Kay Davidson agree that certain recipes from the *Kitāb al-ṭabīḫ* cookbook by Al-Baghdādī (1236) contain desserts made of sweet almond paste, some of which have shapes, and which are today called "marzipan."[133]

At which point in time, then, did sweet almond paste shaped like balls come to be called "mazapán" *(marzapane, marzipan,* etc.*)*? The *Kitāb al-ṭabīḫ* first claims that this sweet was consumed in al-Andalus and in the *Ġarb,* just as it was enjoyed in the East. What remains to be ascertained is who specifically ate it, and what are the first cookbooks to mention *mazapán* as a sweet almond paste that isn't used as a filling. Barbara Santich, in the second edition of *The Original Mediterranean Cuisine: Medieval Recipes for Today,* argues that *marzipan* is a food introduced in "Western Europe by Arabs."[134] She emphasizes both the symbolic value of the dish (at the beginning and the end of a banquet) and the conspicuous sign of wealth that it represented (sugar and almonds were two expensive products in the Latin West). She adds that these practices make it possible to distinguish it from those of ancient Rome, which had "neither sugar nor the technique of making almond paste or *marzipan* . . . both were introduced to Western Europe by the Arabs."[135] *Marzipan,* concerning which Santich cites its frequent use in "Arabic/Persian" food, represents for her "the most splendid association [of sugar and almonds],"[136] served as a sweetmeat at the end of the meal. She mentions the foods served in the Milanese wedding banquet of Marquis Gian Giacomo Trivulzio and Beatrice d'Avalos of Aragon in 1488. As well as pastries made of pine nuts and sugar, there were cakes made with almonds and sugar, "similar to marzipan."[137] *Marzipani* is also the twenty-third of the twenty-four

---

130 Maxime Rodinson, "Ma'mūniyya East and West," in Arberry, Rodinson, and Perry *Medieval Arab Cookery,* 188, 193; *The Redhouse Dictionary: A Turkish and English lexicon* (Constantinople: H. Matteosian, printed for the American Board Mission, 1921), 1661b.

131 Rodinson, "Ma'mūniyya East and West," 193.

132 Davidson and Davidson, *A Drizzle of Honey,* 332.

133 Ibid., 264.

134 Barbara Santich, *The Original Mediterranean Cuisine: Medieval Recipes for Today,* 2nd ed. (Bristol: Equinox Publishing, 2018), 159.

135 Ibid., 11.

136 Ibid., 16.

137 Ibid., 54.

services made by Count Jeronimo, registered in *Cuoco Napoletano* in the fifteenth century.[138]

Libro de cozina by Ruberto de Nola[139] is the first Latin-language cookbook from the Iberian Peninsula that contains a *mazapanes* recipe. Yet the Catalan edition[140] (from a book composed, it appears, by the chef of King Ferdinand of Naples) does not contain the two *mazapanes* recipes. These are only included in later editions in Castilian in 1525 from Toledo and in 1529 from Logroño. Bruno Maggi draws attention to these absences in the original edition in his article about *Il Marzapane*.[141] The Castilian, 1525, contains a recipe of "Marzipan for the sick who have lost their appetite, very good and of good consistency"[142] (a savory recipe, with capon breast), and the Logroño edition of 1529 has, in addition to this recipe,[143] two other recipes—"marzipan"[144] and "marzipan wafer."[145]

In these southern territories (or at least, further south than Barcelona), the largest Jewish and Muslim communities lived (especially Toledo), even if these areas gradually fell into the hands of Christians starting in the eleventh century.

---

138 Ibid., 49.

139 Notaker, *Printed Cookbooks in Europe*, p. 347n1301.1.

140 Carlos Amarós, ed., "Libre de doctrina per a ben servir, de tallar, y del Art de Coch: ço es de qualsevol manera de potages y salses. Compost per lo diligent mestre Robert coch del Serenissimo senyor don Fernando Rey de Napols. Edició digital basada en l'edició de Barcelona" (Ediciones Jistórico Artísticas, 1988).

141 Bruno Maggi, "Il marzapane," *Appunti di gastronomia* 34 (2011): 79: "Se l'origine di questo piatto à araba e il veicolo di trasmissione è rapprresentato da Martino, cuoco di formazione iberica o meglio catalana, sembrerebbe agevole rintracciare il suo archetipo presso la vicina Spagne. Ma anche qui rimaniamo delusi nel constatare la sua assenza, come in Italia, nel più classico ricettari trecenteschi, il Libre de sent sovi, mentre appare improvvisamente e misteriosamente, due secoli più tardi, nel ricettario di Ruperto de Nola ma solo nella redazione castigliana edita a Toledo nel 1525 e più tardi a Logroño nel 1529 dove l'impasto è formato con mandorle pestate nel mortaio, acqua rosata, zucchero ben setacciato, passato al forno non troppo caldo, dalla superficie resa brillante grazie a una glassa di acqua e zucchero." Translated by the author: "If the origin of this Arabic dish is the vehicle of transmission—it is represented by Martino, an Iberian or rather Catalan cook—it would seem easy to trace its archetype to nearby Spain. But even here we are disappointed in noting its absence, as in Italy, in the classic fourteenth-century recipe book the *Libre de sent sovi*. It suddenly and mysteriously appears two centuries later in the cookbook of Ruperto de Nola, but only in the Castilian edition in Toledo in 1525 and later in Logroño in 1529. There, the dough is made with almonds pounded in a mortar, rose water, and well-sieved sugar, baked in a not-too-hot oven, and it has a shiny surface thanks to a glaze made of water and sugar."

142 Original title in the *Libro de cocina de Nola* (1525): "Maçapanes para dolientes que pierden el comer muy buenos y de gran sustancia." Translation by the author.

143 De Nola and Peyrebonne, *Le livre de cuisine*, 98, no. 9: "Maçapanes para dolientes que pierden el comer muy buenos y de gran sustancia."

144 Ibid., 119, no. 135: "Maçapanes."

145 Ibid., 121, no. 139: "Fruta de maçapan."

Should this be considered an adaptation of a part of the original Catalan recipes in this geographic space?[146] Was Toledo influenced by a cuisine that was closer to al-Andalus? Did Toledo, known and recognized for having hosted Jews and Muslims,[147] play an equally important role in integrating these communities' dishes into the recipes of *Libro de cozina*?[148]

Later, *Libro de cozina* by Diego Granado Maldonado mentions a variety of recipes that contain the word *mazapán*: "*Mazapán* Dough" (*Mazapán en masa*), "*Mazapán* Cake"—in three versions (*Torta de mazapán*)—"*Mazapán* Cakes of Different Compositions" (*Tortas de mazapán de diversas composiciones*), and "Cakes of Many Styles Called *Cannelés* and Made of Almond Paste" (*Tortas de muchos tipos llamadas caneladas y mazapanadas*), not to mention "Squash *Mazapán*" (*Mazapán de calabaza*) and "Pink Mazapán" (*Mazapán rosado*).[149]

Spanish literature is not a marginal source when it comes to dealing with this sweet. The famous work by Miguel de Cervantes, *Don Quijote de la Mancha* (1605), is proof. The text mentions *Mazapán*:: "He would cut his head as though he were made of marzipan. . . . Stop, My Excellence, Lord Don Quixote, and know that those who you slay, destroy and kill are not true Moors, but some figurines of dough."[150] In this passage, there is a connection between Moors and the small *mazapán* figurines. That *figurillas* commonly meant "ridicule"[151] demonstrates Don Quijote's contemptuous view of Moors. Is it an accident if Toledo, capital of the current autonomous region Castilla la Mancha, claims to be the original city of *mazapanes*?[152]

But what about the relationship between Jews and this almond paste? The presence of Jewish recipes—whether or explicit or not—in the *Kitāb al-ṭabīḫ*

---

146 Remember that Jews were expelled in 1492 and Muslims in 1609.

147 Louis Cardillac, ed., *Tolède XIIe–XIIIe siècle. Musulmans, chrétiens et juifs: le savoir et la tolérance* (Paris: Autrement, "Mémoires," 2001.

148 The *Livro de cozinha* of the Infanta D. Maria of Portugal: Primeira edição integral do códice português I.E. 33, Biblioteca Nacional de Nápoles, Por Ordem da Universidade, 1967. It also includes a description of the term *macapaaes* (noun from *maçapão*) (210) and a recipe for *maçapão* (136, no. 61). Maria de Portugal, *Livre de cuisine de l'Infante Maria du Portugal*, ed. José Palla (Lisbon: Instituto de Estudos Medevais, 2008).

149 Universidad de Valladolid, http://uvadoc.uva.es/bitstream/10324/7177/1/TFG-M-N113.pdf.

150 Miguel Cervantes, *Don Quijote de la Mancha*, ed. Francisco Rico (Barcelone: Institut Cervantes, 1998), 851–852: "*[L]e cercenara la cabeza con más facilidad que si fuera hecha de masa de mazapán. . . . Deténgase vuestra merced, señor don Quijote, y advierta que estos que derriba, destroza y mata no son verdaderos moros, sino unas figurillas de pasta.*" Translation by the author.

151 WordReference.com, "figurilla," http://www.wordreference.com/esfr/figurilla.

152 Roden, *Le livre de la cuisine espagnole*, 436.

prompts questions about the people who prepared and ate these sweets. Since they were called *sanbūsak* in the East and were a dish for kings, it might therefore be an Eastern food (rather than Andalusian) made by Muslims for Muslim elites. As previously noted, some dishes in the *Kitāb al-ṭabīẖ* clearly refer to the East: either the title explicitly references it or it is stipulated that the dish has another name because it was made in al-Andalus. In terms of sweet almond paste, the preparation does not fit either of these scenarios. The fact that it was made in different forms and that it bears an Eastern name might indicate the interculturality of Spain at the end of the Middle Ages. Sources rarely explicitly connect Muslims and *mazapán*. Yet, for Jews, the opposite is the case. The sweet can be included among the recipes of the *Kitāb al-ṭabīẖ* which are not explicitly Jewish. However, we cannot completely dismiss the hypothesis that Jews and Muslims shared this culinary preparation in al-Andalus.

Nonetheless, its ties to Jewish practices endures. A plethora of different sources show this; and *mazapán* continues to be consumed today by Sephardic Jews from the Iberian Peninsula at marriages, circumcisions, and other celebrations, whatever the country of residence. Muslim North Africa, though, does not seem to include *mazapán*—as a specifically made and shaped sweetmeat almond paste—in its culinary heritage. As for Spain, the IDIME inventory confirms its presence, with six references to *mazapán*. Among these are *Mazapán de Toledo* which was included in the category "Protected Geographical Indication" (IGP) in 2002. Today, no one refers to the preparation and consumption of this sweet among Jews. This is an intriguing fact, given that the historical sources of the Jewish diaspora are proof of this connection.

c. *Orejas de Hamán*

The *hojuelas* preparation, the origins of which are detailed at the beginning of this section, can be related to the "Ears" preparation of the *Kitāb al-ṭabīẖ*. It can also be connected with the "Ears of Haman" (*orejas de Hamán*) in the *Provençal Esther Poem* by Crescas du Caylar (1327), written in the south of France. Remember that *neulas encanonadas* (verses 153–154) are mentioned in the Occitan version of this poem.[153] Nelly Labère translates *neulas encanonadas*

153 Neubauer and Meyer, "Le Roman provençal d'Esther par Crescas du Caylar"; Crescas du Caylar, "Roman de la Reine Esther," 134.

as *orejas de Hamán*, without, however, providing any references;[154] but we can tell that the shape of these two sweets is different. If we focus on the shape of modern day *neulas encanonadas*, we see that they more closely resemble cigars than ears.[155] If the principle of a multilayered pastry (*hojas*) still exists nowadays, the canon-like shape is far removed from the shape of an ear. Yet, this does not mean that there is no link between the *neulas* and the current "ears" of Hamán. Today, Hamán's ears are mainly prepared and enjoyed by Sephardic Jews from the Iberian Peninsula. Prepared in the shape of an ear, these fried pastries are found in the Andalusian preparation called *pestiño*.

The first reference to the term *pestiño* appears in *La Lozana andaluza* (1528) by Francisco Delicado de Cordoba, a young converso. We discover that the protagonist Aldonza learned how to cook from her grandmother and that, thanks to her, she knows how to make many dishes, including *pestiños*.[156] The *Diccionario Crítico y Etimológico Castellano e Hispánico*, by Corominas y Pascual, cites the year 1543 as the first time the word *pestiño* appeared. There, it is written that there is a direct link between *prestiño* and the Occitan word *prestinh*, which means "bakery," *panadería* in Spanish, a place "where bread and cakes are made." The etymology of the word likely comes from the Latin *pristinum*, meaning the workplace of the baker.[157] This pastry therefore be called *prestiño*" in Castilian, which is corroborated by the presence of the word in *La Lozana andaluza*. We have to wait until the *Diccionario de Autoridades* (1726–1739) to read that *prestiño* is defined as a "kind of dough fried in a pan, made of flour, eggs, cinnamon, in the shape of little tubes, which are fried in lard or oil, then glazed with warm creamed honey, and molded like little mounds in the shape of pineapple or other things."[158] The definition of *prestiño* provided by the *Diccionario de Autoridades* also recalls *gañote*, a cylinder-shaped wafer that is one of the

---

154 Analysis from Nelly Labère's research as part of her unpublished HDR. I would like to thank Bruno Laurioux for this information.

155 Jawhara Piñer, *Sephardi*, 132–135.

156 Delicado, Gernert, and Joset, *La Lozana andaluza*: "hojuelas, pestiños, rosquillas de alfaxor, testones de cañamones y ajonjolí, nabos sin tocino y con comino, olla reposada, cazuela de berenjenas, cazuelas de pescado cecial, cabrito apedreado con limón ceutí, pecho de carnero . . ."

157 Antonio Mateos Martín de Rodrigo, "Gañotes, pestiños y prestiños," last modified August 11, 2015, https://miscelaneadesdellerena.blogspot.com/2015/08/ganotes-prestinos-y-pestinosreivindicac.html.

158 Diccionario de Autoridades, 1726–1739: "*pestiño*": "Cierta especie de fruta de sartén, que se hace de massa de harina, huevos y canéla, de la qual se forman unos rollitos de la hechura de piñónes, los quales se frien en manteca ó azeite, y luego se les echa miél muy espumada, y puesta en mucho punto, y se van formando unos montoncillos en figura de piñas ú otras cosas."

culinary specialties of Seville. This food is enjoyed during Holy Week in the south of Spain and is included in the IDIME inventory of the Mediterranean diet.[159] In short, modern day *pestiño*, fried and covered in honey, is eaten today in Spain.[160] It is a pastry disk, the edge of which is pinched, thus forming a cylindrical space above the pressure point. These sweets are common in Andalusia and are made at Christmas or Easter,[161] even though nothing about it reveals its origins. The shape of *pestiño* is that of ear.

Finally, Hamáns are not the only pastries that symbolically represent a part of Hamán's anatomy. The "Eye of Hamán" is another example, mainly prepared by Moroccan Jews. This is an egg without a shell, stuffed into a pastry ball. Two pieces of pastry shaped like a cross are placed on the egg. Both the "ears" and the "eyes" of Hamán continue to preside over Sephardic tables today during the celebration of Purim.[162]

---

159 IDIME, "Cañotes," https://www.inventariodietamediterranea.com/ganotes/.

160 *Las 1000 mejores recetas de cocina*, 272; *Cocina andaluza* (Barcelona: Susaeta Editorial, n.d.), 170; Enrique Sordo, "Gastronomía de la provincia de Málaga," in *Cómo conocer la cocina española* (Barcelona, 1980), 30–33.

161 Pérez Villalón, "El País."

162 Jawhara Piñer, *Sephardi*.

CHAPTER 10

Dishes and Diaspora: From the *Kitāb al-ṭabīẖ* to the Sephardic Culinary Heritage of the Mediterranean Basin

What would Jewish culture be without the diaspora? Probably very different from the culture we know today. Jews have been, from the beginning, a people in motion and a people enriched by that motion. The diaspora—an inherent element of Jewish culture—is only discussed in a few publications from Europe. Yet it arouses increasing interest in the US. Reflecting on the construction of an imagined and real Jewish cuisine is quite interesting.

A thematic analysis of particular dishes belonging to the Sephardic culinary heritage of the Mediterranean Basin, such as *alheiras, boranía,* chickpea croquettes, *mufleta, mazapán,* and other emblematic dishes, offers an overview of the transmission that has taken place as much in Morocco—thanks to diplomats who were stationed there and then returned to Spain—Portugal, Italy, Turkey, the Middle East, and Latin America.[1] Andalusian and African influences are present in Jewish cuisine.

A. The Diaspora: An Inherent Component of Jewish Culture

To define Sephardim as all "Jews who lived in Spain and their descendants throughout the world" could be the best way to refer the them. As Jane Gerber

1 Gerber, *The Jews of Spain,* 149, 147–157; "Cities of Splendour in the Shaping of Sephardi History."

puts it, Sephardic Jews are a "Diaspora within the Diaspora."[2] Part of the complexity of studying Sephardic foods is the scope and spread of the diaspora and the interculturality of certain dishes. It is not possible here to confine one people to one country or continent, as the Sephardic diaspora is located all over the world, wherever descendants of Spanish Jews settled after their official expulsion in 1492.[3] As Yosef Yerushalmi writes:

> Spanish Judaism seemed then to be scattered to the four winds, but dispersion did not mean disintegration. One of the most interesting phenomena of Jewish history throughout the last four centuries is the way that Sephardic Judaism preserved its Hispanic character despite having been expelled from Spain and regardless of the haven where it took refuge.[4]

Jane Gerber states that

> the expulsion of 1492 is a critical watershed for understanding Sepharad. At that time, some Iberian Jews took one path going East and some took a different path that led them to Portugal. We don't know how the decisions were made, probably based on convenience, on how you could find a captain ship to get out, on chance, on luck, to . . . Morocco, Egypt, Portugal, Italy. . . . Those who went openly as Jews into the Ottoman Empire, North Africa, did not have any break in the continuity of their familiarity with Judaism: they retained Hebrew, they generally retained some form of Spanish that then became translated into Ladino or Haketia, they moved to the Balkans, they cherished the ballads of proverbs and cuisine of Spain.[5]

De-territorialization—that is, the diaspora—is thus an vital part of Jewish history. It is, then, essential to focus on Jewish cookbooks concerned with the world of Sephardic Jews.

---

2 Ibid.

3 Yerushalmi, *Sefardica*, 29.

4 Ibid., 31.

5 Gerber, "Cities of Splendour in the Shaping of Sephardi History." Comments by Jane Gerber taken from the text of her oral presentation, transcribed by the author from an audio recording. See also *Cities of Splendour in the Shaping of Sephardi History* (Liverpool: Liverpool University Press, 2020).

a. Publications in Europe and the United States: Explaining the Difference

There is still little acknowledgement in European culinary collections today of an Iberian or even Mediterranean Jewish cuisine. Furthermore, amateur cookbooks are often primarily interested in the short-term history of Sephardic Jews. While recipe books in America are similar to European cookbooks, in that they contain recipes dating back one or two generations, the comparison ends there. Sephardic Jewish cookbooks (and to a greater extent, Ashkenazi cookbooks) abound in the United States. This phenomenon can be explained in three ways. First, this is due to the US having a larger Jewish population than Europe. Second, in Europe there is a taboo around Jewish culture that is not found in the US, or at least to a lesser extent. Finally, the broader publication of Sephardic Jewish cookbooks can be explained by a Jewish American history that is more distant than the history of European Jews. The history I offered in chapter 1 enables a better understanding of this gap in publication quantities. Regardless, both US and European publications are a testimony to the desire to acknowledge the Jewish culinary heritage of the Mediterranean Basin.

b. Reflections on the Construction of a Real and Imagined Jewish Cuisine

The relationship between religion and culinary practices shows us what belongs to one culture and what belongs to another. What indeed does a "Jewish" preparation mean if it is not something that is radically different from something that it is "Jewish? "We symbolically consume identity through our food and drink choices, more specifically by what we don't eat or drink."[6] While a dish is called "Jewish" because it is different from local cuisine, there are nevertheless two types of dishes that are specific to Jewish food. The first is *haroset*,[7] a sweet mix made of dates, cinnamon, and dried fruits, served as a paste or balls or paste. There are as many variations on this dish as there are Jewish diasporas

---

6 "Eating Yourself: We Consume Identity Through Food?" *Culture Decanted*, accessed October 9, 2016, https://culturedecanted.com/2014/10/19/eating-yourself-we-consume-identity-through-food/.

7 Roden, *Le livre de la cuisine juive*, 547; Susan Weingarten, *Haroset* (New Milford-London: Toby Press, 2019).

and families. The second is *matza*,[8] or unleavened bread. Both preparations were used to celebrate *Pessah*, Jewish Easter. But it is especially because they are exclusively enjoyed by Jews that they can be easily distinguished from other foods. Moreover, the specificity of Jewish cooking was also born from the need to adapt food to Kosher laws, as well as to the mobility of Jews. Taking culinary practices to new lands resulted in culinary fusions.

Today, it is difficult to clearly and unambiguously identify dishes that come from an imagined versus a real Jewish cuisine. What I call imagined Jewish cuisine is food that is only based on hearsay. Of course, this is inherent to oral transmission. Yet the greatest difficulty concerns preparations that have been invented to prove belonging to the Jewish culinary heritage. The absence of historical sources thus encourages this kind of drift. It is an imaginary that is imprinted with survival, as nostalgia plays a considerable role in Jewish culture in general. There is a persistent desire to remember and transmit so as not to forget. This phenomenon might be explained by the fact that Jewish history has been constructed in parallel to history as a whole, and that Jews have themselves recovered their culture from fragments that have been spread worldwide. In this sense, cooking, with its smells, foods, dishes, prohibitions, techniques, and celebrations, represents the major—if not the most essential—dimension of Jewish culture—that which endures and never dies.

B. Mediterranean Countries

a. Sausages Without Pork: *Mirkās, Cabaheas, Torteruelos* and *Alheiras*

Sausages were not born in the thirteenth century. Apicius included them among his recipes.[9] There, they are made from pieces of ground meat stuffed into intestine. Sweet varieties also existed. Several kinds of sausages were eaten: smoked (sausages that could also be eaten cold in round pieces), fresh, boiled, and fried. Other cookbooks, such as those from the East, include sausage recipes, like *Sukhtur* and *Kiba*[10] in the *Kitāb al-ṭabīẖ* of Al-Baghdādī (thirteenth century). Cookbooks from the Iberian Peninsula are a part of this tradition. In the

8 Ibid., 42.

9 Apicius, *De re coquinaria*.

10 A. J. Arberry, English trans., "A Baghdad Cookery-Book," *Islamic Culture* 13, no. 1 (1939): 21–47; Davidson and Davidson, *A Drizzle of Honey*, 209, 314.

Kitāb al-ṭabīẖ and the *Fuḍālat al-ẖiwān,* there are several recipes for *mirkās* (merguez). Like all of the other recipes, they do not contain pork.

The ease of transporting sausages, added to the lack of transparency around their origin and what they contained, made this food central to the conversos' attempts to fool the Inquisition orthodoxy that was widespread in Spain from 1480. Like *empanadas,*[11] which crossed the Atlantic several years later with Jewish and Muslims cooks, sausages remain. It turns out that the food also solidified the concerns of the Inquisition because a number of reports from the Holy Office, starting in 1485, stigmatized the consumption of sausages as being the practice of "heretics."

There are many testimonials. Let's take that of a servant named Catalina Sánchez Serrano, who accused her mistress Beatriz of preparing, for Shabbat, a dish that consisted in stuffing a sheep's intestine with ground liver, egg yolk, and spices.[12] Serrano asserted that the family's dishes never contained pork, unlike the servants' food. The accused confessed that she ate neither pork nor fish without scales, and that she respected ritual slaughter (*shehita*)[13] and other Jewish customs. She was burned alive at the stake by the Inquisition in Guadalupe in 1485.

Another example comes from María Sánchez. In 1505, in the city of Almazán,[14] this servant worked for a family of conversos named León. She denounced the cuisine of her mistress, as she prepared, with the servant's help, smoked sausages made from boiled cow and goat heads, which were then cut into thin pieces and stuffed in goat's intestine (*aluillos*) then smoked (*a sahumar*).[15] Smoking and drying was as much crux of the accusation as the composition of the sausage. Jews were identified through the techniques of smoking and drying, as well as from preparing sausages without pork. Thus, one reads the following in the trial against Judeo-conversos in the town of Almazán at the beginning of the sixteenth century:

---

11 Kissane, *Food, Religion and Communities in Early Modern Europe.*

12 Davidson and Davidson, *A Drizzle of Honey,* 219, 315: ". . . en una tripa de carnero o macho echar hígado machado e yemas de huevos e espeçias" (Fita y Colomé, 1893), 301.

13 Deut. 12:20–21.

14 Kissane, *Food, Religion and Communities in Early Modern Europe.*

15 Parrondo and Conde, *Fontes Iudaeorum Regni Castellae,* 4:32: "Las cabezas de buey e cabrones las echase a cozer el domingo en la noche, e después de cozidas las picaua . . .) su ama y las echaua en los aluillos de los cabrones e las ponía a sahumar, e después comía dellas." (A.D.C, Inquisición, leg. 749/15, fol. 22 recto-verso); Davidson and Davidson, *A Drizzle of Honey,* 213, 314.

> . . . intestines from the butcher and lungs [*livianos*][16] and meat, and they gave them to . . . Léonor her daughter, who cooked them like little sausages[17] [*torteruelos*], attached together on a rope, like Jews were accustomed to do . . ., and ate them on days of meat.[18]

In the transcriptions of Inquisition trials, sausages, which were closely related to blood sausage, were often called *cabaheas, longanizas,* or *torteruelos.* The dish refers in particular to dry blood sausages that were prepared by Jews in the region of Almazán. As we can see from the statements below, eating *cahaheas* caused fear,[19] as the dish was so clearly associated with Judaism:

> [D]uring this time, when the witness came to his father's house, . . . some sausages [*longanizas*][20] were hung, and he asked what they were made of, and they answered him . . ., the owners [*sus amos*], cow lungs; and he saw them eat them, and the witness didn't want to eat them because he was afraid they were beef sausages [*cabaheas*], like when they were Jewish; and they had cooked them on coals [*rescoldo*].[21]

---

16 Covarrubias and de Riquer, *Tesoro de la lengua castellana o española:* "Livianos": ". . . aquella parte interna del asadura, que sirue de fuelle al animal para atraer el ayre para refrigerar el coraçon, por otro nombre pulmón y bofes, Latine pulmo, is. Dixeronse liuianos, porque estando llenos de viento pesan poco."

17 Translation by the author. No dictionary since the *Tesoro de la lengua castellana* by Covarrubias (1611) includes the word *torteruelo.* Professor Enrique Cantera, author of several articles on Jewish cuisine in the late Middle Ages, told me that he didn't know the meaning of the term *torteruelos* either. He advised me to leave the original word used in the trial.

18 Parrondo and Conde, *Fontes Iudaeorum Regni Castellae,* 4:117: ". . . unos aluillos de la carneçería e liuianos e carne, e dáuanlos a . . . Lenor su fija, la qual los fasía como torteruelos, todos atados en una cuerda, de manera que los judíos lo solía fazer . . . y los comían en los días de carne." (A.D.C, Inquisición, leg. 748/5–6, fol. 33 r./v.). Translation by the author; Davidson and Davidson, *A Drizzle of Honey,* 213, 314.

19 Santich, *The Original Mediterranean Cuisine.*

20 Parrondo and Conde, *Fontes Iudaeorum Regni Castellae,* 4:56.

21 Ibid., 111–112: ". . . que vido en el dicho tienpo, viniendo este testigo de casa de su padre, que avía ydo a mudar sus vestidos, vido cómo en casa de . . . Antón del Valle—cristiano nuevo vecino de Almazán—tenían colgadas unas como longanizas, e preguntó de qué heran fechas, y le dixeron . . . sus amos que de livianos de buey; e que se las vido comer, e este testigo no quiso comer dellas por miedo que heran cabaheas, como quando heran judíos; e las asavan en el rescoldo." (A.D.C, Inquisición, leg. 748/5-6, fol. 31v.). Translation by the author.

To truly prove Judaism, however, it was important to identify when the *cabaheas* were eaten. Clues from the trials of the Inquisition in the city of Almazán make it possible to understand that while they could be enjoyed every day of the week, they were not eaten on Friday. This observation matches the accusation of María Alvarez. Indeed, in a trial against Judeo-conversos in the city of Almazán (1501–1505), they were accused of making *cabaheas* from the lungs [*livianos*][22] and head of a cow, with its intestines, garlic, and spices, and easting it on Saturdays and the other days of the week.[23] This is also stated in the declaration against Alvaro de Luna (constable of Castile in the mid-fifteenth century and ally of Jewish conversos)[24] and Catalina Laínez, who were accused by their servant for having

> killed a cow and cooked the meat of its head and heart . . . with dry cilantro and tripe and putting in the intestines, and then drying [the sausages] before eating. Yet she did not remember if her masters ate them [*cabaheas*] on Friday or Saturday; she knew that her mistress called the preparation *cabaheas*.[25]

In trials against the Judeo-conversos of Almazán (1501–1505), there were seventeen accusations of consuming *cabaheas*[26] which did not contain pork and were made of the meat, offal, and head of a cow (including *cecina*), as well as spices and garlic.

One might wonder about the origins of the *cabaheas* prepared by Jews in the Aragonese region of Almazán and Soria. And what about the continuity of this

---

22 Covarrubias and de Riquer, *Tesoro de la lengua castellana o española*: *"Livianos." For the meaning, see above.*

23 Parrondo and Conde, *Fontes Iudaeorum Regni Castellae*, 4:37–38, no 39: ". . . cabaheas de lyvyanos de vaca e de cabeca de vaca y de las entrañas y con sus ajos y especias, y las hazían y las comían los sábados y los otros días." Translation by the author.

24 Béatrice Leroy, *Les juifs dans l'Espagne chrétienne avant 1492* (Paris: Albin Michel, 1993), 105–106.

25 Conde, "Las costumbres judaizantes de la comunidad conversa de Almazán a finales del siglo XV y principios del XVI," 450: "Mataron vna vaca . . . e de la carne de la cabeça e del coraçón e baço echáronlo a cozer e, cozido, lo picó este testigo por mandado de . . . su ama, e echaron culantro seco en la carne, e así lo echó . . . su ama en las tripas de la vaca e las pusieron a secar, e comían después dellas . . . sus amos e este testigo e los otros moços e moças pero no se acuerda sy comían dellas viernes o sábados; e que llamaua su ama a aquellas cabaheas." Translation by the author. Concerning the cabaheas, see Parrondo and Conde, *Fontes Iudaeorum Regni Castellae*, 4:23, no 4; 30, no 18; 31, no 19; 43, no 52.

26 Kissane, *Food, Religion and Communities in Early Modern Europe*, 25–29, table 2.5; 169n37 and n38.

dish in current culinary practices? Neither *Tesoro de la lengua castellana o española* by Sebastián de Covarrubias from 1611[27] nor the *Diccionario de Autoridades* from 1726–1739,[28] published by the RAE. refers to the word *cabaheas*, which supports the hypothesis that it was a regional specialty. How did such a central dish in the culinary practices of Iberian Jews disappear from current Sephardic practices? While we can propose that the Inquisition and the statutes of purity of blood eradicated the cuisine of conversos in Spain, we must take into account consider the mobility of the Jewish people, the ease of transporting sausages, and the ability to make them without pork.

The etymology of the term *cabaheas* likely comes from the combination of the word *cabeza* ("head" in Spanish) and the old terms *boe, bofena* ("beef" in Manchego), *bohena* ("beef" in Castilian), *bohena*, or *bueña* (in old Castilian)/ *buena* (in modern Castilian), as it is a dish made of beef or cow head. It refers to a sort of blood sausage made from beef or cow blood that can be eaten on Saturday. As for the term *guëna*, this means cold meats made from pork intestines.[29] Today, the word *cabaheas* is no longer used, but the dish remains. A culinary preparation that resembles *cabaheas* endures today in the Almazán region and the autonomous region of León in the west of Spain called *bojillo* in the cities of Tierra de Campos, Zamora and León, and is also known as *skamba*.[30] The dish is prepared by Sephardic Jews.[31]

What about the porkless sausages that were consumed in the Mediterranean Basin by Jews? It's true that eating sausages is a very old practice, and their consumption by Jews is also very old. Indeed, the presence of sausage in the food practices of Jews is documented in a manuscript of the Jerusalem Talmud found

---

27 Covarrubias and de Riquer, *Tesoro de la lengua castellana o española*. "Longaniza."

28 *Diccionario de Autoridades*, 1726–1739 (Madrid: Real Academia Espannola): https://apps2.rae.es/DA.html.

29 Vicente García de Diego, *Contribución al diccionario Hispánico Etimológico* (Madrid: Revista de archivos, 1923), 39: ". . . con la significación de embutido hecho de hofes hay el cast, 'bofena' y 'bohena;' el manch. 'bofena;' el ant. cast, 'bohena' y mod. 'buena': 'cierto género de morcilla que, según las costumbres de Castilla, se puede comer en sábado, llamado acaso 'bueña' como bovina por hacerse con sangre de buey o de vaca' y el cast, 'guena': "embutido hecho de la picadura de las visceras del cerdo." Translation by the author; Conde, "Las costumbres judaizantes de la comunidad conversa de Almazán a finales del siglo XV y principios del XVI," 450.

30 Known as *chkamba* among Algerians and *chkembe* among Algerian Jews, who prepared it for the celebration of Pessah. The name comes from the Turkish for "tripe," where the dish *İşkembe* comes from. This is proof of the former presence of Ottoman Turks in the territory. Cow stomach stuffed with ground meat, hard-boiled eggs, and garlic is called *hasban* (Jewish Algeria).

31 Montenegro, "La carne y el pescado en el sistema alimentario judío de la España medieval," 35; Parrondo and Conde, *Fontes Iudaeorum Regni Castellae*, 4:24.

in the Cairo Genizah, which contains the term *luqaniqa*—*naqniq* in modern Hebrew. Looking at the Sephardic culinary heritage of the Mediterranean, it is clear that the consumption of sausage has survived. Let's consider the fact that the Inquisition was established in Portugal in 1531,[32] even though the expulsion edict was enacted in 1496. Many Spanish Jews immigrated to this country in 1492, bringing their culinary practices with them. "The cuisine of the special occasions celebrated by the Hebrew people presently gave off a peninsular flavor."[33]

The sausage recipe that is included in the first Portuguese cookbook, the *Cookbook of the Infanta Maria of Portugal* (fifteenth to sixteenth centuries), differs from those in the *Kitāb al-ṭabīḫ* and the *Fuḍālat al-ḫiwān*. The only Portuguese preparation that is close to sausage is in a "blood sausage recipe."[34] And this is what triggers the observation that the earlier recipe does not have a title. Out of the sixty-one recipes that make up the Portuguese cookbook, only one lacks a title, and it is appended to the "blood sausage recipe."[35] The dish does not include meat or eggplant (unlike the recipe in the *Kitāb al-ṭabīḫ*), but it does contain bread, almonds, pine nuts, cinnamon, cloves, orange blossom water, egg yolk, salt, and fresh, melted pork lard. The entire preparation must be put in the stomachs and cooked in broth.

I previously mentioned the importance of the Jewish sausage *cabahea*[36] in the fifteenth to sixteenth centuries in the northern regions of modern Spain and the continuity of the dishes named *bojillo* and *skamba* in their culinary heritage. It is noteworthy that the geographic journey of the dish can be traced from the east to the west, towards Portugal, and on the same longitude as the Portuguese city of Mirandela. This city is located just on the other side of the border with the Castile and León regions, and it is known today in Portugal for *alheira*. It is culinary voyage that parallels the movement of Jews towards a more hospitable land. Let's be clearer. The recipe without a name in the *Cookbook of the Infanta*

---

32 The first edict of expulsion of Jews from Portugal is dated December 5, 1496, under King Manuel I. While still trying to prevent their departure one year later, he forced them to convert. See José Antonio Saraiva, "L'Inquisition portugaise et les nouveaux chrétiens," in *Annales. Économies, Sociétés, Civilisations*, no. 3 (1967): 586–589.

33 Conde, "Las costumbres judaizantes de la comunidad conversa de Almazán a finales del siglo XV y principios del XVI," 435: "La cocina de las grandes ocasiones del pueblo hebreo dejaba escapar su ya peninsular aroma." Translation by the author.

34 De Portugal and Palla, *Livre de cuisine de l'Infante Maria du Portugal*, 41.

35 José Maria Azevedo Santos, "O mais antigo livro de cozinha português—receitas e sabores," *Revista Portuguesa de História* 27 (1993): 63–101.

36 See Manuel Nevot Navarro, "La comunidad judia y conversa de Medinaceli (Soria): 1492–1530" (PhD diss., University of Salamanca, 2015).

Maria of Portugal corresponds to the first recipe for porkless sausages made with bread—and sometimes chicken—that Portuguese Jews ate in order to avoid retaliation by the Inquisition: *alheiras*. This food is the main witness of the persistence of Jewish food practices in the Portuguese culinary heritage.[37]

b. *Almoronía*

We can't talk about Sephardic cuisine, especially that from Morocco, without mentioning *almoronía*.[38] The existence of different names for this dish highlights the fact that it was made in different countries that were home to the Jewish populations that cooked it: *būrāniyya, burāniyya*, or *alboronía* in Spain, and *almoronía, alburnía*,[39] and *brānīya, branya* in Morocco.[40] I will not discuss here the presence of this dish in the culinary heritage of modern Spain, whether Sephardic or not. Still, the dish continues to be prepared today by non-Jews in Spain under the same name. Yet the preparation has almost completely changed, as it almost only contains vegetables from the new world. I will focus on *almoronía*,[41] which is still cooked by Moroccan Jews and whose name, cooking style, and ingredients have not been altered from the original recipe in the *Kitāb al-ṭabīḫ*.

The defining feature of the dish is its main ingredient: eggplant. Let's remember that or "Whole Būrāniyya"[42] in the *Kitāb al-ṭabīḫ* has this name because it brings together several techniques. The dish is made of alternate layers of meat, fried eggplant, and layered meat and eggplant pancakes. Almonds, eggs, and oil are added, and the dish is put in the oven. This recipe is all the more interesting because it mirrors another recipe in the collection, "A Stuffed, Buried Jewish Dish." It is likely that there was a lexical and culinary transmission of this dish, originally present in the *Kitāb al-ṭabīḫ*, into the Jewish culinary heritage of modern Morocco under the name *almoronía*.[43] However, Moroccan Jews are the only ones to not have changed the dish and kept the name. They continue to prepare this dish in the same way as in the *Kitāb al-ṭabīḫ*, namely with meat and eggplant, and without peppers or tomatoes.

---

37 Shira Rubin, "The History of the Inquisition, Wrapped Up in a Sausage," *Tablet Magazine*, March 1, 2018, https://www.tabletmag.com/sections/food/articles/history-of-inquisition-in-a-sausage.

38 Hélène Jawhara Piñer, "Almoronía: A Moroccan-Jewish Recipe from Thirteenth-Century Andalusia," *Sephardi Report* 6, no. 1 (2019): 78.

39 Macías, "Ojos de berenjenas, las mil y una recetas," 267.

40 Manuela Marín, "Sobre būrān y la būrāniyya," *Al-Qanṭara* 2, no. 1–2 (1981): 193–207.

41 Piñer, "Almoronía: A Moroccan-Jewish Recipe from Thirteenth-Century Andalusia."

42 Guillaumond, *Cuisine et diététique dans l'Occident arabe médiéval*, 152, no. 196.

43 The *RAE* records "alboronía" and "almoronía" as being the same term.

Almoronía is a typical dish for Moroccan Sephardic Jews.[44] It is made mostly of chicken, fried eggplant, onions, saffron, honey, salt, and pepper. Interestingly, as regards the inclusion of the recipe in contemporary cookbooks, various books on Jewish cooking from diaspora countries contain *almoronía* recipes. *Olive Trees and Honey*[45] proposes two recipes under the same title, "Moroccan Eggplant Relish," but which include slightly different ingredients, as indicated by their subtitles "*Kahrmus*" (eggplant, olive oil, onions, garlic, red wine vinegar, cumin, paprika, Cayenne pepper, pepper, and sugar or honey) and "*Zeilouk*" (the same ingredients with added peppers, parsley, and cilantro). These dishes do not contain meat, yet their ingredients are different from the original preparation. *Olive Trees and Honey* contains an *alboronía* recipe made with chicken and eggplant cooked in a casserole.[46] The recipe is closer to that contained in the *Kitāb al-ṭabīẖ*. The historic cookbook *Sephardi: Cooking the History* includes an *almoronía* recipe that closely resembles the thirteenth-century recipe and matches the culinary practices of Moroccan Sephardic Jews.[47]

c. Chickpea Croquettes

Of the twelve chickpeas recipes included in the oldest medieval Iberian recipe book, let's focus on the recipe named "Thin Chickpea Croquettes."[48] The simplicity of the recipe is surprising and the final product leads us to think about how it has evolved. In the *Kitāb al-ṭabīẖ* recipe, it is stated that the chickpeas must be shelled and ground. Then, a small amount of yeast, some eggs, and spices are added. Shaping comes later. Finally, the recipe is fried. It is indeed intriguing and is obviously like falafel dishes that are enjoyed today in the Middle East.[49] This is likely the first falafel recipe written in a cookbook in the Muslim West, and it further fuels debate about the geographic and ethnic origin of this emblematic dish in Eastern culinary culture.

---

44 The names *alboronía* or *alburnía* can be used for this dish, which is also enjoyed today beyond the Jewish community. See Macías, "Ojos de berenjenas, las mil y una recetas," 267.

45 Marks, *Olive Trees and Honey* (Boston: Houghton Mifflin Harcourt, 2004), 74, 78.

46 Marks, *Encyclopedia of Jewish Food*.

47 Piñer, *Sephardi*, 22–23.

48 Guillaumond, *Cuisine et diététique dans l'Occident arabe médiéval*, 84, no. 32.

49 Yael Raviv, "Falafel: A National Icon," *Gastronomica* 3 (2003): 20–25; Piñer, *Sephardi*.

d. *Mufleta*

This food is unique in its testimony about Jewish cuisine in the thirteenth century in the south of Spain. It was not easy to discover. The dish, known today as *mufleta,* is an emblematic preparation made by Moroccan Jews to celebrate the end of Jewish Easter, *Pessah*. It is present in the first cookbook in Western Muslim cuisine, the *Kitāb al-ṭabīẖ*, where the dish is called *Murakkaba*. Furthermore, this dish, which means "composed" in Arabic, is the only example of a Jewish preparation in the *Kitāb al-ṭabīẖ*. Keep in mind that the word has the same root as the Hebrew *MuRKaV*, which illustrates a philological interculturality. The term *muārraqa* is included in *Vocabulista arauigo en letra castellana* by Pedro de Alcalá (1505) to define the Castilian word *hojaldre* (which means "pastry").[50]

Louis Bruno and Élie Malka, who put together the *Glossaire judéo-arabe de Fès*, have not been able to provide an explanation about the etymology of the term *mafleta* (مافليطة). They note that it is a "ritual dish made of pastry dough. The very complicated preparation of this pastry creates a certain amount of mess at home."[51] In the *Kitāb al-ṭabīẖ* there are two variants of *murakkaba*. One is simply called "Recipe for *Marakība* (?)"[52] and the other appears to be a variation called "Recipe for *Murakība* Pastry with Dates."[53] The dish is not labelled as Jewish, though, unlike the six other explicitly Jewish recipes included in the cookbook. Does this mean that Muslims also ate it? I think not. The Jews of Morocco are the only Moroccans who prepare *mufleta*, but they are also the only people in the entire Sephardic diaspora to do so.

Let's dwell for a moment on how this festive dish is made. In the *Kitāb al-ṭabīẖ*, it contains semolina, eggs, yeast, and water. The dough is kneaded for a long time until it reaches the consistence of *isfenğ*,[54] a large wafer with a hole in the middle, enjoyed by Moroccans (whether Sephardic or not) today.[55] In a frying pan, the author of the *Kitāb al-ṭabīẖ* instructs, put oil and a thin layer of the dough at the bottom. After flipping it, add another layer of dough on top and flip the whole thing together. Continue until all the layers of dough have been used and form a tower of stacked layers. Once the pile is created, the sides are browned in the

---

50 De Alcalá, *Vocabulista arauigo en letra castellana*, 301.

51 Louis Bruno and Élie Malka, *Glossaire judéo-arabe de Fès*, vol. 37 (Rabat: Publications de l'Institut des Hautes Études Marocaines, 1940).

52 Guillaumond, *Cuisine et diététique dans l'Occident arabe médiéval*, [Recipe for *Marakība*], 188, no. 285.

53 Ibid., 189.

54 Ibid., 268.

55 Rosenberger, "Diététique et cuisine dans l'Espagne musulmane du XIIIe siècle," 181.

pan. Finally, a hole is made in the center and filled with honey and melted butter. As for the other *murakkaba* recipe, it is identical to this one, with the exception that pieces of dates are added between the layers of dough.

The second cookbook written in Arabic, the *Fuḍālat al-ḫiwān* by Ibn Razīn al-Tuǧībī, includes a recipe called *folyāṭil*.[56] The Hispanic origin of the term refers to pastry, as is true for the word *muārraqa*. Fernando de la Granja, who did his doctoral dissertation on this cookbook, establishes a link between *folyāṭil* and a culinary habit of Jews in the Moroccan city of Fes. He demonstrates that the *Fuḍālat al-ḫiwān* includes two preparations whose name "is related to this dough of Jews of Fes." He adds that in the two copies of the *Fuḍālat al-ḫiwān* manuscript—in Tübingen and Madrid—it is stated that *folyāṭil* is a part of a soup (*ṯarīda*) and is Eastern; surprising details given that its name refers to an Andalusian dish. He further explains that *folyāṭil* is the name of a soup (*ṯarīda)* made of pastry (probably pieces of pastry), and that the preparation of this pastry (independently of the dish in which it is used) is called *muwarraqa*. Fernando de la Granja concludes by writing that the

> *ṯarīda* of Spanish Muslims is made of pastry, just like *mafleṭa* is the pastry that Jews of Fes kept, as a hybrid, with the same word in Roman language in the manuscripts. *Mafleṭa* is probably the common form of the feminine past participle in Arabic, "mufalyaṭa" (i.e. "foliácea"), of the hypothetical root "falyaṭa" that perhaps existed in the sense of "giving the shape of pastry dough," the nominal origin of which would precisely be *folyāṭil*.[57]

This explanation sheds light on the reason why the dish is connected with *murakkaba*[58] in the *Kitāb al-ṭabīḫ*.

This "pastry" is still prepared today, but only by Sephardic Moroccan Jews, to celebrate *Mimouna* (a celebration at the end of Jewish Easter, *Pessah*).[59] In short, the *Kitāb al-ṭabīḫ* contains the first recipe for *mufleta* made by Moroccan Jews, while testifying to the existence of a Jewish cuisine in al-Andalus in the

---

56 Ibn Razīn al-Tuǧībī and Marín, *Relieves de las mesas acerca de las delicias de la comida y los diferentes platos*, 91, no. 17. See Fernando De la Granja, "Nota sobre la 'maflêta' de los judíos de Fes," *Al-Andalus* 25 (1960): 235–238.

57 De la Granja, "Nota sobre la 'maflêta' de los judíos de Fes," 237. Translation by the author.

58 Jawhara Piñer, "Making Mufleta, History's Oldest Jewish Pastry, for the Holidays," *Tablet Magazine*, September 7, 2018, https://www.tabletmag.com/scroll/270379/making-mufleta-historys-oldest-jewish-pastry-for-the-holidays.

59 Roden, *Le livre de la cuisine juive*, 492–493.

thirteenth century that is still living today.[60] The second Andalusian cookbook testifies to the connection between the dish and Moroccan Jews.

e. *Maçapães* and *Marzapanes*

As saw in the previous chapter, marzipans—small sweets made of sweet almond paste—have belonged to the culinary habits of the Iberian Peninsula since the Middle Ages. The first book of Portuguese recipes, *Livro de cozinha* (sixteenth century), attributed to the Infanta Maria of Portugal, has a recipe called "Para Fazer Maçapães."[61] The cookbook contains dishes that are present in past cookbooks from the Iberian Peninsula, such as *Libro de cocina* (1529) by Roberto de Nola, and earlier preparations (see the *Kitāb al-ṭabīḫ*).

The Portuguese recipe *maçapães* contains sugar cooked with syrup and flavored water. The same amount of ground almonds and a little bit of flour are added to make the dish moist. The dough is cut into pieces and cooked over a fire. Finally, they are molded to the right shape. The *maçapães* recipe appears to be evidence of continuity in the culinary practices brought from Spain three centuries earlier. This is not surprising, given that the *Livro de cozinha* presents a number of recipes that evoke the cuisine of Spain under Muslim rule—dishes like *maçapães*, which were then passed on to Portugal. The Infanta's taste for these dishes[62] is probably the reason. Still, we cannot rule out the possibility that population movements, and particularly the exodus of Jews from their original land, played a crucial role in spreading the Spanish culinary heritage. The few Iberian sources that exist, however, do not make it possible to establish a link between Jews and *mazapán*. This is where Italian sources come into play.

Let's remember that Jewish communities had been living in Italy since antiquity. The arrival of the Sephardic diaspora can thus be conceived as the continuation of a Jewish presence.[63] The *Grande dizionario della lingua italiana*

---

60 Jawhara Piñer, "Making Mufleta, History's Oldest Jewish Pastry, for the Holidays."

61 De Portugal and Palla, *Livre de cuisine de l'Infante Maria du Portugal*, 5:21, no. 91; María José Azevedo Santos, *A Alimentação em Portugal na idade média*, vol. 61 (Coimbra: Fontes-Cultura-sociedade, 1997).

62 This is if we consider that the infanta was indeed the author of the cookbook.

63 Henri Bresc, "La Sicile médiévale, terre de refuge pour les juifs: migration et exil," *Al-Masāq: Journal of the Medieval Mediterranean* 17, no. 1 (2005): 31–47; Giuseppe Mandalà, "La migration des juifs du Garbum en Sicile (1239)," *Maghreb-Italie. Des passeurs médiévaux à l'orientalisme moderne (XIIIe-milieu XXe siècle)*, ed. B. Grévin (Rome: Ecole française de Rome, 2010), 19–48; ibid., "The Jews of Palermo from Late Antiquity to the Expulsion (598– 1492–93)," in *A Companion to Medieval Palermo: The History of a Mediterranean City*

defines *marzapane*—also called *marciapane, marsapane,* and *marzappane*—as a "sweet almond paste made of egg whites. It is kneaded into different shapes, decorated and colored, molded into figurines, fake fruits or used as a decoration or stuffing."[64] The analyses presented earlier in this chapter show the impossibility of confining marzipan to Italy only. The wide range of names—*mazapán, marzipan, marzapane,* and *massepain*—is evidence the widespread consumption of *marzapane* by various people across different territories for many, many years. The presence of this preparation in cookbooks proves, at the same time, its culinary significance.

Nonetheless, the numerous variations of the term "marzipan" raises questions about its etymology. Venice is the likely origin.[65] But the word *marzipan* also refers to a small box used in the south of France in the fourteenth century.[66] The same term was also employed in Provence and Sicily to designate the same thing. This is interesting because in the fourteenth century, the Italian term *marzipan* was associated with both the container (the small luxury box) and its contents (the sweets). These details come the Florentine merchant Pegolotti's trade manual for the city of Famagusta (northern Cyprus). As for the word *matapan,* it was a currency used in Venice under the rule of Enrico Dandolo in 1193. Thus, there must have been a connection between the name of the currency[67] and the word *mauthabān,* a Byzantine coin on which there is an image of a king sitting down, as we mentioned above.

Maxime Rodinson's suggests that the phonetic proximity of these two words engendered the term "marzipan." Another explanation is that the term derives from the Persian and Armenian word *marzubān*—a unit of measurement—but means "governor." He also referes to the German academic Kluyver, who argues that the unit of measurement gave its name to the container (the box) and then to its contents (the sweets). But there is a great deal of uncertainty

---

from 600 to 1500, ed. Annliese Nef (Leiden: Brill, 2013), 437–485; Michele Amari, *Storia dei Musulmani di Sicilia*, vol. 2, *1933–1939*, 2nd ed. (Firenze: Felice Le Monnier, 2014); Annliese Nef, "Les juifs de Sicile: des juifs de langue arabe du XIIe au XVe siècle," in *Ebrei e Sicilia*, ed. N. Bucaria, A. Tarantino, and M. Luzzati (Palerme: Flaccovio editore, 2002), 169–178.

64 Salvatore Battaglia, *Grande dizionario della lingua italiana* (Torino: Unione tipografico-editrice torinense, 1975), 9:856: ". . . pasta dolce di mandorle pestate e zucchero, resa consistente con albume d'uovo; variamente lavoata, ornata e colorata, viene modellata in figurine, in finta frutta o usata per guernizioni, ripieni." Translation by the author.

65 Rodinson, "Venice and the Spice Trade," 211–213.

66 A. Kluyver, "Marzipan," *Zeitschriftfiir deutsche Wortforschung* 6 (1904): 59–67.

67 Battaglia, *Grande dizionario della lingua italiana*, 9:856: "Dall ar. Mauthāban, originariamente nome di una moneta, poi di una misura di capacità, infine del recipiente o del contenitore nel quale il dole si conservava."

about this interpretation, and it leads to two lines of questioning. Does the term "marzipan" (a sweet)—known in the Middle East and primarily in Syria as *marsabān*—come from its integration into the East, while still considering Italy as its original homeland? Or does the term "marzipan" come phonetically from the word *marzabān* meaning "governor"?[68]

In this section, I will focus on connecting marzipan to its role as a possible marker of Jewish identity in Italy. The Italian sources from the thirteenth century on this topic are too few and do not make it possible to compare the use of marzipan with the preparations in the *Kitāb al-ṭabīḫ*. However, there are specific sources that allow us to solidify the link that between the preparation of sweet almond paste and Italian Jews. Much has already been written about the etymological origin of the term *marzapane* and the initial uses of the sweet. In his article "Il Mazapane,"[69] Bruno Maggi points out a question raised by the dish. He shares the opinion held by Rudolf Grewe and Lucie Bolens that this food was known among Arabs, but that it had no particular name. The author adds that almonds and sugar are two typical ingredients in Middle Eastern cuisine, arriving in Spain and later in Sicily with the Romans. Maggi contests that Europe experienced, with this preparation and many others, a new food reality, thanks to the contribution of Muslim civilization.[70] Nevertheless, if the contributions of Arab civilization to cuisine are undeniable, they didn't extend past the fifteenth century, and the transmission of this culinary heritage throughout Europe remained minimal.

Liber de coquina[71]—the first version of which was in Latin—dates back to 1308. There are three Latin and two Italian versions. It is probably the first cookbook that includes something resembling *marzapane*, then, but is not named as such. The author then focuses on *Libro de arte coquinaria* by Martino,[72] from the mid-fifteenth century (1464–1465), for being the first Italian cookbook

---

68 Rodinson, "Venice and the Spice Trade," 211–213.

69 Maggi, "Il marzapane."

70 Ibid., 76.

71 Ms. 9328, Biblioteca Nazionale in Luigi Sada Vincenzo Valente; Maggi, "Il marzapane," 84n21. Manuscript no. 9328 in the BnF in Paris corresponds to version B. It is the text of the manuscript of the Duke of Berry, written between 1360 and 1370, found in a collection that includes two agricultural books and two dietary books. The full text of the *Liber de coquina* has been digitalized by Justu Liebig Universitat Giessen, Zeitschriftfiir deutsche Wortforschung, and can be found here: https://www.uni-giessen.de/fbz/fb05/germanistik/absprache/sprachverwendung/gloning/tx/mul2-lib.htm.

72 The work can be found here: "Maestro Martino: Libro de arte coquinaria," Justus-Liebig-Universitat Giessen, https://www.uni-giessen.de/fbz/fb05/germanistik/absprache/sprachverwendung/gloning/tx/martino2.htm.

with a *marzapane* recipe. *Libro de arte coquinaria* is thus the first Western cookbook to include the preparation with an explicit title. Indeed, this cookbook is linked with Catalan cuisine, connecting it, geopolitically speaking, to the Iberian Peninsula.

Beyond culinary sources, the word "marzapane" appears in a letter written by one of the most important Jewish bankers from Siena, Jacob di Consiglio da Toscanella, dated May 5, 1463 and addressed to Giovanni di Cosimo de' Medici in Florence. *Marzapane* and other sweets are described as *fatte all'hebrea*, meaning "Jewish made."[73] The sixteenth century *Processi del Santo Uffizio di Venezia contro ebrei e giudaizzanti* (1579–1586)[74] supports this.[75] *Marzapane* is clearly connected with Jewish culinary practices. If preparing and eating *marzapane* had only occasional, it would not have been recorded in the trials of the Inquisition. Ariel Toaff calls *marzapane* a "valued Jewish pastry," a Jewish pastry with an Arab origin that was more or less distant, which later developed independently into a wide range of shapes "with the addition of various essences and flavors (eggs, preserved etrog, rose water and orange blossom water, carnation and cinnamon) as a garnish for cakes and pies and of all different colors."[76] It was eaten upon various occasions, such as circumcisions and other celebrations. The use of citron/etrog among the ingredients made it possible to unite the pleasant flavor of the fruit with the significance it holds in the Jewish liturgy, primarily during the celebration of Sukkot.[77] Thus, in 1568, Leone da Montesanto, a banker in Mantua, gave officers of the city "Jewish marzipan and Malvasia from Candia [wine from the city of Candia]."[78] The existence of a dish made with *marzapane*

---

73 Ariel Toaff, "Marzapani, olive candite e caffè," in *Mangiare alla giudia: la cucina ebraica in Italia dal Rinascimento all'età moderna* (Bologne: Il Mulino, 2000), 101–104.

74 Zorattini, *Processi del S. Uffizio di Venezia contro ebrei e giudaizzanti*, 69–71, 84, 100, 106, 117–118, 142. Fol. 44v., 45v., 46v., 63v., 83r., 91r.

75 Susan Weingarten, "Medieval Hannukah Traditions: Jewish Festive Foods in Their European Contexts," *Food & History* 8, no. 1 (2010): 55.

76 Toaff, "Marzapani, olive candite e caffè," 102: "Questo prezzo pregato dell pasticceria ebraica. . . . con l'aggiunta di essenze e sapori diversi (uova, cedro candito, acqua di rose e di fior d'arancio, garofano e cannela) come ripieno di torte e pasticci e diversamente colorato." Translation by the author.

77 *Sukkot* is a celebration of the divine assistance received by the children of Israel during the Exodus, as well as during the harvest. On the first day of the holiday, *loulav* (made of citron and branches of palm, myrtle, and river willow) is brought to the synagogue. Citron (*etrog* in Hebrew and *utruğ* in Arabic) is essential for this celebration.

78 Toaff, "Marzapani, olive candite e caffè": "marzapani all'hebrea et Malvasia di Candia."

paste called *braciadelli de marzapano all'hebrea* is more evidence of the connection between Jews and *marzapane*.[79]

What is even more interesting is the material link between *marzapane* and Italian Jews. But what should be understood by *fatte all'hebrea*, meaning "Jewish made"? *Marzapane* was indispensable to the Italian elite from as early as the Renaissance. The dish was served in an infinite number of ways. For example, "in the sixteenth century, in the houses of the ghetto of Venice, guests were given, in addition to fresh seasonal fruits (like pears and cherries), some *marzapane* and a little *malvasia* and always these things to eat, Jewish-style, *frittole, rafioli, pignoccata,* things made with sugar that are round-shaped like nuts and fruits with *marzapane* inside."[80]

The attention given to the precision of the shape of *marzapane* should not be underestimated. This aesthetic specificity allowed *marzapane* to be recognized as a Jewish-made dish, which led to accusations against those who prepared it. Indeed, the documents of the Holy Office mention round foods (*son cose tonde*) in the shape of nuts and fruits (*in foza de nosc e de fruti*) and stuffed with *marzapane* paste (*che dentro ve è pasta de marzapane*). In short, the trials of the Inquisition in Venice (sixteenth century) clearly link *marzapane* and other sweets with the Mosaic religion.

Almond pastries and other sweets made with nuts are mentioned in the verses of the *Provençal Esther Poem* by Crescas du Caylar (fourteenth century). These sweets have endured in the preparations for Purim and the collective memory of Sephardic women.[81] Thus, we can understand the significance, within the Sephardic Jewish culinary heritage of the Mediterranean Basin, of *marzapane, massepains,* and *mazapán,* whatever the language used to describe it. If the concept of de-territorialization is needed to trace the trajectory of *marzapane* and Jews who ate it, attention to the regionalization of the sweet (Emilian, Tuscan, Venetian, Mantuan) is just as necessary.[82] This furthermore explains the use of

---

79 Shamuel Shimonsohn, *History of Jews in the Duchy of Mantua* (Jersusalem: Kiryath Sepher, 1977), 264.

80 Toaff, "Marzapani, olive candite e caffè," 103: "Per tormare al marzapane, non c'era ricevimento, che si rispettasse, senza che vi venisse offerto in una pressoché infinita varietà di ricette. Nelle case del ghetto di Venezia nel Cinquecento si offrivano agli ospiti, oltre alla frutta fresca di stagione (particolarmente apprezate le pere e le ciliegie), un pocho de marzapan et un pocho de Malvasia et sempre de queste cose de manzar, fatte all'hebrea, frittole, rafioli, pignoccata, cose fatte de zucharo, che son cose tonde in foza de nose e de fruti, che dentro ve è pasta de marzapane." Translation by the author.

81 Vassas, *Esther*, 109, 126.

82 A regional specialty that is also present in the Jewish culinary practices explained above about *cabaheas.*

"altered terms [that] refer to local Hebrew dialects."[83] Once again, transmission is at the heart of Jewish history.

The precious information concerning the shape of *marzapane* echoes the recipe entitled *sanbūsak*,[84] included in the first cookbook of the Iberian Peninsula, the *Kitāb al-ṭabīẖ*. The transcripts of Inquisition trials and the recipe by the cookbook's anonymous author describe the same aesthetic features of the dish. The existence of Jewish recipes in the *Kitāb al-ṭabīh* raises the question: Who prepared, ate and, sold these sweet almond desserts? Does the connection between the dish and the Jewish people explain why it has no other name besides an Eastern one? There was nothing negative in associating Muslims and *marzapane*.

This was not the case for Jews, however, as attested by a variation found in an anti-Jewish satire[85] from, according to indications, 1497 and written in Terracina, Italy. A sweet named *pignorati* is mentioned,[86]—also called *pinochiati*—made of almond paste and pine nuts. It looks like the modern Italian pastry named *pignoli*. The etymological dictionary of the Italian language (*DELI*) defines *pignoccata* as a sweet (*dolce*) made of sugar paste and pine nuts (*pasta di zucchero e pinoli*) that was eaten in Perugia and Naples in the late fifteenth century. The pastry is discussed in this satire because Jews ate it. Indeed, there is an ironic pun on the verb "pignorare," which means "moneylending" or "seize,"[87] making an obvious allusion to Jewish professions that were denigrated by the rest of the population. It further alludes to the way Jews were perceived by others, namely as miserly and conceited.[88] It is worth pointing out that *pinocc(h)iati* and *marzapane* appear to be juxtaposed in the same verse in Simone Prodenzani's

83 Vassas, *Esther*, 100n27.

84 Guillaumond, *Cuisine et diététique dans l'Occident arabe médiéval*, 197n307.

85 Dozon, "Contributions à l'étude de la civilisation urbaine en Italie."

86 Ibid. See the end of fol. 38. Translation by the author.

87 Manlio Cortelazzo, *DELI-dizionario etimologico della lingua italiana*, 2nd ed. (Bologna: Zanichelli, 1999), 1194: "*Pignoràre*: sottoporre a pignoramento (1280–1297, Statuto di Montagulolo)"; "*Pignoramento*: atto con cui s'inizia l'espropriazione forzata processuale, consistente in un'ingiunzione che l'ufficiale giudiziario fa al debitore di astenersi da atti che possano sottrarre alla garanzia di uno o più creditori dati beni (1289–1309, Statuto dell'Università e Arte della lana di Siena)." Translation by the author.

88 Ibid.: "O. Lurati sposta l'attenzione del sign. Attuale ('pedante') a quello orig. ('avaro'), che si rifà all'immagine del furtto del pino, così difficile da aprire: "Pignolo 'lopseudofrutto che tiene i suoi frutti molto stretti'; 'uomo avaro, che tiene stretti i suoi soldi'; 'persona grettamente avara';'persona gretta irritabilmente meticolosa, pedante, meschina, attacata alla forma e non alla sostanza delle cose.'" See also Manlio Cortelazzo, *Guida ai dialetti veneti*, vol. 13 (Padova: Cooperativa Libraria Editrice Università di Padova, 1991): 10–14.

(1351–1440) *Sallazzo e Saporetto.*[89] In addition to the almond paste preparation, these dishes reveal their link with the Italian Jewish community.

Italian Sephardic Jews continuing preparation and consumption of *marzapane* is primarily revealed during marriages, circumcisions, and other celebrations. This goes for *Monte Sinai*[90] pastry too. The pastry, defined by the *Guide to Italian Gastronomy* as a "Jewish marzipan cake," is also called *sinaini*[91] in Venetian documents. Just like *marzapane di martorana,* the existence of a Jewish cuisine and the integration of Jewish culinary practices into Italian food heritage is in the *Guide.* Furthermore, *sinaini*[92] is included in *piyyut*[93] written in Judeo-Livornese from 1750 onwards, which is riddled with terms in Spanish, Portuguese, Venetian, and Hebrew. The *Guide* refers explicitly to "Mount Sinai." If proof is still needed of the importance of mobility and transmission in Jewish culture, marzipan-based pastries are still prepared today in North Africa.[94]

Claudia Roden has a recipe called *Monte Sinai con uovo filate,*[95] which she describes as "typically Portuguese, almost identical to a dessert called 'bola de amor' in the *Jewish Manual* published in 1846 in London, likely by Judith Montefiore."[96] Ariel Toaff establishes a link between *marzapane* and the dish *marzapane a uova filate,* which dates back to the second half of the eighteenth century. It was a "cake made of almond paste, very widespread among Italian and Sephardic Jews, kneaded in the shape of a braid or in small molds shaped like chestnuts, and cooked in the oven in a few minutes; it was coated in egg yolk and the peel of *melarancia;* finally, a citron confit was added. In Livorno, it was considered to be a typical cake of Iberian Jewish cuisine, and was shaped into small conical mounds and eggs strands, placed on top of pastry wafers, and coated in icing and colored sprinkles."[97] The fact that the Iberian origin of *marzapane* is

---

89 Simone De Prodenzani, *Sallazzo e Saporetto* (Perugia: EFFE Fabrizio Fabri, 1998), 136, verse 5.

90 *Guida gastronomica d'Italia-Introduzione alla Guida gastronomica d'Italia* (2006), 268: "A Livorno si trovano altresì dei dolci d'origine greca, come delle pastine dolci chiamate curambier e la conserva di rose, fatta con i petali delle rose cosidette di Scio, o Chio, nonchè gli orecchi di Aman, specie di "cenci" dolci, e il Monte Sinai, dolce di marzapane, ambedue israeliti." See Szokovski, "Chabad."

91 Toaff, "Marzapani, olive candite e caffè," 102–103. Translation by the author.

92 Vassas, *Esther*, 99. Translation by the author.

93 *A piyyut* is a liturgical poem for any Jewish holiday.

94 Vassas, *Esther*, 100n27.

95 Roden, *Le livre de la cuisine juive*, 432, 512–513.

96 Ibid., 512.

97 Toaff, "Marzapani, olive candite e caffè," 102: "Era un dolce di pasta di mandorle, assai diffuso tra gli ebrei italiani e sefarditi, lavorato in forma di tortiglione o in piccoli pasticci foggiati « a castagna," cotto in forno per pochi minuti, con l'aggiunta di rossi d'uovo, bucce di melarancia e cedri canditi. A Livorno era considerato dolce tipico della cucina ebraica iberica e veniva

mentioned is significant, as is the use of citron in the preparation of the dish, given the importance of this fruit in Jewish culture.

f. *Isfenğ*

Literally "sponge,"[98] the *isfenğ* wafer is the epitome of Moroccan fried pastries. The same terminological root exists in Hebrew, *sfog*, which refers to a round doughnut, *sponğa* in Judeo-Spanish, and *esponja* in Castilian. It is a kind of street food that is prepared by the *šefneğ* and eaten hot or taken home. In the *Kitāb al-ṭabīḫ*, the word *isfenğ* is in the titles of certain recipes, notably the "Preparation of the Original Doughnut."[99] However, none of the *isfenğ* recipes seem to resemble the current Moroccan *sfenğ*, apart from the "Original Doughnut" recipe, due to its distinguishing shape. *Isfenğ* is mentioned in the instructions for several recipes in the *Kitāb al-ṭabīḫ*, particularly in "The making of peot,"[100] a recipe that is similar to the braided *challa* bread discussed earlier.

The second Arab cookbook from Spain, the *Fuḍālat al-ḫiwān*,[101] includes a recipe that can be translated as "Confection of Doughnuts," and which includes the term *isfenğ* in its name. This preparation is made from semolina that is dissolved in hot water with salt and yeast. The recipe specifies that is necessary to first make a hard dough and then add water gradually. It has to be kneaded a lot so that it is thin and so as to remove the air inside. Finally, it must be left to rise. When making the doughnuts, you have to take the dough in your hands, remove the part that comes through the thumb and the index finger, and then put the balls created this way into oil. The large ones are called *aqṣād* and the small ones *mugaddar*. They must be fried and browned on the bottom, but remain white on top. They can be cooked twice, so that they are lighter.[102] The recipe suggests testing the dough before making the doughnut. If the hole of the doughnut stays

---

confezionato in forma di monticelli conici di marzapane a uova filate, posti su cialde di pasta frolla, coperti di glassa e confettini colorati." Translation by the author.

98 *Isfenğ* appears to come from the Latin *spongia* and the Greek *spongiá*, which means "sponge." On "sponge cake" and Jewish food, see Freedman, *Why Food Matters*, 58.

99 Guillaumond, *Cuisine et diététique dans l'Occident arabe médiéval*, 268, no. 488; Ibn Razīn al-Tuğībī and Marín, *Relieves de las mesas acerca de las delicias de la comida y los diferentes platos*, 124–125.

100 Guillaumond, *Cuisine et diététique dans l'Occident arabe médiéval*, 208, no. 336; Piñer, *Sephardi*, 16–17.

101 Ibn Razīn al-Tuğībī and Marín, *Relieves de las mesas acerca de las delicias de la comida y los diferentes platos*, 123, no. 30.

102 Ibn Razīn al-Tuğībī and Marín, *Relieves de las mesas acerca de las delicias de la comida y los diferentes platos*, 123, no. 30. Translation by the author.

open, it rises to the surface of the oil once it is cooked, and the inside collapse, it is a sign that the dough inside the doughnut has risen; if not, the dough must be left to rise longer.

Sfenğ—using the current terminology—is the most commonly consumed fried doughnut in Morocco, by both Jews and Muslims. Interestingly, there is a lexical proximity with the Hebrew word *soufganin*, referring to a specific type of wafer. The word refers to doughnuts that are eaten today for the Jewish festival of lights, *Hanukkah*. Moreover, because the *sfenğ* in the *Fuḍālat al-ẖiwān* are neither dipped in honey or sugar, they can be compared to the *sufganiyot* recipe enjoyed by Israeli Jews. This is included in Talmudic sources, such as the *Mishnah Challa* (1:4; 1:5) and *Jerusalem Talmud Challa* (1:3:1).

The Sevillian Talmudic commentator of the fourteenth century, David Ben Joseph Ben David Abudarham, sheds light on this topic. He writes in the *Sefer Abudarham* that *isfenğ* is the Arabic name for *sufganin*, a term which is already present in the third-century *Mishnah* and the Talmud. These writings support the hypothesis that *isfenğ* have been eaten by the Mosaic people since at least the third century. In addition to this linguistic interculturality, there is also a culinary dimension. Thus, David Ben Joseph Ben David Abudarham proposes that the term *isfenğ* produced the word *zalābīya*, but that the name in the Talmud is *isqariti*. However, the word *isqariti* is found in *Even Bohan* (1322), written by Rabbi Arles Kalonymos ben Kalonymos. He mentions *isqaritin* (*tzapihit bedvah*) as being made of dough cooked over embers, enjoyed hot, and dipped in sugar or honeyed wine. This is an interesting because the term *tzapihit* is connected to *hojuelas*, a Spanish term in the Torah.[103]

---

103 Explanations are provided in the section dedicated to *hojuelas*.

CHAPTER 11

Recipes and Photos of Jewish Dishes from the *Kitāb al-ṭabīẖ*[1]

The copy of the *Kitāb al-ṭabīẖ* that survives today is not written in academic Arabic. As a result, it contains a number of grammatical errors and the syntax is often poor. The translations also respect the fact that there is no list of ingredients that preceded the recipes. The recipes presented in this chapter come from David Friedman's translation, which is based on Charles Perry's work.[2] However, the book *Sephardi: Cooking the History* offers adaptations of all of these recipes, while remaining true to the original recipe.[3]

A. A Stuffed Buried Jewish Dish

Charles Perry writes that "A version of *adafina* (from an Arabic word meaning 'buried treasure,' related to the word *madfûn*, 'buried,' which is found in the name of this dish), the Sephardic equivalent of the Ashkenazi dish cholent, which could be left in the oven overnight on Friday so that Jewish housewives wouldn't have to violate the Sabbath by cooking."

Here is the recipe:

> Pound some meat cut into circles, and be careful that there be no bones in it. Put it in a pot and throw in all the spices except cumin, four spoonfuls of oil, two spoonfuls of penetrating

1 All the recipes presented in this chapter are included in Piñer, *Sephardi.*
2 "An Anonymous Andalusian Cookbook."
3 Piñer, *Sephardi.*

rosewater, a little onion juice, a little water and salt, and cover it with a thick cloth. Put it on a moderate flamb and cook it with care. Pound the meat as for meatballs, season it and make little meatballs and throw them [p. 21, recto] in the pot until they are done. When everything is done, beat five eggs with salt, pepper, and cinnamon; make a thin layer [a flat omelet or egg crepe; literally 'a tajine'] of this in a frying pan, and beat five more eggs into another thin layer. Then take a new pot and put in a spoonful of oil and boil it a little; put in the bottom one of the two layers, pour the meat onto it, and cover with the other layer. Then beat three eggs with a little white flour, pepper, cinnamon, and some rosewater with the rest of the pounded meat, and put this over the top of the pot. Then cover it with a potsherd of fire[4] until it is browned, and be careful that it does not burn. Then break the pot and put the whole mass on a dish, and cover it with 'eyes' of mint, pistachios and pine-nuts, and add spices. You might put on this dish all that has been indicated, and leave out the rosewater and replace it with a spoonful of juice of cilantro pounded with onion, and half a spoonful of *murri naqî'*; put in it all that was put in the first, God, the Most High, willing.[5]

B. A Jewish Dish of Eggplants Stuffed with Meat

Boil the eggplants and take out their small seeds and leave [the skins] whole. Take leg of lamb meat and pound it with salt, pepper, cinnamon, Chinese cinnamon, and spikenard. Beat it with the whites of eight eggs and separate six egg

4 Presumably of coals, as in the Jewish Partridge dish above.
5 "An Anonymous Andalusian Cookbook," 116.

yolks. Stuff the eggplants with this. Then take three pots and put in one of them four spoonfuls of oil, onion juice, spices, and aromatics, and two spoonfuls of fragrant rosewater, pine-nuts, an "eye" of citron [leaves], another of mint, and sufficient salt and water; boil well and throw in half of the stuffed eggplants. In the second pot put a spoonful of vinegar, a teaspoon of *murri*, a grated onion, spices, and aromatics, a sprig of thyme, another of rue, citron leaf, two stalks of fennel, two spoonfuls of oil, almonds, soaked garbanzos, half a *dirham* of ground saffron, and three cut garlics. Boil in sufficient water until it boils several times, and throw into it the rest of the stuffed eggplants. And in the third pot put a spoonful and a half of oil, a spoonful of cilantro water, half a spoon of sharp vinegar, crushed onion, almond, pine-nuts, a sprig of rue, and citron leaves. Sprinkle with rosewater and dust with spices. Decorate the second with cut-up egg yolks and cut rue and sprinkle it with aromatic herbs; cut an egg cooked with rue over the third pot, sprinkle it with pepper, and present it.[6]

C. A Jewish Dish of Chicken

Clean the chicken and take out its entrails, cut off the extremities of its thighs, wings, and the neck, and salt the chicken and leave it. Take these extremities, the neck, and the entrails, and put them in a pot with fine spices and all the

6 Ibid., 316.

flavorings and cilantro juice, onion juice, whole pine-nuts, a little vinegar, and a little *murri*, good oil, citron leaves, and stalks of fennel. Put this over a moderate fire and when it is done and the greater part of the sauce has gone, cover the contents of the pot with three eggs, grated breadcrumbs, and fine flour, crush the liver, add it to this crust, and cook carefully until the liver and the crust are cooked and wrinkled. Then take the chicken and roast it carefully, and strike [cover] it with two eggs, oil, and *murri*, and do not stop greasing [basting] the chicken inside and out with this until it is browned and roasted. Then take a second little pot and put in two spoonfuls of oil and half a spoonful of *murri*, half a spoonful of vinegar, and two spoons of aromatic rosewater, onion juice, spices, and flavorings. Put this on the fire so that it cooks gently, and when it has cooked, cut up . . . [about two words missing] . . . and leave it until it is absorbed. Then ladle it into a dish [and pour the rest of the sauce on it, and cut up an egg and sprinkle with spices, and ladle the preceding almonds into another dish], and garnish it too with egg yolks; sprinkle it with fine spices and present both dishes, God willing.[7]

7 Ibid., 105.

CHAPTER 12

Recipes and Photos of Iberian Medieval Dishes in the Sephardic Culinary Heritage of the Mediterranean Basin

As in the previous chapter, the English translations come from David Friedman, by way of Charles Perry. *Sephardi: Cooking the History* propose adaptations of all the recipes, while remaining true to the original.[1]

A. *Harīsa/Oriza*

The Method of Making It:

Take good wheat and soak it in water. Then pound it in a wooden or stone mortar until it is free from husks. Then shake it and put the clean wheat [its marrow] in a pot with clean red meat and cover it with a lot of fresh water. Put it on a strong fire until it falls apart. Then stir it with the *rikshâb* very forcefully until it becomes blended and one part shades into the other. Then pour on enough melted fresh fat to cover it and beat them together until they are mixed. When it seems that the fat begins to separate and remain on top, turn it onto a platter and recover it with salted fat; dust it with ground cinnamon and use it as you please.[2]

---

1 Piñer, *Sephardi*, 78–79;

2 "An Anonymous Andalusian Cookbook," 404.

a. *Rice Harīsa*

Wash the needed amount of rice and let it sit for a day in enough water to cover it. Then put it in a pot and add what you want of the meat from chicken breasts or fresh mutton; cover it in water and cook it. When it falls apart, stir it vigorously until it is thoroughly mixed up. Put it on a platter and pour on melted fat from a sheep, dust it with cinnamon and use it. You might make this *harisa* in the oven. For that you cover it with a lot of water and fit the pot cover with a hinge and let it spend the night in the oven. Then take it out, pound it and use it with sheep fat.

b. *Recipe for Harīsa Made with White Bread Crumbs Instead of Wheat*

Take crumbs of white bread or of *samid* and grate them until they become grits the size of wheat or a little larger. Spread them in the sun until they dry out and take them up and set apart until needed. Then take the meat from the legs or shoulder blades of a sheep, because you don't make *harīsa* without sheep meat and fat. [p. 61, verso] Put it in a pot with a lot of water. Cook it until the meat falls apart and when you put in a fork [hook?] and it disperses. Then add the needed amount of already mentioned prepared crumbs and let it sit a while until it becomes mushy. Stir it until it is mixed and becomes one mass. Use it with melted sheep fat, dust it with cinnamon, as has been said.

B. *Recipe for Murakkaba*

Knead a well-made dough from semolina like the "sponge" dough with yeast, and break into it as many eggs as you can, and knead the dough with them until it is loose. Then set up a frying pan of clay [*hantam*] on a hot fire, and when it has heated, grease it with clarified butter or oil. Put in a thin flat loaf of the dough and when the bread is done, turn it over. Take some of the dough in the hand and smear the surface of the bread with it. Then turn the smeared surface to the pan, changing the lower part with the upper, and smear this side with dough too. Then turn it over in the pan and smear it, and keep smearing it with dough and turning it over in the tajine, and pile it up and raise it until it becomes a great, tall loaf. Then turn it by the edges a few times in the tajine until it is done on the sides, and when it is done, as it is desired, put it in a serving dish and make large holes with a stick, and pour into them melted butter and plenty of honey, so that it covers the bread, and present it.[3]

C. *Maqrūḍ*

In the *Fuḍālat al-ḫiwān* (thirteenth century) there is a *maqrūḍ*[4] recipe, the preparation of which is as follows. The dough is made of semolina, yeast, and a little bit of water. The stuffing contains sugar and almonds. The semolina dough is

3 Ibid., 428.
4 Ibn Razīn al-Tuǧībī and Marín, *Relieves de las mesas acerca de las delicias de la comida y los diferentes platos*, 121, no. 21.

stretched to make a square and the stuffing is placed inside, before being spread out again. After smoothing the surface, pieces are cut using a sharp knife, about the length of one finger and two fingers wide. The *maqrūḍ* are then fried in oil until brown; they are dried, then placed in a glass dish, and sugar is sprinkled on top. A date-based stuffing can also be made in the same way. The relationship between Jews and *maqrūḍ* is is evident. A historical source about important families in Fes at the end of the Middle Ages attests to the cooking and sale of *maqrūḍ*[5] by the Jewish community in imperial Morocco in the fifteenth century.[6]

5 Ibn al-Ahmar, "Buyūtāt Fās al-Kubrā" (Dhikr mashāhīr a'yān Fās al-qadīm)," *Al-Bahth al-'ilmī* 1, no. 3 (1964): 56; idem, *Buyūtāt Fās al-Kubrā* (Rabat: Dar al-Mansūr li 'l-Tibā'a wa 'l-Warrāqa, 1972), 24–25; Shatzmiller, "Professions and Ethnic Origin of Urban Labourers in Muslim Spain"; Carol Iancu, "Mille ans de vie juive au Maroc. Histoire et culture, religion et magie, bibliographie critique," *Annuaire de l'Afrique du Nord, l'Anthropologie* (1995): 972; Haïm Zafrani, *Mille ans de vie juive au Maroc. Histoire et culture, religion et magie* (Paris: Maisonneuve et Larose, 1983), 315; idem, *Two Thousand Years of Jewish Life in Morocco* (Brooklyn: Ktav Publishing House, 2005), 265.

6 I would like to thank Professor Daniel Newman who shared this information with me. See also Piñer, *Sephardi*, 122–123.

Conclusion

Historical, adaptable, transmittable, territorial, diasporic, and nostalgic best defines the cuisine of Jews and Sephardim. As such, there isn't one Jewish cuisine, but many—as many as there are communities and diasporas. But the rare recognition of the existence of a Jewish culinary culture is confusing. It highlights the great burden place on conscience when it comes to recognizing Jews in history, especially in Spain.

Cuisine is much more than a collection of recipes. It is a language; a universal language which unveils what we are and what we are not. Thus, stressing the relationship between the sacred—language—and daily life (that is, as it interacts with religion) is crucial when it comes to dealing with cuisine and culinary heritage. In short, this book presents religion as the foundation of a culinary system in a formerly multireligious society, through which, by way of historical analysis, can be seen a phenomenon that still endures today. My aim has been to contribute to our knowledge of some of the cuisine of Medieval Spanish Jews and medieval Spanish history more broadly.

It is telling that most of the secondary literature on this topic refers to Muslim sources from the time of Al-Andalus, and that work on medieval Jewish food is, in comparison, quite rare.[1] *Jews, Food, and Spain* examines the Jews of Spain and the evolution if their cuisine from the twelfth century onwards. Looking at the first known cookbook of the Middle Ages is not beside the point. The *Kitāb al-ṭabīẖ*—which is both a cookbook and a dietary manual—shows the existence and recognition of Jewish food in a period dominated by Islamic rule. All the Andalusians from the same social class had access to the same products, and that's why there is little difference between Jewish food and other dishes mentioned in *Kitāb al-ṭabīẖ*.

The practices described in the *Kitāb al-ṭabīẖ* allow us to identify the origin of a dish: burying it, making layers, using various pots, cooking eggplant, and so on. The practices let us discover Jewish traces in the *Kitāb al-ṭabīẖ* and in other kind of sources, whatever the period and place of composition. As the association

---

1 I would like to thank Miguel Ángel Motis Dolader (University of Zaragoza and Complutense University of Madrid) for all his valuable recommendations.

between cuisine and religion is central to Jewish cuisine, this sometimes makes it simple to recognize what dishes are Mosaic. Thus, the presence in a cuisine of the trio "bread–wine–meat" helps us understand which dishes belong to Jews and which to Muslims. These three foods are subject the dietary laws of Kashrut.

Eggplant has to be added to this trio, even if, as a vegetable, it is not under Kashrut laws. It appear as a Jewishness marker, but it is not easy to identify it if we only look at one kind of source, like the *Kitāb al-ṭabīḫ* . Its versatility confused thirteenth- to fourteenth-century Spaniards. Texts written afterwards, under Christian rule, reveal that eggplant was regarded as a sign of Jewishness.

The fourteenth century inaugurated a whole new period of cooking in Spain. The analysis of "Christian" cookbooks proves it, as they record a cuisine which contrasts entirely with former Semitic dishes. The fourteenth century was also the beginning of Spanish culinary uniformity. Food is not only something that is eaten; it is a mirror. It can reveal what you are, but it can also reflect the way of thinking of an entire society. Furthermore, the food of the Jews of Spain became an object of social criticism. Literature offers what cookbooks cannot: irony and hidden meanings.

This book aims to defend the use of food as an identity marker. It highlights the importance of ingredients—cilantro, of pork (which was rejected), and eggplant. These foods formed such a symbolic food group that it was registered in judicial sources. As a result, the culinary customs of the past changes and food styles and practices developed. This book has shown, for the first time, the trio that established what is today the culinary heritage of Spain, that is, the basic ingredients of Sephardic cuisine. The trials of the Inquisition provide much more information than one might think. I do not pretend to have analyzed all the information available; and there is much more to learn. In *Jews, Food, and Spain,* I have not tried to be exhaustive about the cuisine of the Jews who lived on the Iberian Peninsula in the Middle Ages, but I have tried to present what is essential for understanding of this special, people, period and place.

The transcripts of the trials of the Inquisition show us that Jewish cuisine was passed down orally to the following generations; and these same transcripts enable us to cross-check things that are found in literary works. Literature confirms the culinary and religious habits (the two were often combined) of conversos; and their distinctive food proved their guilt in the eyes of the Holy Office. It is important to note the existence of specifically Jewish dishes (in the eyes of both old and new Christians), for which no recipes have ever been recorded. The law of silence; although it shelters an inner identity that the daily act of eating cannot completely conceal.

These dishes were passed down to succeeding generations, however, even if cookbooks were not the vehicle of this transmission.[2] The Sephardic Jewish culinary heritage was little-known and has been the subject of only few works, despite the huge number of dishes prepared nowadays by the Sephardim: *Olla, cecina, cazuela, mazapán,* and so on. The new interest in this cuisine is due to the desire to recognize a past legacy and the wish to discover what Sephardi is. We should actually say Sephardi *cuisines,* as there are many different kinds because of the extent and multifaceted nature of the diaspora. Thus, goring from the *Kitāb al-ṭabīẖ* to the Sephardic culinary heritage of the Mediterranean Basin, *Jews, Food, and Spain* highlights dishes and recipes which are still alive in the hearts and kitchens of the Sephardim.

While some studies have explored Sephardic cuisine, one of my main contributions to the subject is discussion of the entanglement of culture and religion in the food of a territory whose borders did not impose limits on the transmission of knowledge. When faith becomes law, food becomes a tool in the service of religion. A Christian culinary ideology was born at the end of the fourteenth century. It was based on a deliberate erasure of Semitic Andalusians' food and culinary practices. Certainly, Jewish cuisine had to adapt to the new constraints of Christianity on the Iberian Peninsula; so it produced a culinary mix that was essential to its survival and the survival of a culture. But it also spread throughout the diaspora: Sephardic cuisine thrives today, as a result.

For Paul Freedman, "food traditions can reinforce an otherwise weakening religious identity"[3] These words crystalize the current relationship between food and religious identity. Bu they can also apply to the period of the Inquisition, during which some conversos were sincere in their new beliefs while others felt the loss of their original religious identity. Regardless, Sephardic food traditions persisted, regardless of religious identity

The recent book *Gastronomic Judaism as Culinary Midrash*[4] questions Jewish identity through food and modern Jewish food choices. It discusses connections between ancient religious texts and modern Jewish food preferences, and "typifies a sentiment found among Jews whose religious observance has lapsed, but who still consider themselves Jewish because they eat pastrami or celebrate Passover with proper special dishes."[5] Food is a bridge between gen-

---

2 Piñer, *Sephardi.*

3 Freedman, *Why Food Matters,* 58.

4 Jonathan D. Brumberg-Kraus, *Gastronomic Judaism as Culinary Midrash* (Lanham: Lexington Books, 2018).

5 Freedman, *Why Food Matters,* 60.

erations. Although a cuisine can seldom be preserved intact under conditions of assimilation, it survives vestigially as a symbolic language, especially at holidays."[6] The Sephardim's pride about their origins explains why their cuisine is so meaningful and the food prepared for Jewish holidays is symbolic all the way down to its taste

The current desire to recognize Sephardi cuisine is a recent phenomenon, although the first Jews who arrived in the New World (1521) were Sephardim "expelled from Spain or from Portugal, or were descendants of expellees."[7] Many Sephardic cookbooks have been published recently, there are cooking demonstrations dedicated to the cuisine,[8] and there are many new activities that aim to help people discover it.[9] The academic community is involved in this craze;[10] and restaurants now offer so-called Sephardic cuisine.[11] However, this phenomenon is largely restricted to the United States.[12] This North American trend further demonstrates "why food matters" in a country that has seen an increase in restaurants offering Sephardic cuisine and where Ashkenazi culinary culture was, until recently, the most common. Paul Freedman argues that "exile, migration and confinement reinforce the symbolic significance of food." He reflects on the "power of food and memory" demonstrated by a "cookbook put together by Jewish women imprisoned in the Theresienstadt concentration camp (Terezín, Czech Republic) during the Nazi tyranny."[13]

Finally, it has often been written that Jews are the People of the Book; but they also identified themselves through specific culinary practices, especially during Shabbat and at religious holidays. This is one of the links between the practices

---

6 Ibid.

7 Liebman, *The Jews in New Spain*, 52. See also 16–17.

8 The American Sephardi Federation (New York) organized, over a period of one year (August 2020–August 2021), historical and culinary sessions on Sephardic food. I was the speaker.

9 Israeli chef Michael Solomonov is organizing discovery tours in Israel for 2022. Part of his program is dedicated to the discovery of Sephardic cuisine. With Solomonov, we organized a Sephardic dinner at Morcilla restaurant (Pittsburgh) on March 17, 2022.

10 The Jewish Theological Seminary of New York has scheduled a program about Sephardi culinary heritage for April 27, 2022. I was the speaker. Pittsburg University and schools like Contra Costa Midrasha (California) also offer classes that teach the Sephardi culinary past. I was the speaker. A workshop is being scheduled at Carnegie Mellon University (Pittsburgh) for October 2022, with Professor Michal Friedman and Nevine Abraham, in order to present Sephardi and Israeli food.

11 I would like to thank Professor Paul Freedman (Yale) for his interest in this subject—and others—and for sharing the the talk he gave at the University of Haifa on Jewish cuisine in the United States.

12 Alcalá de Henares (Spain) is one of the only universities to offer a special program related to Sephardi studies.

13 Freedman, *Why Food Matters*, 4.

of Jews in both the Middle Ages and today. Food reminds Jews that they are Jews in part because of what they eat to celebrate the holidays; and this, strengthens their unique identity.

While more than five hundred years ago Sephardic cuisine was eaten at celebrations and solely at family gatherings; nowadays, this food is known worldwide and is especially prominent at North American delicatessens and restaurants. In a world where the first Jewish cookbook dates back to the nineteenth century, restaurants offering Jewish cuisine have become a way to preserve and share this ancestral culinary culture. Sephardic Jewish food has spread and is reviving; Israeli cuisine—Michael Solomonov[14] and Adeena Sussman[15] are the most representative chefs—offers healthy dishes with flavors that are different from Ashkenazi Jewish cuisine.. As Paul Freedman writes, "after the evanescence of traditional Ashkenazic cuisine, Israeli food has succeeded in becoming one of the trendiest entries in America's constantly shifting ethnic restaurant categories."[16]

Gerber remarks that "Sephardic Jewry is . . . an attractive kind of prototype to many modern and contemporary Jews."[17] This statement also applies to modern and contemporary Sephardic Jewish cuisines; while they originally developed in a multicultural context, they have not lost their identity and have maintained their unique qualities over the centuries. This identity, must also be understood by acknowledging the various stratifications and entanglements that have made up the history of the Sephardim from Spain to the diaspora. Indeed the Sephardim's pride in their origins and ancestors has remained intact.

To conclude, my book attempts to reaffirm Jewish Sephardic identity through food. Through analysis of the relationship between linguistic patterns, texts, and culinary grammar, *TITLE* gives legitimacy to the Sephardic nostalgia.

To eat is to remember.

---

14 Michael Solomonov and Steven Cook, *Israeli Soul: Easy, Essential, Delicious* (Boston: Mariner Books, 2018); Solomonov, *Zahav: A World of Israeli Cooking* (Boston: Mariner Books, 2015).

15 Adeena Sussman, *Sababa: Fresh, Sunny Flavors from My Israeli Kitchen* (New York: Avery, 2019).

16 These words are part of Paul Freedman's talk at University of Haifa on Jewish cuisine in the United States. I thank him for sharing his paper with me.

17 Gerber, "Cities of Splendour in the Shaping of Sephardi History."

Bibliography

Álvarez, Palenzuela Vicente Ángel. "Judíos y conversos en la España medieval. Estado de la cuestión." *eHumanista/Converso* 4 (2015): 156–191.

Öhrnberg, Kaj, and Sahban Mroueh, eds. *Ibn Sāyyār al-Warrāq,* كتاب الطبيخ*, Kitāb al-ṭabīḫ*. Helsinki: Finnish Oriental Society, 1987.

Abū Marwān ʿAbd al-Malik Zuhr. *Kitāb al-agḏiya*. Edited, translated, and introduced by Expiración García Sánchez. Madrid: CSIC, 1992.

Abū Zacaria Iahia (Al-ʿAwwān). *Libro de agricultura su autor el Doctor excelente Abū Zacaria Iahia* (Spanish-Arabic ed.). Vols. 1 and 2 [1802]. Edited and translated by Josef Antonio Banqueri. Madrid: Clásicos agrarios, 1988.

Abadi, Jennifer. *Too Good to Passover: Sephardic & Judeo-Arabic Seder Menus and Memories from Africa, Asia and Europe*. New York: CreateSpace Independent Publishing Platform, 2018.

Abbott, Lyman, and Thomas Jefferson Conant. *A Dictionary of Religious Knowledge, for Popular and Professional Use: Comprising Full Information on Biblical, Theological, and Ecclesiastical Subjects. With Several Hundred Maps and Illustrations*. New York: Harper & brothers, 1885.

Abulafia, David. "What Happened in Al-Andalus: Minorities in al-Andalus and in Christian Spain." In *Islamic Cultures, Islamic Contexts,* edited by Asad Q. Ahmed et al., 533–550. Leiden: Brill, 2015.

Aillet, Cyrille. "Identité chrétienne, arabisation et conversion à Cordoue au IXe siècle." In *Les Chrétiens dans la ville,* edited by Françoise Thélamon and Cyrille Aillet, 65–77. Mont-Saint Aignan: PU de Rennes et du Havre, 2006.

Al-Arbulī. *Un tratado nazarí sobre alimentos: Al kalam ʿala l-agdiya*. Edited and translated by Amador Díaz García. Mojácar-Almería: Arráez, 2000.

Al-Baghdādī. *A Baghdad Cookery Book: The book of dishes*. Translated by Charles Perry. Totnes: Prospect Books, 2005.

Albertini, Louis. *Apogée des jardins et maraîchages en al-Andalus (Ibérie arabe) Xe-XIVe siècle: nouveaux légumes, fruits et épices. Essor de la cuisine arabo-andalouse*. Paris: L'Harmattan, 2017.

Alexandre-Bidon, Danièle. *Une archéologie du goût. Céramique et consommation (Moyen Âge -Temps modernes)*. Paris: Picard, 2005.

Alhadeff, Ty. "Manna from Heaven: Bumuelos, a Sephardic Hanukkah Treat." Stroum Center for Jewish Studies. Accessed November 20, 2020. https://jewishstudies.washington.edu/sephardic-studies/manna-from-heaven-bumuelos/.

Allaigre, Claude. "La Lozana Andaluza." *Bulletin hispanique* 12, no. 1 (2010): 41–60.

Allard, Jeanne. "Nola: Rupture ou continuité?" In *Du manuscrit à la table. Essais sur la cuisine au Moyen Âge et répertoire des manuscrits médiévaux contenant des recettes culinaires,* edited by Carole Lambert, 149–161. Montréal: Presses Universitaires de Montréal, 1992.

Amari, Michele. *Storia dei Musulmani di Sicilia*. Vol. 2. Firenze: Felice Le Monnier, 2014.

Amarós, Carlos, ed. "Libre de doctrina per a ben servir, de tallar, y del Art de Coch: ço es de qualsevol manera de potages y salses. Compost per lo diligent mestre Robert coch del Serenissimo senyor don Fernando Rey de Napols. Edició digital basada en l'edició de Barcelona." Biblioteca Virtua: Miguel de Cevantes. Accessed September 17, 2017. http://www.cervantesvirtual.com/obra/libre-de-doctrina-per-a-ben-servir-de-tallar-y-del-art-de-coch-transcripcio--0/; http://www.cervantesvirtual.com/obra-visor/libre-de-doctrina-per-a-ben-servir-de-tallar-y-del-art-de-coch-transcripcio--0/html/.

Amran, Rica. "El *Fuero real* de Alonso Díaz de Montalvo y la problemática conversa a finales del siglo XV: ¿puntos de vista e influencias de una minoría?" In *Minorías en la España medieval y moderna (ss. XV–XVII)* [Minorities in medieval and early modern Spain (c. 15th–17th)]. Edited by Rica Amran and Antonio Cortijo Ocaña, 23–37. Santa Barbara: University of California, 2015.

Amran, Rica. "Judíos y conversos en las crónicas de los Reyes de Castilla (desde finales del siglo xiv hasta la expulsión)." *Espacio, Tiempo y Forma, Historia medieval* 9 (1996): 257–275.

"An Anonymous Andalusian Cookbook of the thirteenth century." Edited by David Friedman and translated by Charles Perry. Accessed October 20, 2016. http://www.daviddfriedman.com/Medieval/Cookbooks/Andalusian/andalusian_contents.htm.

Apicius. *L'art culinaire. De re coquinaria.* Edited and translated by Jacques André. Paris: C. Klincksieck, 1965. For English translation see https://www.gutenberg.org/files/29728/29728-h/29728-h.htm

Arberry, A. J., ed. "A Baghdad Cookery Book." *Islamic Culture* 13, no. 1 (1939): 21–47.

Archdekin, Richard. *Theologia tripartita universa: complectens perfectam bibliothecam viri ecclesiastici.* Vols. 1–3. Amstaelodami: Sumptibus societatis, 1737.

Archivo de la Corona de Aragón. *Canc, Reg. 46, f. 86v.* Valence, 27/04/1282.

Arié, Rachel. *L'Espagne musulmane au temps des Nasrides (1232–1492).* Paris: E. de Boccard, 1973.

———. *Éudes sur la civilisation musulmane.* Leiden: Brill, 1990.

———. "Les minorités religieuses dans le royaume de Grenade (1232–1492)." *Revue du monde musulman et de la Méditerranée: Minorités religieuses dans l'Espagne médiévale* 63–64 (1992): 51–61.

Artusi, Peregrino. *La Scienza in Cucina e l'Arte di Mangiar Bene.* Florence: Giunti Gruppo Editoriale, 2017.

Arveiller, Raymond. "Les noms français de l'aubergine." *Revue de linguistique romane* 33, nos. 131–132 (1969): 225–244.

Asheri, Michael. *Living Jewish: The Lore and Law of Being a Practicing Jew.* Pune: Everest House, 1980.

Ashtor, Eliyahu. *The Jews of Moslem Spain.* Vols. 1–3. Philadelphia: Jewish Publication Society of America, 1973.

Aubrun , Charles-V. "Le 'Cancionero General' de 1511 et ses trente-huit romances." *Bulletin Hispanique* 86, nos. 1–2 (1984): 39–60.

Auerbach, David. *Jewish Cultural Nationalism: Origins and Influences.* London: Routledge, 2008.

Azevedo Santos, José Maria. "O mais antigo livro de cozinha português—receitas e sabores." *Revista Portuguesa de História* 27 (1993): 63–101.

Azevedo Santos, María José. *A Alimentação em Portugal na idade média.* Vol. 61. Coimbra: Fontes-Cultura-sociedade, 1997.

Badi, Meri. *250 recettes de cuisine juive espagnole.* Paris: Editions Jacques Grancher, 1984.

Baer, Yitzhak. *Historia de los judíos en la España cristiana.* Zaragoza: Riopiedras, 1998.

———. *A History of Jews in Christian Spain.* Vol. 2. Philadelphia: Jewish Publication Society of America, 1961.

Banegas López, Ramón A. "Una anàlisi dels productes i les tècniques de cuina al Llibre de Sent Soví." In *Llibre de Sent Soví*, edited by Joan Santanach et al., 129–166. Barcelona: Barcino, 2017.

———. "Évolution de la consommation de viande de mouton en Catalogne au long du Moyen Âge. La reconstruction d'un modèle alimentaire." In *Pour une histoire de la viande. Fabrique et représentations de l'Antiquité à nos jours*, edited by Bruno Laurioux and Marie-Pierre Horard, 151–163. Rennes-Tours: Presses Universitaires de Rennes et Presses Universitaires François Rabelais, 2017.

Barkaï, Ron, ed. *Chrétiens, musulmans et Juifs dans l'Espagne médiévale: De la convergence à l'expulsion*. Paris: Cerf, 1994.

Barnett, R. D., ed. *The Sephardi Heritage: Essays on the History and Cultural Contribution of Jews of Spain and Portugal*. Vol. 1, *The Jews in Spain and Portugal before and after the Expulsion of 1492*. New York: Ktav Publishing House, 1971.

Barthes, Roland. "Pour une psycho-sociologie de l'alimentation contemporaine." *Annales Économie Sociétés Civilisations* 16, no. 5 (1961): 977–986.

Barton, Simon. *A History of Spain*. London: Red Globe Press, 2009. (second edition).

Battaglia, Salvatore. *Grande dizionario della lingua italiana*. Torino: Unione tipografico-editrice torinense, 1975.

Bazzana, André, and Johnny De Meulemeester. "La révolution verte." In *La noria, l'aubergine et le fellah. Archéologie des espaces irrigués dans l'Occident musulman médiéval (IXe–XVe siècles)*. Archeological Reports Ghent University—ARGU 6. Cambridge: Academia Press, 2009.

Beinart, Haim. *Records of the Trials of the Spanish Inquisition in Ciudad Real*. Vol. 4, *Documents, Biographical Notes, Indexes*. Jerusalem: The Israel Academy of Sciences and Humanities, 1985.

———. *Records of the Trials of the Spanish Inquisition in Ciudad Real*. Vol. 1, *The Trials of 1483–1485*. Jerusalem: Israel Academy of Sciences and Humanities, 1974.

———. *Records of the Trials of the Spanish Inquisition in Ciudad Real*. Vol. 2, *The Trials of 1494–1512 in Toledo*. Jerusalem: Israel National Academy of Sciences and Humanities, 1977.

———. *Records of the Trials of the Spanish Inquisition in Ciudad Real*. Vol. 3, *The Trials of 1512–1527 in Toledo*. Jerusalem: Israel Academy of Sciences and Humanities, 1981.

Belon, Pierre. *Voyage en Égypte*. Paris: Klincksieck, 1928.

Benarroch, Mois. *Andalusian in Jerusalem*. Independently published: Lulu, 2017.

Benavides Barajas, Luis. *Al-Andalús, la cocina y su historia*. Motril: Dulcinea, 1992.

Benbassa, Esther. *Cuisine judéo-espagnole*. Paris: Edition du Scribe, 1984.

———. "La diaspora juive 1492." *Histoire, économie et société*, no. 3 (1993): 335–343.

Bennison, Amira K. *Almoravid and Almohad Empires*. Edinburgh: Edinburgh University Press, 2016.

Bensadon, Ana. *Recetas endiamentadas*. Alcobendas: Nagrela Editores, 2013.

Bensoussan, Albert. "Les Marranes." *Atalaya* [En Ligne] 14 (2014). https://journals.openedition.org/atalaya/1330

Berg, Nancy E. "Jews among Muslims: Culinary Contexts." In *Global Jewish Foodways: A History*, edited by Hasia R. Diner, Simone Cinotto Cinotto, and Carlo Petrini (intro.), 70–87. Nebraska: University of Nebraska Press, 2019.

Bessière, Jacinthe. "Quand le patrimoine alimentaire innove." *Mondes du Tourisme* 7 (2013): 37–51.

Besson, Florian et al. *Chrétiens, Juifs et musulmans. Pouvoirs et minorités dans l'espace méditerranéen—XIe–XVe siècles*. Paris: Atlande, 2018.

Biblia Online. s.v. "Reina Valeria 1960." Accessed January 12, 2019. https://www.biblia.es/la-biblia-hoy.php.

Biblioteca Digital Hispánica. "Recetas experimentadas para diversas cosas." Mss 2019. Accessed January 12, 2019 http://bdh-rd.bne.es/viewer.vm?id=0000011243&page=1.

Bodian, Miriam. *Dying in the Law of Moses: Crypto-Jewish Martyrdom in the Iberian World*. Bloomington and Indianapolis: Indiana University Press, 2007.

Bolens, Lucie. *La cuisine andalouse un art de vivre, XIe–XIIIe*. Paris: Albin Michel, 1990.

Bonfil, Robert. "El legado historiográfico de los judíos españoles." In *Moreset Sefarad: El legado de Sefarad*, vol. 2, edited by Haim Beinart, 476–493. Jerusalem: Editorial Magnes-Universidad Hebrea, 1993.

Boswell, John. *The Royal Treasure: Muslim communities under the crown of Aragon in the fourteenth century*. New Haven and London: Yale University Press, 1977.

Bourouiba, Rachid. "La doctrine Almohade." *Revue de l'Occident musulman et de la Méditerranée* 1, nos. 13–14 (1973): 141–158.

Brann, Ross. "The Arabized Jews." In *The Literature of Al-Andalus*, edited by M. Menocal, R. Scheindlin and M. Sells, 435–454. Cambridge: Cambridge University Press, 2000.

Bravo Lledó, Pilar. (2012). "Las costumbres judeoconversas en Alcalá de Henares." Exhibit at Museo Casa Natal de Cervantes, Alcalá de Henares: http://www.museocasanataldecervantes.org/escenas-cervantinas-las-costumbres-judeoconversas-en-alcala-de-henares/.

Brenner, Michael. *A Short History of the Jews*. New Jersey: Princeton University Press, 2012.

Bresc, Henri. *Arabes de langue, Juifs de religion: L'évolution du judaïsme sicilien dans l'environnement latin, XIIe–XVe siècles*. Paris: Bouchène, 2001.

———. "Cultures et nourritures de l'Occident musulman." *Médiévales: Cultures et nourritures de l'Occident musulman. Essais dédiés à Bernard Rosenberger*, no. 33 (1997): 5–8.

———. "La Sicile médiévale, terre de refuge pour les juifs: migration et exil." *Al-Masāq: Journal of the medieval Mediterranean* 17, no. 1 (2005): 31–47.

Fiero, Maribel. "Al-Turtushi." In *Christian-Muslim Relations 600–1500*. Brill Online. Edited by David Thomas and Alex Mallet. Accessed March 22, 2022. https://referenceworks.brillonline.com/entries/christian-muslim-relations-i/al-turtushi-COM_23895.

Brillat-Savarin, Jean Anthelme. *Physiologie du goût ou Méditations de gastronomie transcendante*. Vol.1. Paris: Sautelet, 1826.

———. *The Physiology of Taste or, Meditations on transcendental gastronomy*. Edited and translated by M. F. K Fisher (New York: Vintage Books, 2011).

Brisville, Marianne. "Meat in the Urban Markets of the medieval Maghrib and al-Andalus: Production, Exchange and consumption." *Food and History* 16, no. 1 (2018): 3–20.

———. "Plats sûrs et plats sains dans l'Occident musulman médiéval. La harīsa comme contre-exemple?" In *De la nature à la table au Moyen Âge: L'acquisition des aliments. Actes du 138e Congrès du CTHS: Se nourrir. Pratiques et stratégies alimentaires, Rennes, 22–26 avril 2013*, edited by Bruno Laurioux, 112–113. Paris: CTHS, 2017.

———. "Préparer et consommer la viande dans l'Occident musulman au Moyen Âge (XIIe–XVe siècles)." Presented at Religion et interdits alimentaires. Archéozoologie et sources littéraires, Actes du Colloque de Paris, Paris, Avril 3–5, 2014.

Brumberg-Kraus, Jonathan D. *Gastronomic Judaism as Culinary Midrash*. Lanham: Lexington Books, 2018.

Bruno, Louis et Élie Malka. *Glossaire judéo-arabe de Fès*. Vol. 37. Rabat: Publications de l'Institut des Hautes Études Marocaines, 1940.

Brunschvig, Robert. *La Berbérie orientale sous les Hafsides des origines à la fin du XVe siècle*. Vol. 2. Paris: Maisonneuve, 1982.

Buresi, Pascal. "L'Empire Almohade. Le Maghreb et Al-Andalus (1130–1269)." In *Les Empires. Antiquités et Moyen Âge. Analyse comparée*, edited by Frédéric Hurlet, 221–237. Rennes: PU de Rennes, 2008.

Caldarella, Sergio. "The Jews of Sicily: A Unique Culture." *Philadelphia Jewish Voice*. Accessed March 22, 2022. http://www.pjvoice.com/v33/33004sicily.aspx.

Campbell, Jodi. *At the First Table: Food and Social Identity in Early Modern Spain*. Lincoln: Nebraska Press University, 2017.

Cancionero general: que contiene muchas obras de diuersos autores antiguos con algunas cosas nueuas de modernos, de nueuo corregido e impresso Martin Nucio. Anvers: n.p., 1557. See https://books.google.fr/books?id=frsCXnbQZJAC&printsec=frontcover&hl=fr&source=gbs_ge_summary_r&cad=0#v=onepage&q&f=false.

Cantera Montenegro, Enrique. "La carne y el pescado en el sistema alimentario judío de la España medieval." *Espacio, tiempo y forma. Serie 3: Historia medieval*, no. 16 (2003): 13–51.

———. "El pan y el vino en el judaísmo antiguo y medieval." *Espacio, tiempo y forma. Serie 3: Historia medieval*, no. 19 (2007): 13–48.

Capatti, Alberto et Massimo Montanari. *La cucina italiana. Storia di una cultura*. Roma-Bari: Laterza, 1999.

Capel, José Carlos. "¿La ensaimada mallorquina, un dulce de origen judío?" *El Pais*, February 8, 2019. https://elpais.com/elpais/2019/02/06/gastronotas_de_capel/1549480805_687074.html#?prm=copy_link.

Cardillac, Louis, ed. *Tolède XIIe-XIIIe siècle. Musulmans, chrétiens et juifs: le savoir et la tolérance*. Paris: Autrement, "Mémoires," 2001. [1st ed. 1991].

Carlin Officier, Maura. "Eggplant." In *The Oxford Encyclopedia of Food and Drink in America*, vol. 1, edited by Andrew Smith and Bruce Kraig. Oxford: OUP USA, 2013.

Carr, Raymond. *Spain: A History*. Oxford: Oxford University Press, 2000.

Carrete Parrondo, Carlos. *Fontes ludaeorum Regni Castellae*. Vol. 3, *Proceso Inquisitorial contra los Arias Dávila segovianos: un enfrentamiento social entre judíos y conversos*. Salamanca: Universidad Pontificia de Salamanca, Universidad de Granada, 1986.

Carrete Parrondo, Carlos, and Carolina Fraile Conde. *Fontes Iudaeorum Regni Castellae*. Vol. 4, *Los judeoconversos de Almazán 1501–1505. Origen familiar de los Laínez*. Salamanca: Universidad Pontífica de Salamanca, Universidad de Granada, 1987.

Carrete Parrondo, Carlos, and María José Castaño González. *Fontes ludaeorum Regni Castellae*. Vol. 2, *El tribunal de la Inquisición en el obispado de Soria (1486–1502)*. Salamanca: Universidad Pontificada de Salamanca, Universidad de Granada, 1985.

Castro, Américo. *España en su historia; cristianos, moros y judíos*. Buenos Aires: Editorial Losada, 1948.

———. *La Realidad histórica de España*. México: Editorial Porrúa, 1954.

Caussin de Perceval, Armand Pierre. *Essai sur l'histoire des Arabes avant l'islamisme: pendant l'époque de Mahomet, et jusqu'à la réduction de toutes les tribus sous la loi musulmane*. Paris: Firmin Didot, 1847.

Cejador y Frauca, Julio. *El libro de buen amor*. Madrid: Espasa Calpe, 1967.

Cervantes, Miguel. *Don Quijote de la Mancha*. Edited by Francisco Rico. Barcelona: Institut Cervantes, 1998.

Chauvet, Michel. *Encyclopédie des plantes alimentaires*. Paris: Belin, 2018.

Cocina andaluza. Madrid: Susaeta Editorial, n.d.

Cocina Marroquí. *Almodrote de berenjenas*. Accessed March 2019. https://decaminoamicocina.blogspot.com/2013/11/almodrote-de-bernejena.html.

Cohen, G. D., trans. *A Critical Edition with a Translation and Notes of the Book of the Tradition by Abraham ibn Daud*. London: Routledge and Kegan Paul, 1969.

Cohen, Stella. *Stella's Sephardic Table: Jewish Family Recipes from the Mediterranean Island of Rhodes*. Cape Town: Hoberman Collection, 2012.

Cole, Peter. *The Dream of the Poem: Hebrew Poetry from Muslim and Christian Spain 950–1492*. Edited, translated, and introduced by Peter Cole. New Jersey: Princeton University Press, 2007.

Cooper, John. *Eat and Be Satisfied*. Northvale: Jason Aronson INC, 1993.

Coran. Saudi Arabia: Al-Madinah Al-Munawwarah, 2001.

Corriente, Federico. *Diccionario de arabismos y voces afines en Iberorromance*. Madrid: Gredos, 1999.

Corriente, Federico et al. *Dictionnaire du faisceau dialectal arabe andalou. Perspectives phraséologiques et étymologiques*. Berlin: De Gruyter, 2017.

Cortelazzo, Manlio. *DELI-dizionario etimologico della lingua italiana*. 2nd ed. Bologna: Zanichelli, 1999.

Cortelazzo, Manlio. *Guida ai dialetti veneti*. Vol. 13. Padova: Cooperativa Libraria Editrice Università di Padova, 1991.

Costa, Marithelma. "La contienda poética entre Juan de Valladolid, el Comendador Román y Antón de Montoro." *Cahiers de linguistique hispanique médiévale* 23 (2000): 27–50.

Crescas du Caylar. "Roman de la Reine Esther." In *Nouvelles courtoises occitanes et françaises*, edited by Suzanne Méjean-Thiolier and Marie-Francoise Notz, 124–157. 3 vols. Paris: LgF, 1997; 2005; 2010.

Crespo García, Herminia. *Trabajo de fin de grado: La Judería de Segovia como recurso didáctico. Una propuesta educativa multidisciplinar*. Unpublished PhD diss., 2014.

Cubero S., José Ignacio. *El Libro de agricultura de Al Awan*. Edited and translated by Banqueri. Sevilla: Junta de Andalucía, 2003.

"Cuisine." *JudaicAlgeria*. Last modified August 28, 2021. https://www.judaicalgeria.com/pages/arts-culture-traditions/cuisine.html.

Daunay, Marie-Christine. "Eggplant." In *Vegetables II: Fabaceae, Liliaceae, Solanaceae, and Umbelliferae*, edited by Jaime Prohens-Tomás and Fernando Nuez. New York: Springer Science & Business Media, 2007.

Davis-Secord, Sarah, Belen Vicens, and Robin Vose, eds. *Interfaith Relationships and Perceptions of the Other in the Medieval Mediterranean: Essays in Memory of Olivia Remie Constable*. Cham: Springer Nature Switzerland, 2022.

De Alcalá, Pedro. *Vocabulista arauigo en letra castellana*. 1505. Granada: Juan Varela de Salamanca. https://archive.org/details/ARes193062/page/n299/mode/2up.

De Baena, Juan Alfonso. *El Cancionero. (Siglo XV): Ahora por primera vez dado a luz, con notas y comentarios*. Madrid: La Publicidad, 1851.

De Beauvais, Pierre. "Bestiaire." In *Bestiaire du Moyen Âge*, edited by Gabriel Bianciotto. Paris: Stock, 1995.

De Covarrubias, Sebastián, and Martín De Riquer, eds. *Tesoro de la lengua castellana o española*. Barcelona: Horta, 1943.

De Eguilaz y Yanguas, Leopoldo. *Glosario etimológico de las palabras españolas de origen oriental*. Granada: Edition La Lealtad, 1886.

De Gayangos, Pascual. *Introducción a Libros de Caballería*. Madrid: Rivadeneyra, 1857.

De la Granja, Fernando. "Nota sobre la 'maflêta' de los judíos de Fes." *Al-Andalus* 25 (1960): 235–238.

De la Granja, Fernando. *La cocina arabigo-andaluza según un manuscrito inédito. Thèse de doctorat (non publiée) menée sous la direction de Terés Sádaba*. Madrid: Universidad Complutense de Madrid, 1960.

De Nebrija, Antonio. *Gramática sobre la lengua española. Vocabulario español-latino*. Madrid: Real Academia Española, 1494.

De Nola, Roberto, and Nathalie Peyrebonne, eds and French trans. *Le livre de cuisine*. Paris: Classiques Garnier (Textes de la Renaissance), 2011.

De Portugal, Maria, and Maria José Palla, eds. and trans. *Livre de cuisine de l'Infante Maria du Portugal*. Lisbon: Instituto de Estudos Medevais, 2008.

De Prodenzani, Simone. *Sallazzo e Saporetto*. Perugia: EFFE Fabrizio Fabri, 1998.

De San Juan, Huarte, and Fernando Serrano Larráyoz . "La edición del 'Regalo de la vida humana de Juan Vallés (c. 1496–1563): un proyecto en curso." *Geografía e Historia* 13 (2006): 341–354.

Del Castillo, Hernando. *Cancionero general*. poem 997. Madrid: Sociedad de Bibliófilos Españoles, 1882.

Delgado José, Martínez. "Ibn Janāḥ, Jonah (Abū' l-Walīd Marwān)." In *Encyclopedia of Jews in the Islamic World*, edited by Norman A. Stillman. Leiden: Brill, 2010.

Delgado José, Martínez, and Amir Ashur. *La vida cotidiana de los judíos de alandalus*. Vols. 10–13. Córdoba: UCO Press, 2021.

Delicado, Francisco. *La Lozana andaluza*. Alicante: Biblioteca Virtual Miguel de Cervantes, 2003.

Delicado, Francisco. *La Lozana andaluza*. Edited by Carla Perugini. Sevilla: Fundación José Manuel Lara/Clásicos andaluces, 2004.

———. *La Lozana andaluza*. Edited by Carla Perugini. Alicante: Biblioteca Virtual Miguel de Cervantes, 2011.

———. *La Lozana andaluza*. Edited by Folke Gernert and Jacques Joset. Madrid: Real Academia Española, 2013.

———. *Retrato de la Loçana andaluza*. Edited by Rocío Díaz Bravo. Estudio y edición crítica. Cambridge: MHRA, 2019.

Denjean, Claude. "Pourquoi parler de civilisation juive médiévale?" *Cahiers de civilisation médiévale* 62, no. 1 (2019): 17–47.

Díaz-Mas, Paloma, ed. "Entre el pasado y el futuro: La Cultura sefardí." *Insula* 647 (2000): 3–28.

Díaz-Mas, Paloma. *Los Sefardíes. Historia, lengua y cultura*. Barcelona: Riopiedras, 1997.

Diccionario de Autoridades. 1726–1739.

Diccionario Etimológico Castellano en Línea. http://etimologias.dechile.net.

Diner, Hasia R., and Simone Cinotto Cinotto, eds., with an introduction by Carlo Petrini. *Global Jewish Foodways: A History*. Lincoln: University of Nebraska Press, 2019.

Doron, Aviva. "Le dialogue littéraire andalou: modèle de dialogue interculturel." In *Les routes d'al-Andalus: patrimoine commun et identité plurielle*, UNESCO, 2011. Accessed September 25, 2016. https://unesdoc.unesco.org/ark:/48223/pf0000123370.

D'Ottone, Arianna. "The Tale of Bayād and Riyād." In *Arabic Manuscripts of the Thousand and One Nights*, edited by A. Chraïbi. Paris: Espaces & Signes, 2016.

Dozon, Martine. "Contributions à l'étude de la civilisation urbaine en Italie (XIIIe–XVIe). Hommage à Ida Maier." Nanterre: Centre de recherches de langue et littérature italiennes, 1974.

Dozy, Reinhart. *Recherches sur l'Histoire*. Vol. 1. Paris: Maisonneuve, 1881.

Dufourcq, Charles-Emmanuel. "La coexistence des chrétiens et des musulmans dans Al-Andalus et dans le Maghrib du Xe siècle." In *Actes du 9e congrès des congrès de la Société des historiens médiévistes de l'enseignement supérieur public, Dijon, 1978*. Paris: Société Les Belles Lettres, 1979.

Dutton, Brian. "Brian Dutton Corpus." Accessed March 21, 2017. http://cancionerovirtual.liv.ac.uk.

———. "El cancionero del siglo XV." Accessed March 21, 2017. http://cancionerovirtual.liv.ac.uk.

"Eating Yourself: We Consume Identity Through Food?" *Culture Decanted*, accessed October 9, 2016. https://culturedecanted.com/2014/10/19/eating-yourself-we-consume-identity-through-food.

Einbinder, Susan L. *No Place of Rest: Jewish Literature, Expulsion, and the Memory of Medieval France*. Philadelphia: University of Pennsylvania Press, 2009.

El aderezo. "hojuelas de la abuela germana." Accessed February 21, 2016. https://www.eladerezo.com/recetas/hojuelas-de-la-abuela-germana.html.

Em Bible. Accessed February 21, 2016. https://emcitv.com/bible/strong-biblique-hebreu-ham-1990.html.

Epafras, Leonard C. "Judeo-Arabic: Cultural Symbiosis of Jews in the Islamicate Contex November." *Journal of Islam and Humanities* 1, no. 1 (2016): 1–14.

Epstein, Isidore. *The "Responsa" of Rabbi Solomon ben Adreth of Barcelona (1235–1310) as a Source of the History of Spain: Studies in the Communal Life of Jews in Spain as Reflected in the "Responsa."* New York: Ktav Publishing, 1968.

Escartín González, Eduardo. *Estudio económico sobre el Tratado de Ibn Abdún. El vino y los gremios en Al-Andalus antes del siglo XII*. Séville: Fundación del Monte, 2006.

Espadas Burgos, Manuel. "Aspectos socioreligiosos de la alimentación española." *Hispania* 131 (1975): 537–566.

Fellous, Sonia. *Histoire de la Bible de Moïse Arragel. Quand un rabbin interprète la Bible pour les chrétiens*. Paris: Somogy Éditions d'Art, 2001.

Fenton, Paul. "Jonah Ibn Ǧanāḥ's Medical Dictionary, the Kitāb al-Talḫīṣ: Lost and Found." *Aleph* 16, no. 1 (2016): 107–143.

Ferhat, Halima. "Le patrimoine gastronomique andalous." In *El banquete de las palabras: la alimentación de los textos árabes*, edited by Manuela Marín and Cristina De la Puente, 11–28. Madrid: CSIC, 2005.

Fernández Suárez, Luis. *Judíos españoles en la Edad Media*. Madrid: Rialp, 1980.

Ferre, Lola, ed. and trans. *El régimen de salud (Fi Tadbir al-Sihhah). Obras médicas I*. Barcelona: Herder Editorial, 2016

Fierro, Maribel. "Conversion, Ancestry and Universal Religion: The Case of the Almohads in the Islamic West (Sixth/Twelfth–Seventh/Thirteenth Centuries)." *Journal of Medieval Iberian Studies* 2, no. 2 (2010): 155–173.

———. *Judíos y musulmanes en al-Andalus y el Magreb. Contactos intelectuales*. Madrid: Casa de Velázquez, 2002.

———. "Le mahdī Ibn Tûmart et al-Andalus: l'élaboration de la légitimité almohade." *Revue des mondes musulmans et de la Méditerranée* 91–94 (2000): 107–124.

The Filāḥa Texts Project. Accessed November 1, 2016. http://www.filaha.org/introduction.html.

Fita y Colomé, Fidel . "La Inquisición en Guadalupe." *Boletín de la Real Academia de la Historia* 23 (1893): 283–343.

Flandrin, Jean-Louis. "Internationalisme, nationalisme et régionalisme dans la cuisine des XIVe et XVe siècle: le témoignage des livres de cuisine." *Manger et boire au Moyen Âge.* Actes du colloque de Nice 15–17 octobre 1982. Vol. 2, *Cuisines, manières de table, régimes alimentaires* (Paris: Les Belles Lettres, 1984).

Fraile Conde, Carolina. "Las costumbres judaizantes de la comunidad conversa de Almazán a finales del siglo XV y principios del XVI." *Helmántica* 49, no. 150 (1998): 435–455.

Frans Ijzereef, Gérard. "Social Differentiation from Animal Bone Studies." *British Archaeological Reports.* British Series. Amersfoort: ROB, 1989.

Freedman, Paul. *Why Food Matters.* Yale: Yale University Press, 2021.

Freidenreich, David M. *Foreigners and Their Food: Constructing Otherness in Jewish, Christian and Islamic Law.* Berkeley: University of California Press, 2011.

———. "Sharing Meals with Non-Christians in Canon Law Commentaries, Circa 1160–1260: A Case Study in Legal Development." *Medieval Encounters* 14 (2008): 41–77.

Perry, Charles, trans. *An Anonymous Andalusian Cookbook of the Thirteenth Century.* Accessed October 20, 2016. http://www.daviddfriedman.com/Medieval/Cookbooks/Andalusian/andalusian_contents.htm.

Gallego, María Ángeles. *El judeo-árabe medieval: edición, traducción y estudio lingüístico del Kitāb al-taswiʾa de Yonah ibn Ǧanāḥ.* New York-Bern: Peter Lang AG, 2006.

Gallego, Olga. "Receta de Hojeulas." *Recetas gratis,* March 23, 2022. https://www.recetasgratis.net/receta-de-hojuelas-12531.html.

García-Arenal, Mercedes and Gerard Wiegers. *Polemical Encounters: Christians, Jews, and Muslims in Iberia and Beyond.* Iberian Encounter and Exchange, 475–1755. University Park: Penn State University Press, 2018.

García de Diego, Vicente. *Contribución al diccionario Hispánico Etimológico.* Madrid: Revista de archivos, 1923. Al-Šaqundī, Abū-l-Walīd Ismāʿīl Ibn Muḥammad,. *Elogio del islam español (Risāla fī faḍl al-Andalus).* Spanish translation by García Gómez. Madrid: Maestre, 1934.

García Sánchez, Expiración. "La alimentación de los andalusíes: entre las normas médicas y la vida cotidiana." In *El saber en al-Andalus. Textos y Estudios V. Homenaje a la profesora Doña Carmen Ruiz Bravo-Villasante,* edited by Julia María Carabaza Bravo and Laila Carmen Makki Hornedo, 121–134. Seville: Universidad de Sevilla, 2011.

———. "La alimentación en la Andalucía islámica." In *Andalucía Islámica. Textos y Estudios II-III (1981–1982),* edited by J. Bosh Vilá and W. Hoenerbach, 139–178. Granada: Universidad de Granada (Granada: Anejos de Cuadernos de Historia del Islam, 1983).

———. La alimentación en la Andalucía Islámica. Estudio histórico y bromatológico. In *Andalucía Islámica. Textos y Estudios IV-V (1983–1986),* edited by J. Bosh Vilá and W. Hoenerbach, 237–239. Granada: Universidad de Granada (Granada: Anejos de Cuadernos de Historia del Islam, 1987).

———. "Comida de enfermos, dieta de sanos: procesos culinarios y hábitos alimenticios en los textos médicos andalusí." In *El banquete de las palabras: la alimentación en los textos árabes,* edited by Manuela Marín and Cristina De la Puente, 57–87. Madrid: CSIC, 2005.

———. "La consommation des épices et des plantes aromatiques en al-Andalus." *Médiévales: Cultures et nourritures de l'Occident musulman. Essais dédiés à Bernard Rosenberger* no. 33 (1997): 41–54.

———. "El sabor de lo dulce en la gastronomía andalusí." In *La herencia árabe en la agricultura y el bienestar de Occidente*, edited by Fernando Nuez, 165–204. Valence: Universidad Politécnica de Valencia, 2002.

García Sanjuán, Alejandro. "Violencia contra los judíos: el pogromo de Granada del año 459 h/1066." In *De muerte violenta: política, religión y violencia en Al-Andalus*, edited by Maribel Fierro, 167–206. Madrid: CSIC, 2004.

García, Jacinto, and Rosa Tovar. *Un banquete por Sefarad: cocina y costumbres de los judíos españoles*. Gijón: Trea, 2007.

García-Sánchez, Expiración, Julia María Carabaza Bravo, and J. Esteban Hernández Bermejo. *Flora agrícola y forestal de al-Andalus*. Vol. 1, *Monocotiledóneas: cereales, bulbosas y palmeras*. Madrid: Escuelas de Estudios árabes (CSIC Granada), 2012.

Gerber S., Jane. *Cities of Splendour in the Shaping of Sephardi History*. Liverpool: Liverpool University Press, 2020.

———. "Cities of Splendour in the Shaping of Sephardi History": A Conversation with Jane S. Gerber. *JBS*, December 1, 2020. Video, 54:32. https://www.youtube.com/watch?v=2vuuD2xdRwQ.

———. *The Jews of Spain: A History of the Sephardic Experience*. New York: The Free Press, 1992.

Gitlitz, David. *Secrecy and Deceit: The Religion of Crypto-Jews*. Philadelphia: The Jewish Publication Society, 1996.

Gitlitz, David, and Linda Kay Davidson. *A Drizzle of Honey: The Lives and Recipes of Spanish Secret Jews*. New York: Saint Martin's Press, 1999.

Graboïs, Aryeh. "La description de l'Égypte au XIVe siècle par les pèlerins et les voyageurs occidentaux." *Le Moyen Âge* 109, nos. 3–4 (2003): 529–543.

Granado, Diego. *Libro del arte de cozina*. Lleida: Pagès, 1991.

Graysel, Solomon. *The Church and Jews in the XIIIth Century*. Vol. 2, *1254–1314*. Edited and arranged with additional notes by Kenneth R. Stow. New York: The Jewish Theological Seminary Press, 2012.

Grewe, Rudolf. "Hispano-Arabic Cuisine in the Twelfth Century." In *Du manuscrit à la table. Essais sur la cuisine du Moyen Âge essais sur la cuisine au Moyen Âge et répertoire des manuscrits médiévaux contenant des recettes culinairesm*, edited by Carole Lambert, 142–148. Montréal: Presses Universitaires de Montréal, 1992.

Guichard, Pierre. "Alimentation et cuisine en Al-Andalus." *Pratiques et discours alimentaires en Méditerranée de l'Antiquité à la Renaissance. Actes du 18e Colloque de la Villa Kérylos, Beaulieu-sur-Mer, octobre* 2007, edited by Jean Leclant, André Vauchez, and Maurice Sartre, 337–357. Paris: Académie des Inscriptions des Belles Lettres, 2008.

———. "La trajectoire historique des mozarabes d'Espagne." In *Mutations, identités en Méditerranée. Moyen Âge et époque contemporaine*, edited by Henri Bresc, 111–122. Saint-Denis: Bouchène, 2000.

Guida gastronomica d'Italia-Introduzione alla Guida gastronomica d'Italia (rist. anast. 1931). Touring: Ia Edizione, 2006.

Guillaumond, Catherine. *La cuisine dans l'Occident arabe médiéval. Étude de textes. Thèse de doctorat sous la direction d'Ameur Ghedira, Université Jean Moulin Lyon III, soutenue en 1991*. Unpublished PhD dissertation.

———. *Cuisine et diététique dans l'Occident arabe médiéval. D'après un traité anonyme du XIIIe siècle. Étude et traduction française*. Paris: L'Harmattan, 2017.

Haliczer, Stephen. *Inquisition and Society in the Kingdom of Valencia: 1478–1834*. Berkeley: University of California Press, 1990.

Hamesse, Jaqueline, ed. *Roma, magistra mundi. Itineraria culturae medievalis: Mélanges offerts au Père L.E. Boyle à l'occasion de son 75e anniversaire*. Turnhout: Brepols Publishers, 1998.

Harvey, L. P. *Muslims in Spain, 1500 to 1614*. Chicago: University of Chicago Press, 2005.

Horard, Marie-Pierre, and Bruno Laurioux, eds. *Pour une histoire de la viande*. Rennes-Tours: PUR et PUFR, 2017.

Huetz de Lemps, Alain. *Boissons et civilisations en Afrique, Grappes et Millésimes*. Bordeaux: Presses Universitaires de Bordeaux, 2001.

Huici Miranda, Ambrosio. "La cocina hispano-magribī durante la época almohade." *Revista del Instituto de Estudios Islámicos en Madrid* 5 (1957): 137–155.

Huici Miranda, Ambrosio, ed., with an introduction by Manuela Marín. *La cocina hispano-magrebí en la época almohade Según un manuscrito anónimo del siglo XIII*. Gijón: Trea, 2005.

Hussein, Mahmoud, and Philippe Calderon, dirs. *L'âge d'or de l'Islām. L'épopée andalouse*. France Télévisions Distribution, n.p., 2001.

Iancu, Carol. "*Les Juifs du Midi. Une histoire millénaire*." Avignon: Ed. Barthélemy, 1995.

Ibn Ğanāḥ, Yonah. *The Book of Hebrew Roots*. Edited and translated by A. Neubauer. Oxford: Clarendon, 1875.

Ibn Ḫalṣun. "Troisième partie. L'hygiène générale." In *Kitāb al-Aġḏiya (Le livre des aliments)*, edited by Suzanne Gigandet, 67–92. Damas: Presses de l'Ifpo, 1996.

Ibn al-Ahmar, Ismā'īl. "Buyūtāt Fās al-Kubrā (='Dhikr mashāhīr a'yān Fās al-qadīm')." *Al-Bahth al-'ilmī* 1, no. 3 (1964): 56; idem, *Buyūtāt Fās al-Kubrā*. Rabat: Dar al-Mansūr li 'l-Tibā'a wa 'l-Warrāqa, 1972.

Ibn Razīn al-Tuğībī. *Fuḍālat al-Ḫiwān fī ṭayyibāt al-ṭa'ām wa-l-alwān* [Relieves de las mesas acerca de las delicias de la comida y los diferentes plato]. Edited and translated by Manuela Marín. Gijón: Trea, 2007.

Ibn Razīn al-Tuğībī. *Fuḍālat al-Ḫiwān fī ṭayyibāt al-ṭa'ām wa-l-alwān.* [The Most Delectable Foods and Dishes from al-Andalus and al-Maghrib: A Cookbook by the Thirteenth-Century Andalusi Scholar Ibn Razīn al-Tujībī (1227–1293)]. Edited and translated by Nawell Nasrallah. New York: Brill, 2021.

Iván Pini, Antonio. "La viticoltura italiana nel Medioevo. Cultura della vite e consumo del vino a Bologna dal X al XV secolo." *Studi Medioevali* 3, no. 15 (1974): 795–884.

Jawhara Piñer, Hélène. "Almoronía: A Moroccan-Jewish Recipe from the Thirteenth Century Andalusia." *Sephardi Report* 6, no. 1 (2019): 78.

———. "Évolutions et transmission du patrimoine culinaire de l'Espagne à travers les réceptaires anciens: le cas de la cuisine juive." Paris: CTHS, forthcoming.

———. "Making Mufleta, History's Oldest Jewish Pastry, for the Holidays." *Tablet*, September 7, 2018. https://www.tabletmag.com/scroll/270379/making-mufleta-historys-oldest-jewish-pastry-for-the-holidays.

———. *Sephardi: Cooking the History. Recipes of Jews of Spain and the Diaspora from the Thirteenth Century to Today.* Boston: Cherry Orchard Books, 2021.

———. "The Sephardi Origin of the Challah Braided Bread." *Meldar: Revista Internacional De Estudios sefardíes* 1 (2020): 65–74.

Jewish Encyclopedia. "Book of Obadia." Accessed February 21, 2017. https://www.jewishencyclopedia.com/articles/11642-obadiah-book-of.

———. "Sephardim." Accessed February 21, 2017. https://jewishencyclopedia.com/articles/13430-sephardim.

Joaquín Domínguez, Ramón. *Diccionario universal francés-español: Español-francés.* Madrid: la Viuda de Jordan e Hijos, 1846.

Juderías, Alfredos. *Alfredos Juderías, Viaje por la cocina hispano-judía.* Barcelona: Seteco, 1990.

"Julep." Centre National des Ressources Textuelles et Lexicales. Accessed March 10, 2019. http://www.cnrtl.fr/definition/julep.

Jurado, José . *El cancionero de Baena: problemas paleográficos.* Madrid: Editorial CSIC, 1998.

Kakon, Maguy. *L'oriental marocain. Des siècles d'art culinaire Juif.* Casablanca: La croisée des chemins, 2018.

Kaye, Alexander, and David N. Myers. *The Faith of Fallen Jews: Yosef Hayim Yerushalmi and the Writing of Jewish History.* Lebanon, NH: Brandeis University Press, 2013.

Kehayan, Nina. *Voyage de l'aubergine. Préface de Philippe Meyer.* Avignon: L'aube cuisine, 2016.

Kissane, Christopher. *Food, Religion and Communities in Early Modern Europe.* New York: Bloomsbury Academic, 2018.

Klein, Ernest. *A Comprehensive Etymological Dictionary of the English Language.* Vol. 1 [1967] and 2 [1971]. Amsterdam: Elsevier, 1967 and 1971.

Kluyver , A. Marzipan. *Zeitschriftfiir deutsche Wortforschung.* Vol. 6. N.p: n.p., 1904.

"Knowing Jesus." "Hojuelas". https://bible.knowing-jesus.com/Españal/words/Hojuelas.

Koening, Leah. *The Jewish Cookbook.* New York: Phaidon, 2019.

Kraemer C, David. *Jewish Eating and Identity Through the Ages.* London: Routledge, 2008.

Kriegel, Maurice. *Les Juifs dans l'Europe méditerranéenne à la fin du Moyen Âge.* Paris: Hachette Pluriel Référence, 2006.

La Bible, Traduction œcuménique française. Paris: Cerf, 2010.

Lacalle, José María. *Los judíos españoles.* Barcelona: Sayma, 1961.

Laliena Corbera. Carlos, ed. *Documentos municipales de Huesca, 1100–1350.* Huesca: Crónica, 1988.

Las 1000 mejores recetas de cocina. Madrid: Editorial Optima, 2001.

Laurens, Henry, John Tolan, and Gilles Veinstein, eds. *L' Europe et l'Islam: Quinze siècles d'histoire.* Paris: Odile Jacob, 2009.

Laurioux, Bruno. "Le festin d'Assuérus: femmes – et hommes—à table vers la fin du Moyen Âge." *Clio: Histoire, femmes et sociétés. Festin de femmes* 14 (2001): 47–70.

———. "Le goût médiéval est-il arabe? À propos de la "Saracen connection." In *Une histoire culinaire du Moyen Âge,* edited by Bruno Laurioux, 305–335. Paris: H. Champion, 2005.

———. *Une histoire culinaire du Moyen Âge.* Paris: Honoré Champion, 2005.

Laurioux, Bruno. "Des lasagnes romaines aux vermicelles arabes: quelques réflexions sur les pâtes alimentaires." In *Hommes et campagnes médiévales: L'homme et son espace. Études offertes à Robert Fossier,* edited by Elisabeth Mornet, 199–215. Paris: Publications de la Sorbonne, 1995.

Laurioux, Bruno, and Martin Bruegel, eds. *Histoire et identités alimentaires en Europe.* Paris: Hachette littératures, 2002.

Lecker, Michael. *Jews and Arabs in Pre- and Early Islamic Arab.* London: Routledge, 1998.

Leroy, Béatrice. *Les juifs dans l'Espagne chrétienne avant 1492.* Paris: Albin Michel, 1993.

León Tello, Pilar. "Costumbres, fiestas y ritos de los judíos toledanos a fines del siglo XV." In *Symposium "Toledo judaico (Toledo 20–22 abril 1972).* 2 vols." Toledo: Centro universitario de Toledo, 1973.

Levi-Provençal, Évariste. *Histoire de l'Espagne musulmane III, Le siècle du califat de Cordoue*. Paris: Maisonneuve et Larose, 1999.

———. *Séville musulmane au début du XIIe siècle. Le traité d'Ibn 'Abdun sur la vie urbaine et les corps de métiers*. Paris: Maisonneuve et Larose, 2001.

Lévi-Strauss, Claude. *Totemism*. Translated by Rodney Needham. Boston: Beacon, 1963.

Hussein, Mahmoud, and Philippe Calderon, dirs. *L'âge d'or de l'Islām. L'épopée andalouse*. France Télévisions Distribution, n.p., 2001.

Liebman, Seymour B. *The Jews in New Spain: Faith, Flame, and the Inquisition*. Coral Gables: University of Miami Press, 1970.

Llibre de Sent Soví. Edited by Joan Santanach et al. Barcelona: Barcino, 2014.

Llorca, Bernardino. "La Inquisición Española Incipiente. Nuevos Datos Sobre Su Primera Actuación." *Gregorianum* 20, no. 1 (1939): 101–142.

Lopes De Baros, María Filomena, and José Ramón Hinojo, eds. *Minorías étnico religiosas na Península Ibérica*. Évora: Edições Colibri, 2008.

Macías, Uriel. "Ojos de berenjenas, las mil y una recetas." In *La mesa puesta: leyes, costumbres y recetas judías. XVI curso de cultura hispanojudía y sefardí de la Universidad de Castilla-La Mancha: en memoria de Iacob M. Hassán*, edited by Uriel Macías and Ricardo Izquierdo Benito, 241–269. Cuenca: Universidad de Castilla la Mancha (UCLM), 2010.

"Maestro Martino: Libro de arte coquinaria." Based on *Arte della cucina. Libri di ricette, testi sopra lo scalco, i trinciante e i vini. Dal XIV al XIX secolo. A cura di Emilio Faccioli*. Vol. 1. Milano: n.p., 1966. https://www.uni-giessen.de/fbz/fb05/germanistik/absprache/sprachverwendung/gloning/tx/martino2.htm.

Maggi, Bruno. "Il marzapane." *Appunti di gastronomia* 34 (2011): 73–84.

Maíllo Salgado, Felipe. *Los arabismos del castellano en la Baja Edad Media*. Salamanca: Universidad de Salamanca, 1998.

Maimonides, Moses. *Hanhagat ha-Beri'ut (Regimen Sanitas)*. And by Solomon Munter and translated by Moses Ibn Tibbon. Jerusalem: Mosad ha-Rav Kook, 1957.

———. *Qusṭā ibn Lūqā's Medical Regime for the Pilgrims to Mecca: Risālā fī tadbīr safar al-ḥajj*. Edited and translated by Gerrit Bos. New York: Brill, 1992.

———. *El régimen de salud (Fi Tadbir al-Sihhah). Obras médicas I*. Edited and translated by Lola Ferre. Barcelona: Herder Editorial, 2016.

———. *On the Regimen of Health: A New Parallel Arabic-English Translation*. Vol. 12 of The Medical Works of Moses Maimonides, edited and translated by Gerrit Bos, with critical editions of medieval Hebrew translations by Gerrit Bos and Latin translations by Michael R. McVaugh. Leiden and Boston: Brill, 2019.

Mandalà, Giuseppe. "The Jews of Palermo from Late Antiquity to the Expulsion (598– 1492–93)." In *A Companion to medieval Palermo: The History of a Mediterranean City from 600 to 1500*, edited by Annliese Nef, 437–485. Leiden: Brill, 2013.

———. "La migration des juifs du Garbum en Sicile (1239)." In *Maghreb-Italie. Des passeurs médiévaux à l'orientalisme moderne (XIIIe-milieu XXe siècle)*, edited by B. Grévin, 19–48. Rome: Ecole française de Rome, 2010.

Mankowski, P. V. *Akkadian loanwords in biblical Hebrew*. Eisenbrauns: Warsaw, 2000.

Marín, Manuela. "La alimentación en las culturas islámicas." In *La alimentación en las culturas islámicas*, edited by Manuela Marín and David Waines, 89–110. Madrid: Ediciones Mundo Árabe e Islam, 1994.

———. "Cuisine d'Orient, cuisine d'Occident." *Médiévales: Cultures et nourritures de l'Occident musulman. Essais dédiés à Bernard Rosenberger*, no. 33 (1997): 9–22.

———. "From al-Andalus to Spain: Arab Traces in Spanish Cooking." *Food & History* 2, no. 2 (2004): 35–52.

———. "Matériaux pour l'histoire de l'alimentation hispano-maghrébine: ʿAlī B. Ibrāhīm al-Andalusī et son Urǧūsaï al-fawākih." In *Islão e arabismo na Península Ibérica: actas do XI Congresso da União europeia de arabistas e islamólogos, Évora, Faroi, Silves, 29 set.-6 out. 1982*. Évora: Universidade de Évora, 1986.

———. "Sobre būrān y la būrāniyya." *Al-Qanṭara* 2, nos. 1–2 (1981): 193–207.

Marks, Gil. *Encyclopedia of Jewish Food*. Boston: Houghton Mifflin Harcourt, 2010.

———. *Olive Trees and Honey*. Boston: Houghton Mifflin Harcourt, 2004.

Martínez Crespo, Alicia, ed. *Manual de mugeres en el qual se contienen muchas y diversas reçeutas muy buenas*. Salamanque: Ediciones universidad de Salamanca, 1995.

Martínez Delgado, José. *Ibn Janāḥ, Jonah (Abū' l-Walīd Marwān)*. Edited by Norman A. Stillman. Encyclopedia of Jews in the Islamic World. Leiden: Brill, 2020.

Martinez-Gros, Gabriel, and Sophie Makariou. *Histoire de Grenade*. Paris: Fayard, 2018.

Márquez Villanueva, Francisco. "El mundo converso de la 'Lozana Andaluza.'" *Archivo Hispalense* 96, no. 291–293 (2013): 31–39.

Méchoulan, Henry, ed., with an introduction by Edgar Morin. *Los judíos de España. Historia de una diáspora (1492–1992)*. Madrid: Editorial Trotta, 1992.

Meddeb, Abdelwahab, and Benjamin Stora. *A History of Jewish-Muslim Relations: From the Origins to the Present Day*. New Jersey: Princeton University Press, 2013.

Métailié, Georges, and Alice Peeters, "Origine des légumes en Chine." *Journal d'agriculture traditionnelle et de botanique appliquée* 42 (2000): 165–186.

Michel, Francisque. *El Cancionero de Juan Alfonso de Baena*. Leipzig: Brockhaus: n.p., 1860. https://archive.org/details/elcancionero01baenuoft.

Milgrom, Génie. *Recipes of My 15 Grandmothers: Unique Recipes and Stories from the Times of the Crypto-Jews during the Spanish Inquisition*. Jerusalem, New York: Gefen Publishing House, 2019.

Milner Silberstein, Susan. "The Provençal Esther Poem Written in Hebrew Characters c. 1327 by Crescas de Caylar: Critical Edition." PhD diss., University of Pennsylvania, 1973.

Miscelanea desde Llerena. "Gañotes, pestiños y prestiños." Accessed August 11, 2015. https://miscelaneadesdellerena.blogspot.com/2015/08/ganotes-prestinos-y-pestinosreivindicac.html.

Molénat, Jean-Pierre. "Le passage des mozarabes d'Al-Andalus vers l'Espagne chrétienne." In *Passages, Déplacements des hommes, circulation des textes et des identités dans l'Occident médiéval*, edited by Joëlle Ducos and Patrick Henriet, 67–76. Toulouse: Presses universitaires du Midi, 2013.

Montanari, Massimo. *La chère et l'esprit. Histoire de la culture alimentaire chrétienne*. Paris: Alma Éditeur, 2017.

———. *Gusti del Medioevo. I prodotti, la cucina, la tavola*. Rome-Bari: Laterza, 2012.

Montserrat, Piera. *Forging Communities: Food and Representation in Medieval and Early Modern Southwestern Europe*. Fayetteville: University of Arkansas Press, 2018.

Motis Dolader, Miguel Ángel. "L'alimentation juive médiévale." In *Histoire de l'alimentation*, edited by Massimo Montanari and Jean-Louis Flandrin, 367–387. Paris: Fayard, 1996.

———. "Claves e identidades de los judeoconversos de Lleida según los procesos inquisitoriales a finales del siglo xv." *Tamid: Revista Catalana Anual d'Estudis Hebraics* 10 (2014): 81–124.

———. "Regimen alimentario de las comunidades judías y conversas en la Corona de Aragón en la Edad Media." In *Actes Ier Col.loqui d'Història de l'Alimentació a la Corona d'Aragó*, 205–362. Lleida: Institut d'Estudis Ilerdencs, 1995.

———. "Ritos y festividades de los judeoconversos aragoneses en la Edad Media: la celebración del Yon Kippur o Día del Perdón: ensayo de etnología histórica." *Revista Zurita* 61–62 (1990): 59–92.

Mubārak Shāh. *The Sultan's Feast. A Fifteenth-Century Egyptian Cookbook*. Edited, translated, and introduced by Daniel L. Newman. London: Saqi Books, 2020.

Múñoz Solla, Ricardo. "Los conversos judaizantes de Berlanga de Duero (s. XV-XVI)." PhD diss., Universidad de Salamanca, 2003.

Nadeau, Carolyn. "Contributions of medieval Food Manuals to Spain's Culinary Heritage." *Writing about Food: Culinary Literature in the Hispanic World*, no. 33 (2012): 59–77.

———. "From Kitāb al-ṭabīḫ to Llibre de Sent Soví: Continuities and Shifts in the Earliest Iberian Cooking manuals." In *Forging Communities: Food and Representation in Medieval and Early Modern Southwestern Europe*, edited by Piera Montserrat, 21–34. Fayetteville: University of Arkansas Press, 2018.

———. "Constructions of Taste in Francisco Martínez Montiño's Cookbook." March 3, 2018. https://soundcloud.com/culinaryhistory/constructions-of-taste-in-francisco-martinez montinos-cookbook.

Nasrallah, Nawel. *Annals of the Caliph's Kitchen: Ibn Sayyar al-Warraq's Tenth-Century Baghdadi Cookbook*. Leiden: Brill, 2007.

———. ed. and trans. *Best of Delectable Foods and Dishes from al-Andalus and al-Maghrib: A Cookbook by Thirteenth-Century Andalusi Scholar Ibn Razīn al-Tujībī (1227–1293)*. New York: Brill, 2021.

Nathan, Joan. *King Solomon's Table: A Culinary Exploration of Jewish Cooking from Around the World*. New York: Alfred A. Knopf, 2017.

Nebrija (De-), Antonio. *Gramática sobre la lengua española. Vocabulario español-latino*. Madrid: Real Academia Española, 1494.

Nef, Annliese. "Les juifs de Sicile: des juifs de langue arabe du XIIe au XVe siècle." In *Ebrei e Sicilia*, edited by N. Bucaria, A. Tarantino, and M. Luzzati, 169–178. Palerme: Flaccovio editore, 2002.

———. "La Sicile de Charybde en Scylla? Du tout culturel au transculturel." *Mélanges de l'École française de Rome – Moyen* Âge, 128-2 (2016). Accessed April 29, 2020. https://doi.org/10/10.4000/mefrm.3394.

Neubauer, Adolf, ed. *Abu 'l-Walīd Marwān Ibn Janāḥ: The Book of Hebrew Roots, Kitāb al-Uṣūl*. Oxford: Oxford University Press, 1875.

Neubauer, Adolf, and Paul Meyer. "Le Roman provençal d'Esther par Crescas du Caylar, médecin juif du XIVe siècle." *Romania* 21, no. 82 (1892): 194–227.

Neuman, Abraham A. The Jews in Spain: Their Social, Political and Cultural Life during the Middle Ages. Philadelphia: JPS, 1942.

Nevot Navarro, Manuel. "La comunidad judia y conversa de Medinaceli (Soria): 1492–1530." PhD diss., University of Salamanca, 2015.

Niederehe, Hans-Josef. "La lexicographie espagnole jusqu'à Covarrubias." *Histoire Épistémologie Langage* 8 (1986): 9–19.

Nirenberg, David. *Communities of Violence: Persecution of Minorities in the Middle Ages*. New Jersey: Princeton University Press, 1996.

———. *Neighboring Faiths: Christianity, Islam, and Judaism in the Middle Ages and Today*. Chicago: University of Chicago Press, 2014.

———. "Was There Race before Modernity? The Example of 'Jewish' Blood in Late Medieval Spain." In *The Origins of Racism in the West*, edited by Miriam Eliav-Feldon, Benjamin Isaac, and Josep Ziegler, 232–264. Cambridge: Cambridge University Press, 2009.

Notaker, Henry. *A History of Cookbooks: From Kitchen to Page over Seven Centuries*. Berkeley: University of California Press, 2017.

———. *Printed Cookbooks in Europe, 1470–1700: A Bibliography of Early Modern Culinary Literature*. New Castle, DE: Oak Knoll Press, 2010.

Nuevo Diccionario histórico del Español. Madrid: Real Academia Española, n.d.

Old cook. 2002–2020. "O Livro de Cozinha da Infanta D. Maria de Portugal." Accessed June 1, 2022. http://www.oldcook.com/medieval-livres_cuisine_portugais.

Oubahli, Mohamed. *La main et le pétrin. Alimentation céréalière et pratiques culinaires en Occident musulman au Moyen Âge*. Casablanca: Fondation du Roi Abdul-Aziz Al Saoud pour les Études Islamiques et les Sciences Humaines, 2011.

Oukosher. "The Birds of the Bible, or, Solving the Mystery of Which of the Species Are Kosher and Which Are Not." Accessed April, 27, 2017. https://oukosher.org/blog/articles/the-birds-of-the-bible-or-solving-the-mystery-of-which-of-the-species-are-kosher-and-which-are-not/?fbclid=IwAR32frb2RGShOs9jw0-8mzFXLvhR.

Pansier, P. "Le roman d'Esther de Crescas du Cailar." *Annales d'Avignon et du Comtat Venaissin* 11 (1925): 5–18.

Pasqualone, Antonella. "Traditional Flat Breads Spread from the Fertile Crescent: Production Process and History of Baking Systems." *Journal of Ethnic Foods* 5, no. 1 (2018): 10–19.

Pelletier, André. "De la culture sémitique à la culture hellénique. Rencontre, affrontement, pénétration." *Revue des Études Grecques* 97, no. 462–464 (1984): 403–418.

Pérez, Béatrice. "Conversos sevillanos a principios de la época moderna. ¿Élites financieras o familias relacionadas?" In *Los judeoconversos en el mundo ibérico*, edited by Enrique Soria Mesa and Antonio Díaz Rodríguez. Ediciones Universidad de Córdoba, UCO Press, 2019. EPUB.

———. *Inquisition, pouvoir et société. La province de Séville et ses judéoconvers sous les Rois Catholiques*. Paris: Honoré Champion, Collection Études d'histoire médiévale, 2007.

———. "Aux premiers temps de l'Inquisition: une institution dans la genèse d'un État moderne." In *Aux premiers temps de l'inquisition espagnole (1478–1561)*, edited by Carrasco Raphaël, 9–49. Montpellier: P.U de la Méditerranée, 2002.

Pérez, Joseph. *Andalousie. Vérités et légendes*. Paris: Tallandier, 2018.

———. *Histoire de l'Espagne*. Paris: Fayard, 1996.

Pérez Alonso, María Isabel. "La olla judía el Šabbat: estudio lexicológico y lexicográfico de adafina, ḥamín, caliente(s) y otras denominaciones." *Espacio, tiempo y forma, Historia medieval*, 3rd ser., 28 (2015): 441–458.

Pérez Ramírez, Dimas. *Catálogo del Archivo de la Inquisición de Cuenca*. Madrid: Fundación Universitaria Española, 1982.

Pérez Sámper, María Ángeles. *La alimentación en la España del Siglo de Oro. Domingo Hernández de Maceras "Libro del arte de cocina."* Huesca: La Val de Onsera, Colección Ali Farra Estudios, 1998.

Pérez Villalón, Clara. "Pestiño de Semana Santa." *El Comidista,* March 27, 2018. https://elcomidista.elpais.com/elcomidista/2018/03/14/receta/1520989775_726854.html.

Perry, Charles. "The Description of Familiar Foods." In *medieval Arab Cookery*. Edited by A. J Arberry, Maxime Rodinson, and Charles Perry, 273–465. Totnes: Prospect Books, 2006.

———. "Tracta/Trachanas/Kishk." *Petits propos culinaires* 14 (1983).

———. "Trakhanas revisited." *Petits propos culinaires* 55 (1997): 34–39.

———. "What was Tracta?" *Petits propos culinaires* 12 (1982): 37–39.

Perry, Charles Perry, Maxime Rodinson, and A. J. Arberry, eds. *Medieval Arab Cookery*. Totnes: Prospect Books, 2001.

Perry, Charles, ed. and trans, with and David Waines. *Kitāb al-wuṣla ilā -ḥabīb fī waṣf al ṭayyibāt wal-ṭīb / Scents and Flavors: A Syrian Cookbook*. New York: New York University Press, 2017.

PhiloBiblon. http://vm136.lib.berkeley.edu/BANC/philobiblon/index.html.

Pignon, Tatiana. "Les dhimmi dans l'Empire islamique." *Les clés du Moyen Orient*. March 18, 2013. https://www.lesclesdumoyenorient.com/Les-dhimmi-dans-l-Empire-islamique-medieval.html.

Pike, Ruth. "The Conversos in La lozana andaluza." *Modern Languages Notes* 84, no. 2 (1969): 30–48.

Pitchon, Véronique. *La gastronomie arabe médiévale—Entre diététique et plaisir*. Paris: Erick Bonnier, 2018.

Pitrat, Michel, and Claude Faury. *Histoires de légumes: Des origines à l'orée du XXIe siècle*. Paris: Editions Quae, 2003.

Plouvier, Liliane. "Regards nouveaux sur la cuisine provençale du bas Moyen Âge: le témoignage des livres de cuisine." *Revue Provence historique* 54, no. 218 (2004): 431–462.

Pomeroy, Hilary. "Ojos de Berenjena: Some Literary Links between Food and Religious Identity." *Proceedings of the Thirteenth British Conference on Judeo-Spanish Studies, 7–9 September 2003,* edited by Hilary Pomeroy, 137–149. London: Queen Mary University of London, 2006.

Pottier, Bernard. "Les lexicographes espagnols du XVIe siècle." *Comptes rendus des séances de l'Académie des Inscriptions et Belles-Lettres* 3 (135e année, 1991): 591–604.

Rabi Saadia Gaon (Rassag). *Sefer Ha-Egron*. Edited by Nehemiah Aloni. Jérusalem: Académie de la langue hébraïque, 1969.

Raviv, Yael. "Falafel: A National Icon." *Gastronomica* 3 (2003): 20–25.

Redhouse, James William. *A Turkish and English Lexicon*. Constantinople: H. Matteosian, printed for the American Board Mission, 1921.

Remie Constable, Olivia. "Food and Meaning: Christian Understandings of Muslim Food and Food Ways in Spain (1250–1550)." *Viator: Medieval and Renaissance Studies* 44, no. 3 (2013): 199–235.

———. *Housing the Stranger in the Mediterranean World: Lodging, Trade, and Travel in Late Antiquity and the Middle Ages*. Cambridge: Cambridge University Press, 2004.

———. *To Live like a Moor*. Edited by Robin Vose, with a foreword by David Nirenberg. Philadephia: University of Pennsylvania Press, 2018. Kindle.

———. *Medieval Iberia: Readings from Christian, Muslim, and Jewish Sources*. Philadelphia: University of Pennsylvania Press, 2011.

Riera i Sans, Jaume. "La conflictivitat de l'alimentació dels jueus medievals." In *Alimentació i societat a la Catalunya medieval,* 294–314. Barcelona: CSIC, 1988.

———. "Judíos y Conversos en los reinos de la Corona de Aragón durante el siglo, XV." In *La Expulsión de los Judíos de España*. Vol. 2, *Curso de cultura hispano-judía y sefardí de la Universidad de Castilla-La Mancha (Toledo)*, 71–90. Castilla-La Mancha: Asociación de Amigos del Museo Sefardí, 1993.

Riveline, Claude. "Le monde Juif et l'Islam." *Akadem*. Accessed October 21, 2017. https://akadem.org/sommaire/cours/juif-et-non-juif-approche-traditionnelle/le-monde-juif-et-l-islam-03-05-2007-6927_4298.php.

Roden, Claudia. *The Food of Spain*. London: Penguin, 2012.

———. *Le livre de la cuisine espagnole*. Paris: Flammarion, 2012.

Rodinson, Maxime. *Recherches sur les documents arabes relatifs à la cuisine*. Paris: Geuthner, Revue des études islamiques, 1950.

———. "Studies in Arabic Manuscripts Relating to Cookery." In *Medieval Arab Cookery*, edited by A. J. Arberry, Maxime Rodinson, and Charles Perry, 92–164. Totnes: Prospect Books, 2006.

———. "Sur l'Etymologie de 'losange.'" *Studi orientalistici in onore di Giorgio Levi Della Vida* 2 (1956): 425–435.

———. "Venice and the Spice Trade." In *Medieval Arab Cookery*, edited by A. J. Arberry, Maxime Rodinson, and Charles Perry, 199–215. Totnes: Prospect Books, 2006.

Rojo Valles, Julio. *Cocina y alimentación en los siglos XVI y XVII*. Valladolid: Junta de Castilla y León, 2007.

Romero, Elena. "Canciones y coplas sefardíes de contenido gastronómico." In *La mesa puesta: leyes, costumbres y recetas judías: XVI curso de cultura hispanojudía y sefardí de la Universidad de Castilla-La Mancha: en memoria de Iacob Hassán*, edited by Uriel Macías and Ricardo Izquierdo Benito, 171–214. Cuenca: Universidad de Castilla la Mancha, 2010.

———. "El olor del sábado: la adafina, del Arcipreste de Hita a las versiones 'light.'" In *La mesa puesta: leyes, costumbres y recetas judías: XVI curso de cultura hispanojudía y sefardí de la Universidad de Castilla-La Mancha: en memoria de Iacob Hassán*, edited by Uriel Macías and Ricardo Izquierdo Benito, 215–240. Cuenca: Universidad de Castilla la Mancha, 2010.

Romero, Elena, and Carmen Valentín. *Seis coplas sefardíes de 'castiguerio' de Hayim Yom-Tob Magula*. Edición crítica y estudio. Madrid: CSIC, 2003.

Romoli, Domenico. *La singolar dottrina*. n.p.: n.p, 1560.

Rosell, De Cayetano, ed. *Crónica de Enrique*, vol. 3, 161–271. Madrid: Atlas, 1953.

Rosenberger, Bernard. "Dietética y cocina en el mundo musulmán occidental según el Kitāb al-ṭabīj, recetario de época almohade." In *Cultura alimentaria Andalucía-América*, edited by Antonio Garrido, 13–35. México: Universidad Nacional Autónoma, 1996.

———. "Diététique et cuisine dans l'Espagne musulmane du XIIIe siècle." In *Le désir et le goût, une autre histoire (XIIIe–XVIIIe). Actes du colloque international à la mémoire de J.L. Flandrin*, edited by Odile Redon, L. Sallman, and S. Steinberg, 175–180. PU de Vincennes, 2003.

Rubin, Shira. "The History of the Inquisition, Wrapped Up in a Sausage." *Tablet*, March 2, 2018. https://www.tabletmag.com/sections/food/articles/history-of-inquisition-in-a-sausage.

Safra, Edmon, ed., and Aharon Marciano, trans. *Chumash*. New York: ArtScroll Series, 2017.

Sagaert, Claudine. "L'utilisation des préjuges esthétiques comme redoutable outil de stigmatisation du juif. La question de l'apparence dans les écrits antisémites du XIXe siècle à la première moitié du XXe siècle." *Revue d'anthropologie des connaissances* 7, no. 4 (2014): 971–992.

Salvator, Israël. "Les Marranes." *Revue des études juives* 1, no. 118 (1959–60): 29–77.

Samrakandi, Mohammed-Habib, and Georges Carantino, eds. *Manger au Maghreb*. Vol. 2, *Approche pluridisciplinaire des pratiques de table en Méditerranée du Moyen Âge à nos jours*. Toulouse: Presses universitaires du Mirail: 2006.

Sánchez Moya, Manuel. "El ayuno del Yom Kippur entre los judaizantes turolenses del siglo xv." *Sefarad* 26 (1966): 273–304.

Sánchez-Albornoz, Claudio. *España, un enigma histórico*. Buenos Aires: Editorial Sudamericana, 1956.

Santanach, Joan, et al. *Llibre de Sent Soví*. Barcelona: Barcino, 2014.

Santa María, Ramón. "Ritos y costumbres de los hebreos españoles." *Boletín de la Real Academia de la Historia* legajo 299 (1893): 181–188.

Santich, Barbara. *The original Mediterranean Cuisine: Medieval Recipes for Today*. 2nd ed. Bristol: Equinox Publishing, 2018.

Saraiva, José Antonio. "L'Inquisition portugaise et les 'nouveaux chrétiens.'" *Annales. Économies, Sociétés, Civilisations* 22, no. 3 (1967): 586–589.

Savy, Pierre, Katell Berthelot, and Audrey Kichelewski. eds. *Histoire des Juifs. Un voyage en 80 dates de l'Antiquité à nos jours*. Paris: PUF, 2020.

Sefaria. "Exodus 16." Accessed April, 18, 2017. https://www.sefaria.org/Exodus.16?ven=The_Koren_Jerusalem_Bible&lang=bi&aliyot=0.

Sefaria. "Shabbat 119a" Accessed April, 18, 2017. https://www.sefaria.org/Shabbat.119a.8?lang=bi&p2=Jastrow%2C_תָ%D6%BC1.בָל&lang2=bi&w2=Shabbat&lang3=en.

Sefarim. "Sefarim.fr: la Bible en hébreu, en français et en anglais." Accessed April, 18, 2017. http://www.sefarim.fr.

Serventi, Silvano, and Françoise Sabban. *Pasta: the Story of a Universal Food*. New York: Columbia University Press, 2002.

Sesma Muñoz, J. Ángel. *El establecimiento de la Inquisición en Aragón (1484–1486), Documentos para su estudio*. Zaragoza: CSIC, 1987.

Shatzmiller, Maya. "Professions and Ethnic Origin of Urban Labourers in Muslim Spain: Evidence from a Moroccan Source." *Awraq* 5 (1983): 152–153.

Shimonsohn, Shamuel. *History of Jews in the Duchy of Mantua*. Jersusalem: Kiryath Sepher, 1977.

Siete Partidas [1436]. Translated by S. P. Scott and edited by R. I. Burns. Philadelphia: University of Pennsylvania Press, 2001.

Simnegar, Reyna. *Persian Food from the Non-persian Bride: And Other Sephardic Kosher Recipes You Will Love*. New York: Philipp Feldheim, 2011.

Singerman, Robert. *The Jews in Spain and Portugal: A Bibliography*. New York: Garland Publisher, 1975.

———. *Spanish and Portuguese Jewry: A Classified Bibliography*. Westport: Greenwood Press, 1993.

Solomonov, Michael, and Steven Cook. *Israeli Soul: Easy, Essential, Delicious*. Boston: Mariner Books, 2018.

———. *Zahav: A World of Israeli Cooking*. Boston: Mariner Books, 2015.

Sordo, Enrique. "Gastronomía de la provincia de Málaga." In *Cómo conocer la cocina española*. Barcelona: Argos Vergara, 1980.

Soria Mesa, Enrique. *La realidad tras el espejo. Asenso social y limpieza de sangre en la España de Felipe II*. Valladolid: Ediciones Universidad de Valladolid, 2016.

Soussen, Claire, "La cacherout ou le besoin d'une expertise juive en matière alimentaire." In *Expertise et valeur des choses au Moyen Âge*. Vol. 1, *Le besoin d'expertise*, edited by Claude Denjean and Laurent Feller, 37–52. Madrid: Casa de Velázquez, 2013. http://books.openedition.org/cvz/24427.

Spivakovsky, Erika. "The Jewish Presence in Granada." *Journal of Medieval History* 2, no. 3 (1976): 215–237.

Stroumsa, Sarah. *Andalus and Sefarad: On Philosophy and Its History in Islamic Spain*. Princeton: Princeton University Press, 2019.

———. "Between Acculturation and Conversion in Islamic Spain: The Case of Banū Ḥasday." *Mediterranean International Journal for the Transfer of Knowledge* 1 (2016): 9–36.

Sussman, Adeena. *Sababa: Fresh, Sunny Flavors from My Israeli Kitchen*. New York: Avery, 2019.

Szokovski, Di Miriam. "Torta del Monte Sinai." IT.Chabad.ORG. Accessed April, 18, 2017. https://it.chabad.org/library/article_cdo/aid/3691031/jewish/Torta-del-Monte-Sinai.htm.

Tanara, Vicenzo. *L'Economia Del Cittadino In Villa*. Venice: Stefano Curti, 1674.

The Schechter Institutes, Inc. "Why Do Ashkenazic Jews Eat Hamentashen on Purim?" October 3, 2014. http://www.schechter.edu/why-do-ashkenazic-jews-eat-hamentashen-on-purim/.

Tixier Du Mesnil, Emmanuelle. "La tolérance andalouse a-t-elle existé?" *L'Histoire* 452 (2018): 64–71.

Tixier du Mesnil, Emmanuelle, and Brigitte Foulon. *Al-Andalus: Anthologie*. Paris: Flammarion, 2009.

Toaff, Ariel. "Le couscous et l'histoire des juifs en Italie." In *Couscous, boulgour et polenta. Transformer et consommer les céréales dans le monde*, edited by Hélène Franconie, Monique Chastanet and François Sigaut, 141–144. Paris: Karthala, 2010.

———. "Marzapani, olive candite e caffè." In *Mangiare alla giudia: la cucina ebraica in Italia dal Rinascimento all'età moderna*, edited by Ariel Toaff, 101–104. Bologne: Il Mulino, 2000.

———. "Pranzi quotidiani, di sabato, di festa." In *Mangiare alla giudia: la cucina ebraica in Italia dal Rinascimento all'età moderna*, edited by Ariel Toaff, 132–133. Bologne: Il Mulino, 2000.

———. *Il vino e la carne. Una comunità ebraica nel Medioevo*. Bologna: Il Mulino, 1989.

Tolan, John. "Le statut légal des minorités religeuses dans l'espace euro-méditerranéen (ve–xve siècle)." *Relmin*. Accessed July 1, 2018. http://www.cn-telma.fr/relmin/auteur1507/.

Tolan, John, Stéphane Boissellier, and François Clément, eds. *Minorités et régulations sociales en Méditerranée médiévale*. Rennes: PU Rennes, 2010.

Trémolières, Jean. *Biologie générale*. 4 vols. Paris: Dunod, 1969.

Tzvia Piudik, Jaclyn. "Hybridity in the Fourteenth-Century Esther Poems of Israel Caslari." PhD diss., University of Toronto, 2014. https://tspace.library.utoronto.ca/bitstream/1807/74812/1/Piudik_Jaclyn_T_201411_PhD_thesis.pdf.

Ullman, B. L. "Horace *Serm*. I.6.115 and the History of the Word *Laganum*." *Classical Philology* 7, no. 4 (1912): 442–449.

UNESCO. "Formulaire de proposition d'inscription Registre international de la Mémoire du monde." Accessed March 1, 2022. http://www.unesco.org/new/fileadmin/MULTIMEDIA/HQ/CI/spain_sentsovi_eng_01.pdf.

Valenzuela-Lamas, Silvia, Lua Valenzuela-Suau, Oriol Saula, Anna Colet, Oriol Mercadal, Carme Subiranas, and Jordi Nadal. "Shechita and Kashrut: Identifying Jewish Populations through Zooarchaeology and Taphonomy: Two Examples from Medieval Catalonia (North-Eastern Spain)." *Quaternary International* 330 (2014): 1–9.

Vallés, Juan, and Fernando Serrano Larráyoz, eds. and trans. *Regalo de la vida humana*. 2 vols. Pamplona: Gobierno de Navarra-Österreichische National bibliothek, 2008.

Vassas, Claudine. *Esther. Le nom voilé*. Paris: CNRS Éditions, 2016.

Velsid. "Receta de Hojuelas." *República de las ideas,* April 20, 2011. https://gastronomiaycia.republica.com/2011/04/20/receta-de-hojuelas/.

Vercier, Joseph. "Culture potagère." *Encyclopédie des sciences agricoles.* Paris: Hachette, 1965.

Villanueva, Jaime. *Viaje literario por las iglesias de España.* Vol. 18. Madrid: Imprenta de Fortanet, 1851.

Vose, Robin. *Dominicans, Muslims and Jews in the Medieval Crown of Aragon.* Cambridge: Cambridge University Press, 2010.

Wachtel, Nathan. *Entre Moïse et Jésus. Études marranes (XVe–XXIe siècle).* Paris: CNRS Éditions, 2013.

Waines, David. "The Culinary Culture of al-Andalus." In *The Legacy of Muslim Spain,* edited by Khadra Jayyusi, 725–738. Leiden: Brill, 1992.

Wasserstein, David. "Islamisation and the Conversion of Jews." In *Conversions islamiques: identités religieuses en islam méditerranéen* [Islamic Conversions: Religious Identities in Mediterranean Islam], edited by Mercedes García Arenal, 49–60. Paris: Maisonneuve et Larose, 2001.

———. "The Muslims and the Golden Age of the Jews." In *Dhimmis and Others: Jews and Christians and the World of Classical Islam,* vol. 17, edited by Uri Ruben and David Wasserstein, 179–196. Eisenbrauns: Israel Oriental Studies, 1997.

Watson, Andrew. "Eggplant, Aubergine, Brinjal, Solanum Melongena L." *Agricultural Innovation in the Early Islamic World: The Diffusion of Crops and Farming Techniques, 700–1100.* Cambridge: Cambridge University Press, 2008.

Webster's New World College Dictionary. 4th ed. Cambridge: Cambridge University Press, 2004.

Weingarten, Susan. "The Debate about Ancient Tracta: Evidence from the Talmud." *Food & History* 2, no. 1 (2004): 21–40.

———. *Haroset.* New Milford-London: Toby Press, 2019.

———. "Medieval Hannukah Traditions: Jewish Festive Foods in Their European Contexts." *Food & History* 8, no. 1 (2010): 42–62.

Weinstock, Nathan. *Le 'Livre d'Esther' dans la tradition occitane judéo-comtadine.* Puylaurens: Institut d'Estudis Occitans, 2018.

Wilson, Anne. "The Saracen Connection: Arab Cuisine in the Medieval West." *Petits propos culinaires* 8 (1981): 13–22.

Wolfenzon, Carolyn. "La Lozana andaluza: judaísmo, sífilis, exilio y creación." *Hispanic Research Journal* 8, no. 2 (2007): 107–122.

Wolff, Philippe. "The 1391 Pogrom in Spain: Social Crisis or Not?" *Past & Present* 50 (1971): 4–18.

Word Reference. "Figurilla." Accessed by November 2019. http://www.wordreference.com/esfr/figurilla.

Yanklowitz, Shmuly. *Kashrut and Jewish Food Ethics.* Boston: Academic Studies Press, 2019.

Yerushalmi, Yosef Hayim. *Sefardica.* Paris: Chandeigne, 2016.

Yungman, Limor. "Beyond Cooking: The Roles of Chefs in Medieval Court Kitchens of the Islamic East." *Food and History* 15, nos. 1–2 (2017): 85–114.

Zafrani, Haïm. *Two Thousand Years of Jewish Life in Morocco.* Brooklyn: Ktav Pub Inc, 2005.

———. *Juifs d'Andalousie et du Maghreb.* Paris: Maisonneuve et Larose, 2002.

———. *Mille ans de vie juive au Maroc. Histoire et culture, religion et magie.* Paris: Maisonneuve et Larose, 1983.

Zinato, Andrea. "El viaje de la Lozana andaluza entre Edad Media y Edad Moderna." forthcoming.

———. "'¿Y cuándo quiere Usted que partamos?': le mappe virtuali della Lozana Andaluza." *Estratta da quaderni di lingue e letterature* 33 (2008): 179–194.

Zorattini, Ioly, Pier Cesare. *Processi del S. Uffizio di Venezia contro ebrei e giudaizzanti.* Vol. 5, *1579–1586.* Florence: Ed. Olschki, 1980–1999.

Zuhr, Abū Marwān 'Abd al-Malik. *Kitāb al-agḏiya.* Introduced and translated by Expiración García Sánchez. Madrid: CSIC, 1992.

Index

"In this fascinating study, which will appeal to readers (and cooks!) interested in the intersecting histories of food, Sephardic Jewish culture, and the Mediterranean world of Iberia and northern Africa, Hélène Jawhara Piñer studies *Kitab al-tabikh,* a cookbook of uncertain authorship written in Arabic around the year 1200 which also includes dietary advice about which foods to eat to address individuals' variable health needs. Remarkably, this volume includes several recipes which its author describes as explicitly Jewish, such as 'Jewish Partridge' and 'A Jewish Dish of Eggplants Stuffed with Meat.' Piñer uses this volume and these recipes as her point of departure to investigate far-reaching questions: What is Jewish cuisine, what is Sephardic culture, and how can we use the history of food to trace Jewish experiences in the Iberian Peninsula and later, following Jewish and Muslim expulsions from Spain? Piñer makes a case for the role of ingredients, methods, cultural associations, and even utensils or cooking pots that probably once made a recipe discernibly Jewish."

— Heather J. Sharkey, Professor and Chair, Department of Near Eastern Languages & Civilizations, University of Pennsylvania, Philadelphia

"Hélène Jawhara Piñer's new book, *Jews, Food, and Spain,* is a wonder. Her research is deep and comprehensive, her presentation detailed and wise, and her 'gift' to the reader generous. Her work answers every question about the Sephardic culinary heritage you have ever had, and many questions you didn't even know how to ask. This is a book anyone interested in food, its history, and its meanings, will want to read."

— Dr. David Kraemer, Jewish Theological Seminary Librarian and Professor of Talmud and Rabbinics. Author of Jewish Eating and Identity Through the Ages

"In *Jews, Food, and Spain,* Hélène Jawhara Piñer invites us into the medieval kitchens of Muslim Spain, where she uncovers compelling evidence of several unknown, distinctively Jewish culinary practices that over the centuries have been integrated into Spanish cuisine. Her meticulous research into the foodways of Spain's Sephardim will be eye-opening to all those with an interest in the food, history, and culture of the region."

— Darra Goldstein, Food historian and founding editor of the journal Gastronomica

"'To eat is to remember.' These words which conclude Piñer's fascinating book are its basic postulation. *Jews, Food, and Spain* unfolds the story of the of Sephardic Jews through the unique perspective of its cuisine. It starts with a brilliant reconstruction of the medieval Arabic cookbook *Kitāb al-ṭabīẖ* in which Piñer uncovers the Jewish layers through a painstaking linguistic and textual analysis and goes on in the footsteps of the almost invisible traces left by Jewish cuisine in Spain after the expulsion as well as in the Sephardic diasporas around the Mediterranean and in the new world. Through the history of food and foodways, Sephardic identity is discovered and reaffirmed. This is a captivating book with enormous erudition which brings new insight into the history of Sephardim, Spain and the Mediterranean."

— *Miriam Frenkel, Menahem Ben-Sasson Chair in Judaism & Islam Through the Ages, The Hebrew University of Jerusalem*

"Through a refined 'counter-hair' reading of historical sources (Islamic texts in the Middle Ages, then Christian texts), Hélène reconstructs the identity (not only culinary, since what we eat is what we are) of a people of which others speak, to describe and mark its diversity. It is an exciting detective story that reveals not only the characteristics of Jewish cuisine in those distant centuries, but also the strength with which those characteristics have been transmitted over time, until today."

— *Massimo Montanari, Professor of Food History, Bologna University*

Printed in the USA
CPSIA information can be obtained
at www.ICGtesting.com
JSHW011019300424
62199JS00001B/1

9 781644 699188